The Politics of School Choice

The Politics of School Choice

Hubert Morken
and
Jo Renée Formicola

ROWMAN & LITTLEFIELD PUBLISHERS, INC.
Lanham • Boulder • New York • Oxford

ROWMAN & LITTLEFIELD PUBLISHERS, INC.

Published in the United States of America
by Rowman & Littlefield Publishers, Inc.
4720 Boston Way, Lanham, Maryland 20706
http://www.rowmanlittlefield.com

12 Hid's Copse Road
Cumnor Hill, Oxford OX2 9JJ, England

British Library Cataloguing in Publication Information Available

Library of Congress Cataloging-in-Publication Data

Morken, Hubert.
    The politics of school choice / Hubert Morken and Jo Renée
Formicola.
        p.   cm.
    Includes bibliographical references and index.
    ISBN 0-8476-9720-7 (alk. paper)
    ISBN 0-8476-9721-5 (pbk. : alk. paper)
    1. School choice—United States.   2. School choice—Political
aspects—United States.   3. Education and state—United States.   I.
Formicola, Jo Renée, 1941-   II. Title.
    LB1027.9.M68   1999
    379.1'11'0973—dc21   99-36303
                                                            CIP

Printed in the United States of America

⊗ ™ The paper used in this publication meets the minimum requirements of American
National Standard for Information Sciences—Permanence of Paper for Printed Library
Materials, ANSI/NISO Z39.48–1992.

Contents

Acknowledgments

We gratefully acknowledge the indispensable assistance of the many people who helped us complete this study: Dr. Mary Boutilier and Dr. Barbara Feldman critiqued the survey; Dr. Allan Formicola aided in the analysis of the statistics; Ms. Rasheeda Morris assisted in putting the data into statistical order; and Ms. Jaymie Virok helped with charts and graphs. Seton Hall University granted release time to work on the book. Thomas Roepke of the Ashland Center, Ashland University, facilitated research in Ohio. Regent University awarded time and funding for a sabbatical and travel. David and Lisa Helm provided a most hospitable research base in the Midwest. Jay Duggan and Peter Gustafson helped to produce the appendix and index. Mary Carpenter and Steve Wrinn were supportive editors. Most of all we thank all the people we interviewed who are the brains and backbone of the school choice movement, including the many organizations, entrepreneurs, scholars, educators, attorneys, pastors, and activists, who discussed the effectiveness of their efforts to promote educational alternatives for parents and children.

Two people deserve special note, William Bentley Ball, Esq., distinguished school choice litigator, and Dr. Quentin L. Quade, of Marquette University, founder of the Blum Center in Milwaukee. Both passed away in early 1999. Both made acute observations on recent developments for this book. We wish to acknowledge their labors and insights.

We dedicate this book to our families: our spouses, our children and our grandchildren. Furthermore, we commend it to all families, who, as the prime educators, are most impacted by the debate and the politics about school choice.

Introduction

In 1997, we published *Everson Revisited,* a book to commemorate the fiftieth anniversary of the landmark church-state education case, *Everson v Board of Education.* In that original law suit, a New Jersey taxpayer challenged the right of the state to pay for the bussing of students to a parochial school with public monies. The decision of the Supreme Court was ambiguous: The justices ruled that the cost of transportation was part of every student's "child benefits," so that New Jersey could pay for busing to private religious schools; but it also said, nevertheless, that a high wall of separation must exist between church and state.

Everson Revisited emphasized the fact that education and the law are at a crossroads today in the United States. Shortly after its completion, other events challenged us professionally, directing our concerns more broadly to the future of American education. In the same year that our book was published, Mayor Rudolph Giuliani of New York asked that the Catholic schools take the overflow of students from the city's crowded public schools, and John Cardinal O'Connor agreed—reminding the mayor of his earlier offer to educate the worst of the city's students in a better and cheaper way! In 1997, as well, the Supreme Court agreed to rehear *Aguilar v Felton* and subsequently reversed itself, allowing remedial education to be carried out in parochial schools. Around the nation African-American ministers were establishing parish schools of their own, new Catholic schools were under construction for the first time in decades, and Evangelicals and Muslims too were active, building schools. Jewish Hasidim were given the opportunity to create a mechanism to found special schools for their handicapped children in New York State with public monies as a result of their Supreme Court challenge in *Board of Education of Kyrias Joel v Grumet.* Charter school legislation was proliferating across the country; home schooling was developing as more than a trend in the South and the Midwest. Milwaukee and Cleveland had flourishing programs in place to provide tuition funds to the disadvantaged. Furthermore, entrepreneurs pledged millions of dollars for schol-

1

arships for inner-city children. In short, it seemed as though everywhere we turned there were movements underway to promote school choice in the education of America's children. The confluence of these events led us to take a closer look at U.S. education policy: the variety of calls for change; the myriad methods being tried to leverage school choice, and the proliferating politics of diverse groups to create educational options in the United States.

Defining School Choice

In public discussion today, there are many definitions and views of "school choice." The topic can be confusing and difficult to comprehend. It is easier to understand, however, if one were to imagine an educational spectrum with one end representing the status quo, i.e., with most public funding limited to public schools, and the other end representing the ability of a parent to purchase any kind of education at any time, anywhere for his/her child.

On this type of a continuum, those who support the status quo would claim that public education in America is adequate, sufficient, and in many cases superior to all forms of private education. Logically from this position, all children should be able to attend a public school in their school district, if they choose to do so; and public schools exclusively should continue to be funded by local real estate taxes and state governments. Private schools should operate on private funds.

Further along the spectrum are those parents and groups who support some options within the public school system, considering them necessary to meet the different needs of a variety of children. They advocate "magnet," or specialized schools, such as computer schools or music schools, and some experimental schools, usually "charter" schools. Most charter schools have significant autonomy, allowing variations in the curriculum, but they often employ only accredited teachers, must adhere to state regulations for licensing, and are accountable for the performance of their students to the state or local school district. Both magnet and charter schools are publicly funded, and charter schools have been growing in numbers in a variety of states during the last decade. In addition, public school choice may include transfers inside or outside the district to other public schools, something called an intradistrict or interdistrict transfer.

Nearer the center of the education spectrum are programs that provide public or private scholarships to students, allowing them to use from several hundred to several thousand dollars per year to attend the public or private school of their choice. Most of these programs are available only for the economically disadvantaged.

It should be noted that entrepreneurial schools play a role in both charter and voucher programs. These schools are established by educational companies that require government reimbursement in the case of charters, or require tuition payments by parents, private scholarships, or vouchers. Some are operated for a profit. These kinds of schools are a business, promise high achievement with innovative methodologies, and will go bankrupt unless they can deliver their educational product with success. Some new charter schools are being run by nonprofit entrepreneurial or philanthropic organizations, as well.

Further along the spectrum are those who advocate school "vouchers" for all children, that is, full, public educational funding that follows children wherever they attend. Vouchers in principle could cover from part to all of the cost of education within a particular district, and be spent at *any* school inside or outside the district, including public, private, or religious schools. This kind of system is in place to some degree in nations like Holland and France and has not yet been adopted in any state in America.

Tax credits are also an alternative and are favored especially by those who fear the potential for government regulation that might well come with vouchers. This choice is further along the spectrum, closer to those who want a robust private system to replace government operated and funded schools, who see the need to provide additional funding to the middle class as well as the poor but who are leery of vouchers.

At the end of the spectrum are those who advocate that all education should be privately funded, or that "home schooling" be the norm. In the former, supporters would abolish all public schools and tax subsidies for education, opting instead for a pure market approach. In the latter, parents take the responsibility to teach their own children in their own homes. In reality, however, some students who do home school attend local public schools for special classes, like chemistry, and participate in sports or extra-curricular activities. Home schooling parents in most states do not receive any funding for providing this service to their children, but can, in many states, avail themselves of some part of the public education offerings.

This book explores only the activities of those promoting a free market system of education using various means, including charters, tax credits, private scholarships, public vouchers, and by some, withdrawal from public schools. As worthy as they are of study, little is said about home schooling or other reforms internal to public and private education, except as these reforms relate directly to school choice legislative strategies.

We have found that information on school choice is readily available yet at the same time relatively unknown, sometimes held in secret, and generally enlightening and fascinating. Our research has led us to this basic hypothesis: that school choice, *as a political movement,* is coalescing slowly and unevenly around the United States across racial, religious, economic, moral, and ideological lines. This is due, first and foremost, to the fact that choice advocates are themselves diverse, working with different methods and motives. All are working to bring educational options to parents who are looking for better, yet affordable schools, to neighborhoods without either, and to states that are willing to use private or public resources to benefit all students. But agendas vary and there are rivalries within the school choice coalitions.

At one time this was merely a Catholic issue, based on a religious challenge to the Protestant-created public schools. But that paradigm is now all but gone, replaced by a largely secular system. School choice today is much more than the right to a religious education. It focuses on parental resources and responsibilities, which may have little to do with religion. And, it addresses a variety of issues, including academic standards, access to quality schools especially for the inner-city poor, violence and disorder in classrooms, ideology, the value of competition, and the cultivation of morality and civic virtue.

As a matter of public policy, school choice may well replace the model of the single common school, the neighborhood public school. Across the United States there are efforts to create, on the one hand, charter schools, magnet schools, experimental schools, new private schools, and home schools, and, on the other, vouchers and tax credits to support parental choices. Increasingly students may transfer to the public school of their choice inside or outside the district. Attendance zones for public schools are not the restrictive walls they once were, in law and increasingly in practice.

Second, remedies and tactics to shift public policy in the direction of one school choice plan or another vary widely. Increasingly grassroots coalitions of parents, entrepreneurs, scholars, think tanks, confessional groups, corporate visionaries, local politicians, taxpayer organizations, and mayors and governors are working together. This has especially been true in Minnesota, Wisconsin, and Ohio. They are the Midwest vanguards of choice, where advocates for change have achieved substantial unity. They are now exporting their model for other states to replicate, joining and helping to construct a truly national movement.

Third, school choice is viewed from a wide variety of perspectives across the United States. Religious leaders have told us that educational options are a moral question, one that must be measured in terms of equity. Businessmen claim that it is a matter of market competition, of using public monies in the most efficient way. Racial activists see the issue in terms of equality. Liberals believe that government should take the lead in providing as much freedom as possible in as many areas as possible. Conservatives believe that school choice is about empowering parents. Libertarians want to go back to American assumptions and question why government plays any role at all in education. In short, there are as many reasons supporting school choice as interest groups!

While there is much speculation about the future of choice and how far it will go, it is too early in the political process to know the answer. What it is possible to do at the present time is to examine the reformers, their efforts, and the visible trends in the early stages of this movement. What are the tactics and organizational efforts of school choice advocates? What are their politics? How do they operate? What steps do they take to persuade others to join their movement? How do they leverage change and where do they fail? No thorough and systematic study as yet been done to get at these political questions. This book is such an effort. The authors, having spent two years doing extensive interviews from coast to coast, have uncovered school choice "stories" developing in a variety of states. Buttressed by survey materials and other empirical evidence, this information paints a picture of a growing, but complex, state and national political movement.

Methodology and Research Access Issues

Our efforts to gain information have been met with a variety of reactions. On the one hand, there were those who did not want to speak to us. Often locked in conflict with education interest groups, choice advocates are sometimes reluctant to be studied because they are more than just philosophers, more than just idea people who love a good debate. They are all activists in this inquiry—even the scholars among them—and they want to win, to waken the public to their cause, to achieve majorities, to forge coalitions. They want to pass laws, to be vindicated in the courts, and they understand that to accomplish this they must sometimes keep some things secret. They have their own interests to protect. The strength of their forces and their next move will not be broadcast to adversaries in what some perceive to be a war. So those supporting school choice in this conflict, clearly a political dogfight with dust swirling and some blood and broken bones, are wary of too much public disclosure. Publicizing how they are working to bring change has its down side; they believe it can hurt the cause.

On the other hand, there were those most anxious to get their stories on the record. Not surprisingly, political conflicts in a democracy that prizes open discussion and rational debate include elements of concealment, but also openness. This does not prevent the study of activists; it just limits it, in this case to what they are willing to disclose and to what is part of the public record. Not everything activists think and do can be discovered or known. However, there are strong reasons why activists also want to be understood and talked freely for this study despite their necessary caution.

First, the process of leveraging change in education policy requires the public to know who the activists are and to approve their recommended program. Gaining public trust forces the advocates of choice to unveil their agenda to secure the approval of community leaders, parents, and voters. Clearly to be too public too soon may provoke attacks from opponents and raise expectations too high among supporters, courting disaster. But to remain concealed is to guarantee remaining weak and on the margins of politics. This means that information on the school choice advocates, including their organizations, strategies, and methods, must be released to the public, sooner rather than later and more rather than less, especially as they gain strength, success, and influence. This is a reason for their cooperation with the press and scholars.

Second, public actions must be defended. The public activity of any movement begs for further understanding. Who are these people? What are they doing? Why are they so motivated? What will their next step be? Can they win? Relentlessly the spotlight descends on the personal and the procedural. Are these people to be trusted in so delicate a matter as reconstructing a system for educating the young? Can they carry out the reforms they are advocating? Is their enough political strength and wisdom in a particular program to give it any chance of success? Can they prevail over opponents that are so formidable? The press and public want to know answers to these questions even before they give a full hearing to its claims. Questions about a movement and its viability can only be put off so long. Total concealment from the adversary for tactical political reasons is impossible to maintain once serious and significant attempts to influence policy begin.

Third, supporters and potential supporters must be recruited. Financial and political realism dictate that outcomes be considered positive and probable before money is contributed and grassroots efforts are started. Resources are scarce and people want to gauge potential risks before they commit to help.

In sum, to gain a public hearing, to answer questions posed in the policy process, and to win supporters, activists have given us considerable personal and organizational access. There will always be surprises, new leaders and new tactics. But studying the politics of school choice, discovering who these people are, their motivation, plans, organizations, and activities, has been accomplished in this study with the cooperation of many school choice advocates who see the value of having their stories told and critiqued.

Organizing energetically for choice as they do, often at great personal sacrifice, is difficult and even grueling activity, especially when a tradition like public education is at stake and when there is active opposition. Gathering data on an active, embattled, national political movement has been a challenge. Each state is different: much is happening in some places, little in others. There are diverse groups and organizations operating nationally and locally. Through personal and telephone interviews, mail and e-mail, we have gathered a great deal of information. For researchers this has been an embarrassment of riches, difficult to bring together systematically, yet making possible insights and conclusions about the politics of school choice advocates.

At the same time, because we are political scientists, it has also been important to seek out empirical evidence to substantiate or challenge the information that was being gathered from interviews in the field. Thus, a survey was created to bring together confidential, objective information on over 200 choice organizations that are working to change public educational policy in the United States. Our results have been surprising, but our statistics can be reconciled with our research in the field. We found that school choice, as a political issue, is coalescing very slowly as a political movement, and that it is proceeding at a different pace in different places. We found fragmentation, differences on what kind of school choice most advocates support, a lack of national leadership, and a need for more unity within advocacy ranks.

We believe that the research that we have done is significant because it is the first to look at school choice through a political lens and to do so on a national level. We also believe that we are in a position to present that picture accurately and objectively to the public at this time.

Perspective and Scope of the Book

As authors we carry with us our own histories, proclivities, and commitments that influence this study. Between us, we have attended public, private, and parochial schools; we have taught at the junior high school, secondary, university, and post-graduate levels. And, we have sent our own six children to a variety of schools. Thus, we partly look at school choice though a kaleidoscope, which reflects many experiences both personal and professional.

As political science professors, researchers, and authors, we looked at the school choice question and realized that most books on the subject dealt with education quality and the benefits or deficiencies of choice programs. Usually, the literature compared public with parochial schools. Frequently, the advocates taking sides in the controversy or those critiquing the claims of both sides wrote books. What we do best—studying activists to see how they are doing politics to support their cause—was missing, perhaps because the issue was so new.

By 1990 and accelerating thereafter, school choice politics reached a level of significance worthy and capable of study. One recent indication is that at the 1998 American Political Science Association convention in Boston several panels discussed education reform and school choice. There are now enough school choice programs in place or contemplated for us to study how they got there. Furthermore, the movement is no longer simply state-based with local activists lobbying elected officials. School choice is emerging at the end of the decade as a critical issue with national and local structures in place that are spreading the vision and coordinating efforts and the investment of resources. Granted that school politics in America remains mostly under state and local administration, activists are, nevertheless, looking for break through states where the most well conceived and broadly supported school choice programs can be implemented.

Significant Players and Factors

Who, specifically did we study and why? Originally, we started in New Jersey, were one of the authors had convened a conference at Seton Hall University on "Religion and Education at the Crossroads." It afforded us the opportunity to meet many of the school choice advocates in the northeastern part of the country, particularly Bret Schundler, the mayor of Jersey City. A committed, open, and vocal spokesman for school choice, he shared his philosophy and political agenda with us. His interview was soon followed by an interesting discussion with state Senator Joseph Doria (D-Bayonne), who enacted the first state charter legislation in New Jersey. While both political leaders' methods, goals, and philosophies conflicted, they were working toward the same goal: educational reform. That intrigued us. How could they be so different, yet so alike? They led us to other people—politicians, ministers, policy experts, litigators, and many other diverse, committed, dedicated activists.

Among these were many experienced leaders, including Susan Miller, who heads up the American Education Reform Foundation, funded in part by John Walton of Wal-Mart fame; Howard Fuller, an activist from Milwaukee who until recently headed the public schools in the city; Representative Dwight Evans, running for mayor of Philadelphia; Representative Polly Williams, the initiator of public vouchers in America; and the Reverend Floyd Flake, former Congressman and now a leading spokesman for school choice. We traveled to Washington D.C., New York, Indianapolis, Chicago, Milwaukee, Boston, and to Pennsylvania, Michigan, Ohio, California, Colorado, and elsewhere to talk to the leaders of organizations with a national focus who are sponsoring conferences and communicating widely by magazines and on websites.

We also dealt with exciting new leaders, such as Benno Schmidtt, who are playing an increasingly large role in the movement in several ways. They are important school choice players because newly created profit-making education providers are setting up schools and selling their services where school choice has been successful. In addition, new private schools, many not for profit and attached to churches, are being funded by local business leaders and church parishioners. At the same time, existing parochial school systems are expanding their efforts to raise support and even to build new schools. We found that public funds are flowing to charter schools and to private schools in the form of transportation and support services. We also found that private scholarship programs for public school students to attend private schools of their choice are being initiated in major cities paid for by entrepreneurs. Some funds are also being invested by businessmen in political campaigns to pass legislation, to get friendly politicians elected, and to educate the public through TV and radio. We were surprised to learn that a lot of new, corporate, and individual money is being put into choice organizations to fund their activities.

We also met with policy experts and school choice advocates, such as Terry M. Moe, Quentin L. Quade, Myron Lieberman, and Paul E. Peterson. Their influence is growing in importance on the school choice issue. For example, Milton Friedman, the Nobel Prize winning economist who took up the cause of school choice and public vouchers in 1962, is now boosting choice via the Milton and Rose Friedman Foundation. Other prominent scholars have been active too, including John E. Coons, Stephen D. Sugarman, and John E. Chubb. There are several roles these scholars play. Some articulate and defend school choice as an idea, a vision, and a program. Some defend it from other scholarly attacks, arguing that the facts do not discredit choice. Some are also working to demonstrate that in fact choice works to improve learning for the students so empowered to study where they wish. Some wear two hats, functioning as consultants giving counsel on where to set up choice programs and how to run them, and some are highly public in electoral battles, speaking out for choice. In such a heavily politicized controversy academic neutrality is rare and objectivity at risk. One solution adopted by the scholars who support choice is to make their study so methodologically rigorous, supported by external authorities, that it is not only accurate but also credible.

Politicians, such as mayors John Norquist (Milwaukee, Democrat) and Brett Schundler (Jersey City, Republican) and legislator Dwight Evans (Philadelphia, Democrat), have solid school choice commitments fully integrated with their political ideology and sense of mission. They all gave us access and time. In principle they support choice because they see it as necessary for the health of the city—without it, people who can afford it, leave the city when their children reach school age, and parents and children who stay in the city tend to become passive and poorly educated. From the point of view of Norquist, Schundler, and Evans, the future of cities hangs in the balance. For them school choice is now the top priority on their agendas, more important today than welfare reform. Other politicians are not driven so much by a vision as they are by hard political facts, including the visible discontent of parents expressed by protests measured by surveys and potential votes. Politicians will also work to defuse an issue looking for the most convenient compromise, adopting a restricted form of charter schools to prevent more liberal charters or tax credits.

We heard governors speak on the issue of school choice, and we recount a speech given by Arne Carlson of Minnesota. Governors are in especially critical positions provided that they aggressively support choice. Frequently legislatures are deeply divided on choice with most Democrats and some Republicans opposed and a few hard-core Republican supporters. To keep Republicans together and to win significant Democrat defections requires strong leadership from a governor's office. Even with this support, governors will often wait until after an election before they push for choice reform because they do not want to inflame teacher unions at the polls. Former governors like Arne Carlson (Minnesota, Republican) and George Voinovitch (Ohio, Republican) proved to be effective political counterweights to union opposition.

Corporate executives gave us business insight into their concern for school choice, particularly Pat Rooney of Indianapolis. Corporations have long supported the public schools and have avoided divisive political controversies. Often the health and success of their businesses depend on amicable relations with major unions. Yet today choice activists view corporations as likely allies. Work force issues loom large. How can semi-literate workers face the task of dealing with computers and the demands of overseas competition? Companies spending a great deal to educate and train their employees ask why primary and secondary schools have failed to do the job. If pouring even more money into existing schools has not worked then choice begins to look attractive to corporate leaders. This happened in Milwaukee, and in Cleveland, key beachheads for choice. Some Chambers of Commerce are taking the lead for choice and more are looking into it.

Church leaders helped to clarify the Catholic stance on school choice. Monsignor Thomas McDade of the United States Catholic Conference, Dr. Leonard DiFiore of the National Catholic Education Association, and John Cardinal O'Connor of New York were especially helpful, as were Catholic lobbyists and educators. Churches are maintaining and even establishing more schools. Some large parochial school systems are learning new approaches to choice, abandoning at least temporarily their support for voucher legislation, opting instead to work for tax credits or cooperating in private voucher initiatives. Building coalitions with market-oriented libertarians, Evangelicals, and the business community deflects critics from the Catholic church. Cardinals and bishops assisted by effective church lobbyists are going public once again on choice.

Evangelicals were more than open with us, particularly Ken Smitherman of the Association of Christian Schools International and the staff of Focus on the Family, in Colorado Springs. We found that they remain divided on some forms of choice, particularly vouchers, which some think will result in more government regulation of schools. However, those active in home schooling are beginning to warm to some choice programs, especially tax credits. Charter schools are also very popular with Protestants who feel at home in schools that stress traditional learning and conventional morals. Some charter schools are much like the old public schools, locally controlled and influenced by the parents who help to start and run them. They are a model familiar to Evangelicals, except for the absence of school prayer, and have the substantial benefit of public funding.

Black pastors opened our eyes. The newest school choice pioneers with whom we spoke, the Reverend Floyd Flake, Reverend Steve Gardner, Reverend Marlon Moss, and Reverend Ann Byfield, also have the potential to make the greatest contribution to the success of school choice in the next phase of the movement because they are African-American pastors. Developing and maintaining schools are difficult to do under any circumstances but doing so in tough neighborhoods and without external funding is almost folly. Black pastors and even denominational leaders are forging alliances with choice leaders to tap private and public resources to help them start and maintain schools.

Grassroots leaders are perhaps born and not made. State Representative Polly Williams in Milwaukee and Cleveland's Bert Hall helped us to understand this in our conversations with them. They opened the modern school choice door. Other cities, such as Minneapolis and Chicago, have looked for such individuals in their backyards, but they have failed to find them. Experienced leaders, like Representative Dwight Evans in Philadelphia and former Congressman Reverend Floyd Flake of New York, are playing larger state and even national roles. But in the down and dirty legislative fights, mobilizing mothers and children to descend on the statehouse or the court house is a tactic that still needs a school choice advocate with a local following.

Lawyers were also on our "to be interviewed" list. William Bentley Ball, recently deceased, Philip Murren, Conn Chapman, and Clint Bolick have been and are also involved significantly in choice, helping to draft legislation and to defend it in court once it is adopted. Litigation is their distinctive role, augmented by the crafting of *amicus* briefs to support a variety of school choice challenges. Lawyers also participate in coalition building and organization activities, often working to help other activists to compromise their differences in the light of political reality. Some attorneys contribute pro-bonum time to the cause; others, such as Chip Mellor of the Institute for Justice in Washington, D.C., and Kevin Hasson of the Becket Fund, work in public interest law firms taking cases that have the potential to set constitutional precedents. Lawyers serve the movement and often get financial support from it. They are indispensable in taking claims for school choice forward.

Entrepreneurs especially have played key roles from the early 1990s on. Pat Rooney and Don Laskowski in Indianapolis, David Brennan in Ohio, Steve Schuck in Colorado, and Reed Hastings in California helped us to see why. John Walton in California, Peter Flanagan, and Ted Forstmann in New York are examples of independently wealthy individuals who have already made significant contributions. Providing scholarships on the K–12 level, they continue their work, strategizing, organizing, and donating time and money to the effort. While these magnates have their differences, each has found a niche and an outlet for his creative energy. There is a consensus in the movement, for example, that without David Brennan's leadership little would have happened in Ohio. Certainly private vouchers owe their existence to the entrepreneurs.

Foundations and their leaders too have added vital strategic advice and resources at critical times. We met with Gordon St. Angelo in Indianapolis for example. In Milwaukee, among the long-term activists no one is held in higher regard than Michael Joyce of the Bradley Foundation. His conviction that all efforts, even private vouchers, should be used to promote public policy reform, kept the efforts of disparate groups focused on the prize of public funding for students attending private schools. Funding litigation, contracting surveys, recommending electoral strategies, and supporting academic studies and publications are all part of foundation efforts. The newly formed Friedman foundation under the leadership of Gordon St. Angelo is active all across the school choice landscape, putting on conferences and lending a hand where needed.

Think tanks, local and national, are contributing vital information to activists. James G. McGann helped us to understand their function at breakfast in Philadelphia one cold and windy Saturday morning. In Washington, D.C., the Center for Education Reform headed by Jeanne Allen is active in disseminating data on charter schools. The Heritage Foundation monitors federal efforts in Washington. The Heartland Institute (Chicago), headed by Joseph L. Bast, is active in Illinois and publishes the *School Reform News*. The Friedman-Blum Center for Parental Freedom in Education at Marquette University, founded by Quentin Quade, recently deceased, maintains an archive of school choice research materials and publishes a newsletter. The Buckeye Institute (Ohio), the Mackinac Center (Michigan), and the Pacific Research Institute (California) are all examples of active idea-generating organizations feeding the movement.

Single-issue organizations have the distinctive role of initiating particular school choice alternatives. Douglas Dewey and Paul DeWeese spent much of their time explaining the philosophy and goals of their organizations. CEO America, headquartered in Bentonville, Arkansas, under the leadership of Fritz Steiger, supports private vouchers and public initiatives. In New York, Washington, and other major cities, the Children's Scholarship Fund, headed by Ted Forstmann and John Walton is implementing a $200 million private voucher initiative. Teach Michigan, founded by Dr. Paul DeWeese, M.D., has been a prime supporter of voucher initiatives and is heavily involved assisting choice in Detroit and in efforts to amend the Michigan constitution. Charter schools have organizations to support their efforts, too, including public offices within each state that has a charter school and private offices to support the movement in other states. Getting these organizations to cooperate when they each have a clear vested interest in promoting their cause is one of the biggest challenges facing the school choice movement.

Unanswered Questions

Although we were able to uncover a tremendous amount of information, this study is by no means complete. We hope that Thorsten Veblen's critique of valuable research will apply here: that this study raises further questions still to be explored. Even as we write this introduction, new events occur daily that will require further scrutiny and synthesis to give deeper understanding to the politics of school choice: New York State adopted charter schools in 1999; Arizona enacted scholarship tax credits in the same year; Florida adopted a state wide public voucher program for all students in failing schools; Texas, Illinois and Pennsylvania are debating school choice legislation; New Mexico's Governor, Gary Johnson introduced legislation for vouchers for public and private schools to every child in the state below the poverty level; the Supreme Court has been petitioned to hear a challenge on school choice. These events and proposals, even if only some of them succeed, will indeed change education in the United States as we now know it.

Finally, we note, this study has taken us on a journey through a labyrinth. There were times when we thought we would never emerge from the school choice maze. It was filled with too many details, it was too secretive, it was too conservative, it was too religious, it was too libertarian, it was too altruistic, it was too political, it was too entrepreneurial, it was too naive, it was too Catholic, it was too black, it was too free-market, it was too Evangelical, it was too local, it was too monetary, it was too new, it was too loose, it was too complex, it was too overwhelming. But, because it is *what it is,* we can also say from our research: We have found that the political strategies for school choice are innovative, and in some cases daring; that they are supported by committed and determined individuals and groups; that these are developing into a vital and critical political movement; and, that this is an issue that will not go away in the future.

Chapter 1

The Federal Government, the Courts, and School Choice

In America, the principle that education is a parental right and responsibility is more complex than it seems. If it were not, the President, the Congress, and the courts, along with state governments and interest groups, would all be working together to implement consistent programs encouraging a wide range of educational choices for children. Right? Again the answer is more complicated than it seems. There are many demands on the public sector to balance the prerogatives of parents and students with regard to education, with the perceived obligation of the government to provide schooling for America's children. As a result, there is a constant, yet subtle, dynamic interplay between politics, the law, and interest groups; an internal tension that simultaneously mitigates against, and makes possible, school choice in the United States now and in the future. This chapter will explore those forces.

The President, the Congress, and the Law

The development of educational policy in America has reflected the religious and political interests of the white, Anglo-Saxon, Protestant majority in the United States—from the era of Founding Fathers to the twentieth century. The dominance of the "WASPS" as civil officials, especially as members of local school boards and teachers, helped to make Bible reading, Christian character building, and school prayer part of every student's daily educational experience until very recently. So influential were the Protestants and their post–Civil War radical wing known as "nativists" that President Ulysses S. Grant supported a constitutional amendment in 1875 to protect their monopoly over public education. The Blaine Amendment, as it was called, denied financial assistance to any school that "advanced sectarian or atheistic dogmas" and was aimed specifically at the growing number of Catholics who were entering the United States and establishing their own schools. Although the Blaine Amendment failed enactment by only two votes in the Senate, it was understood, by "gentlemen's agreement," that the use of tax monies for religious schools on both the national and state levels was unacceptable. As a consequence, the Blaine effort resulted in a presidential-congressional consensus to discourage the Catholic school movement in the United States, and it became the unofficial, but prevailing, public policy from the turn of the century forward.

Questions of recognition and government aid to parochial schools, however, emerged in the twentieth century as contentious political issues for both the President and the Congress. As Catholic immigration soared and social marginalization became more pronounced and chronic, the now largest minority in the United States still could find no support for its schools. Therefore, Catholics pursued what they believed to be the only avenue of redress open to them: the courts. They sought judicial remedies on two specific aspects of U.S. education practice: the legality of compulsory state education laws, and the legitimacy of "child benefit theory."

In 1922, Catholics brought suit against the state of Oregon for enacting a law that required all children to attend public school. This law, in effect, banned private and parochial schools. In the suit, Catholics asserted their parental rights over education, maintained the legitimacy of their schools, and questioned the validity of the Oregon law. The Supreme Court vindicated Catholics in *Pierce v Society of Sisters,*[1] ruling that the "child is not the mere creature of the state," and thus, preserved the right of parents to school choice.

In a second major confrontation, on "child benefits," Catholics found themselves at the center of another legal controversy in 1930. Generated by the fact that the state of Louisiana permitted the lending and/or supplying of textbooks for secular subjects to students in parochial schools, Catholics had to defend themselves against the charge that such an action authorized the use of public funds for a private purpose. And again, the Court sided with the Catholics. Broadening education policy in *Cochran v Board of Education,*[2] the Court ruled that state support for textbooks constituted a "child benefit," and justified the use of tax monies because the children and the state, rather than a particular school, were the beneficiaries of the aid.

The two legal victories in *Pierce* and *Cochran* were eventually challenged by an irate New Jersey taxpayer. In 1947, Arch Everson, with the support of a local anti-Catholic organization, brought suit against the state for using tax monies to pay for the transportation of Catholic students to a parochial school. Their contention was that the action was illegal and that it constituted a violation of the principle of separation of church and state, the underlying premise of the First Amendment.

Ruling narrowly, the Court upheld the right of the state of New Jersey to use tax money to pay for the bussing of students to Catholic schools. As a result of *Everson v Board of Education,*[3] then, transportation was considered a "child benefit." Thus, it followed the precedent in *Cochran.* However, the *Everson* decision was also critical because it went beyond the tax matter and dealt with the second complaint about separation of church and state. Ruling broadly, the Court defined the establishment clause of the First Amendment, maintained that neither the church nor the state could participate in the affairs of the other, and applied this principle to religious education as well. This seemingly ambiguous decision led to the proliferation of a series of legal challenges and soon the Supreme Court was petitioned to examine a growing number of aspects about the relationship between education, religion, and the law.

Concern about the decisions of the Court, and the types of cases that were emerging, soon prompted a serious congressional response to stave off anything that appeared to be an encroachment on the American, still Protestant dominated, public educational system. Designed to end even the perception of a judicial accommodation to Catholics and/or religious schools, the Congress gave legal force to the executive-legislative consensus established by the Blaine Amendment earlier. It enacted the Barden Bill in 1948, officially denying the expenditure of federal monies to non-public schools. It was so staunchly supported that even three major attempts to overturn the bill in later years failed: the Mills-Byrnes Bill in 1972, the Roth Amendment in 1977, and the Vanik Tuition Tax Credit Act in 1978.

Various presidents, however, treated private/parochial aid in different ways. Viewed as a sacrosanct policy until 1961, funding for non-public schools was not challenged until President John Kennedy took office. The first Catholic president requested $2.3 billion for construction costs and teachers' salaries in private/parochial schools, but he was, of course, turned down by the Congress. The best Kennedy could do was to secure passage of the Higher Education and Facilities Act, making funds available for buildings for non-public colleges.

It was Lyndon Johnson who effected the most significant change in financial assistance for both public and private education. As part of his "Great Society" legislation, the Elementary and Secondary Education Act, better known as "Title One," was enacted, permitting *direct* school funding for a variety of remedial and other child benefits.

Thus, the policy of the federal government toward financial education assistance to private and parochial schools was inconsistent throughout the first half of the twentieth century. A pseudo-accommodation existed between the parochial schools and the Supreme Court, a sense of hostility pervaded the actions of the Congress, and an air of complacency characterized the agendas of most of the Presidents. That changed, however, in 1980, when the interest in funding non-public schools found a supporter in Ronald Reagan.

The Republican platform had supported tuition tax credits as vital planks in 1972, 1976, and 1980, but no presidential candidate had aggressively pursued the issue before Reagan. So, when he promised the membership of the Catholic Education Association, one month before his election, that tuition tax credits would be an integral part of his future legislative agenda,[4] most felt that some federal program to support parochial education was at hand. A confluence of political, ideological, and religious events seemed to bear this out. The Senate shifted from a Democratic-controlled body to a Republican dominated one. The House saw an increase in Republican membership, as well. A national ideological transposition had occurred, with the right overshadowing the left. Religious activism by both Protestants and Catholics was on the rise. In fact, the chief educational lobbyist for the United States Catholic Conference, who represented all of the Catholic school interests in America, optimistically reported that "there has never been a better political climate in Washington for successfully pursuing congressional enactment and presidential approval of education tax credit legislation."[5]

Within months of the Reagan presidential victory, a loose coalition of private/parochial groups began to form to support a tuition tax credit bill. The supporters included fundamentalists, particularly, the Moral Majority and the National Association of Evangelicals; Jewish organizations such as Aguduth Israel; and Catholic groups such as the Federation of Catholic Teachers, the National Catholic Education Association, the Knights of Columbus, and the United States Catholic Conference. Private agencies such as the Association for Public Justice, Citizens for Education Freedom, and the Council for American Private Education also worked within the network.

True to his word, Reagan sent a White House version of a tuition tax plan to the Senate (S2673) and the House (HR1635) in July 1982. Aimed at middle- and lower-income families, it would have allowed a $500 tax credit per child for the cost of tuition at any non-public school. But both bills were killed in congressional finance committees, as was another attempt to enact the bills later on that same year.

A revised plan in 1983 (S528) also died, but it is mentioned here because it foreshadowed some of the school choice legislation that has appeared during the 1990s. Originally, S528 had three parts. The first section would have allowed tax credits of $100 in 1983, $200 in 1984, and a maximum of $300 from 1985 forward. A second part of the bill included a voucher system to help parents of disadvantaged children to receive federal aid from states or individual schools districts so that they could choose the school they wanted their children to attend. A third part of the bill proposed to allow parents to save $1,000 for their children's college education with no tax on the interest.

By the time the bill reached the House, sections two and three were already deleted.

Two ironies accompanied the abbreviated bill. The Carnegie Commission issued its famous report, *A Nation at Risk,* decrying the state of American education that year. And, within a month of the introduction of Reagan's bill, the Supreme Court also ruled, in *Mueller v Allen*[6] that a state tax deduction for educational expenses was constitutional. Perhaps sensing that financial relief would ensure greater school choice as well as difficulties in the public schools, the Senate dug in its heels, ignored both events, and tabled what was left of S528. More significantly, the White House did nothing to push the bill. Staffers at the United States Catholic Conference, who had so much hope and so much at stake at the time, reported that they had been waiting for administration action,[7] but to no avail. Finally, White House strategists said why: they admitted that they could not support a tuition tax credit bill that would cost between 245 and 779 million dollars by FY 1987,[8] *and* tax reform, which was President Reagan's top economic priority. Thus, in 1985, the Reagan administration scrapped the tuition tax credit plan completely, in favor of "Reaganomics."

President Reagan's Secretary of Education William Bennett, however, tried to salvage part of the plan. He urged the passage of a law that would institute a voucher system designed to give low-income families $600 per year so that they could choose from a variety of public and private schools for their children. Emphasizing economic parity and equality of opportunity rather than tax relief, the Department of Education, under Bennett, attempted to enact the first school choice initiative; but it went no further for lack of congressional support.[9] A similar attempt to create legislation for public funding for remedial education through school choice also died.

Comparatively speaking, President Reagan and his administration made the most aggressive attempts to advance educational reform through school choice in the twentieth century and gave it the highest federal priority to date. At the other end of the spectrum, President Clinton has done just the opposite. He has consistently supported strengthening the public schools in America and outlined early in his campaign his plans to put education back on track. In the book, *Putting People First,* candidate Clinton, in 1992, called for fully funding Head Start, establishing national education standards, and instituting a federal system of examinations to measure students' and schools' progress. He supported raising the high school graduation rate to 90 percent, increasing Title One funds, reducing class size, supporting incentives to recruit and hire teachers, as well as helping states to "develop public school choice programs" within the public schools.[10] However, within a presidency committed to health care reform, job creation, and welfare change, the early attention given to education legislation was only negligible:

tinkering with tax credits for college tuition; allowing access to IRA's for college payments, and increasing Pell Grants.

In the 1996 campaign, however, challenged by Senator Robert Dole's support for vouchers, the President responded with a financial package for public education in order to stave off school choice. Calling for more teacher training grants to improve reading instruction, Clinton also sought voluntary national standards to test students in basic subjects. The latter idea met with opposition from teachers' organizations and minority groups. The NAACP and the Mexican Legal Defense and Education Fund feared that students would be subjected to biased testing.[11] And the National Council of Teachers of Mathematics complained that the lack of the use of calculators would limit the number of questions that could be asked in arithmetic and more advanced subjects. In October 1997, the testing plan was suspended by the Secretary of Education and, by November, the House imposed a moratorium on all federal mathematics testing.

President Clinton has adamantly opposed any type of federal funding that might support school choice. Claiming that such spending would hurt average families, that it would be a give-away to the wealthy, and that it would siphon off limited federal funds and resources from public schools, the chief executive vetoed all such efforts in the first six years of his presidency. In his State of the Union address in January 1999, the President did unveil a plan to make changes in the funding of public education. He called for reapportioning the twenty billion dollars that the Federal government spends annually on education in a new way—by rewarding school districts that follow federal guidelines on teacher training, enforcing classroom discipline, reporting school performance to parents, and ending the promotion of unqualified students. Using the carrot-and-stick approach, he announced that school districts that did not comply with these regulations would risk losing some or all of their federal assistance.

Even without presidential support, however, two major bills were introduced to advance school choice in the 105th Congress. The first was a voucher/scholarship program for impoverished children living in the District of Columbia, and the second was an educational savings account bill that would have applied to all elementary and secondary students in the United States.

In September 1997, in an attempt to overhaul the District of Columbia's 4.2 billion dollar budget, Rep. Charles Taylor (R-N.C.), chair of the House Appropriations subcommittee on the District, recommended that the poorest children in Washington each receive a $3,200 voucher. These were intended to help defray the cost of public, private, or religious education in Maryland, Virginia, and the District of Columbia. Members of Congress, particularly House Speaker Newt Gingrich (R-Ga.), Senate Majority Leader Trent Lott (R-Miss.), and Sen. Joseph Lieberman (D-Conn.) proposed a similar plan, one that would have given 2,000 scholarships to low-income students in the District of Columbia. Passed by the House and the Senate, the plan, however, was vetoed by President Clinton on the claim that it had the potential of undercutting public education.

At the same time, Sen. Paul Coverdell (R-Ga.) and then, Representative Robert Torricelli (D-N.J.) jointly introduced S. 1133 and HR2646, bills that would have allowed parents, corporations, and foundations to put up to $2,500 a year in after-tax dollars into tax-free savings accounts. Their bill would have allowed the funds to be used later to pay for tutoring, school fees, home computers, preparatory test courses for college, or private/parochial school tuition for grades K–12. Approved by both the House and the Senate, with a $2,000 cap, the educational savings accounts (ESA's) represented a bipartisan shift in congressional sentiment, and set a new precedent with regard to education policy. Again, the legislation was vetoed by the President.

The bill was actually a culmination of Republican attempts to enact an "Agenda for the American Learner."[12] Two of its six planks were choice items: one designed to give $100 million for charter schools and the other to make $310 million available from another federal education fund to establish scholarships for children from low-income families. Neither of the measures moved very far along the legislative path. The charter-school bill passed in the House, but died in the Senate. The scholarship bill never made it beyond the House. Because of pressure from the NEA and the NAACP, the Congressional Black Caucus, which had originally supported the bill, dropped its support, thus deserting J. C. Watts (R-Okla.), its sponsor, and the Reverend Floyd Flake (D-N.Y.) its chief supporter. At the same time, the House lacked internal constituents for education reform, except possibly Peter Hoekstra (R-Mich.) and Frank Riggs (R-Calif.). The United States Catholic Conference, a key player, also feared that such legislation would jeopardize its own Title One funds, and refused to support the bill. Thus, school choice scholarships had nowhere to go at the time.

On the other hand, school choice advocates considered the fact that the ESA bill overcame so many obstacles as significant and encouraging. Some supporters hailed it and maintained that the "United States Congress has now affirmed parental rights in education as a national priority."[13] Polls showed that minorities agreed.[14]

Other groups, such as the powerful and politically influential National Education Association, opposed the ESA's. Education Secretary Richard Riley echoed the views of the educational establishment when he called the Coverdell-Torricelli bill "a regressive tax policy that is masquerading as something good for education."[15] Without a veto-proof majority in the Congress, and with strong union opposition, the measure was, of course, vetoed by the President.

As the end of the century approaches, it is possible to conclude that the current congressional attitude toward school choice has, indeed, begun to change. However, presidential behavior still generally reflects opposition to any reform that would advance school choice and possibly compromise the public educational system. Thus, it is important to track the area where school choice is most likely to advance, if at all, at the federal level: that place is the Supreme Court.

The Supreme Court

Since *Everson* (1947), many judicial challenges to educational policy have been couched in church/state terms. However, a brief overview of the most recent cases reveals that these claims have broadened and shifted to include a range of questions about student's rights, parent's rights, and school choice. Forming a jurisprudence that reflects an emerging and changing legal interpretation of the tripartite relationship between the state, students, and various types of schools, the Supreme Court and in some cases state courts have engaged in a strange dance. They often take two steps forward, and one step back, doing a political fox-trot with state legislatures and local politicians to implement school change.

The three facets of educational policy most challenged are those areas that deal with: (1) equal opportunities, (2) child benefits, and (3) equal access. Taking their lead from the Supreme Court, many state courts are also turning their legislative partners around and providing the impetus to force a constitutional confrontation on the issue of school choice in the United States.

Educational Opportunities

The most significant legal transformation, in terms of educational opportunity, came about in 1954 with the Supreme Court's landmark ruling in *Brown v Board of Education*.[16] That case struck down "the separate but equal" doctrine in American education, a policy that had prevailed since *Plessy v Ferguson*,[17] and effectively ended school discrimination based on race.

Brown has been important to education jurisprudence because it also serves as an example of judicial activism. In that case, the Court went beyond simply handing down a decision; it also designated a plan for mandated bussing to make educational integration a reality. Since that time, the Supreme Court has heard other cases, issued remedial integration orders, and played a growing role in implementing school change. For example, in *Swann v Charlotte-Mecklenburg Board of Education*,[18] the court held that racial balance could be achieved in public schools by a variety of techniques, including quotas, transportation, the design of new attendance zones, and the pairing of schools. Thus, in some cities, magnet schools, charter schools, and other kinds of experimental schools were established as a way to integrate district schools.[19]

While the Court has ruled so aggressively on this matter, it has also recently recognized that it cannot make changes in the "quality" of education in low-income areas without some limits. In Missouri, for example, higher taxes were used to pay better salaries for teachers and staff within the Kansas City school district for the last eighteen years in order to provide better education in the inner city. But in a legal test of state legislative and judicial power, the Supreme Court ruled in *Jenkins v Missouri*[20] that remedial action is limited, and that it may not be extended beyond desegregation to effect "quality education."

In other equality challenges, lower courts have also mandated open enrollments plans, particularly in Nebraska, Arkansas, and Minnesota.[21] But often, judicial decrees that have called for intra-district and inter-district school choice plans to bring about desegregation and greater equity were struck down as well.[22]

These challenges, however, are clearly expected to continue and proliferate. The judicial-political dance continues. Just recently, for example, a case was brought before the Connecticut Court of Appeals in which the plaintiffs argued that the state is responsible to correct alleged constitutional violations to assure public school children an equal education opportunity. Agreeing with the claimants, the Court ruled that the state, alone, had the obligation to provide a substantially equal education opportunity, particularly in light of the dual condition of poverty and racial/ethnic isolation. Thus, the implementation of a policy requiring a "thorough and efficient" education, as it is often called, has now been placed at the door of the Connecticut General Assembly by the Court.[23]

In some states, like New Jersey, the state Supreme Court has already charged the legislature with equalizing education opportunity, but has rejected as inadequate a variety of plans that have been drawn up by the State Assembly.[24] As a result, the judicial-political dance provides a reason to change partners in the political arena frequently.

The Garden State is unique in that it passed an enabling statute in 1987 allowing the state Department of Education to take over school districts that were not providing a thorough and efficient education to its students. Additionally, it allowed the state to create and operate school districts to provide corrective budgetary and administrative actions. As a result, in 1989, the functioning of the Jersey City schools, one of the worst school systems in the state, passed from the hands of the district board of education and its officials to the control of the state.

The action had the unintended effect of giving rise to a variety of plans to change the way that education was being delivered, not only in Jersey City but across the state, as the Court had mandated earlier. Two critical state officials supported different approaches, namely, charter schools for educational reform, versus scholarships to bring about equality of educational opportunity.[25] Leading the charge for change were Joseph Doria, the Minority Leader of the State Assembly, a limited charter schools advocate, and Bret Schundler, the mayor of Jersey City, who supported equal opportunity scholarships.

Doria, a former history teacher and past president of the Bayonne Board of Education, now heads the human resources division of St. Peter's College in Jersey City along with his position in the legislature. Determined and well versed in educational theory, he completed all of the course work for his doctorate in education—twice. After his initial studies, he ran out of time to finish the writing of his dissertation, so he took all the course work all over again at Columbia Teacher's College in New York, where he is again in the throes of attempting to complete the research part of his degree. Extremely knowledgeable in pedagogy, he is also master of the political infrastructure within the New Jersey legislature. And so, when he perceived a movement toward education reform in the state, he designed a charter school bill in 1995 in order to control both the substance and the process of that desired change. A true political pragmatist, Doria is also the consummate backroom, deal-making, politician. The first person to realize that only an incremental approach to reform under state control could work, he rejected the notion of radical change administered by local municipalities, the courts, or the teachers' unions. Instead, Doria combined his educational expertise with his political savvy, and was a natural to bring together enough Democrats and Republicans in the legislature to place school funding and accountability in the hands of the state government. His plan gave parents and teachers the opportunity to create experimental, or charter, schools within the public school system, i.e., new schools that were basically paid for by the state. Viewing this as a way to ensure legislative, rather than judicial, control over the school reform question, Doria created a pressure valve to let off some of the steam in the education reform movement. Most important, he and the legislature controlled the change that was about to occur. Doria led the judicial-legislative dance.

Republican Bret Schundler, the mayor of Jersey City, on the other hand, is more philosophical and continues to see school choice as the "civil rights issue of this generation." A committed Evangelical, this young millionaire made his fortune on Wall Street in the 1980s, but decided to leave stocks and bonds behind and to spend the next part of his life in public service. He has been influenced by both his religion and his economics, and he can theorize on the ideas of the Founding Fathers or Milton Friedman with the best of scholars. Schundler won election to the New Jersey State Senate in 1991 and, soon thereafter, became the first Republican mayor of blue-collar, Democratic Jersey City for the first time in history. His wife, an attorney, works as a consultant to the city for a dollar per year.

Schundler's first political challenge was, and remains, turning around the failed schools in Jersey City. He stepped into office after the schools had been taken over by the state, and he has been working to bring education back to a level of competency that will make Jersey City's schools free of state control. Schundler supports school vouchers and sees equality opportunity scholarships as the critical step to implement school choice. Religiously, ideologically, and politically, he believes that school choice empowers parents, creates civic virtue and responsibility in students, subjects the public schools to the market forces of supply and demand, and provides equality of opportunity to all children.

Schundler attempted to get legislation enacted in 1996 that would have permitted the state to fund scholarships for low-income students in Jersey City, but he failed. This was due, in part, to the fact that the scholarship program only applied to Jersey City, and that most of the legislators were loathe to vote funding for such an expensive project without getting something for their own districts. He also lacked the backing of the Republican governor at the time, Christine Todd Whitman, herself an ostensible advocate for school choice.

The governor had promised, during the campaign, to give Schundler's plan her support if he could deliver Democratic Jersey City for her. Schundler provided 87,000 votes for the Republican candidate, assuring her victory, but was jolted into political reality when he found that Whitman did not want to use her political currency to advance his agenda after the election. Instead, she pushed her own issues and did nothing about school choice for a year.

In 1997, Governor Whitman created her own gubernatorial educational reform plan. An inter-district experiment in school choice, Whitman's pilot program was struck down by the New Jersey Supreme Court immediately, thus leaving only Doria's charter school plan in place.

Whitman has now been reelected for a second term, but has done nothing further to advance school choice in the Garden State. Doria is still the Minority Leader in the Assembly and presides over his charter school experiment. Schundler remains as Jersey City's mayor, and is stumping nationally for school choice. He waits patiently to see if the governor has higher political aspirations and will need his help again—hoping that this time, his support will be the leverage to get voucher legislation enacted in New Jersey in the future. The legislature continues to wrestle with ways to implement its judicially mandated responsibility to provide a thorough and efficient education to all students within the state. The court waits to rule on the next education opportunity initiative. The judicial-political dance continues.

Child Benefits

In the second category of cases, those dealing with educational benefits, the Supreme Court has made a variety of decisions since *Everson* that indicate its continued concern for students *qua* students and parents *qua* parents. Recognizing that all students, and in some cases their parents, are eligible for particular "benefits," these rulings have continued to expand and to include broader financial assistance to the families of those attending non-public schools. This can be seen in the Court's rulings in *Board of Education v Allen*,[26] *Wolman v Walter*,[27] *Mueller v Allen*,[28] *Witters v Washington Services for the Blind*,[29] *Zobrest v Catalina Foothills Board of Education*,[30] *Board of Education of Kyrias Joel v Grumet*,[31] and *Agostini v Felton*.[32]

Beginning in 1968, the Court enlarged the principle of indirect assistance to students as "child benefits." In *Board of Education v Allen*, it reiterated the funding for text books, and in *Wolman v Walter* added testing, diagnostic services, and guidance fees to the list of child benefits allowed to students in non-public schools. The most important case dealing with child benefits occurred in 1983, however, when the Court considered the question of whether or not parents, who sent their children to *any school* in Minnesota, could take a tax deduction for certain education expenses, including private school tuition. In *Mueller v Allen*, the Court upheld the benefit. Reasoning that it impacted a large segment of society directly and that individual parochial or private schools were effected only indirectly, the Court maintained that the tax credit should be construed as having a secular rather than a religious purpose. Thus, the benefit was ruled legal, opening the door for school choice advocates to implement tax credits for education scholarships, most notably in Minnesota and Arizona.[33]

In 1986, in *Witters,* the state of Washington denied vocational funds to a blind man because he wanted to use the benefit to attend a seminary. Again, the Court ruled that such public monies were available to *everyone* and that they encompassed a broad classification of citizens, and, therefore, could not be denied on the basis of religious affiliation. In 1993, a similar situation occurred. In that year, the Court heard the case of a student who attended a parochial high school and was denied the right to a deaf interpreter because he attended a religious institution. Ruling in *Zobrest* that the student had been denied his free speech rights and had been discriminated on the basis of his religion, the Court upheld the right of all students to receive certain educational benefits without regard to religious affiliation. More recently, the Court took up the case of *The Board of Education of Kyrias Joel,* which sought to establish a separate school district within its incorporated village in order to use the taxes of that newly formed district to fund a school for handicapped Hasidic children. Although the Court held that the action did violate the separation of church and state, it did allow the Hasidim to recreate another school district based on a specific mechanism applicable to the entire state of New York. While the final disposition is again being challenged in the federal courts, the matter may be moot, since the Court's most recent decision in *Agostini v Felton* reversed its previous ruling of remedial education. Holding that such education could be provided by public school teachers within the buildings of parochial schools, the Court, in effect, maintained that remedial education was a "child benefit." Thus, the Hasidim might still be allowed to provide special education to their students in their own school buildings in New York in the future.

Equal Access

Equal access to school facilities is a third area of educational change that has been addressed by the Supreme Court, particularly in the cases of *Widmar v Vincent*[34] *Board of Education v Mergens,*[35] *Lamb's Chapel v Center Moriches School District,*[36] and *Rosenberger v Rector.*[37] In each of these cases, religious groups sued for the right to use public school buildings, university facilities, or university funds to carry out their religious purposes. In 1981, in *Widmar,* a group of college students wanted to use university facilities to hold meetings for their Bible study club. Denied access by the administration, the students sued, claiming religious discrimination. The Court held for the students, maintaining that the school had created a public forum for its students, and that to deny access to one group solely on the basis of religion was a violation of the Fourteenth Amendment. Some scholars see this as a turning point in the Court's treatment of religious groups, contending that "the Court now found that an equal access policy was compatible with its establishment clause jurisprudence."[38] In fact, this same right was granted to high school students in 1990, when secondary school youngsters wanted to establish religious clubs able to receive treatment equal to that of other clubs. Denied that, they appealed to the Supreme Court, which ruled that to deny equal access is an act of hostility toward religion. One year later in 1992, the principle was tested again in *Lamb's Chapel.* In that case, a group of parents from a particular church requested the right to use public school facilities that were routinely rented out for social, civic, and recreational purposes. They wanted to show a movie about family and child rearing issues. Although the district provided a limited forum for such activities, the Court ruled that to deny the particular church group from airing its views on the topic was, nevertheless, a violation of the free speech clause of the First Amendment. Finally, and most recently, students at the University of Virginia brought suit again its administration, claiming in 1995 that the university denied funds for the publication of a Christian journal. Citing that the university funded fifteen other student opinion publications, the students maintained that their free speech rights had been violated, but that funding would not compromise the establishment clause of the First Amendment. Again the justices agreed with them.

Clearly, it has been demonstrated that the Supreme Court has already articulated significant changes in educational policy with regard to the principles of equality of opportunity, child benefits, and equal access in the United States during the last half century. But in a number of state cases, the lower federal courts have gone even further, prescribing some types of school choice as the legal remedy for a lack of thoroughness, efficiency, and efficacy in the public school system, particularly as it effects the financially disadvantaged in America's inner cities. As a result, the range of issues and players in the school choice arena has grown. It now encompasses not only Catholics and Evangelicals but also Hasidim and Islamic believers, black church groups, tax reformers, entrepreneurs, policy researchers, and foundations. Thus legal challenges to education policy are being brought on diverse grounds. The school choice suits are no longer "Catholic" or "Hasidic" or "black" issues, but they are instead claims about religious, racial, and economic discrimination, unfair taxation, and limitations on due process. In response, the traditional roles of interest groups to educate, monitor, and lobby on behalf of school choice have been augmented by that of public interest law firms that now litigate for a change in American educational policy before local, state, and federal courts.

Public Interest Law Firms

Currently, the majority of school choice lawyers represent religious, conservative, and libertarian legal organizations that are committed to help individuals and others to challenge educational policy within the United States. These firms are proliferating and include the Institute for Justice, the Becket Fund, the United States Catholic Conference, the Landmark Legal Foundation, the American Center for Law and Justice, the Christian Legal Society, the Liberty Counsel, the Rutherford Institute, and the Western Center for Law and Religious Freedom. They have become major players to leverage school change in the United States by taking on the liberal and "establishment" legal coalitions, most notably the National Education Association, the American Civil Liberties Union, Americans United for Separation of Church and State, and People for the American Way.

Public interest law firms work for school choice in a variety of ways. Often they act as counsels, co-counsels, or intervenors before a variety of state and federal courts. Sometimes they serve as activists in the court of public opinion, and, just as important, they also represent particular interests by filing as *amicus curiae* in specific cases. Although there are also a variety of private law firms[39] that operate in the school choice arena, they will not be examined here because often their main focus is on a wider range of private issues. Instead, this section will focus on those public interest firms most active today in attempting to bring about educational options through judicial tactics.

The Institute for Justice

First among these in influence today is the Institute for Justice. A self-described libertarian law firm, the Institute was founded in 1991 by William Mellor and Clint Bolick. Mellor is the Institute's President and General Counsel. He formerly served as deputy general counsel at the U. S. Department of Energy and as senior attorney at the Mountain States Legal Foundation.

Bolick is the Institute's Vice President and Director of Litigation. He served previously in the Reagan administration; the Civil Rights Division of the U. S. Department of Justice, and the U. S. Equal Employment Opportunity Commission where he worked for Clarence Thomas. Subsequently, Bolick headed the Landmark Center for Civil Rights. A certified teacher before going to law school, Bolick became interested in school choice when he read about Polly Williams and her attempts to get public vouchers enacted in Milwaukee in 1990. He contacted her and offered legal help, but recounts that her first comment was, "Why do I need a lawyer?" According to him, the rest is history. His motto is: "If you have a school choice program you have a lawyer." In fact, he assumes that if a school choice initiative does not end up in court, it is doing no good![40]

More than a litigator, Bolick is another one of those rare individuals who can blend intellectualism with pragmatism. He is the author of several major articles and books, the most recent being *Transformation: The Promise and Politics of Empowerment*.[41] Bolick draws a philosophical comparison between charter schools and *perestroika*—they are a step with more to come. He sees the variety of choice cases that he handles as a teaching tool for the public and a way to build support for the issue, but despite this active writing agenda, he handles most of the major litigation for the Institute for Justice.

Located in Washingtonm D.C., the Institute for Justice through "strategic litigation, training, communications, and outreach, attempts to advance a rule of law under which individuals can control their own destinies as free and responsible members of society."[42] It has been known to support, among other issues, vouchers and other kinds of school choice. It opposes the ideology of the welfare state and is, therefore, funded primarily by private donations, foundations, and corporations. It has a yearly budget of over one million dollars and interacts politically with the Heritage Foundation, CEO America, the Center for Educational Reform, the American Education Reform Project, the Center for Equal Opportunity, and other like-minded organizations.[43]

It was Clint Bolick who brought some of the earliest school choice litigation before the courts. In 1992, representing over a hundred low income families, he argued against the Chicago public school system in *Jenkins v Leininger*[44] and the Los Angeles School District in *Arviso v Honig*,[45] because both had failed to provide quality public education. Subsequently, Bolick and the Institute have represented school choice advocates in Maine, Vermont, Ohio, Arizona, Pennsylvania, and Wisconsin, thus being in the center of most of the major cases dealing with school choice litigation in the United States today.

One such example is in Maine, where many small towns do not have their own public high schools. There, the state often pays the fees for students who opt to attend private or public schools in adjacent districts. This practice, known as "tuitioning," allowed subsidies to be used in both religious and non-religious private schools. In 1983, however, the state legislature reversed that policy, excluded sectarian schools, and justified its action citing the need to maintain the principle of separation of church and state.

In almost duplicate cases involving children from the Minot and Raymond school districts, the Institute has represented Maine families that recently sought public payment for the cost of their children's tuition at Roman Catholic schools.[46] In effect, the parents were requesting state vouchers to cover the cost of paying the tuition of their children's education. Both suits contended that because the state pays tuition to some private schools it should not discriminate between private schools that are religious and those that are not. In nearly identical opinions in U.S. District Court, and in a Maine superior court, two different judges, rejected Bolick's arguments. Both ruled narrowly that there was no constitutional authority for such requirements in the Maine constitution. These decisions have also been upheld in the Maine Supreme Court and the First Circuit Court of the U.S. Court of Appeals.[47]

Although Bolick and the members of the Institute for Justice were disappointed by the decision, the experience served as the basis for a second, similar suit in Vermont. In that state, the constitution requires that towns furnish a high school education, in any of three different ways, to its citizens. The state permits the operation of individual or collective public schools, private schools designated to function as a town's high school, or the payment of the tuition of students to attend other high schools in a different district. Tuition fees were regularly paid to religious schools, but the practice was ended in 1961. Three decades later, however, when a parent petitioned the board of education for the tuition fee for his child to attend a sectarian school, the state again allowed the payment. Citing the evolution in First Amendment establishment clause jurisprudence, the Vermont Circuit Court seemed to reopen the matter. In the confusion, eighty-eight school districts, which were involved in tuitioning situations by 1995, sought a new state opinion on the matter of reimbursement.

The Commissioner of Education, with the approval of the state Attorney General, issued new regulations in an attempt to try to clarify the issue. He required districts now to send tuition payments directly to the schools selected by the parents. The Chittenden Town School District, attempting to obey the new directive, transmitted tuition payments to the Catholic high schools that the parents in their district chose for their children. But the Department of Education responded by terminating all general state aid to the district! The town, in confusion and anger, turned to the Institute for Justice.

Acting on behalf of the Chittenden Town School District, the Institute for Justice argued its case for state tuition payments to religious/private schools on several fronts. First, it maintained that tuition payments were neutral, child benefits neither hindered nor advanced religion, and the choice of where to use the benefit should be left to the individual beneficiary. Second, the Institute argued that neither the U.S. Constitution nor the Vermont constitution would be violated by the payment of tuition to a parochial high school because the tuition benefit does allow a parent to choose a particular school. As neutral, rather than institutional, aid, the plaintiffs maintained that to deny payment to religious schools was an act of discrimination. Citing both *Everson* and *Mueller,* the Institute also argued that Chittendon's actions were neutral as to religion and that they provided benefits to families rather than to schools. However, on appeal the Vermont Supreme Court decided that state support for religious education is the same as state support of religious worship and denied the argument.[48]

The Institute was also involved in the case of *Gatton v Goff*[49] in Ohio. As an intervenor, the Institute represent concerned parents and the organization known as "Hope for Cleveland's Children." In this particular case, the then Governor, George Voinovich, proposed the use of public funds to help low-income students receive tuition and tutorial assistance grants. These were to be applied toward tuition eligible participating private schools within a particular district or a public school in a participating adjacent district. Capped at $2,500 or the cost of tuition, whichever was less, the funding was distributed by lottery and could be applied to any school that did not discriminate on the basis of race, religion, or ethnicity. Among those schools were private ones, some of which were new, some non-sectarian, and some religious that were operated by Catholics, Protestants, and Moslems.

Plaintiffs in this case argued that the Cleveland Pilot Scholarship Program was enacted illegally, that it violated the religious clause of the Ohio state constitution, and that it did not meet the *Lemon* test.[50] Answering these

complaints, the Institute for Justice contended that the Program was a legitimate attempt to equalize educational opportunities and to remedy the educational deprivations facing Cleveland school children. It maintained, first,
that it is the right of the parents to choose the education of their children.
Second, it claimed that the Pilot Project conforms to the three-prong *Lemon*
test; namely, that it has a secular purpose, that its primary effect is to neither
advance nor prohibit religion, and that there is no entangling alliance between church and state due to the statute. Third, it argued that the Program
follows in a line of child benefit precedents, thus contesting that scholarships
constitute a direct subsidy or financial assistance to religious schools. In
short, the Institute's arguments were based on the fact that the program was
about broadening educational options for disadvantaged families rather than
subsidizing religion to religious schools. The case, however, was decided on
behalf of the defendants.[51] The decision, which struck down the voucher
program on federal establishment clause and state constitutional grounds,
was appealed to the state Supreme Court. There, the court reversed those
issues, only to deny the program on a technicality.[52] Bolick is again considering another appeal to the U.S. Supreme Court.

The number of decisions of state courts and lower federal courts disallow-
ing various aspects of school choice, however, should not be interpreted as a
macabre dance in preparation for the death of the issue. Rather, the situation
is quite the reverse. Recently, the Supreme Court of Arizona upheld the use
of tax credits for tuition-aid donations,[53] thus giving encouragement to those
in Cleveland and elsewhere who would support the use of public monies to
provide equal educational opportunities.

In April 1997, the Arizona State Legislature enacted a law that allowed
individuals to receive a tax credit for donating up to $500 to a "school tu-
ition organization" that would provide scholarships for students to attend
private schools, including religious ones. A challenge to this law had been
mounted by a coalition of education and civil rights groups, and the Institute
became involved to support the tax credit law in the state. A special action
was filed by the Americans United for Separation of Church and State, but,
in early 1999, the Arizona Supreme Court ruled that the scholarship donations were legal. More important to school choice advocates, it also contended that "the encouragement of private schools in itself is not unconstitu-
tional. Such a policy can properly be used to facilitate a state's overall
educational goals."

Another voucher initiative case is also wending its way through the courts
in Pennsylvania.[54] There, the South East Delaware County (Delco) School
Board passed by a 7-0-2 vote, a voucher plan which would have allowed
taxpayers to use public funds to pay part of the cost of tuition at a private or
religious school. Struck down in the county court, the legal decision is being
appealed by the Institute and other groups to advance the case to higher
levels within the state. It represents an interesting challenge because it would

allow individual school districts within Pennsylvania to reimburse parents who send their children to private and religious schools. Their reimbursements would include $250 dollars for kindergarten, $500 for grades 1–8, and $1,000 for children in high school. The plan, according to its supporters, is meant to stabilize enrollments in local public and private schools, and has been touted as a way for the district to save more than a million dollars a year. Should it be successful, Pennsylvania's 501 school districts would have the option to change the funding of education within the state, district by district.

Of all these cases, the most successful one that the Institute has litigated and has gone the farthest in the judicial infrastructure has been the challenge to the expanded Milwaukee Parental Choice Program (MPCP). Argued in *Jackson v Benson*,[55] the program was originally enacted in 1990 and held constitutional at the state level in 1992. The program allowed up to 1 percent, or 1,000 economically disadvantaged pupils in the Milwaukee public schools, to use their state share of education funds as full payment of tuition in nonsectarian private schools that met certain state standards and agreed to participate in the program. The new plan, enacted as part of the 1995 state budget bill, increased the number of children eligible for the program to 15,000, and it included religious schools among the educational options. In a 1998 suit brought by Warner Jackson, the Milwaukee Teachers Education Association, and others, the plaintiffs contended that the MPCP violated the First Amendment of the U.S. Constitution, as well as the religion provision, the local bill provision, and the public purpose doctrine of the Wisconsin Constitution. And, in a more specific challenge, they also questioned the continued legality of those children who were enrolled in the program in September 1995 as still being eligible even if they met the prescribed economic criteria. Representing a variety of parents and the organization known as "Parents for School Choice," the Institute for Justice acted as an intervenor in the case. It defended the legality of the state's actions on three claims: that its purpose in founding the MPCP was to equalize educational opportunity for all; that the state assured adequate institutional accountability, and that it provided direct aid to parents rather than to educational institutions.

The critical nature of the case was underscored by the fact that six *amicus* briefs were filed, representing approximately fifty individuals and organizations. Perhaps the most important of these was the brief presented by David Riemer, Milwaukee's attorney on behalf of the city and its mayor, John O. Norquist.[56]

The mayor, committed to the notion of parental school choice, is another one of those few intellectual, yet pragmatic, individuals who can make educational options work in his city. Norquist believes that school choice will prevail and that it will revitalize the city. He sees the remaining barriers to school choice—income limits for vouchers and the establishment of more charter schools, including religious charter schools—as the wave of the future.

Riemer reflects the mayor's thinking, both philosophically and legally. His brief contained a series of innovative arguments crafted to reframe the school choice question. He indicated that this was done to influence Sandra Day O'Connor, who is viewed by many as the swing vote on the school choice issue, should the case ultimately be heard in the United States Supreme Court. In his brief, Riemer argued that the MCPP had been enacted to apply competitive pressure on the Milwaukee school system in order to improve it, and to afford low-income students more educational options. Citing the fact that Wisconsin had traditionally empowered parents to have greater choice in school preference, he maintained that it was the state's obligation to establish a wider range of options. Thus, reasoned Riemer, only by putting pressure on the public school system to improve itself could the state's education crisis be solved.

In a landmark decision, the Wisconsin Supreme Court held the Milwaukee Parental Choice Program to be legal on all counts. In a 4-2 ruling, the Court reasoned that the MPCP did not violate Wisconsin's existing ban on spending state money for religious schools, or the separation of church and state clause of the state's constitution. Instead, it maintained that the state had the responsibility to eliminate government preferences with regard to religion, rather than to constrain individual preferences for religion or to discriminate against it. Basing its decision on the principles established in *Everson,* the Court held that the expanded Milwaukee Parental Choice Program provided public funds for the benefit of children, rather than for the benefit of religious institutions. And, in essence it held that mere reimbursement is not aid.[57] The Court also maintained, on the basis of the *Lemon* test, that state oversight for the payment of funds to religious schools did not constitute an excessive entanglement and that the funds served a secular purpose, that is, they "provide[d] greater prospects for education" for low income families and they placed public and private school choice options on an equal footing. As a result, the state actions did not have the primary effect of advancing religion. Finally, the Court maintained that the MPCP program was designed to provide accountability to the state, and to serve the needs of a large, disadvantaged segment of the state population.

The politics surrounding the case are escalating. With Clint Bolick immediately declaring the decision to be "a total, unconditional victory for school choice" the Institute declared that "David has beaten Goliath on a very important one."[58] Other choice groups claimed that "common sense returned to the law of religious liberty."[59] And, buoyed by the decision, business leaders pledged to raise $200 million for a national voucher program for urban and particularly poor education districts.[60]

Opposition groups like the American Civil Liberties Union, Americans

United for Separation of Church and State, People for the American Way, and the NAACP had attacked the original suit and the decision on establishment and equality grounds. And, as could be expected, the case gave rise to some strong educational and political reactions in Wisconsin. The Superintendent of Education, along with the majority of members of the Board of Education of Milwaukee, began using delaying tactics in threatening to raise taxes and claiming that the financial viability of the Milwaukee school system was now in jeopardy. Further, the state Department of Public Instruction also sought to impose increasing state and federal regulations on private schools, leaving themselves open to the criticism that they intended to limit participation by private schools in the MPCP. The Institute monitored those actions, but, in the end, the growing regulations were not imposed.

Even more seriously, a developing polarization is becoming apparent between unions, teachers, and superintendents across the state with school choice Republican advocates, the latter of whom are becoming a critical mass in Wisconsin. At the same time, state Democrats who want the support of the white working class and the blacks in the cities are at odds with the mayor of Milwaukee, certain members of the board of education, the business community, African-American ministers, the Catholic establishment, and some members of the town council. Others are trying to make the school choice issue a racial matter in order to split the supporters of the school choice plan in the city.

On the whole, however, both sides did become divided, with various factions supporting and opposing motions to bring the case to the Supreme Court. The Institute for Justice had petitioned for a writ of certiorari and, in anticipation of its involvement in the case, announced that it had convened a group of constitutional scholars, Supreme Court experts, and Wisconsin lawyers "to help guide our strategy."[61] However, other supporters subsequently opposed the writ, fearing that the state might risk the loss of its case in order to uphold the new type of school financing for the other states where it is still in question. In November 1998, however, the Supreme Court denied certiorari in the Wisconsin case; therefore, the Institute is currently taking a "wait and see" attitude. It is hoping that one of the other four pending cases will convince the Supreme Court to back the issue of school choice in the future.

The Becket Fund

Another public interest law firm that litigates on behalf of school choice is the Becket Fund. A bipartisan, ecumenical, and non-profit organization, the Becket Fund describes its mission as the protection of the free expression of all religious traditions. Its advisory board boasts the likes of Senator Orrin Hatch (R-Utah) and U. S. Representative Henry Hyde (R-Ill.), constitutional scholars such as Douglas Kmiec of Pepperdine University, Michael McConnell of the University of Utah Law School, and Mary Ann Glendon of Harvard. William Barr, former U.S. Attorney General, along with Sargent Schriver and Eunice Kennedy Schriver, founders and chair of Special Olympics International, add a sense of credence to its work. Jay Lefkowitz, former Director of Cabinet Affairs in the White House and one of the lawyers who argued *Jackson v Benson* before the Wisconsin Supreme Court, gives significant legal stature to its advisory board. John Cardinal O'Connor, the Rev. Richard John Neuhaus, and Dr. Ronald B. Sobel, add the "ecumenical" dimension to the organization.

Located in Washington, D.C., the fund is headed by Kevin Hasson, who served at the former Attorney-Advisor for the Office of Legal Counsel of the U.S. Department of Justice. There, one of his responsibilities included advising the Reagan administration on church-state issues. After his government service, Hasson worked for a large Washington, D.C.-based law firm before founding the Becket Fund. Financed by voluntary grants and contributions from individuals, foundations, and corporations, the Fund mainly deals with fundamental questions of religious liberty. Recently, however, it has also been working to advance school choice in acting as lead counsel in *Gatton v Goff,* working with the Institute for Justice, and currently representing the plaintiffs in a unique legal situation in Massachusetts.

Boyette v Galvin[62] is a case that addresses two complex issues: religious discrimination and school choice. The first matter deals with the legality of the Massachusetts Anti-Aid Amendment adopted at the state's constitutional convention in 1917–18. A result of the Blaine Amendment, mentioned earlier, the meeting was held at the height of the nativist movement, and, according to the plaintiff, overwhelmingly controlled by members sympathetic to the ideas of the American, or Know-Nothing Party. The governor at the time, also a member of the Know-Nothings, was reputed to have discriminated against the Catholics who were pouring into the state. In retaliation or defense, the legislature enacted an amendment to the Massachusetts constitution that tightened state appropriations for religious undertakings and higher educational institutions, and totally denied the founding, maintenance, and aiding of any denominational schools, institutions, colleges, infirmaries, or hospitals. In 1974, the Anti-Aid Amendment was changed by the legislature again, this time allowing the state to give grants-in-aid to private higher educational institutions, students, parents, or guardians of students attending such institutions.

The second question in *Boyette* challenges the state's Anti-Initiative Amendment, also adopted at the constitutional convention in 1917–18. It contests the prohibition of the right of citizens to petition on behalf of any matters related to religion, religious practices, or religious institutions, especially those mentioned in the Anti-Aid Amendment. In short, plaintiffs in this case, who claim to be financially disadvantaged, are seeking state aid in the form of vouchers or scholarship to help pay the elementary and secondary tuition costs for their children who attend parochial schools.

Before plaintiffs can pursue legislative remedy and challenge the Anti-Aid Amendment, however, they must first initiate a petition request for a constitutional amendment that would enable the state of Massachusetts to enact a parental choice in education program. The crux of the plaintiff's arguments is that they are substantially burdened for religious reasons by the Anti-Initiative Amendment in their pursuit of this redress. The regular legislative process would require an affirmative vote of the majority of the members of the Massachusetts legislature in two successive joint sessions, and the initiative process would require only a one-fourth vote before the matter could be submitted to the voters.

The Becket Fund is arguing the case on five principles. First, it contends that the free speech of the plaintiff has been violated. Second, it is claiming that the free exercise of religion has been denied. Third, it is maintaining that the equal protection clause of the United States Constitution has been compromised. Fourth, it is alleging that the plaintiff's right to petition has been denied. Fifth, it is citing the state of Massachusetts with violating the establishment clause of the U.S. Constitution.

As of this writing, the Becket Fund has achieved part of its goal. The Massachusetts Circuit Court has allowed plaintiffs to solicit signatures to initiate a petition request for a constitutional amendment, holding the Anti-Initiative Amendment to be illegal. The other aspects of the case are pending.

Understandably, the school choice issue has brought other public interest lawyers into the fray and created a firestorm in Massachusetts. On the one side, the Parents Alliance for Catholic Education (PACE) has taken up the cause of school choice.[63] Founded in 1994 by the four Catholic bishops of Massachusetts, the organization's main purpose is to educate Catholic parents about school choice, to monitor legislation on the matter, and to publicize the church's position to the public and the government. It seeks primarily to influence Catholic parents, as well as state, local, and national policy makers, by supporting tuition tax credits and voucher programs. PACE is funded by contributions and grants of over a half million dollars a year that are donated by the four Bishops of the state, private foundations, and the Catholic schools within the state.

Steve Perla, the head of PACE, has established a successful grass-roots organization, having brought together a coalition of taxpayer and eighteen other organizations on a public level. He does not want school choice to be viewed as a "Catholic issue," and points to the fact that PACE has been successful in collecting over 65,000 signatures to petition the Massachusetts state legislature to consider school choice in the future.

What Next?

Some public interest law firms and other school choice litigators thought that the Supreme Court would hear *Jackson v Benson* on appeal during its 1998–99 session. Their hopes were based on the fact that, since the Wisconsin Supreme Court had upheld all the aspects of the case, it would surely win on the federal level and bring scholarships, vouchers, and other aspects of school choice to the rest of the United States. This was the view of Clint Bolick and the staff of the Institute for Justice, particularly, as they filed for a writ of certiorari. However, the Institute lacked the support of the other parties to the claim. The major power players, such as the Wisconsin state legislature, Polly Williams, the originator of the plan, and Mayor John Norquist of Milwaukee, feared that the gains made in the area of school choice would be lost if the Supreme Court ruled against Milwaukee's plan. The Landmark Legal Foundation, an *amicus* on the original suit, also withdrew its legal support.

Thus, the politics, the internal fragmentation of the legal groups, and the lack of cohesive support on the writ could be cited in speculating as to why the Supreme Court did not feel enough pressure to rule on the case in its 1998–1999 session. It is also possible to conjecture that the Court did not see school choice as a "clean" issue. It has been reported that only Justice Stephen Beyer supported hearing the case, leaving room for the belief that there was no consensus or clear majority coalescing within the ranks of the justices to assure a "win" for either side. Inside sources have claimed that until the justices are sure that a strong view is emerging, either for or against school choice, no legal decision will be made.

Two things are clear, however. The number and complexity of school choice cases are proliferating and they will have to be addressed soon. Without a constitutional standard on which to judge such efforts, state legislatures will continue to have to deal with a variety of individual, local, state, and national school advocates and organizations across the country in addition to judicial challenges to the equality, efficiency, and thoroughness of the status quo. Rising pressures for a federal ruling on the legality of current funding and spending for public and private education is simply a matter of time, and it holds with it the possibility of changing education in the United States as we now know it.

Until a Supreme Court decision is handed down, however, the complex interplay of inconsistent federal and state initiatives for educational reform will continue its strange dance. A series of steps that are currently constrained within a political process that is historically, philosophically, and legally limited in what it can and wants to do, the dance now includes some new and liberating movements. Tax credits for scholarship donations, scholarship vouchers, and the distinct possibility of educational savings accounts are small strides, but steps that have the potential to change the entire educational reform exercise in the United States.

Notes

1. *Pierce v Society of Sisters,* 268 U.S. 510 (1925).
2. *Cochran v Board of Education,* 281 U.S. 370 (1930).
3. *Everson v Board of Education,* 330 U.S. 1 (1947).
4. See his speech to the members of the Catholic Education Association in Cincinnati, Ohio, October 1979.
5. Frank Monahan, "Memorandum, Tax Credits for Education: Background and Analysis," unpublished, February 23, 1981, p. 5. Available from the United States Catholic Conference. Hereafter UCCF.
6. *Mueller v Allen,* 463 U.S. 388 (1983).
7. Correspondence of Father Thomas Gallagher, Secretary of Education for the USCC, August 20, 1985, p. 1.
8. "Bell Is Criticized on Tuition Credit," *New York Times,* April 29, 1983, p. A19.
9. Dr. Edward Anthony of the USCC, former Director of the Office of Educational Assistance for the USCC and former Assistant to the Director of the Office of Private Education of the Department of Education, interview by Jo Renee Formicola, August 28, 1986.
10. Bill Clinton and Al Gore, *Putting People First* (New York: Times Books, 1992), pp. 85–86.
11. Tamara Henry, "Clinton Pushes for National Exams," *USA Today,* August 29, 1996, p. 9D.
12. Robert W. Sweet, Jr., staff member of the House Subcommittee on Education and the Workforce, interview by Hubert Morken, November 20, 1997.
13. USCC, Federal Legislative Action Call, June 26, 1998.
14. Donald Lambro, "House Passes No-Tax Tuition Savings Plans," *Washington Times,* October 24, 1997, p. A24.
15. Lizette Alvarez, "House Approves Special Accounts for School Costs," *New York Times,* October 27, 1997, p. A29.
16. *Brown v Board of Education,* 347 U.S. 483 (1954).
17. *Plessy v Ferguson,* 163 U.S. 537 (1896).
18. *Swann v Charlotte-Mecklenburg Board of Education,* 402 U.S. 1 (1971).
19. For an in-depth discussion, see May Haywood Metz, *Different by Design: The Context and Character of Three Magnet Schools* (London: Routledge and Kegan Paul), 1986.
20. *Jenkins v Missouri,* 110 S. Ct. 1651 (1990). For a discussion of the case see Deborah. E. Beck, "*Jenkins v Missouri*: School Choice as a Method of Desegregation and Equity," *California Law Review,* July 1993, and Thomas J. Walsh, "No Taxation without Representation unless Desegregation. The Power of Federal Courts to Order Tax Increases to Desegregate Schools: *Missouri v Jenkins,*" *Hamline Journal of Public Law and Policy* (spring 1991).

21. See for example, the order of the Eighth Circuit Court of Appeals to the Omaha School District, in July 1975.

22. For a discussion of the legal principle see Angela G. Smith, "Public School Choice and Open Enrollment: Implications for Education, Desegregation and Equity," *Nebraska Law Review, 1995.* Also see the cases: *Milliken v Bradley,* 481 U.S. 717 (1974) and *Freeman v Pitts,* 503 U.S. 467 (1992).

23. *Sheff v O'Neil* 238 Conn. 1: 678 A.2d. 1267, 1996. On appeal 1998.

24. Many pieces of legislation had been considered in response to suits brought for a thorough and efficient education as guaranteed in the New Jersey State Constitution. See the cases *Abbot v Burke (Abbot II)* 119 NJ 287 (1991) and *Abbot v Burke (Abbot IV)* 149 NJ 145 (1996). In 1996, Governor Christine Todd Whitman signed P. L. 1995, c.426 into law, thus enacting charter school legislation for the Garden State.

25. Mayor Bret Schundler of Jersey City and Minority Leader Joseph Doria of the New Jersey State Assembly, interviews by Jo Renee Formicola and Hubert Morken, September 12, 1997.

26. *Board of Education v Allen,* 392 U.S. 236 (1968).

27. *Wolman v Walter,* 433 U.S. 229 (1977).

28. *Mueller v Allen,* 462 U.S. 388 (1983).

29. *Witters v Washington Services for the Blind,* 474 U.S. 481 (1986).

30. *Zobrest v Catalina Foothills Board of Education,* 509 U.S. 1 (1991).

31. *Board of Education of Kyrias Joel v Grumet,* 512 U.S. 687 (1994).

32. *Agostini v Felton,* 117 S. Ct. 1997.

33. See for example, the state of New Jersey, where Governor Brendan Byrne had attempted to establish a tuition tax credit plan as early as 1978. *Public Funds for Public Schools v Byrne,* F. 2d 514 (1979).

34. *Widmar v Vincent,* 454 U.S. 263 (1981).

35. *Board of Education v Mergens,* 496 U.S. 226 (1990).

36. *Lamb's Chapel v Center Moriches School District,* 508 U.S. 384 (1993).

37. *Rosenberger v Rector,* 115 S. Ct. 2510 (1995).

38. See Angela Carmella, " '*Everson* and its Progeny' Separation and Non-Discrimination in Tension," in *Everson Revisited,* Formicola and Morken, eds. (Lanham, Maryland: Rowman and Littlefield, 1997), p. 110.

39. See Ball, Skelly, Murren, and Connell, among other partnerships.

40. Clint Bolick, interview by Hubert Morken, Washington, D.C., November 20, 1997.

41. His major publications include: *The Affirmative Action Fraud: Can We Restore the American Civil Rights Vision?* (1996), *Grassroots Tyranny: The Limits of Federalism* (1993), *Changing Course: Civil Rights at the Crossroads* (1988), *Supreme Court and Civil Rights: A Challenge for George Bush* (1989), and *Unfinished Business: A Civil Rights Strategy for America's Third Century* (1991).

42. Internet transmission of Maureen Blum, Outreach Director of the Institute for Justice, November 9, 1998, www.mblum@ij.org.

43. Survey of the authors.

44. Filed in Cook County Circuit Court on June 10, 1992.

45. Filed in Los Angeles County Superior Court on June 10, 1992.

46. See *Bagley v Department of Education*, Slip Op., No. CV-97-484 (Ma. Superior Ct., April 20, 1998) and *Strout v Commissioner, Maine Department of Education*, 113 F. Supp. 2d 112 (D. Me. 1998).

47. *Bagley v Raymond School Department*, 1999 ME 60, 728 A. 2nd 127 (1999).

48. See *Chittenden Town School District v Vermont Department of Education*, Slip Op. No. SO-478-96 RcC (Vt. Sup. Ct., Rutland Co., June 27, 1997); *Swart v So. Burlington School District* 167 A. 2nd 514 (Vt. 1961); Chittenden Town School District v Vt. Dept. of Education (97-275), Slip Op. (Vt. Sup. Ct. June 11, 1999).

49. *Gatton v Goff*, No. 19970117, Slip Op. (Ohio Sup. Ct. May 27, 1999).

50. *Lemon v Kurtzman*, 403 U. S. 602 (1971). The case set up a three-pronged test to determine if a statue violated the principle of separation of church and state. It asked if a statute had a secular purpose as its primary effect, if it hindered or advanced religion, or if it created an entangling alliance between church and state.

51. See *Simmon-Harris v Goff*, No. 96 APE08–982-1997 WL 217583 (Ohio Ct. Appeals, May 1, 1997).

52. On appeal the case was turned back because it violated the "single subject" requirement of the Ohio Constitution. It was created as part of the omnibus budget bill. See *Simmons-Harris v Goff*, No. 97-1117 Slip Op. at 18 (Ohio May 27, 1999).

53. *Kotterman v Killian* 972 P. 2d 606 (Ariz. 1999).

54. *Giacomucci v Southeast Delco School District*, No. 98–5805 (Pa. Common Pleas Ct., Delaware Cty., October 14, 1998).

55. *Jackson v Benson* 578 N. W. 2nd 602, 620 (Wisc. 1998).

56. David Riemer, Esq., interview by Jo Renee Formicola, Madison, NJ, July 23, 1998; Mayor John Norquist, interview by Hubert Morken, Milwaukee, WI, July 30, 1998.

57. The ruling follows the reasoning and precedents of *Mueller v Allen; Witters v Washington School for the Blind*, and *Zobrest v Catalina Foothills School District*.

58. Internet transmission of the Institute for Justice June 10, 1998, www.m-blum.ij.org.

59. Kevin Hasson of the Becket Fund as quoted by Ethan Bronner in "Wisconsin Court Upholds Vouchers in Church Schools," *The New York Times,* 11 June 1998.

60. It was at this time that Ted Forstmann and John Walton came forward with their scholarship initiative. At first they offered to put 100 million dollars into it. See *The International Herald Tribune,* June 10, 1998, p. 83. Later they increased their donations to 200 million dollars.

61. Memo from Clint Bolick. Internet transmission of the Institute for Justice, August 19, 1998. www.mblum.ig.org.

62. *Boyette v Galvin*, No. 98-CV-10377-GO filed in Fed. Dist. Ct. (June 12, 1998).

63. Steve Perla, Executive Director, interview by Jo Renee Formicola, September 18, 1998.

Chapter 2

Elections and Legislation:
Colorado and California

In 1998, the Colorado tax credit initiative and the California charter school legislation had two things in common: both began as ballot initiatives and each was the brainchild of a businessman. Otherwise they were different in terms of expectations and strategies. Initial prospects in Colorado for a tax credit initiative victory were high, but unrealized. In California the reverse happened—anticipated failure for the charter school legislation resulted in success. How and why did school choice in these two states meet such unanticipated and different fates? In Colorado, sufficient grassroots and interest group support simply was not there. In California, however, where leadership and political tactics were superb and the objective of charter school expansion was less ambitious, success was achieved.

One thing was new and of strategic importance in both cases—the intense involvement of local businessmen Steve Schuck in Colorado and Reed Hastings in California, respectively, and their high-tech computer industry friends. Because of people like them, school choice politics has gone modern with leaders arising unattached to old ethnic, religious, or political loyalties. They want change because they consider the current system irrelevant and outdated, especially for the poor and for technology-based industries lacking competent workers. Neither Schuck nor Hastings is hostile to public education, but they think a traditional government monopoly of tax funding for education is disastrous. Their immediate goal in 1998 was to get the public to agree and to pass initiatives expanding school choice in their respective states.

Using initiatives to advance school choice is a hotly contested subject within the education reform community. A total of twenty-four states and the District of Columbia have used the initiative process to pass laws and amend constitutions. Essentially, the process involves voters petitioning for

42

a change in the law by having it put on the ballot, thus allowing a majority vote of the people. This is direct democracy and considered to be especially useful when legislatures are resistant to an issue such as school choice. Initiatives help to generate civic discussion and voter participation in decision making; they can also be used to place pressure on legislatures as was done by Steve Schuck in Colorado. Scholars note that initiatives have their weaknesses as well: they can be manipulated by big money special interests, they can be decided by TV ads, they can be poorly drafted, they may be hard to implement, and they can abuse the interests of minorities. Despite these drawbacks they are now used frequently; in fact, in 1996 alone there were ninety initiatives on the ballot in a total of twenty-two states.[1]

Those who support initiatives claim that they speak for the people and a good cause. They may be the brainchild of a visionary who taps into the popular needs of the day. This was true of the famous 1978 tax limitation initiative in California, Proposition 13, and two other tax initiatives in Massachusetts (1980) and Colorado (1992). The underlying organizational support structures, financing, and political tactics varied, but all three shared the presence of a visionary leader, respectively, Howard Jarvis, Barbara Anderson, and Douglas Bruce. All also received somewhat favorable press coverage and all were able to use TV to reach the public effectively. Voters enthusiastically responded even when the initiative organizations were small and their message simple. Few people campaigned. Supporters did *not* march in the streets, ring doorbells, raise money, write letters, make phone-calls, send faxes, or lobby. Instead, attention grabbing TV spots did the trick.[2]

Asked why so few people care enough to study an issue and campaign for it, these tax-crusading visionaries, somewhat ironically in the context of this discussion, blamed the failing education system. As citizens are less able to think, visionaries suggest, they are also less active in politics. As school standards decline the people will be less likely to reform the system. Why then even try to use an initiative to pass school choice? Will enough voters care for children to overcome all the negative propaganda? The answer taught by tax crusaders is to use creative marketing, using power symbols that capture the imagination of poorly educated voters with pictures and a few words.[3]

Businessmen, like Steve Schuck and Reed Hastings, understand the use of power and symbols. Freshly arrived in the education reform battle like young generals ready to fight in an old war, they are not handicapped by fatigue and disappointment. Confident they can succeed where others have failed, Schuck and Hastings launched initiative campaigns, which renewed the school choice movement. What is new in school choice politics is the arrival of entrepreneurs—activists who are independent, freewheeling, sensitive to marketing issues, and able to move with lightening speed and chutzpah.

Colorado School Choice Strategies

Steve Schuck is a land developer in Colorado Springs who came originally from New York. His brother is a law professor at Yale University. In 1986 Schuck lost a bid to become governor. Two years later Schuck lost his considerable fortune and even his home (he did not declare bankruptcy), as a result of the Savings and Loan collapse. For the past decade he rebuilt his business. This one-time math teacher, football coach, and recovered businessman has no desire to lose at anything, but he has a history of taking risks.[4]

In Colorado in 1998 the tax credit initiative lost by a vote of 780,496 to 514,263, with 39.7 percent of the vote in favor. This was the only school choice initiative on the ballot in the fifty states. A voucher initiative in Colorado lost by the slightly larger margin of 37 percent to 62 percent in 1992. So what has changed? On the surface the answer is, "not much." Coloradans do not yet support an ambitious statewide program—except for charter schools—and a choice initiative failed again. Governor-elect Bill Owens (R), supporter of the tax credit, commented after the election that the issue would not be brought up again in the legislature for a few years because the voters had spoken.[5]

There was some good news for supporters of choice. Tom Tancredo (R), the primary crafter of the language in both initiatives and former Director of the Independence Institute that helped to spearhead the effort, won election to Congress from the 6th district by a large margin. School choice will have a strong advocate in Washington D.C. There were also other positive things to remember, even in defeat, according to its leaders.[6]

Sitting in his Denver offices, Eric Sondermann, the general campaign consultant for the Proposition 17 Colorado Tax Credit Initiative, discussed distinctive features of the campaign just concluding. Proposition 17 was behind in the polls 42 percent to 52 percent with 6 percent undecided. He expected to lose. It was October 29, days before the Tuesday election, and he had just returned from a small school choice demonstration in front of the Colorado Education Association building. Supporters handed out certificates to the "Hypocrites Hall of Shame," awarded by name to the leaders of the opposition who sent their children to private schools. Sondermann, a relatively young man, is an old salt in Colorado politics, with more then twenty years working on campaigns for Democrats. In fact, he observed with a wry grin, the Colorado Education Association was on his client list, if it had not been purged. He is, he noted, a liberal and a Jew, not the usual conservative Republican one might expect in his position.[7]

What was the most significant, positive development in the Tax Credit Initiative? According to Sondermann, it was the large influx of contributions made by local entrepreneurs. He had never seen so much money given by a few individuals to such an initiative. This was a first compared to other campaigns. The Tax Credit effort received a cluster of large contributions from $1,000 to $25,000, at least forty of them, with fifteen of these over $10,000. Although such donations were not new to Sondermann, what did come as a surprise were the $75,000 and above donations. There were a number of them, topped by the $250,000 sums given by local contributor and cable pioneers John Saeman and Bill Daniels, software developer C. Edward Mc-Vaney, a recently minted billionaire, and Ralph Nagel, a home developer. John Walton of San Diego, a son of Sam Walton the founder of Wal-Mart, also gave $250,000. Others promised large donations, including one for $1 million from Alex Cranberg (oil and gas businessman) for a student tuition loan fund. Such sums, gratefully spent by Sondermann, are impact money designed to take away the funding advantage long enjoyed by the opposition. The campaign received more in-state money than expected.[8]

He was impressed not just by the size of the contributions, said Sondermann, but by the motivation behind them, proving to him that local businessmen really do care about school choice. This surprised the opposition, too, because among political professionals the street talk was that tax credits were just a stalking horse, particularly for Steve Schuck. Some believed that Schuck, the campaign co-chairman, would simply use this issue to put himself in the running for governor again. That Schuck might be altruistic in this matter and gather a small band of like-minded fellows was something unexpected and difficult to combat. It had other implications too as Schuck himself then explained.[9]

Altruistic entrepreneurs, he argues, are an antidote to career-minded politicians. There is a need for people who stand for good public policy even if it is unpopular with powerful interest groups, unlike politicians, "whose primary need is to stay in office rather than to set good policy, and who think they must stay popular and get along with everyone rather than to do what is right." Once a politician is focused on who he or she is, not on what they can do to bring change, they are, said Schuck, effectively neutered. He understands personal ambition from the inside—running for governor as a Republican in 1985–86, campaigning for eighteen months, losing his party's nomination narrowly. From his experience, Schuck is convinced that if school choice is to succeed in Colorado, it must be pushed by people of means, those not afraid to make enemies, leaders with no personal stake in the outcome. Few unfortunately qualify.[10]

Schuck contrasts his allies with the Republican state legislators. "We had a veto proof Republican majority in Colorado one-third of the time in recent years and they could not get the legislature to support school choice because the Colorado Education Association (CEA) controls too many Republicans." In his view, genuine commitment to this cause matched by political independence is a rarity. There are different motivations in his band, Schuck commented, with some more attached to parochial schools, for example, but he perceives this to be a public policy issue pure and simple.[11] He notes:

> We need an intelligent active citizenry to be a functioning democracy—we cannot be passive and ignorant. School choice is necessary for the republic to survive. We need leaders like the patriots of 1776, to fight for it, pledging personal sacrifice to get it done. The education monopoly cannot heal itself. It produces mediocrity and a 'Gimmick du Jour' of phony reforms.[12]

This is not a personal issue with Schuck. He distinguishes between the public school teachers and the principles that are trying to make it happen and the system that inhibits initiative and excellence and slows them down. Entrepreneurs by contrast understand the need for competition and choice almost instinctively and also are confident that effective change in education can happen quickly. Those in the computer and cable industries expect change and not inertia to govern. They know how to overcome seemingly impossible obstacles—"they said it couldn't be done"—and relish doing so. With his band of can-do entrepreneur school choice brothers and sisters in place, Schuck said he is not deterred by the weakness of politicians and educators, the indifference of the public, or the opposition of unions. However, as he was to discover, success with voters in an initiative is a complex, and often unpredictable, struggle for success.

Strategies for the 1998 Initiative

In 1992, Schuck had supported vouchers and in 1996 attempted to put a new voucher initiative of his own on the ballot. Crafted by Tom Tancredo of the Independence Institute, the initiative was delayed by the state Supreme Court and, as a result, Schuck opted to wait until 1998 to introduce it. During the interim, it was decided that the time would be used to lay the foundation for refundable tax credits, rather than for vouchers.[13]

Studying the vulnerabilities of 1992, Schuck decided to put together a bipartisan, all-inclusive campaign for 1998. He reached out to both the rich and the poor, Republicans, Democrats, Catholics, minorities, and supporters of public education. The goal of the campaign was to break out of the stereotypical mold—white, conservative, Republican, and suburban—and to expand the base of support dramatically. Quoting Lao-Tsu, a Chinese philosopher, he warned himself, "Insanity is doing the same things in the same way and expecting different results." Nothing in 1998, he hoped, will be a repeat of 1992.[14]

At the start he hired Democrat Eric Sondermann as the campaign consultant. "Republicans have good ideas," he said, "but Democrats know how to win." Behind the scene Schuck tried to make in-roads with Democrats such as Governor Dick Lamm, and to contact 25–30 of the key Democratic public education supporters. He found to his chagrin and utter disappointment that no one would join him.[15]

The minority community leadership also generally resisted his overtures. One exception was Reverend Bowman of the Union Baptist Church, who he met through Tom Tancredo. Over time, Schuck was able to win Bowman's support, meeting every two weeks at the Excel Institute, a school operated by the church. With this small beachhead in the African-American community, Schuck went on the offensive to bring attention to the problems in public schools. In the struggles ahead he found Vivian L. Wilson, administrator at Excel, a superb exponent of choice. Later on young black pastors also responded, but not the mainstream minority leadership that he had hoped for.[16]

Schuck succeeded with the business community whereas he had largely failed to gain new support among Democrats and the ethnic minorities. Ten business leaders agreed to give at least $25,000 for the effort and others even more. In addition, he found the Roman Catholic Church hierarchy ready to back the initiative, and to ask the public, church members, and priests to help. Writing an opinion article in the *Wall Street Journal* in September 1997, Most Reverend Charles J. Chaput, Archbishop of Denver, strongly endorsed the coming Colorado initiative, saying vouchers "should" and someday "will" win.[17] Later, perhaps slightly disappointed that Schuck had substituted a refundable tax credit for a voucher, he wrote to all pastors of the archdiocese:

> While no measure is perfect, I believe this initiative helps to empower parents and serves as an important first step toward serious educational reform. I would therefore encourage priests and people of the archdiocese to consider giving their support, as I do, to this valuable initiative.[18]

Schuck contacted national Evangelical leader and radio host Dr. James Dobson of Focus on the Family, headquartered in Colorado Springs. He was assured of his support. The campaign counted on conservatives, Evangelicals, Republicans, Catholics, and parents to be its base. With Evangelical and Catholic leadership on board, Schuck now sought to mobilize the suffering poor of Denver to complete his new school choice coalition.[19]

Steve Schuck wanted to enlarge the coalition, making it bipartisan. Broadening the base was a necessity; conservatives and Catholics by themselves could not win. But when liberals and Democrats refused to join him, for various reasons including their political attachments to education unions, he made the decision to launch a confrontation with the Denver Public Schools (DPS) to attach the campaign to the very families it was designed most to help. Writing in the summer of 1997 Sondermann commented privately to Schuck:

> So a decision was made to go in a very different direction. Instead of conserva-
> tive ideologues going solo in publicly advancing this issue, we wanted to bring
> in some left-of-center constituencies. Instead of lily-white faces, we wanted
> some people of color. Instead of looking to boardrooms to pick up one or two
> names out of the Democratic elite, we decided to take it to the streets. Instead
> of looking to Republican strongholds in the suburbs and rural Colorado, we
> brought the issue home to the core city and its troubled school system.[20]

Sondermann was referring to a class action suit filed by his allies against the Denver Public Schools. On May 8th, a handful of parents and children and the Denver Parents Association (DPA), represented by local African-American attorney and past Republican congressional candidate Joe Rogers, sued the district. Eventually over 3,500 people joined the suit as plaintiffs.[21]

The genesis of the suit lay in a program implemented by Tom Tancredo to produce a "Parent Information Center," which put information "Report Cards" out on every Colorado public school using the Iowa Achievement (ITBS) test as the standard. Overcoming opposition by the district, threaten-ing a lawsuit if they refused to cooperate, Tancredo secured the information through the Freedom of Information Act. Scores for the worst performing schools, populated largely by minority students, were so low and drop out rates so high that the schools were blamed for failing to educate children. This violated the state Constitution, Rogers argued, in Article 9, Section 2, which states that there is an "obligation of the state of Colorado to provide educational opportunities to students which challenge them and enable them to lead fulfilling and productive lives. . . ." Rogers and the parents asked for immediate improvement in reading, writing, and math education programs and the right for lower-income parents in these schools to use tax dollars to procure a quality education in a public or private school of their choice—in other words, vouchers.[22]

Supporters took to the streets. Several hundred kids and parents marched downtown eight to ten blocks to stand in front of DPS offices. Superinten-dent Irv Moskowitz would not speak with them. The case, funded largely by Schuck, in the fall of 1998 was still under appeal. The *Denver Post* editorial-ized that the plaintiffs raised "valid complaints" but did so in the wrong way—in the courts, and with the wrong solution, vouchers.[23] The *Rocky Mountain News* preferred that Rogers seek vouchers through the political process, but saw this case contributing to the debate:

> Achievement in some Denver schools is abysmal, as the lawsuit alleges. If it
> weren't, Superintendent Irv Moskowitz wouldn't have authorized the
> "blowup" of two elementary schools—the military-like parlance for replacing

their entire staffs in a total restructuring. Nor would he have mandated a summer school program for thousands of students who test well below grade level, or replaced so many principals in the recent past.[24]

This in-your-face strategy adopted by Schuck and his allies certainly aroused the DPS and put them on the defensive. The superintendent commented that parents have an obligation to turn off the TV at night and make sure their kids take books to school. Rogers attacked this response as another example of blaming the parents for the schools' failures. One positive outcome of the litigation was its emphasis on standards of accountability. A year later, in October 1998, once again the DPS was put under the spotlight: low performance scores demonstrated little or no improvement.[25]

Al Knight, *Denver Post* columnist and editorial writer, understood immediately the political impact of waking up the poor to education quality issues and enlisting their assistance. The class action suit filed by Rogers might not win in court, but it would prove that school choice was not a "white middle-class" way to escape integration. The lawsuit could prepare the way for an initiative. The *New York Times* reported 3,500 parents already participating by December 1997, with as many as 6,000 more ready to sign up. Rogers then closed the roll of plaintiffs. Opinion polls also indicated, the *Times* said, strong support for vouchers among blacks and Hispanics nationwide while whites were split almost evenly.[26]

Pleased with the reception of the lawsuit in the community and by the press, Steve Schuck and the other supporters of the initiative turned their attention to the 1998 election. A lawsuit and an initiative were complementary means to the same ends, providing, it was hoped, resources and alternatives to parents. The suit, however, was focused exclusively on students in collapsing schools. Targeted vouchers in distressed schools were only a step, in this view, and charter schools were not enough. As Schuck explained: "This Colorado initiative is not designed to make a statement. It is not about making incremental progress towards the ultimate goal of school choice. *This is about winning.*" A law, or even better a constitutional amendment, that in principle set aside substantial state resources for any child to attend any school, including home schools, was his goal. There might need to be compromises to get the support needed to pass it, but the core principle—aid available to all, funds permitting, was to be inviolate to Schuck in this election. He wanted more than vouchers for the poor. He wanted to force all public schools to improve and to meet the needs of parents and students.[27]

Crafting the Initiative

A standard procedure today in politics is to use surveys and focus groups to shape proposals that must be submitted to the public for approval. The sur-

veys commissioned in December 1997 and July 1998 by Coloradans for
School Choice tested support and alternative language in proposed initiatives. Ninety percent said some change in education was needed. The terms
"parochial" and "religiously affiliated," for example, were equally acceptable.
Tax credits, however, were more positively received than "opportunity scholarships" by a margin of 18 percent, with support levels for the former at 69
percent. Demographically, those who favored choice were social conservatives and lower-income parents, confirming the earlier adopted strategy. Two
money questions, the impact of the initiative on public school funding and
on taxes, made clear the hostility of voters toward any reduction of support
for existing schools or any increase in taxes—the initiative had to be revenue
and tax neutral. The pollsters concluded, "Giving parents the power to make
decisions about their kid's education is the most powerful message at our
disposal." Almost 70 percent of those surveyed responded positively to this
message. A vulnerability, the survey noted, was the charge that the initiative
helped the rich kids and not the poor. Among other objections raised in the
survey, this one resonated most strongly with the public.[28]

Obviously one of the greatest limitations of a pre-election survey is that it
is not taken in the midst of an actual media battle when the ads have their
impact. One way to dig more deeply into the thinking and leanings of voters
is to use focus groups to anticipate how they will respond in an ad battle.
The school choice campaign used several focus groups to test the initiative
concepts in October 1997. Most participants had attended public schools,
which they liked. Most thought school quality was declining and some
schools were much worse than others. They considered private schools better
than public schools. Reforms like charter schools barely showed up in their
responses, and most were not familiar with them at all.[29]

Two issues the focus groups dealt with made it clear that any reform program would have to pass a relatively high credibility threshold before it
would be approved. First, the groups held parents and not schools accountable for low performance. This could easily be translated into contempt for
the poor and not concern for their schools, or into fatalism—nothing can be
done for the poor in the inner city. Neither of these responses would help
the initiative. The possibility that schools do make a large difference was
given less credence than the role of parents in preparing and encouraging
children to learn.[30]

Second, when school choice was presented, participants found it relatively
easy to raise objections, pointing to pitfalls. It was much easier to imagine
reasons not to change the relatively simple and predictable public education
system than to transition to choice—"Better the devil we know than the one
we don't." They asked, Would public schools suffer? Would some children
be left out? What about community unity? What about costs? Would kids
in the rural areas be left out? Surprisingly few questions were raised about

religion and the issue of aid to parochial schools. Although Denver participants were more supportive of choice and critical of schools than groups in the suburbs, the focus groups made it clear that until the public has a clear understanding of how choice will work to the benefit of all, it will be relatively easy for opponents to prey on fears. Choice was a new idea to most. Opinions were more malleable than rigid, but in a campaign, if there is substantial doubt, people ask, "Why change?"[31]

Adopt a "both/and" strategy—both school choice and public schools—is the answer that emerged from these studies and from the consultations that went on with school choice experts outside the state. Public schools must not be touched and their finances must be left intact. Private schools must be protected, too, from any additional state regulations. This is to allay fears, especially in the parochial schools, that with government money will come state control. Clearly tax credits were less objectionable and more saleable than scholarships. The wording of the initiative, Schuck knew, needed to anticipate objections encountered in earlier elections and uncovered in this research, and then be drafted so as to neutralize them.[32]

The 1998 initiative, a constitutional amendment, was called the "Educational Opportunity Tax Credit Initiative." It fit on one page in fine print and contained two short introductory paragraphs, a complex nine-part description of how the credit would be distributed, and five other paragraphs with particular restrictions or requirements. Funding was to be not less than one-half of the per student state funding of a public school student (about $2,500) or 80 percent of the tuition, whichever was less. The remainder of the per student amount (approximately $2,500) was to be placed in an Educational Opportunity Fund when a child left a public school and went to a private school. This fund would cover overhead costs and help to pay for tax credits to be granted to lower income and other students already in private schools or even in public schools. Savings by public schools from students transferring to private schools were to be placed in the fund also. Eligibility was prioritized, with the poor helped first and others qualifying later as funds lasted. There were other details, including coverage of special needs students and for materials and supplies for home school students as well as support for those who stayed in public schools. Essentially all students got something as long as the money lasted.[33]

Protective measures included a provision that per-student school expenditures would neither be reduced nor raised as a result of this program. Children who attended schools that were racially discriminatory or taught hate on the basis of "race, ethnicity, color, national origin, religion, or gender" or employed persons convicted of sexual crimes or child abuse were excluded from participation. Any increase in government regulation of private schools as a result of this amendment was forbidden. The complexity of the initiative was to cause some problems (i.e., details confuse) but it certainly was a sophisticated effort to manage tax credits, given the several concerns and political liabilities.[34]

Selling the Initiative to Outside Supporters

From the beginning Steve Schuck counted on outside contributors to subsidize the effort by as much as $2 million if necessary, which was one-half the total costs or more. In the end this was not to be. There were some large gifts, from John Walton for example, and early on substantial sums were promised. The issue of why this funding did not materialize or why it took other forms (indirect soft money) is worth some explanation although it probably did not affect the ultimate outcome of the election.[35]

In 1997, early in the campaign, Steve Schuck at his initiative met John Walton in a meeting of the Philanthropy Roundtable in Rhode Island and made his pitch for outside support for the Colorado initiative. He met with Virginia Gilder and others, who later helped him, but he received little or no encouragement to do an initiative. David Brennan, the legendary school choice businessman from Ohio, was not positive. Behind this courteous but skeptical reception that Schuck later recounted lay a history.[36]

The initiative is the amphibious landing of the school choice movement. To win an initiative is to crush the enemy with one blow, avoiding the heavy fortifications built by unions in the education committees and party leaderships of state legislatures. In military history, however, to lose badly on the beach is a catastrophe because it means being thrown back into the sea with heavy losses. California's Proposition 174 in 1993, for example, was not only a heavy loss largely inflicted by union media attack ads—the school choice supporters were out spent five to one and lost two to one—but it poisoned public opinion, making vouchers appear un-American and their supporters a maverick fringe. Such a defeat is never forgotten. Furthermore, different lessons learned from the same event divide the school choice movement today.[37]

The dominant perspective among school choice leaders is that initiatives are a lost cause because they are so visible. There can be no backroom maneuvering in a legislative committee chamber here, no collecting political debts, and thus school choice is easily defeated by the large union war chest that pays for attack ads. Out-spent, out-maneuvered, out-gunned by unions claiming to speak for the children and the public good and by unions expertly twisting and shaping public opinion negatively against them, school choice fleets have always sailed away with nothing to show for their initiatives, except their own casualties and the loss of their good name.[38]

Yet there is a minority view, held by Schuck among others, that sees the initiative as the only possible way to succeed when other avenues are blocked. If the votes are not there in the legislature and the governor is not sympathetic or is weak, an energized electorate is the only way to win. The answer, in this view, is very much like the one proposed and executed by the United States Marine Corps in the Pacific in World War II.[39]

For those not familiar with this history, Marines carefully studied the most famous amphibious landing disaster of all time, the battle of Gallipoli, fought on the coast of Turkey in World War I during which tens of thousands of British and allied troops died needlessly, mowed down by artillery and machine guns. Other armies concluded that an amphibious landing should never be made, but this was not the lesson Marines learned from Gallipoli. Machine guns can be overcome—by air and shore bombardment, by coordinated landings in newly designed vehicles, by skipping islands where advisable, by the sheer intensity of a strongly focused attack. With virtually no external help the Marines worked to perfect the systems and tactics later used against Germany and Japan. All this was possible because they approached past mistakes with a winning spirit, knowing that in the next war such attacks would have to be made, preparing realistically for the inevitable.

According to Schuck, the initiative was the only available option, despite its bad press. He wanted to learn from the mistakes of Colorado in 1992 and California in 1993 prior to his campaign. There is no concealing an initiative so in order to win the preparations must be carefully made. The Colorado initiative deserves careful study to see how school choice tactics are evolving and maturing in the crucibles of defeat. Other states will also use the initiative, such as Michigan and California.[40]

Given the bad past experience with school choice initiatives, national foundations and large contributors are reluctant to commit to them. Local entrepreneurs tend to hold back too until national money comes in. Why should local donors give when it is known from the outset that the campaign requires national funding to be viable? With so little encouragement from outside Colorado, Schuck eventually sought help from Fritz Steiger of Children's Educational Opportunity Foundation America (CEO America), the leader of this national school choice organization, who put him in touch with Kevin Teasley, an experienced initiative campaigner active in California in 1993. Schuck brought in Teasley to help with the campaign in the late spring and summer of 1998, making him responsible for external fund raising.[41]

Steve Schuck also attended the Jackson Hole CEO America school choice retreat in the summer before the election—John Walton, James Leininger, Congressman Frank Riggs, James Mansour, Virginia Gilder, and others nationally known in school choice politics attended. Restless with the discussion—all about goals and private scholarships that he says are a drop in the bucket—and reluctant to speak as an invited guest, Schuck had to listen as one leader attacked initiatives, claiming the only way to get choice was through legislation. Responding, Shuck recounted his woes with the Colorado legislature. He said that even with a veto-proof Republican majority they would do nothing. He told them the goal of CEO America should be to put itself out of business in five years. He argued:

> Private philanthropy, while very generous, has two flaws that prevent it from being the answer. First, there simply is not enough money available to scholarship even a fraction of the kids in poor schools. Second, private scholarships do not bring enough pressure to bear on the public system. The primary goal of vouchers or tax credits is to change, improve, the public education system by threatening its complacency with real competition.

No one in his view should plan to make a career, philanthropic or otherwise, out of fighting for school choice. His strategy, Schuck said, was to push public vouchers or tax credits in strategic locations, where you can win. Like an old football coach, he says find the weak spot in the line and play your strengths to the opposition's weakness. He then asked for help. Promises were made to give outside funding and Schuck viewed the approaching fall with confidence that the original game plan was in reach.[42]

The initiative campaign's summer petition drive for signatures netted 90,000 names, many more than the 55,000 needed to put Proposition 17 on the ballot. Schuck prepared to fight, buoyed by survey reports that 70 percent of likely voters indeed favored tuition assistance. Given a relatively predictable turn out he thought he needed as many as 900,000 + votes to win. Sondermann warned, however, that positive polls could backfire, fueling more campaign ads by the opposition.[43]

Controversy over alleged money laundering of contributions to the campaign through the Independence Institute suddenly blew up in Schuck's face, barely eight weeks before the election. Schuck had served as chairman of both the school choice effort and the initiative campaign until August 11, when he resigned from the Institute position. Campaign consultant Kevin Teasley and others discovered the problem in July and moved to correct it. All funds donated to the campaign had been routed through the Institute first, to obtain a tax deduction and to prevent disclosure of contributors. Money given for direct campaign costs, however, is not tax deductible and contributions must be identified. So-called soft money spent to educate the public on issues, that is spent totally independent of a campaign, is tax deductible and donors and contributions do not have to be disclosed.[44]

In a flurry of controversy, Coloradans for Public Schools, an umbrella group of those opposed to the tax credits, filed a complaint against Coloradans for School Choice in state court, claiming that contributions from the Independence Institute were illegal. Schuck responded with a lawsuit of his own arguing that the Colorado Education Association was funding the opposition and should also be required to identify its donors. In late October both sides agreed to drop the complaints to avoid mutual embarrassment and months of dispute. Other issues, such as Schuck's complaint against the opposition's use of public school facilities, went forward.[45]

This controversy, briefly described, could not have come at a worse time for two reasons. First, the fall initiative campaign was in full swing. Such charges damaged the image of responsible community leadership that must be carefully cultivated and maintained if one is to win a tough race. Second, and far more serious, outside donors chose not to contribute. This was devastating. Mailings could not be sent out and TV time could not be bought.[46]

At this critical point in the campaign a national school choice foundation sent in a representative to review the situation. Meanwhile, Denver businessmen John Saeman, Bill Daniels, and Edward McVaney came to the rescue by increasing their contributions. Outside contributors, after receiving information and counsel from their representative, chose a middle course. Instead of pulling out altogether they opted for independent expenditures. They would buy their own TV and radio time to back tax credits. They thought if media expenditures were maintained then the race would at least be close and not a blowout that would be used by the opposition to discredit choice efforts elsewhere. "Win if we can but keep it close we must," was the watchword of the moment.[47]

Schuck would have preferred less outside money spent indirectly and more given directly to his effort. Still smarting from this decision a week before the election, Schuck commented that when the campaign was attacked, which the national school choice leaders predicted would happen, instead of giving more support the foundations and entrepreneurs with some notable exceptions pulled out to save their own reputations. "Better to lop off a branch then to risk losing the tree," was one defense given to Schuck. He was angry—the national movement was AWOL—he felt more hurt by friends than by the enemy. "School choice is really about experimentation, risk taking, and an entrepreneurial spirit, yet when Colorado creates its own initiative the national supporters of choice focused on small flaws, rather than putting their shoulder to the wheel." The perfect is ever the enemy of the good, he thought; people quibble over details. To conclude, Schuck's biggest complaint against the school choice movement is, "We don't know how to win. There is too much comfort with losing. These attitudes in our friends are our worst enemy and we tend to shoot our wounded."[48]

Such comments come from line officers in every army that has ever fought. George Patton said the same in World War II, as did Douglas MacArthur. Give me gasoline and bullets and I will do the job. In a very real sense state political battles are the front lines and the national choice organizations have a larger vision, more responsibility, greater resources, but ultimately less to do with winning then the courage and sense of local commanders who must push the enemy over the next hill. Steve Schuck is fully aware that he must have the trust and assistance of out-of-state supporters to win but this dependence on them rankles and his own mistakes must burn.

Final Election Push

The last demonstration of this campaign (the first was the march for the class action suit) took place in Denver, October 29, at 2:00 p.m. outside the Colorado Education Association building. There were no TV cameras. About ten supporters stood with posters on the sidewalk. A few countermarchers showed up and a loud speaker pick-up truck rolled by pulling a lemon-colored old Cadillac with banners attached saying, "Proposition 17 is a lemon." Janet Bingham, a reporter for the *Denver Post*, began her interview of Steve Schuck and Vivian Wilson. One African American counter-demonstrator accused Wilson of being "used." This set her off and she responded, "You're using our children, while I am trying to protect them." The demonstration ended shortly after the interview was complete. Meanwhile, the battle of TV ads and talk show interviews continued.[49]

What Happened?

The public survey data on the tax credit initiative was solidly positive a month before the election. Tracking polls showed 52 percent of the public in support and 41 percent opposed with 7 percent not committed on the issue. This changed slightly two weeks later, with an increase in the number of voters opposed. But by the end of October, after commercials had their full impact, the position of the two sides reversed with 51 percent of electorate opposed to the voucher initiative, 42 percent in favor, and 7 percent still uncommitted. If these numbers held or improved to a 45/55 split this would have been considered a victory, or even evidence of progress, an improvement on 1992. However, the final tally of 39.7 percent was a defeat, given the investment of time, effort, and money.[50]

So, what went wrong? Why didn't money—real money—make a difference in Colorado? The answers seem so simple now. Voters must be sold on the plan. Schuck and friends could not do it alone and even solidly-funded initiatives are always tough to win against well-financed opponents.[51] There were tactical errors; the problems with the Independence Institute campaign expenditures were a blow; more out of state funding for advertising would have helped. The initiative was also complicated and lies played their part. Al Knight, *Denver Post* columnist, wrote of the misrepresentations by opponents and the confusion wrought by election laws:

> Opponents of Amendment 17, the Educational Opportunity Tax Credit initiative, have apparently renounced all standards of integrity. The plain provi-

sions of the act have been deliberately turned on their head. The opponents' claim that "not one public school family can get the tax credit until all private school families get theirs" is designed to obscure the fact that first priority goes to families that currently live in poor-performing public school districts. Opponents have also falsely claimed that student safety can't be regulated under the initiative. This is nonsense. No school, public or private, is immune from a whole variety of state and local safety regulations. . . . Finally, there are the confusing issues of what constitutes candidate advertising, issue ads, independent expenditures and voter guides. The U.S. Supreme Court has said there can be no limit on issue ads that stop short of asking voters to cast ballots for a specific candidate. As this election proves, the court has underestimated the cleverness of groups who have twisted the language into previously unrecognized shapes to endorse a specific candidacy. Only experts can spot differences in issue and candidate advertising.[52]

Independent campaign expenditures by out-of-state supporters were not sufficient to dull the edge of negative and false campaigning (opponents reported to have spent $1.1 million in direct expenditures, $635,000 of this from the National Education Association; supporters spent $1.3 million directly, most from Colorado). Nor were all the finely crafted efforts to deal with objections, nor major newspaper endorsements, nor talk show hosts able to convince the public that now was the time to try tax credits. Of even more concern, however, is the issue of the support base for the initiative. Conservative social issues' people are the identified base for school choice outside the inner city. Problems surfaced here among Evangelicals even before the contribution scandal and the negative ads. Where were the conservative Christians so visibly lead by James Dobson, for example, on Election Day?[53]

Charter laws, passed in Colorado after the defeat of vouchers in 1993 and again in 1996 were the prime obstacle to Evangelical mobilization for tax credits in 1998. By the fall, sixty charter schools were in operation. Evangelicals in particular flocked to them as an immediate relatively cost-free alternative. Tom McMillan, Rocky Mountain Family Council, affiliated with Focus on the Family, is one of these strong supporters of charter schools—he sends his children there. Evangelicals, he said, are getting power and control, quietly putting in curriculums friendly to their beliefs—celebrating Christian holidays, teaching creation as alternative explanation of origins, supporting moral absolutes. Most, he said, have a wait-and-see attitude on the tax credit initiative—not confident that additional state regulation will be prevented by the initiative and secure for the time being in their newly built shelters.[54]

Denise Mund, Republican candidate in State House District 27 (she lost by 1 percent in a three-way race) illustrates the problem. The mother of four children, Mund also operates a charter school—her school is in its fifth year. Her passion, she says, is for "parental involvement" and that gets education unions upset with her. In this campaign, although she favored the tax credit initiative, her own primary education agenda was pressing for an automatic waiver of public school requirements for charter schools. This illustrates how other more immediate charter school concerns diluted commitments made by strong supporters. School choice for conservatives is now so complicated that one form of choice competes with another. The variety of remedies— tax credits, vouchers, charter schools, home schools—diminish commitment and blur focus.[55]

Of even more import and largely ignored in this campaign were parents who support choice in theory but have more concrete concerns to deal with daily. "Where should my children go to school?" trumps other questions and led to problems for the tax credit initiative among those who held the power to pass it. Parents were already occupied, pursuing the charter school option, and paid little attention to Proposition 17 because even if it passed it would be cheaper and better, they thought, to put their children in charter schools. From this perspective, good private schools are too expensive or simply do not exist.

Interviews with friends in the state confirmed this finding. Some of the most active and aggressive young Evangelical families, people who could and do influence others, have put their children in charter schools where as parents they are investing hours and dollars in making them run properly, sitting on boards, and volunteering to help. The tax credit initiative presumed that parents would opt for private schools if given a chance—the suburbs and smaller cities and towns chose otherwise. Charter schools and home schools rule the day for the discontented.[56]

One school choice advocate, Dr. Perry Glanzer, who is responsible for education policy issues at Focus on the Family, attributed this strategic insensibility in 1998 to a lack of understanding about what private Christian education can do. In their ignorance, he remarked, Evangelicals settle for less than they ought.[57]

What about the inner cities? Having support from some families, even thousands of them as in the class action suit, is not the same as capturing the leadership of the community or at least getting them to listen and consider the merits of school choice. One incident, three weeks before the election, speaks directly to this never solved problem. Reverend Floyd Flake, the well-known African Methodist Episcopal pastor and recently retired former Democratic Congressman from New York, came to Denver to speak on behalf of choice. The pastors of the city were invited to attend, but none would come. Steve Schuck related this with regret.[58]

In conclusion, voting was exceptionally heavy on the tax credit initiative: More people voted on this issue than for other controversial propositions on the ballot like abortion. Opponents successfully got out their vote. The natural allies of choice identified by the campaign, the social issue conservatives and inner city minorities, did not mobilize in sufficient numbers.

Retrospective on What Was Accomplished

Because of this campaign one can now imagine a future combination of social conservatives and inner-city minorities led by community leaders and funded by entrepreneurs leading the fight for choice. Some progress was made toward this goal by breaking the old rigid stereotype. As Steve Schuck and Eric Sondermann observed:

> Go for an "Opportunity Tax Credit" not a voucher. We are a multi-ethnic coalition not a conservative movement. This is a new civic vision not a religious right reflex. Who says libertarians, evangelicals, and liberals can't work together in one campaign team, we did. The rich still care.[59]

Sondermann commented on how inspiring it was for him personally to visit the Excel school. To support schools like Excel, an ethnically diverse, bipartisan coalition was inspired to fight regardless of the odds. A fierce energy was unleashed, he said, despite the outcome. "The tides of history are turning," Sondermann observed. "This monopoly cannot sustain itself. At some point the war ends and you start negotiating the terms of surrender."[60]

Looking Ahead

When school choice prevails, at the ballot or in the legislature, the other side loses something permanently. This is one reason the opposition fights so fiercely, because for them to lose a battle may well be to lose a war. On the other hand, when the advocates of choice lose as they did in 1998, they can always return for another go-round. Schuck and Sondermann commented that from the education union's point of view it is better to lose less than to lose more. This means compromise can look very attractive when the prospects of a bigger loss are real. They expect the opposition to negotiate at some point to prevent full school choice from being adopted.

Meanwhile, Schuck and Sondermann predict, politicians will want the issue to go away—they will be looking for some form of accommodation. With Bill Owens as newly elected governor the other side will expect another round eventually. The opposition will fear another campaign, they suggest—so at some point it will be opportune to play on this fear and to use it to get a legislative solution. If this does not happen, and it may not given the power of the unions in the legislature, Schuck and Sondermann will have learned how to campaign better on this issue for a round three initiative.[61]

The most striking feature of this campaign to these leaders was the new entrepreneurial money that made it possible. This will not likely go away though it may be spent more prudently next time with fewer campaign glitches. The absence of Evangelicals and African-American pastors also stands out. It will take more than a letter written by James Dobson, a demonstration in Denver, or campaign telephone get-out-the-vote efforts to break the inertia in the suburban and inner-city communities. Catholics and free-market libertarians by themselves cannot win it.

A grammar school in Colorado Springs put up a sign that said, "Life for a child is a journey not a race." Whoever wrote that obviously had forgotten playgrounds where play is both a journey and a race, and more often a race. A new magnet school in the city of Colorado Springs was designed to be "paperless," using laptops instead of books, so they built no lockers. The children there now have to lug around heavy forty-pound packs with all their books. Such follies almost guarantee discontent even in the most effective schools. Yet until more parents prefer private schools or public schools in the inner city start closing their doors, more choice will have to wait in Colorado.[62]

California School Choice Strategies

Reed Hastings, software developer, has the ready smile, cordial hospitality, and blue jeans informality of the successful young. Nothing easily stops him. His public success came recently when he took up the cause of education reform in his home state of California. With no history of involvement in politics or education policy, in a few months he educated himself on school choice issues, spoke with experts in the field, designed a school choice initiative to expand charter schools, bargained successfully with the state education unions, and won. His plan (with some modifications) passed the legislature with bipartisan backing and Governor Pete Wilson signed it into law on May 7, 1998. Nothing in politics happens in a vacuum. A number of things made this victory possible, including the initiative process, pressure from Democrats, and assistance from like-minded entrepreneurs.[63]

Experts had good reasons to be discouraged about school choice prospects in the Golden State. The original charter school law, passed in 1992, was said to be something of an accident, sponsored by State Senator Gary Hart (D) and signed by Wilson. It was heavily encumbered by restrictions—no more than 100 schools in a state with over 5,000,000 students and no more then ten charter schools in one school district. Charter approvals took no fewer than 10 percent of the teachers in the district or 50 percent of the teachers in the school. The state legislature refused to amend this law to lift the cap on charters or make it easier to get charters. Efforts to get vouchers also failed dismally, in the 1993 failed voucher initiative and in the legislature, and subsequently another initiative was not launched after supporters counted the negatives—they might lose even if they spent $30 million—and they failed to get unity among pro-voucher forces. If initiatives don't work, the legislature is not cooperative, and supporters are divided, why try? To his advantage, Reed Hastings was not a school choice movement person, he did not buy into the conventional wisdom that counseled delay, and he had friends ready to act.[64]

Laying the Foundations for the 1998 Initiative

Hastings studied computers at Stanford, and taught third grade in the Peace Corps. In April 1997 he sold his software company and unexpectedly took up the cause of school choice. Why? Reed states that first of all he was offended. "In America there is meritocracy—the market rewards excellence—without opportunity." Children who have a poor education or fail to graduate are doomed to low paying manual jobs at best. This was not just. Second, he saw how difficult it was to find well qualified people who were educated in America to fill positions in his industry. Third, he thought an open, innovative, competitive, system could turn things around for all schools, including public schools. The schools simply were not preparing people for good jobs.[65]

Initially interested in vouchers, Hastings talked with Professor Terry Moe (Stanford) and others, and concluded that vouchers were not yet politically viable in California. In fact, in 1993 he had opposed Proposition 174 because it had too small a voucher—only $2,600—to do much good. He saw charter schools as a reasonable alternative. They were free to all students, provided complete tuition, and were open to all students, yet were independent and competitive. These features placed them squarely in the American tradition of education, accessible to everyone at public expense but without the ill effects of a monopoly. Private schools have a big liability in Hastings's view because they are selective in admissions. He supports open admissions. Also he is convinced that any voucher system will subject private schools to the same regulations as charter schools.[66]

Leaning toward a charter initiative, Hastings sought advice on the political viability of an initiative from Dan Schnur, a Republican consultant, former Director of Communications for Governor Wilson and a protégé of the legendary Lee Atwater of the National Republican Committee and the George Bush campaign. Schnur worked for TechNet in the spring of 1997, a political/educational firm with concern for public policies favorable to the computer industry. Reed Hastings was on the TechNet board. Schnur told Hastings that passing a charter bill through the legislature would be tough, and he advised going with the initiative. He said they could either win the initiative or possibly use the threat of the initiative to prod the legislature to act.

Realistically, Schnur said he did not think using the initiative as a club would actually work—it was just a long shot possibility. Having no real hope for legislation, he did think that an initiative backed by a minimum of $15 million would pass.[67]

Schnur was surprised at Hastings's interest in education. When TechNet was founded it had two purposes—tort reform and education reform. Initially Schnur was surprised at Hastings, cynically thinking the education mission statement was social policy window dressing, a front for more selfish purposes. Then when he discovered they really were serious about education, he guessed they were altruistic, that these were simply good people. Later, he concluded that this was enlightened self-interest—they were alarmed that poor workers would undermine the computer industry and the country's ideals.

Schnur relates, "You must understand that leaders in Silicon Valley like Hastings are not patient—they are used to moving fast in quick monthly cycles." In their experience they succeeded when everyone told them it could not be done, that it was impossible—so school choice was just another challenge. Lastly, many of Reed's circle of associates are young, have children of their own, can identify with the problem of bad schools, and so are motivated by that. But most important, in Schnur's explanation of Hastings's motivation, is the workforce crisis—there are not enough smart people.[68]

Silicon Valley computer industries woke up to politics in 1996 when they fought Proposition 211 that would have made it easier to file class action suits against companies that were in financial trouble. Computer entrepreneurs raised $38 million in six months to oppose this initiative. Even President Clinton backed them. They defeated it with a 75 percent *no* vote. Schnur knew that when the word was out that these same people, or some of them at any rate, were behind a charter bill, opponents would consider this a real threat.[69]

Concluding that the initiative was the route to take, Hastings worked with Don Shalvey, Superintendent of the San Carlos School District (which had the first charter school in California), to put together the charter initiative. He tapped entrepreneurial business contacts to be ready to fund $15 million at the start. He got help in drafting the law from Ted Kolderie, a consultant on charter schools, and others. This initiative was to be aggressive—no cap on the number of schools and no teacher credentials. It would make it almost impossible to turn applications down and guarantee safety from regulations that bind other public schools. If the charter were a start-up, it could be independent of the collective bargaining unit in the district. Union and local school district controls were effectively shut down.[70]

Going Public with the Initiative

Forming an organization, Californians for Public School Excellence, Hastings began selling his plans. The group put up a home page on the Internet with a California School Report Card, assigning state schools an F in reading, D- in math, F in science, and F in the high school graduation rate. Much of the blame was placed on the bureaucracy and its "40 pounds of paperwork-generating rules," and low salaries for teachers. The page practically shouted:

> California has the worst public school system in the United States. Half of our fourth-graders can't read at the fourth-grade level. Our eighth-graders trail most of the country and much of the world in science and math. California ranks dead last in the percentage of those between 18 and 24 years of age that have earned high school diplomas. Half the incoming freshmen in the California State University system need remedial math and reading courses. . . . California's public schools were once the envy of the world, and some of our schools are terrific. In general, however, our schools don't make the grade. Unless we are willing to condemn future generations of Californians to low-paying jobs and unless we are willing to bear the economic and social costs of an undereducated society, we must reform our public school system. No issue of public or social policy is more important.[71]

Yet as bad as the public schools were, Hastings was not open to the radical solution of privatizing schools. Privatization is not the answer, he asserts, because it is a hard sell.

> Public education is the American heritage—we are not ready to give it up—people love their schools. So rather than attacking public education we must redefine what "Public Education" means. It does not mean government education delivery—education by the state—but rather education for the benefit of all.[72]

With the initiative prepared to go, Reed Hastings decided to give the strategy mentioned earlier by Dan Schnur a try. Why not try to negotiate a solution? Hastings supports unions. He sees their positive contributions, e.g., bringing professional standards to education and removing once common political patronage from the system. He wanted an open, innovative, competitive, system, not a private one. With a conciliatory attitude, he met with the head of the California Teachers Association (CTA) early on. Choice must be built gradually—it will take twenty years in his view—and must be built incrementally. This was to be another step.[73]

Negotiating a Legislative Solution

Between February and March 1998 Hastings sat down with the unions to negotiate in order to find charter legislation they both could support. His focus was on common ground. Charter schools per se do not scare unions, he says, vouchers do. The union knew he had strong Democratic and Republican backing, was not anti-public schools, and was prepared to spend a great deal of money to win the initiative. Hastings had been very public about the $15 million minimum budget. Education was the hottest issue in 1998, and both the public and business were concerned.[74]

Hastings and the union hammered out an agreement that passed the legislature with huge majorities—90 percent—in both houses. Instead of no cap on the number of schools Hastings accepted 150 new schools the first year and 100 a year thereafter. In addition, unions received a concession that all teachers in charter schools must be certified—a tactical retreat to get the bill. It then moved fast. Almost everyone was on board for charter schools. It was fully bipartisan. After it passed, Hastings said, the CTA was helping to defend it in litigation.[75]

Reed Hastings avoided polarization by working from the center. Commenting on the pure politics of it, Schnur said, Democratic legislators were the key brokers with the unions. If $20 million had been spent by the union to fight the charter initiative, that is $20 million not going into Democratic coffers in legislative races. Democratic legislators were the keys to victory in his view—they feared losing both the initiative and the campaign contributions that unions put into their races. It was time to broker a deal beneficial to all.[76]

Calling his strategy "Embrace and Extend," Hastings says he adopted a model Bill Gates followed when dealing with the Internet and its challenge to Microsoft. This advice cuts both ways. To the public schools it says embrace and extend school choice on your terms, avoiding vouchers if at all possible. To school choice people it says embrace and extend public education on your terms to bring competition. By extending charter schools we change the definition of public to mean, "run for the public benefit." He advises, "Wrap reform in the flag of public education." Charter schools embody that American tradition.[77]

Hastings also warns that "a holy war over school choice has not begun when only 1–5 percent of students go to publicly funded alternatives. But when 10–15 percent are involved watch out." In view of this coming conflict, Hastings gives this piece of advice. The school choice movement must come to terms with unions and let them organize unions at charter schools. In his opinion, charter schools sell well when politicians visit them and the unions should not be excluded.[78]

Future Reforms in California

Opening the doors to charters may well lead to more education experimentation. In Oakland, for example, Mayor Jerry Brown is considering the possibility of promoting charters. Before his recent election in 1998 Brown met with people from the School Futures Research Foundation, an organization that runs charter schools in the state, to discuss possibilities. Though not directly responsible for schools Mayor Brown saw education reform as important. Brown is not a supporter of public vouchers, but he has no objection to charters.[79]

Hastings wants facility funding for charter schools, a minimum of $1,000 per student. Preparing for this battle in the next two years Hastings says, "The business of schools is the business of buildings." There is a shortage of useable buildings. When available space is over 90 percent occupied there can be no competition; he says this is true for hotels and for schools. Today when the state has full enrollment in private and public schools, there is a capacity problem. California needs 80 percent occupancy to insure competition, and this will cost, Hastings argues, $50 billion for new facilities in the next few years. It will be important to help charter schools build aggressively to meet this demand.[80]

In Hastings's opinion when California is 10 percent charter this should be enough to motivate the rest of the system to excel. The purpose of charters is to improve all schools. He is taking politicians to visit charter schools to help persuade them that they do work and are worth supporting with capital funds and not just tuition. His hope is that by freeing teachers to teach in new creative ways schools will improve and politicians will rally in support.[81]

Looking down the road toward broader reforms, Hastings says parents in an area should own the facilities. Parents should decide who should run the school in an attendance area, by a 50 percent plus one vote, removing any agency they do not want. In his view this would give parents more power than in any voucher system. Hastings notes that too few groups or agencies want to run charter schools—more education providers are needed. One remedy for all public schools, he says, is to allow parents to receive open bids from different groups who desire to run the school. Most of these agencies will be non-profit, drawn by a "Mission to Serve." If parents controlled facilities, teachers, and budget without excessive regulation from the state, which is his dream, they could insure that good schools were maintained. Republicans and Democrats both try to control schools from the top down, and Hastings asserts this is bad. What we need, according to him, is the freedom to fail at the local level with clear accountability so that the schools that have a problem can be fixed quickly.[82]

Daniel Schnur is more sanguine about the future of vouchers in California than Reed Hastings. Proposition 174 poisoned the well for years making it impossible to discuss vouchers. That has changed, Schnur asserts, after the charter school victory. He favors vouchers for poor who cannot afford tuition and for those attending the worst schools, and he thinks it is possible to gradually grow the program. He likens it to progress in a football game. "It's all about first downs—keep the chain moving." He also wants tuition tax credits similar to those that exist in Minnesota and the recent federal Coverdale legislation for Washington, D.C. The benefit of opportunity scholarships is that they get the public used to the idea of using public funds for students attending private schools. Schnur gives this overview:

> The school choice movement in California is moving forward but has not taken a defined shape. Like welfare reform people know something must be done but the remedies are not clear. No one has recruited black Democrats yet. There is no grass-roots leader like a Polly Williams. California is so large and diverse it is hard to mobilize the grass roots and hard to build coalitions. People in this state live in separate universes. There is no consensus yet but it will come. When the school choice movement coalesces it will include Silicon Valley entrepreneurs, academicians, conservative ideologues, Roman Catholics, inner city grass-roots leaders, and parents; but there is no structure in place to keep these people together.[83]

One reason why Schnur is confident is because 70 percent of Latinos are pro vouchers, many attend parochial schools, and more would if they could afford to. These are upwardly mobile Catholics who need help, and their support for vouchers will accelerate. The year 2000 election will put school choice before the public again, he said, and Republicans will likely grab this opportunity and use it to win support from blacks and Latinos. The best means to use in his view will be an initiative, particularly because a Democratic governor is not inclined to help. Initiatives do work, he argues, if they are timed, crafted, and funded properly. An opportunity scholarship initiative could pass in the near future.[84]

Governor Pete Wilson, commenting on school choice at the same time, also was optimistic about vouchers. There had been a huge decline in education quality in the state between 1960 and 1990, he said. During his years as governor, spending reached $5,700 per pupil, $250 billion in eight years for all education in the state. Despite all this funding the CTA opposed accountability and opportunity scholarships for the bottom 5 percent of performing schools in 1996, 1997, and 1998. This would have impacted only 250,00 of nearly six million children. More recently as governor he backed a 15,000-student voucher pilot, which also was rejected. To win against such opposition he advised school choice supporters to do six things: match money spent by unions in campaigns, end the automatic union check-off for dues spent in political campaigns, pass school choice in a smaller state first, persuade the grass roots to demand it perhaps by seeing the value of private vouchers first, consider refundable tax credits for the poor, and give parents information on school performance in using school accountability to stir parents up. These points are not groundbreaking. What they indicate is that consensus among school choice supporters for the next step is not as far off as it seems.[85]

Lessons from the California Initiative—Legislation

Even tax credits are hard to pass in an initiative, as Colorado demonstrated in 1998. This would have been the case in California as well. Charter schools are much easier to win in any state. It is also true that in California the pressure placed on unions by voucher legislative proposals and by Proposition 226 (the initiative forbidding automatic deductions for union dues used in elections) helped to win support for charter schools as the lesser of two evils. Comparing initiatives to a wartime amphibious landing, charters are a smaller beach more lightly defended. However, even in the California victory there are lessons for supporters or opponents of choice.

First is the stereotype-breaking leadership that was neither conservative nor self-serving. When high-tech leadership raises the alarm it is hard to call this a throwback to some earlier era. Getting new high-profile leadership to commit to school choice has to be a top priority in any school choice initiative effort.

Second, the sums of money committed in advance by a few individuals were of a new order of magnitude—ten times greater than even the Colorado entrepreneurs managed to contribute. Having a large sum from sources hard to discredit is an immense political asset. However, knowing that those sums will also be there for a second and third round of campaigns is more significant than the size of one campaign's contributions and this has usually been the opposition's advantage.

Third, discovering ways to get Democrats to put pressure on unions turns the whole lobbying process upside down. This position of strength for advocates normally reliant on Republicans is never easy to achieve, requires some public discontent with the status quo, and requires securing support from politicians willing to find a middle ground not too threatening to unions.

Fourth, the advocates were ready to compromise on non-essentials to win. Defining the core charter school program that could not be given up was vital to victory. But given the high stakes, the intense feelings, and the issues that involve private schools, drawing these lines on tax credit and voucher laws will be equally vital but more difficult to do in practice.

Tactically there is a real dilemma facing the school choice movement when opting to use initiatives. In electing not to advertise heavily they will lose to unions as they did in California in 1993. Concentrating on voter turn out using quiet behind-the-scenes methods, as some recommend, may not work either especially if the groups that support choice are passive, distracted, or unreached as apparently was the case in Colorado. Having equal or even superior exposure on TV is no guarantee of success either. Still, as difficult as it is to win a school choice initiative in some states, this is the only avenue available. In Michigan, for example, the state constitution and the legislature are a double barrier that only an initiative can overcome. In the past initiatives heave worked in Michigan when nothing else would. The same is true in California.

The 1998 California charter school story is an example of the adroit use of power. If this example is any measure, initiatives will succeed when they have leaders who are hard to discredit and are well funded, bipartisan based, and tactically flexible, containing compromises on non-essentials. Context and circumstances make a difference too. The opposition feared vouchers were coming so they gave in; and when public schools are in deep trouble and other reforms fail the public is more inclined to look at school choice. This is especially true in inner cities like Detroit and Philadelphia where interest in school choice is now rising.

Notes

1. Daniel A. Smith, *Tax Crusaders and the Politics of Direct Democracy* (New York and London: Routledge, 1998), 1–16.

2. Ibid., 156–64.

3. Ibid., 164–67.

4. Steve Schuck, interview by Hubert Morken, Denver, CO, October 29, 1998.

5. 1998 General Election, "Results in Key Races," *Denver Post Online,* denverpost.com (November 4, 1998); "School Choice Programs 1998, Colorado," *Heritage Foundation Online,* heritage.org (November 5, 1998); Bruce Finley, "Education Splits Governor Hopefuls," *Denver Post Online,* (August 27, 1998); Carla Crowder, "Reforms Will Be Gradual, Owens Says," Election '98, *Rocky Mountain News,* InsideDenver.com (November 5, 1998).

6. Janet Bingham, "Tancredo Backs School 'Separation' Plan," *Denver Post Online: Election '98* (June 24, 1998); Stacie Oulton, "6th CD Race Features Clash of Styles," *Denver Post Online: Election '98* (October 16, 1998).

7. Eric Sondermann, interview by Hubert Morken, Denver, CO, October 29, 1998; "Coloradans for School Choice . . . For All Kids," and "School Choice Opponents Named to 'Hypocrites Hall of Shame,'" News Release, October 29, 1998; "Latest Tracking Poll," *Denver Post Online: Election '98* (October 29, 1998).

8. Sondermann, interview, October 29, 1998; Janet Bingham, "Big Shots Bankroll School Measure," *Denver Post Online: Election '98* (October 13, 1998); Mike Soraghan, "Newest Billionaire Boosts State GOP," *Denver Post Online: Election '98* (August 8, 1998); Janet Bingham, "Fund Kicks in if Tax Credit OK'd," *Denver Post Online: Election '98* (October 28, 1998); Patty Price, Memorandum to John Saeman, October 27, 1998, files of Steve Schuck; Coloradans for School Choice, Memorandum to Interested Parties, July 28, 1998, files of Steve Schuck.

9. Sondermann, interview, October 29, 1998.

10. Steve Schuck, October 29, 1998.

11. Ibid.

12. Ibid.

13. Ibid.; Eric Sondermann, Memorandum to Steve Schuck, Tom Tancredo, and

Ed Graham, June 25, 1996, files of Steve Schuck; draft of voucher initiative, May 2, 1996, files of Steve Schuck; Steve Schuck, "School Vouchers," arguments in defense of, undated, files of Steve Schuck.

14. Ibid.; for an example of Hispanic support see, Robert Armendariz, Steve Schuck, and Vivian Wilson, "The School Solution," *Rocky Mountain News*, 1B (October 4, 1998); Lao-Tsu quote, cover page of packet of materials, 1998, files of Steve Schuck.

15. Ibid.

16. Vivian L. Wilson, interview by Hubert Morken, Denver, October 29, 1998; Schuck, interview, October 29, 1998.

17. Rev. Charles J. Chapur, "Fighting for School Choice: Its Time Has Come" *Wall Street Journal* (September 11, 1997), files of Steve Schuck.

18. Chaput, letter by Fax, "To All Pastors of The Archdiocese," June 16, 1998, files of Steve Schuck.

19. Schuck, interview, October 29, 1998; Coloradans For School Choice For All Kids, "Campaign Plan: A Winning Strategy for the 1998 Colorado School Choice Tax Credit Initiative," summer 1998.

20. Eric Sondermann and Eric Anderson, Memorandum, p. 2, July 8, 1997, files of Steve Schuck.

21. District Court, City and County of Denver, Colorado, Class Action Complaint, Parents and Children by and through the Denver Parents Association, plaintiffs v. Denver Board of Education et al., defendants, May 8, 1997; Alan Gotleib, "Black Parents File DPS Lawsuit," *Denver Post*, 1B (May 8, 1997); Brian Weber, "Moskowitz Lashes at Demand for Vouchers," *Rocky Mountain News*, 5 A (May 8, 1997).

22. Schuck, interview, October 29, 1998; Class Action Complaint; Eric Sondermann, Memorandum to Steve Schuck, et al., June 5, 1997; The Sondermann Group, draft of a strategic plan for "Lawsuit and Related School Voucher Issues," May 17, 1997, files of Steve Schuck.

23. Editorial, "Voucher Suit Misguided," *Denver Post*, undated, files of Steve Schuck; Schuck, interview, October 29, 1998.

24. Editorial, "Joe Rogers' Fiery Crusade," *Rocky Mountain News*, undated, files of Steve Schuck.

25. Gotleib, " Black Parents"; "Denver Public Schools Reading Scores," *Rocky Mountain News*, 11A (October 22, 1998); Diane Carman, "Scores Fail Test at DPS," *Denver Post Online*, October 1, 1998.

26. Al Knight, "Challenging Educational Paternalism," *Denver Post* (May 12, 1997), files of Steve Schuck; James Brooke, "Minorities Flock to Cause of Vouchers for Schools," *New York Times*, A1, 6 (December 27, 1997); Brian Weber, "Thousands Join Suit against DPS," *Rocky Mountain News*, 4A (November 18, 1998).

27. Schuck, "Colorado School Choice Ballot Measure: Summary," Memorandum, undated, files of Steve Schuck.

28. Survey, "Colorado School Choice Statewide Public Opinion Strategies," July 15–16, 1998; "Presentation of Key Data: Colorado's School Choice Initiative," July 22, 1998, files of Steve Schuck.

29. The Sondermann Group, "Focus Group Research Concerning Colorado Ed-

ucation Issues and Reform Proposals," October 1997; Ciruli Associates, "Focus Group Report: School Issues," October 15, 1997; files of Steve Schuck.

30. Ibid.

31. Ibid.

32. Coloradans for School Choice, "Amendment 17: The Educational Opportunity Tax Credit, A white paper prepared for Colorado editors, publishers, and reporters," September 1998; Coloradans for School Choice, "Colorado School Choice Ballot Measure Fact Sheet," 1998, files of Steve Schuck; Eric Sondermann, Memorandum to Core Campaign Team, July 17, 1998, files of Steve Schuck.

33. Coloradans for School Choice, "Amendment 17: The Educational Opportunity Tax Credit."

34. Ibid.; Coloradans for School Choice, "Educational Opportunity Tax Credit: Summary" talking points, 1998, files of Steve Schuck.

35. Eric Sondermann and Eric Anderson, Memorandum to Steve Schuck, May 11, 1988; Jeanne Adkins, Memorandum to Steve Schuck, et al., September 8, 1998.

36. Schuck, interview, October 29, 1998.

37. "School Choice Programs 1998, California," *Heritage Foundation Online,* heritage.org (November 5, 1998).

38. The Buckeye Institute, "Draft of a Report on the History of Ohio School Choice," pp. 2–3, 1998.

39. Schuck, interview, October 29, 1998; Kevin Teasley, interview by Hubert Morken, Indianapolis, July 22, 1998; and Kevin Teasley telephone interview, fall 1998.

40. Joseph P. Overton, Matt Brouillette, and Dan Cassidy, interview by Hubert Morken, Mackinac Center, Midland, MI, July 24, 1998; Gary Glenn, interview by Hubert Morken, School Choice Yes, Midland, MI, July 24, 1998.

41. Schuck, interview, October 29, 1998; Kevin Teasley, telephone interview, fall 1998.

42. Schuck, interview, October 29, 1998; Polling data remained positive at the end of August, see Eric Sondermann, Memorandum to Steve Schuck, August 27, 1998, files of Steve Schuck.

43. Janet Bingham, "Education Petitions Turned In," *Denver Post Online: Election '98* (August 4, 1998); Sondermann, Memorandum to Steve Schuck, August 27, 1998, files of Steve Schuck.

44. Mike McPhee, "Schuck IRS violations alleged"; Kevin Teasley, telephone interview, fall 1998.

45. Mike PcPhee, "Financing Flap Ends up in Court," *Denver Post Online: Election '98* (October 13, 1998); Mike Mcphee, "Tax-Credit Foes Settle," *Denver Post Online: Election '98* (October 24, 1998); Schuck, interview, October 29, 1998.

46. Schuck, interview, October 29, 1998; Coloradan's for School Choice For All Kids, "Amendment 17—Education Tax Credits for Colorado Families, a colored brochure, October, 1998, files of Steve Schuck; Jeanne Adkins, Memorandum to Steve Schuck, August 27, 1998, files of Steve Schuck.

47. Schuck, interview, October 29, 1998; Interviews by Hubert Morken with leaders of national school choice organization, unnamed, fall 1998.

48. Schuck, interview, October 29, 1998.

49. Morken witnessed the demonstration, Denver, October 29, 1998.

50. 1998 General Election, "Results in Key Races," *Denver Post;* "Latest Tracking Poll," *Denver Post Online*; Karen Abbott, "Amendment 17 Opponents Paint Picture of Education Devastated by 'Yes' Vote," and, "Ads about Education—and Money," *Rocky Mountain News*, InsideDenver.com (October 17, 1998).

51. Ibid.

52. Al Knight, "Who Called off Search for Truth?" *Denver Post Online: Opinion* (October 29, 1998); Eric Sondermann, Memorandum to *Rocky Mountain News* reporters Karen Abbott and Brian Weber, on opposition TV ads false statements, October 12, 1998.

53. Editorial, "'Yes' to School Tax Credits," *Rocky Mountain News*, (October 16, 1998); Editorial, "Amendment 17," *Pueblo Chieftain*, 4A, Pueblo, Co (October 20, 1998); Editorial, "End Monopoly on Education," *Colorado Springs Business Journal*, Colorado Springs, CO, p. 3 (October 23, 1998); Coloradans For School Choice, "Campaign Plan: A Winning Strategy" Summer 1998; Morken, personal interviews in Colorado Springs, October 27–29, 1998; Janet Bingham, "School Tax Credit Soundly Defeated," *Denver Post Online: Primary Election '98* (November 4, 1998).

54. Tom McMillan, telephone interview by Hubert Morken, September 17, 1998.

55. Denise Mund, telephone interview by Hubert Morken, September 18, 1998.

56. Morken, personal interviews in Colorado Springs, October 27–29, 1998.

57. Dr. Perry Glanzer, interviews by Hubert Morken, Focus on the Family, Colorado Springs, CO, July and October, 1998.

58. Schuck, interview, October 29, 1998.

59. Author's paraphrase summary of comments made by Steve Schuck and Eric Sondermann, Denver, CO, October 29, 1998.

60. Eric Sondermann, interview, October 29, 1998.

61. Schuck and Sondermann, interview, Denver, CO, October 29, 1998.

62. Morken, personal interviews in Colorado Springs, October 27–29, 1998.

63. Reed Hastings, interview by Hubert Morken, Palo Alto, CA, October 7, 1998.

64. "School Choice Programs, 1998—California," *Heritage Foundation Online* (November 5, 1998).

65. Reed Hastings, interview, October 7, 1998.

66. Ibid.

67. Daniel Schnur, interview with Hubert Morken, Sacramento, CA, October 7, 1998.

68. Ibid.

69. Ibid.

70. Ibid.; Californians for Public School Excellence, "Chapter One: The Problem," Internet homepage, CPSE.ORG (November 9, 1998).

71. Ibid.

72. Reed Hastings, interview, October 7, 1998.

73. Ibid.

74. Ibid.

75. Ibid.

76. Daniel Schnur, interview, October 7, 1998.

77. Reed Hastings, speech given at the Milton and Rose Friedman Foundation Conference, San Francisco, CA, October 10, 1998.

78. Ibid.

79. Ibid.; Jerry Brown, telephone interview with Hubert Morken, October 1998.

80. Reed Hastings, interview, October 7, 1998.

81. Ibid.

82. Ibid.

83. Daniel Schnur, interview, October 7, 1998.

84. Ibid.

85. Pete Wilson, Governor, speech given at the Milton and Rose Friedman Foundation Conference, San Francisco, CA, October 10, 1998.

Chapter 3

Consensus Building:
Michigan and Pennsylvania

When it comes to coalition building Michigan and Pennsylvania are models of "adolescent" and "mature" politics. Michigan is in the throes of trying to figure out how to get different groups to work together for a common school choice program. Obstacles abound especially when people sincerely differ. It is easier to compromise merely political differences than to get principled people to bend. This is the problem in Michigan. Pennsylvania, on the other hand, is completely different. All sides of the school choice coalition in the Commonwealth know how far to push and when to be flexible—they may have friction but they get along—they just do not win, and that is their problem. In a political sense, there is a lot than can be learned from their stories.

Michigan Politics: Justice for the Poor vs. Free Market Principles

Across the country two mighty forces for school choice meet like rivers, turbulent at their confluence, conflicting, yet each increasing the strength of the other. One is motivated religiously, by a passion for justice, a concern especially for the poor of the inner cities whose dysfunctional schools are getting worse. The second is motivated by economic theory, free market principles, and a desire for educational liberty and is committed to opening up school choice for all, including those who live in the suburbs and attend the best schools. The school choice movement in Michigan is being led, on the one hand, by religiously inspired groups focused on justice, particularly the TEACH Michigan Education Fund, which supports vouchers. The free market motivated school choice organizations, with whom they conflict, are led by the Mackinac Center for Public Policy, a group that promotes Universal Tuition Tax Credits (UTTC). Michigan is one of many states where these

73

two movements compete and struggle together in an effort to cooperate or dominate.[1]

Professor Bruce Fuller of Fordham University, a specialist in education unions in Europe and America, commented on these two different approaches, with their radically different perspectives, at an education policy conference at Harvard in the fall of 1998:

> People fail to see that in the USA (and unlike Europe), there are two powerful forces that cannot be held back forever: (1) entrepreneur capitalism—businesses ready to run or help to run schools; and (2) religion, that creates schools and that demands support for schools. The whole process will take fifty years—and cannot be stopped.[2]

What brings the two together in Michigan is a common state constitutional problem: No tax money—whether voucher or tax credit, given directly or indirectly—may be used to assist private schools (transportation excepted). Michigan's Constitution in Article VIII, Section 2, forbids the following:

> No public monies or property shall be appropriated or paid or any public credit utilized, by the legislature or any other political subdivision or agency of the state directly or indirectly to aid or maintain any private, denominational or other nonpublic, pre-elementary, elementary, or secondary school. No payment, credit, tax benefit, exemption or deductions, tuition voucher, subsidy, grant or loan of public monies or property shall provide, directly or indirectly, to support the attendance of any student or the employment of any person at any such nonpublic school or at any location or institution where instruction is offered in whole or in part to such nonpublic school students.[3]

School choice legislation would probably pass in Michigan if this airtight barrier were not in place. But it takes a two-thirds vote of the legislature to amend the constitution by a legislative proposal and the votes to support it are never going to be there. It will take an initiative to bring school choice to Michigan and an initiative requires Teach Michigan and the Mackinac Center to come up with common wording for a constitutional amendment that the governor will support. Neither group sees eye-to-eye on most matters, when everything about them, including their ideology, history, operating styles, and choice programs are so different, but they have no choice. Other interested parties, including Governor John Engler and key entrepreneurs who support choice and help to fund these very organizations, will not proceed until there is agreement or at least a willingness to work together for the amendment. If there is to be a school choice initiative on the ballot in the year 2000 TEACH Michigan and the Mackinac Center must concur.[4]

In the early 1990s, five new organizations were created quickly: (1) TEACH Michigan, (2) The Mackinac Center for Public Policy, (3) The Acton Institute, (4) Michigan Family Forum, and (5) Citizens for Traditional Values—all are for school choice and each has some impact on Michigan politics. The two most active in school choice politics are TEACH Michigan and The Mackinac Center, the former with education reform as its only issue and the latter involved in a variety of issues and the originator of the Universal Tuition Tax Credit (UTTC) plan. To understand these rivals and their prospects for an effective alliance and in order to understand similar organizations in other states as well, it is important to examine their differences.[5]

TEACH Michigan

Paul DeWeese, M.D., founded the TEACH Michigan Education Fund in 1990.

A non-profit corporation (501c-3), TEACH publishes a bi-monthly full-color magazine, *Michigan Learning*, in its role as education consumer advocate. The magazine is subscription based, with corporate and school sponsors providing distribution to groups and to targeted low-income families. *Michigan Learning's* website, http://teach-mi.org/learning, provides an interactive forum where parents air problems and share solutions. Using press releases, a syndicated column, and other media, *Michigan Learning* wages education related public information campaigns. Bryan Taylor, the Executive Director of TEACH, reports that parents, community activists, and public officials make use of its 1–800 help line for research and referrals, frequently working in partnership with the Department of Education Ombudsmen office. TEACH research, Taylor says, focuses on the way public policy issues impact education consumers: parents, students, employers, and the community at large. Taylor comments on the TEACH agenda and its accomplishments:

> TEACH policy development has focused on school choice, student-based funding, site-based management, accountability standards, distance learning, career preparation, educational alternatives and parental involvement. TEACH is perhaps best known for providing the research blueprint for Michigan's charter school law, leading Gov. John Engler to write on its cover, "TEACH Michigan made this possible." In the years following passage of the law TEACH's charter school center helped launch the first generation of new schools. TEACH seeks to equip urban community officials to lead the reform debate. TEACH's urban initiative has included an education summit, clergy conferences on reform, special reports published in partnership with local community groups, research analyses, policy forums and fact-finding studies. TEACH provides a nonpartisan forum for reformers from a variety of perspec-

tives to talk about what the future of schooling should look like. TEACH Michigan Education Fund does not endorse political candidates.[6]

TEACH is especially concerned, Taylor says, to encourage active participation by parents in the education of their children and in education policy debates. This focus reflects the founding perspective of its physician founder.

Paul DeWeese, M.D.

A practicing physician, Paul DeWeese switched medical specialties from internal medicine to emergency medicine to devote more time to education choice, his primary passion, and to public affairs. He says he is not opposed to public schools or to unions, a critically important fact for Michigan politics. He takes great pride in helping to pass the 1994 charter school legislation in the state, now heavily attended by minority students. He has an intense dedication to issues of "dignity, and public justice for each child, especially the vulnerable." Morally driven, and personally ambitious, he is on a civic mission.[7]

In the 1998 election DeWeese, a Republican, ran for the state legislature, winning his Lansing seat by 60 percent in the largely Republican district. The Republican Party then selected him to be majority party whip, the fourth highest position of responsibility in the House, a sign of honor and respect for the freshman legislator. During the election his Democratic opponent, Bill Keith, a former representative from a different district, attacked DeWeese on school choice but failed to make this much of a liability for him. Prior to the election a voter survey in the district indicated strong approval for school choice: DeWeese knew the voters were with him. This fact is deeply satisfying to DeWeese, a personal vindication for one who has sought for a decade to put choice on the policy agenda of the state. Ironically, during the campaign, his opponent was endorsed by a former Republican governor, William Milliken, who opposed choice, and DeWeese was endorsed by "The Detroit Council of Baptist Pastors," long a power in Democratic city politics, because he supported choice. How urban Democrats came to support a rural Republican is the story of TEACH and its founder.[8]

Preparation for Choice

DeWeese, who describes his father was a violent man, "a cop kicked off the police force," strongly identifies with Detroit kids and wants a safe harbor for children. Schools must be a positive community asset, he observes, partly to make up for problems at home.[9]

DeWeese attended public schools in Grand Haven, Michigan. As a graduate of Hope College, in Holland, Michigan, he paid for his education with government loans, private scholarships, and his own work. He sees a public role in education, in partnership with charitable giving, and self-help. Strongly preferring mixed public and private solutions to community problems, DeWeese is proud that he is not an economics purist. He is not a free-market Republican; he rejects efforts to base social policy on economic theory alone and sees Democrats blindly pursuing well-intentioned but destructive policies.[10]

Sharply etched memories shape the DeWeese perspective on politics and policy. While at Hope College he went to Pakistan and saw deep poverty. He then went to Taiwan in the summer before medical school, visiting a place, he says, with no natural resources that was booming because of freedom, with the unleashed creative power of the human spirit and the protection of law.[11]

After these trips DeWeese went to Wayne State University for medical school, located in Detroit. There, in neighborhoods decimated by riots in 1967, he saw no hope in people despite material wealth greater than that which existed in Pakistan. He worshiped in the biracial "Church of the Messiah," an Episcopal Church on the east side, which had a school for fifty to sixty children. These were the poorest kids, he recalls, but there was a great atmosphere; they were motivated students with joy on their faces, who were learning in safety (real learning), with parents active at school. Then tragically the parochial school closed for lack of funds and the children were placed in public schools, leaving the parents in despair as the "lights went out" in their children. DeWeese asked himself the following questions: What is it about public policy that strips parents of their dignity? What is it about public policy that calls some schools "public" when in fact they are anti-public, immersing students in chaos? Why not call the Episcopal school public? He was offended at what he saw, but he had no answers.[12]

DeWeese did nothing initially for school choice. He made a trip to the Ivory Coast, and again saw vulnerable people; and he visited Mother Theresa in Calcutta in 1981. Then, in 1985, as he finished his residency, he moved to Lansing to start his career. As he looked for a house to buy for his family, realtors said to him, "We are only going to show you places where there are good schools." This angered him. He saw access to excellent schools based on wealth. "If you have money choice is available." Convinced a good education is a universal need, he could not tolerate this. "Income should not decide whether or not you receive a quality education and the worst schools could be so much better."[13]

Looking back on these formative moments in his life, DeWeese thinks a change-agent needs vision, but he began, he says, not with vision but with an ache in his spirit caused by the suffering of students and their parents. He had no solution or plan of action. This "gut" pain, as he calls it, which came before his understanding of solutions, was the necessary remedy to callousness that breeds indifference to injustice. Subsequently he was influenced by James Skillen, who is an articulate Evangelical defender of school choice and by Catholic thinking. Scholars and church teaching helped him discover a remedy: publicly funded vouchers especially targeting the poor. Equipped with compassion, vision, and a plan for a better way to educate the young, DeWeese soon tackled the problem of an indifferent public.[14]

School Choice Activist Vision

DeWeese spoke out at Rotary and other service clubs, seeking available forums in 1988–89. In 1990–91 he formed TEACH Michigan, shortly experiencing fierce attacks from the Michigan PTA and education union. His concern was for the poor—not successful suburban schools—but he recalls the unions treated him as an enemy out to destroy the whole system. Given the heat of opposition he said one needs a moral base to sustain participation.[15]

As he entered the fray, DeWeese formulated the following principles:

1. Parents select schools for their children not the state. Parents have the right to ask, "Which school do I want my child in?"
2. Children are different and need a variety of schools and programs to meet needs (this argument, he says, is won).
3. Each school should determine what pedagogy works best for their children. A true pluralism needs to be recognized that makes room for diversity of worldviews in different schools (this argument has yet to be won).
4. There must be tax funds for choice, vouchers or refundable tax credits, because there are equity issues in financing. There is a state obligation to make a quality choice available to all.
5. The state has a legitimate interest in requiring that certain subjects be taught, e.g., American history, and that assessment tools be used to measure outcomes.
6. Virtue must be taught in all schools. Education must have a moral compass, which is essential for self-government and love of community.[16]

Developing his rhetorical weapons for this contest, DeWeese calls school choice a second American Revolution. In the first Revolution, in 1776 and 1787, he says the people secured their liberty from Great Britain and gave limited powers to a representative federal government, defined by the Constitution. In the second Revolution, which he anticipates, government will return tax dollars back to the people. The public school monopoly of tax revenue for education is a tyranny, DeWeese argues, like old King George. "In Europe kings were safe and the people were vulnerable; in America the people are safe and the rulers are vulnerable." He says, "We need a system that puts every school administrator and teacher at risk for failure to perform—and where every child is safe."[17]

DeWeese predicts that if Michigan passes an initiative in 2000, this will lead to the collapse of the whole monopolistic public education system—like the Berlin Wall. Recently he studied *The Fourth Turning* (1997), a bookin which authors by William Strauss and Neil Howe discuss systemic change and generational politics. Agreeing with the Strauss and Howe analysis, DeWeese says that hard times are coming (in the economy, in foreign affairs, and in domestic politics), which will create new opportunities for school choice. Leadership will need to be decisive in a time of troubles, he says, and he plans to be part of the government in such a time, to implement a policy revolution. "Democratic leadership requires having people with one foot in the present and one foot in the future."[18]

Coalition Building

Visiting Detroit often in the 1990s, DeWeese built bridges to community leaders and especially to pastors. He said this was a slow process. Winning the confidence of the reverends Eddie Edwards, Edgar L. Vann, Samuel Bullock, and Ned Adams Jr., to name a few African-American ministers, could not happen over night. Pastors wanted to know why this white doctor who lived in the country would bother to spend time with them with no connection to his own self-interest. Over the years these labors eventually bore fruit. After a careful study of school choice efforts in Milwaukee and Cleveland, the Council of Baptist Pastors of Detroit and Vicinity elected to support choice. Not until the 1998 election did DeWeese ask for something in return, requesting a pastoral endorsement for his election candidacy, which they granted. Grateful for this support that helped to nullify accusations that he was an extremist, DeWeese is slow to ask for political favors.[19]

Republicans, in his view, have little credit with African Americans in Detroit. DeWeese notes that in 1996, Senator Bob Dole refused to come to the NAACP convention meeting in the city. In contrast President Clinton came, not only to speak, he said, but also to hear their concerns. "Republicans must learn to show respect for all groups," he contends, "including those who do not vote for them." Republican leadership, in his view, has a lot to learn if they are to win personal trust, friendship, and rapport in Detroit. Relationships count not only in politics, they are at the heart of the process. TEACH took thirty black pastors to Milwaukee to view school choice in operation and to talk to local leaders. They also sponsored a trip to Cleveland. The pastors commented, "All of our grandparents were Republicans." DeWeese now wants Republicans to earn the right to win back the loyalty of African Americans.[20]

This will require action. DeWeese would like to see the Michigan Republican Party draft a new manifesto with the help of African-American pastors. It would have a realistic social policy component. He would give the draft to the Michigan House Republican caucus, help them to discuss it, adopt it, and use this statement to form new ties and a renewed agenda for the party. The key, he said, is a joint effort, reaching out to the black community and to other groups politically vulnerable, like the large and growing Michigan Arab community.

DeWeese predicts that there will be new coalitions based on school choice and public/private partnerships. In Detroit, the city owns houses. He asks: "Why not give local agencies including churches and mosques the right of first refusal to own and rehabilitate the houses if they wish?" Black pastors, he relates, want this change in the law. DeWeese now sees school choice as the first step for an attractive urban agenda and he wants Republicans to begin constructing a new social policy. This will take a common program and personal relationships, both lacking at the moment.[21]

To make this work, on both sides, DeWeese believes that Detroit pastors need to see this as a civil rights movement, a new civil cause. Only a minority of them support choice, he notes, and they do not fully trust the "white" school choice crowd. There needs to be a homegrown Detroit organizational effort. As one pastor commented, "information" needs to be communicated in a big community meeting, followed by a sermon of "inspiration," finally concluding with an action plan for "transformation." DeWeese argues vehemently, that the preeminence of the black church in the harshest environment must be respected. Detroit, he reminds his listener, is under black control. Chicago, by contrast, is under white control. Yet Detroit has so many problems—so the system is not working. People in Michigan are looking for answers, not others to blame, so change may come sooner rather than later for Detroit, DeWeese hopes.[22]

DeWeese holds that victory in an initiative requires a broad-based, head-turning leadership from the community and corporations—a true civic coalition. The Michigan Chamber of Commerce supports school choice, he says, but widespread corporate support will come only after Governor Engler discreetly leads and blacks are also active. A key corporate leader is Dick DeVos, President of AMWAY Corporation and a board member and major contributor to TEACH, and Bob Lutz, head of Chrysler. Dave Bing, a black businessman, is also active. To sustain such a broad-based effort, the school choice movement will need a new organization to help bring people together and keep operational unity. DeWeese doubted that the organizations in existence in 1998, or at least their current leadership, could fill that public role.[23]

In conclusion, DeWeese considers school choice a life calling that will likely take the balance of his professional career. It is a winnable cause, in his view, because he is confident of God's help as he witnesses to the truth on behalf of vulnerable children. Furthermore, he sees the public education system today imploding and parents coming forward with the help of community leaders, calling for change. The law sanctions parental authority in education and, just as one or two positive steps encourage more steps, DeWeese foresees demand for school choice rising. He is forthrightly, even stubbornly, optimistic on the destiny of school choice.[24]

The Mackinac Center for Public Policy

The Mackinac Center for Public Policy (MCPP), founded in 1988, is a non-partisan, non-profit (501c-3) public policy research and education organization that seeks major influence on the institutions and culture of Michigan. No task is too large or too difficult for the Center to tackle, in fact, it specializes in "long-term consequences." When solutions require non-governmental remedies MCPP recommends them in preference to more "government intervention." The Center will not accept any government funding for its operations. It is a free-market public policy think tank that strives to see its ideas heard and then adopted.[25]

Located in Midland, Michigan, far up the peninsula, several hours north of Lansing, the state capital, the MCPP recently moved into a new and remarkably efficient and comfortable facility that occupies most of a city block and gives them room to grow. Nothing about the organization appears second rate. The facilities, the personnel under its President, Dr. Lawrence W. Reed, and the publications of the center all reflect a serious and professional purpose. This is a place designed for impacting the future of one state, bringing together the best available analytical talent to ask the hard questions (especially economic questions), and proposing solutions to problems often created or made worse by government.[26]

Senior vice president, Joseph Overton, one of the authors of the Center's Universal Tuition Tax Credit (UTTC) proposal spoke of the recent efforts to build support for it. Every available medium of communication for the UTTC message is being tapped, including Michigan Education Report (a quarterly twelve-page paper), an Internet website, radio broadcasts, e-mail, faxes to legislators, studies and white papers, meetings with legislators in Lansing, a freshman legislator orientation, an 800-word op-ed each month on school choice together with responses to attacks by the opposition, and a rally in Detroit. This in basketball terms is a communication full-court-press. The goal, Overton said, is to lay the groundwork for public affirmation of a school choice education initiative in November 2000.[27]

Influencing policy outside of Michigan is another of the Center's goals. If the MCCP has a good idea for Michigan why not export it? Overton commented that eight states have already expressed interest in the UTTC. Recently the Center held a conference in Midland for teachers committed to education choice, a "National Summit of Teachers for Education Reform" with about fifty participants. The goal is to begin the serious recruitment of teachers to the cause and enlist their help in public advocacy.[28]

The distinctive contribution of the Mackinac Center is the UTTC, the product of much research and thought. The original proposal is a seventy-five-page document that includes projections on how the plan would impact student enrollments, education costs, and state and local revenue over a ten-year phase in. This truly is a master plan for school choice designed to change the structure of education in an entire state. It is not a plan of experiments and pilot projects but a bold statement that claims, first, that it has anticipated the costs and, second, that the projected benefits far outweigh them.[29]

What precisely is a tax credit? Tuition tax credits return to parents some or all of the money they spend on tuition or other education-related costs by reducing their tax liability to the state when they file their income tax return. It is not a tax deduction but a credit: If parents owe $500 in taxes and have a $500 credit they pay no tax. It is not money granted directly to a parent to cover private education costs but a reduction of taxes. There is an exception to this rule if a tax credit is refundable. Refundable means that if a parent paid no taxes because of a low income, they would receive a check in the amount of the tax credit. This functions like a delayed voucher and would be paid by the state after the parent filed a tax return. The UTTC by design contained no refundable tax credit provision. Refundable credits appear to be an attractive modification to the UTTC, and they received attention and discussion in the process of drafting the proposal. However, the MCCP concluded they were too much like another entitlement; they were, in effect, a voucher that violates free-market principles.[30]

The chief innovation of the UTTC is its "universal" feature. Young families with school age children are among the most vulnerable people in the population with relatively low incomes and high expenses. This is true of the middle class as well as the poor. The UTTC recognized this problem and dealt with it by making it possible for any Michigan taxpayer, individual or corporate, to contribute and receive a credit if they gave toward the tuition of a student attending a primary or secondary school in the state. The credit in Michigan would apply to three different state taxes, the individual income tax, a business tax, and an education tax. The goal of this feature is to release the extended family, grandparents, aunts, and uncles to give, and to encourage charitable efforts by corporations.[31]

To ease the impact in Michigan on the regular public schools the UTTC would phase in the credit (up to 80 percent of tuition) gradually, starting with a maximum of about $600, which is 10 percent of the per pupil public school revenue. In ten years this would reach a maximum figure of about $3,000, i.e., 50 percent of per pupil public school revenue. To encourage contributions for students from families whose income is below the federal poverty line, the corporate and charitable donors would receive a credit for 100 percent of the tuition provided to the poor. All tax credits would still be limited to 50 percent of the per pupil public school figure.[32]

This plan provides some tax relief to any individual and organization that pays taxes in Michigan and helps pay tuition costs for students in a primary or secondary school—including the wealthy. There is no income cap for this credit. On the other hand, the poor who do not pay taxes, receive nothing directly, because UTTC defenders are confident that philanthropic efforts will cover the needs of those unable to pay tuition, who are not qualified for the credit.[33]

The Mackinac Center in its publication of the UTTC plan, presents the strongest objections to vouchers or government opportunity scholarships, as they are often called, without saying that vouchers are "bad" policy. These objections, which it calls voucher "weaknesses," include:

1. Any direct transfer of government funds to religious schools encounters resistance from some taxpayers who do not want to contribute to religious schools.
2. Government regulation of private schools is more likely with vouchers because some will demand accountability for the quality of education being paid for.
3. Vouchers will encourage dependency and place pressure on legislators to increase the funding, in effect creating a new special-interest group.
4. First amendment issues involving religion make it difficult to include or exclude religious schools—if they are included this may be considered an establishment of religion and if they are excluded they are not being given equal treatment.[34]

On the other hand, the Center supports private vouchers. One of the benefits of the private voucher programs expanding across the nation, the MCCP says, is that they demonstrate that corporate America is indeed ready to help the poor to send their children to the schools of their choice. Voluntary contributions do not have the respect they deserve in social policy discussions, in this view, and private vouchers have more in common with the UTTC than public vouchers. Tax credits and private vouchers are both based on voluntary contributions.

Overton reports that corporations backed choice in the state but were waiting for a plan that all school choice organizations could agree on and which the governor would approve. The Center is the education arm of the UTTC effort, but it also remains in contact with a parallel political organization.[35]

The Public Face of Campaigning

About a mile from the Mackinac Center in an old wooden storefront are the offices of Gary Glenn, president of "School Choice YES" (SCY). This organization, one that he calls a "ballot campaign committee," has one purpose, to pass a school choice initiative in Michigan in the year 2000. Glenn works independently of the Mackinac Center to protect its Internal Revenue Service 501c-3 status. His duties are purely political so the Center must keep its distance, befitting its role as an educational research institution. Recently, the Michigan Education Report published an interview with Glenn discussing his strategies for the coming campaign.[36]

SCY backs the Mackinac tax credit plan. It makes no effort to conceal this fact. Unlike what must be kept secret in a campaign—fund raising information, marketing plans, surprise endorsements, outside help, and the timing of events and advertising—the strategic elements of this effort are regularly announced to the world by Gary Glenn on his Internet site or by news releases. His purpose, two and a half years before the election, is to build confidence in supporters and to enlarge his base. Glenn's initial goal is to obtain 300,000 signatures to put the constitutional amendment on the ballot.[37]

The coalition Glenn has announced includes African-American church leaders in Michigan, some Democratic legislators (Representative James Barcia of Bay City), most of the Republican Senate and House leadership and rank-and-file members. When Governor Engler received over a quarter of the black vote in the 1998 election, double the percentage in 1994, Glenn publicly attributed some of this increase to the tax credit movement. CNN found that blacks favor the tax credit idea and the "universal" feature of the credit Glenn states, is a welcome improvement over other forms of tax credit, because it rewards philanthropic and business assistance to poor families.[38]

Glenn is especially pleased to have the support of Dr. Arthur J. Pointer, president of the 400,000 member Wolverine State Missionary Baptist Convention, who has personally endorsed the initiative. Dr. E. Edward Jones, head of the National Baptist Convention of America, after a meeting in Grand Rapids, in May 1988, came on board too and a letter by him was sent by Pointer to all the Missionary Baptist pastors in the state. Dr. Pointer proposed setting up a denominational education scholarship fund and formally backing the initiative.[39]

Like any focused political operative would do, Glenn produces regular news releases to announce the latest number-count of backers in the legislature and in the Michigan congressional delegation: "Ten out of eleven Republicans elected this week to Senate leadership posts." He gives tax credit pledges, and he names the leaders and their positions:

> The lone exception, newly-elected Senate Majority leader Dan DeGrow, R-Port Huron, said in response to the Michigan Family Forum that he is 'undecided' on the issue. . . . The House will include 44 members who pledged to support a K–12 tuition tax credit amendment, only 22 members who responded in opposition, and 44 members who are "undecided" or did not respond.[40]

The larger strategy is to create a momentum for choice and for tax credits that appears irresistible, that will pull in the undecided. When there is positive survey information, "Tuition tax credits are favored 64–30 in Michigan (66–30 nationally, Gallup)," as the *Detroit Free Press* poll announced, Glenn immediately sends the good news to supporters. When tax credits are more popular than vouchers (10 points more favorable) he lets that be known too. Of great significance, to him, are the indications that suburban voters are also finding good reasons to back choice. Catholic schools in the Detroit metropolitan area, the *Free Press* reports, are investing some $60 million into "new or renovated classrooms, libraries and gymnasiums." Enrollment in the Detroit Archdiocese schools was 53,743 in 1997–98 and numbers are increasing gradually.[41] A *Free Press* article, noted by Glenn, printed comments by its pollster on the results of the poll:

> In urban centers, they just want better schools. . . . Urban residents prefer vouchers, but if that's not available, they will support a tax credit. The lower your income, you don't see how you're going to have the money necessary to spend before you get that credit. . . . Suburban parents are not dissatisfied with public schools. But they want schools to teach morality and values as well as reading and writing, and believe this is more likely to be found in private and parochial schools. It's not so much that people think public schools are bad. . . . They are looking for something that public schools aren't offering.[42]

Responding to the November 1998 news of the Colorado tax credit defeat, Glenn stressed the positive results. He affirmed there was a five percent increase in the vote compared to previous elections and that initiative did not have a "universal" tax incentive feature encouraging business and individuals to give. He noted the superiority of a UTTC initiative and favorable trends nationwide.

Glenn is especially critical of campaigns that go on the defensive, much preferring a hard-hitting aggressive strategy. This is reflected in his own carefully chosen arguments. "The current government education monopoly fails poor families because they cannot afford to pay twice for their children's education—once in taxes for the government-run school that is not educating their children and again for tuition for a better or safer school." Hammering the point, that without a tax credit only the rich can afford choice, Glenn says the leaders of the opposition, "The Michigan Education Association and the Michigan Federation of Teachers—whose officials draw six-figure annual salaries . . ." are those who resist choice for the less affluent. Glenn is determined to seize the high ground, first, asserting that this initiative is in the public interest; second, affirming that it is needed for average and disadvantaged people; and third, noting that powerful and wealthy interests oppose it. He wants to win the class warfare argument to totally undermine the credibility of his opponents. Some call this negative campaigning; he calls it the truth and he is confident it will sell. If Glenn is able to help make key decisions on how to market the 2000 initiative, he will not flinch from conflict, rather, he will seek it out.[43]

The Private Face of Campaigning

One reason a school choice initiative was not on the ballot in Michigan in 1998 had little or nothing to do with needing two more years to campaign, as Glenn in fact preferred. SCY was ready to commence operations in February 1998, with its office and staff in place. By early spring, however, one development led to delay. Governor Engler did not want the school choice initiative on the ballot in November. He did not, presumably, wish to campaign on the issue during his reelection effort and risk stirring up the unions. It would be better politically for his effort to wait until after the election; and Glenn thought it made victory more likely. Adjusting its timetable to this delay, SCY prepared for the year 2000 instead.[44]

Soon, however, another difficulty surfaced in an open conflict between TEACH Michigan and the MCPP. This was dealt with publicly by a joint statement issued by Paul DeWeese and Lawrence Reed, representing their two organizations. The two announced their commitment to work together for choice despite differences on vouchers and tax credits. The press had reported that the Mackinac Center opposed vouchers and this was denied—there were "trade-offs" with each remedy, DeWeese and Reed said, and they pledged to work together to craft the "best school choice proposal." Committing themselves to an open discussion with all school choice groups, they announced their intent to come up with a "united" proposal, thus averting civil war within the Michigan school choice movement.[45]

Left to themselves it might be impossible to keep conflicts muted between these two protagonists. Each is heavily invested in the struggle and they have strong differences. What helps to keep them members of a coalition is that the governor will not go forward with any school choice proposal until they agree. The Catholic Church and the business community also await a common plan before committing to the initiative. The Board of Directors for the Michigan Chamber of Commerce, for example, wants the state constitutional prohibition of assistance to private schools removed, to make room for "universal tuition tax credits, vouchers, or similar approaches." But formal endorsement of an initiative by the Chamber awaits consensus.[46]

Before an initiative campaign for 2000 is formally launched with a petition drive, the supporters, including TEACH Michigan and the Mackinac Center, must agree on the wording. To facilitate this process, something akin to diplomatic negotiations took place behind closed doors. Both sides were equally represented in these meetings and a variety of proposals were put on the table for discussion. The governor and the Catholic Conference sent representatives to participate. Reverend Eddy Edwards from Detroit chaired sessions, seeking principles that all could agree on, and looking for a common understanding of public opinion surveys. Richard McClellan, an attorney who drafted Michigan constitution proposals for both TEACH Michigan and The Mackinac Center, participated with the intent of contributing balance and impartiality.[47]

TEACH has long supported voucher pilot programs in Detroit and elsewhere and continues to argue that the poor must be guaranteed help by government. It is not enough, according to DeWeese, to promise the poor— "Private voluntary assistance encouraged by tax credits might be available." A voucher-entitlement in his view is a good thing when it is given to the most vulnerable families. A middle position is a UTTC with a refundable tax credit. The Mackinac representatives point out that the UTTC with or with out the refundable provision has the advantage of higher public approval ratings in the surveys. In a hard fought political campaign, which this will surely be, the plan that has the best chance of winning has an advantage in these negotiations. However, if the Mackinac Center insisted on making no concessions, standing by its principles, and TEACH Michigan refused to budge, no common plan could ever emerge from these meetings.[48]

Negotiations like these are almost bound to fail given the depths of the disagreement, unless there is outside direction or pressure, from Governor Engler or some other player. Richard "Dick" DeVos, for example, has sufficient clout politically and financially to forge a common plan. Essential to the process of negotiating, perspective must be maintained if action is to follow. Activists heavily engaged in cutting wood may lose sight of the forest. One of the more difficult questions is what to amend in the constitution and what to leave to the discretion of the legislature. Allowing some problems to be solved later may be enough to get the ball rolling.[49]

In fact, after a somewhat arduous half year process of negotiating and fact finding, Dick DeVos announced a common plan on the front page of the

Detroit News and Free Press on April 25, 1999, to be called the "Kids First! Yes!" coalition and ballot initiative. Attorney Richard McLellan and economist Patrick Anderson, the former deputy budget director for Govenor Engler, helped to draft the plan with the advice of a group of civic and religious leaders. Reporting the results, TEACH Michigan said, "The final plan was built around extensive public opinion studies and a consensus achieved between urban leaders, Catholics, non-public school parents, and business representatives." The Michigan State Chamber of Commerce and black religious leaders in Detroit reportedly endorsed it. Cardinal Adam Maida of Detroit said he would support it and DeVos welcomed his positive words. The governor initially would not endorse the initiative but was said to be interested.[50]

The Michigan 2000 initiative balanced the concerns of all the players and incorporated provisions that survey research indicated the public would support. It includes:

- Removing the language in the Michigan Constitution prohibiting indirect funding of religious schools—vouchers, tax credits, or other per pupil measures.
- Giving parents whose children attend schools with low graduation rates in "at risk" districts (below two out of three graduating), a tuition voucher worth one half of the per pupil state spending rate, about $3,000, to select the school of their choice. Thirty-eight of the state's 560 school districts qualify in 1999, including Detroit, which encompasses about 250,000 students of 1.7 million in public schools.
- A local option that will permit voters or school boards in all Michigan school districts to adopt school choice measures. Petitions signed by only 10 percent of the number voting in the previous school board election would be required to put choice on a ballot in a district.
- Requiring teacher testing in all public schools and private schools that accept tuition vouchers.
- Guaranteeing that per pupil funding levels for districts will not be reduced.[51]

In survey research the advocates of school choice in Michigan discovered one fact—most voters were satisfied with their local schools and timid about change but wanted to help those locked into poorly performing public schools. They were ready to help with vouchers. To receive support from all coalition members any initiative needed to include something for average suburban voters, hence the embrace of local options for districts so inclined. The initiative also leaves open the possibility of a tax credit at a later time. With these bases covered, and all school choice advocates on board, including TEACH Michigan and the Mackinac Center, DeVos promised a vigorous campaign to get over 300,000 voter signatures for the initiative and to help raise a minimum $5 million for the campaign. Kids first! Yes! will lead the effort and will hire a director and staff.

When and if school choice reaches the ballot in 2000 and it is voted on, it will have survived intense internal bargaining within the movement and will have gained outside political and financial leadership from entrepreneurs and the governor. Without clear direction from outside the choice organizations it is hard to see how this initiative would have ever seen the light of day. United in their opposition to a monopoly of funding for government-run public schools, but divided on the solution, choice advocates tend to engage in fratricidal conflicts that intensify as success in the larger battle appears near. But in the case of Michigan such an impasse was avoided by the strong leadership of Dick DeVos and ultimately the cooperation of all the school choice players.

Lessons Learned from Michigan

The motivation behind school choice is significant in shaping legislation and conducting negotiations. Some activists like Paul DeWeese are intensely personal about the issue. Choice to him means that the lives of children in this and future generations are in his hands much like they are in the emergency room. For DeWeese, vulnerable people and supportive relationships come first. He spends time with pastors in Detroit, earning their trust the hard way. Vouchers are something tangible that directly helps people, like dressing a wound. He will not betray his cause, the little ones, or his friends.

The free-market libertarian motivation of the Mackinac Center brings an intensity of feeling and commitment to the process that is ideological more than personal. Convinced that their ideas are the best on the market, that they are politically viable and thus will help more children, they defend the clarity, simplicity, and symmetry of the plan. The plan, the UTTC, is their baby, a policy creation, and they want to see it come to reality. A compromise, such as a refundable credit, potentially mars the creation, defiles its architecture as a free-market solution, corrupting the cause. Politics as the art of the possible makes demands on this approach that appear unreasonable to the MCPP. Some tax credit supporters argue: Why should the poor demand guarantees, a refundable credit, when we know the market will work? Why should we surrender because of irrational fears? And besides, we are convinced vouchers lead to government entanglement, and they cannot help the poor who do not file any tax returns. From this perspective a refundable tax credit would be a big improvement over the status quo but would also be a liability in some ways.

Statecraft is more than loyalty to persons or principles when it is done right. Listening to the concerns of TEACH Michigan and the Mackinac Center must be fatiguing for the power brokers of the state. Such strong wills and bright minds rarely give ground gracefully and compromise will not come easily for them, yet without it little can be done. Leaders, such as Governor Engler and Richard DeVos, must give direction to the school choice movement, or the activists, left alone to make plans and to wage war, will likely fail by holding fiercely to their dreams and thereby miss opportunities to act. On the other hand, as Gary Glenn commented after the new plan was adopted, if the tax credit plan had not been promoted so vigorously maybe nothing would have been done in Michigan with respect to the ballot initiative in 2000.[52]

Legislating Vouchers in Pennsylvania: The Long Journey

The vision for school choice—bright, clear, and multidimensional—is alive in Pennsylvania where supporters are slow to settle for modest or incremental change. Rejecting tax credits—some claim they violate provisions of the state constitution—and rejecting pilot projects for the inner city as insufficient, advocates are asking for an aggressive voucher program. This is not a new demand. It is one they very nearly achieved in 1995 and came closer to achieving in 1998. The turn of the millenium, may be years of victory for this most persistent of school choice movements.[53]

Much is in their favor. Philadelphia schools are in a state of perpetual budget crisis and are severely under performing academically. Prominent African-American Democrats, including Representative Dwight Evans and Senator Anthony Williams, have come out for choice. Governor Tom Ridge, his Secretary of Education Dr. Eugene Hickok, and legislative leaders, such as Representative John Perzel, House Republican majority leader, favor it. Organizations, including Catholic, Evangelical, free-market, black, and corporate groups, have formed strong working relationships. Other school reform measures have already passed, including a charter school law, leaving only school choice on the unfinished legislative agenda. Encouragingly, the Supreme Court allowed the pilot voucher law in Wisconsin to stand.[54]

Some thought that the lame duck session in November 1998 was the perfect time to act. They prepared a plan, yet chose not to act, no legislation was put on the table, and no votes were taken. Instead the legislature at the governor's urging attempted to deal with the stadium issue in Pittsburgh and Philadelphia. Not surprised by this delay, which is so characteristic of legislative politics, action was expected sometime in the spring of 1999, timed to coincide with voucher initiatives elsewhere.[55]

School choice politics in Pennsylvania is a mature politics. The players all know how the game is played in Harrisburg. There are no newcomers, either to the political process or to school choice issues. Some have changed sides, many have remained neutral—not everyone takes sides—and most would probably like the issue to be resolved. Outside players like CEO America, and The Center for Education Reform, make minor contributions of ideas and resources, but this is very much a local high-stakes battle with the major in-state supporters playing the leading roles. Governor Thomas Ridge may have the final say, but that is yet to be seen.[56]

If vouchers are passed in Pennsylvania statewide or nearly statewide this will be a first for the nation. Success or failure may well depend on the choices of a very few individuals in the legislature. Swing votes are key in such closely divided contests. In fact, some think the one or two people who are conservative and back choice but oppose vouchers may block progress. But more than principled support or opposition plays into the process. This is backroom politics, the politics of the smoke-filled room, where deals are brokered and votes committed for unknown reasons. Certainly the full story of victory or defeat for vouchers in Pennsylvania will never be told. However, what can be known is well worth the telling. This account shows how a principled vision combines with a defense of vested interests and personal ambition to produce a rather conventional politics distinguished by its longevity and intensity.[57]

Retrospective on the 1990–91 School Choice Defeat

Don E. Eberly, then-chairman of the REACH Alliance (The Road to Educational Achievement through Choice), the Pennsylvania school choice coalition, was in many ways the father of contemporary conservative coalition politics in the state. He dreamed of combining the efforts of free-market and social conservatives, of Evangelicals and Catholics, helping to multiply their effectiveness in Harrisburg by cooperative efforts where possible. The Pennsylvania Family Institute (PFI) and the other family policy offshoots of Focus on the Family were in part his idea. In fact, he helped to recruit Michael Geer to found the PFI. Heading the Commonwealth Foundation, a free-market think tank, Eberly was not blind to the possibilities of working with Catholics and Evangelicals on issues like school choice. The REACH Alliance that continues to serve as a mechanism to promote school choice was also fruit of his labor.[58]

Eberly wrote a memorandum for the leaders of REACH, in January 1992, on "Pennsylvania's Educational Choice Battle," just completed.[59] A fairly detailed and long memo (six pages, single space), this was his analysis of why vouchers lost in the House by thirteen votes the previous December, after winning in the Senate twenty-eight to twenty-two.

Eberly celebrated the fact that an aggressive bill had made it to the legislative floor, succeeded in one house, and, most important, by so doing put this issue squarely before the public. Debate on education reform, in his view, would never be the same because the need for substantial change was now assumed. No one was defending the status quo any longer, just how to change it. This was, he said, a political victory with far reaching consequences even though it was a legislative defeat. But there was one other more fundamental defeat he acknowledged—"we completely lost control of the public debate." He blamed a combination of media distortions and radio attack ads for this outcome:

> The bill was derailed by distortions perpetrated by the media and by our opponents' radio ads. I have never seen the media conduct itself with such systematic determination to stop an idea. I still can't recall one article that clearly communicated the problems in education and how choice might cure them. What we saw instead was a constant drumbeat about the bill's costs and multiple flaws. It was obvious that the media accepted several of our opponents' premises, particularly that the REACH Alliance was launching a sneak attack on the taxpaying public, that it was mostly religious interests doing it, and that its purposes were selfish.[60]

Eberly admitted that these tactics—race, class, taxes, and extremism—had taken him somewhat by surprise, and that only one newspaper, the *Philadelphia Inquirer,* came to his group's assistance, labeling them "sneak attack" ads. Average people, generally cautious of change, drew back, fearful of what choice might do to public schools. Aware that they could not possibly win against this onslaught, REACH might have withdrawn the bill instead of pressing ahead on a vote to protect supporting legislators from retaliation by education unions. Instead, to honor the long hours of effort on its behalf by so many grass-roots supporters, they pressed ahead and had the vote. Eberly commented, "To walk away without a vote would have been like sending workers home without a pay check." Reviewing the damaging charges made against choice, Eberly concluded, that the threat of more taxes ($300 million) was the most devastating. A total of forty-five Republicans voted against the bill, many because choice would increase taxes. The charge of religious favoritism—helping parochial schools—also hurt. To win, Eberly concluded, choice must go on the offensive in the public debate, mobilize its own base, and target the legislative districts where grass-roots support is strong, all this to shift twenty or thirty votes.[61]

Altering the public debate most interested Eberly. Shifting attention to the failures of public schools, to their high costs, to their academic mediocrity, will prepare the way, he thought, for the consideration of choice as the only remedy sufficiently powerful to work. Educators had tried other reforms and these had not reversed the tide. He thought contrasting these failures to the successes of parochial schools at a fraction of the cost will help to force people to ask themselves—What is wrong with public schools? In fact, Eberly noted, parochial schools are reducing education costs that otherwise would be much higher for taxpayers. He wanted to press other issues too, including parental rights and issues of order and discipline.

To strengthen the coalition Eberly talked of getting additional backing from the business community and from city minorities. Maintaining the loyalty and confidence of his own Catholic and Evangelical base also concerned him. Affluent and indifferent Republicans needed persuading. They needed to be won over gradually by helping them see how the current system was not doing well even in the suburbs and how it could be improved by choice. Lastly, he favored more organizational resources and staffing for REACH.[62]

Retrospective on the 1995 School Choice Defeat

The next big effort at school choice legislation in Pennsylvania took place four years later. The newly elected Governor Tom Ridge and his Secretary of Education Dr. Eugene Hickok put a large school reform package before the legislature in 1995. Calling it the "Keystone Initiative for a Difference in Our Schools (K.I.D.S.)," it included regulatory reforms, charter schools, public-to-public school transfers, distance learning, and school choice. In the fall, K.I.D.S. II was unveiled, with slight modifications.[63]

The Educational Opportunity Grant portion of K.I.D.S. was exceptionally ambitious, going far beyond what was attempted in other states. Beginning in the first year with the poorest families (under $15,000 federal taxable income) living in the poorest school districts in the state (measured by percentage of low-income families), the state would provide grants for children to attend public or private schools K–12. If a grant were used in a public school in a different district the grant would help to defray additional costs in the receiving district. In the following five years, eligibility expanded to include all of the state's 501 school districts and families with up to $70,000 income. Grants were to be $350 for half-time kindergarten, $700 for full-time K–8, and $1,000 for high school or 90 percent of tuition, whichever was less (with a $1,500 high school grant for the poorest families). Governor Ridge called this a pilot program because it was to be evaluated annually and at the end of the phase in process. However, if the program was determined to be successful by third-party evaluators, as provided in the law, it in fact would be a comprehensive school choice program covering all but those who could afford to send their children to private schools.[64]

In one legislative package Governor Ridge called for charter schools, public school transfers to other districts, and public vouchers. Some critics argue that this was too much and that he should not have included public school transfers because many suburban and rural districts oppose them more than vouchers. What is astounding is how close he came to winning in his first effort. There was intense opposition in the month leading up to the first vote in June. In an initial procedural vote the bill lost 95–106 with 102 required to win, slightly narrowing the 1991 margin. Not wanting the supporters to pay a high price for this defeat the bill was removed from consideration without a recorded roll call vote, much to the consternation of the opposition.[65]

In the following three-and-one-half years the Ridge administration took up its education reforms one by one and passed them, except for vouchers. It took two years to get charter schools, for example. They also tackled teacher preparation, professional development, teacher recertification, deregulation, and new technologies. Reflecting on the 1995 defeat and his subsequent victories, Secretary Hickok, himself a political scientist, commented that change had to come incrementally partly because Republican legislators simply were not used to initiating creative structural reform and, of course, there was much opposition. He said that once legislators warmed to the idea that changes could be made without wrecking the system it was less difficult to get their votes.[66]

Secretary Hickok is still an outsider in education circles. A former professor at Dickinson College, with some experience in school board politics, he was not an education specialist and was selected by Ridge after others refused to serve in a reform administration sure to antagonize the unions. When he assumed his position in 1995, Hickok refused to be a member of the Council of Chief State School Officers because that organization opposed school choice. Instead he joined with other state education department heads from Arizona, Georgia, Florida, Michigan, and Virginia to form the Educational Leaders Council. He got help to do this from his former student, Jeanne Allen, of the Center for Education Reform.[67]

The council first held a conference in Dallas, where secretaries of education discussed school choice, standards, local control, teacher reform, and freedom from federal control. The council also gives technical support to secretaries on reforms and how to formulate them. Periodically they have telephone conference calls of several hours to discuss ideas and to solve problems together. Commenting on these discussions, Hickok has noticed in the last year or two that other state secretaries of education are not as pro voucher as they once were—and he does not know why. He thought they may have lost support for the idea inside their state or are occupied with charter schools. One reason some governors are pushing for vouchers, Hickok thought, was that wherever they succeed, the person responsible would be in a stronger position for the national Republican ticket in the year 2000. The first state to have a statewide voucher law will make history.[68]

Hickok wants systemic change and not mere improvements in the current system. For him the moment of truth came on a seventeenth of September at a Constitution Day celebration in Philadelphia, when he remembers, four students, the best in the city, got up to speak, and they were totally inarticulate. They could hardly utter coherent sentences in public; to his and to their own embarrassment, and before the leadership of the city, their performance exposed the weakness of the public schools. Given the educational deficiencies in evidence, charter schools, Hickok thinks, may not be enough to solve the problems. Pennsylvania, by 1998, had thirty-one charter schools operating, with no limit on the number that can be chartered. In the fall of 1999 there will be a state appeals board to hear appeals from people turned down for charters by the school districts. Hickok supports rapidly expanding the number of charter schools, but he continues to push for vouchers.[69]

Hickok admits that vouchers are harder to sell than charter schools. Marketing them properly will be crucial, he says, and who the salesmen are counts most of all. He was tremendously encouraged when Philadelphia state Representatives Dwight Evans and Anthony Williams, acknowledged senior African-American Democratic leaders, announced their support for choice and vouchers in 1997. It will take inner-city votes to win in Harrisburg, Hickok knows, because so many suburban or rural Republicans oppose it. In addition, business support in Philadelphia is still weak, unlike Pittsburgh, where, he said, Paul O'Neill, President of ALCOA Corporation, is a great encourager of choice efforts.

The hardball game of legislative politics teaches that losses are not to be repeated. Governor Ridge and the Republican legislative leadership will not offer a school choice bill until they know that they have the votes for passage. Delay is better than defeat, they say, when a loss exposes legislators to the wrath of the opposition. Hickok observed that one key to winning is making choice "no-cost" or budget neutral. The current system of education is so expensive that no one wants to raise taxes.[70]

Expanding the Coalition

Surveys guide politicians and give them the confidence to support school choice when they might not have the courage of their convictions. As school choice appears more attractive to the public, politicians in turn warm to the issue. In Pennsylvania, as elsewhere, the numbers vary with the poll but the message is the same—voters with the passing years consider choice to be less a problem and more a solution. The Commonwealth Foundation survey of October 20–24, 1998, for example, asked this question: "Do you support or oppose using public funds to pay for scholarships to students to attend the public, private, religious, or parochial school of their choice?"[71] The results show school choice growing in favor with new potential constituencies:

- 58 percent of liberals
- 53 percent of Democrats
- 64 percent of African Americans

- 59 percent of those that think public schools have improved
- 61 percent of women age 18–44
- 71 percent in Philadelphia
- 57 percent in Pittsburgh

The lowest figure reported by the Foundation was 51 percent in the Philadelphia suburbs where Republicans are much stronger. Opposition numbers in most groups ran about 33 percent, and overall, 58 percent of the voters were positive. Public perceptions do influence leaders, who face severe sanctions especially if they break ranks. Legislators ask, "Will voters stay with me if the unions oppose me in the primaries?" In the end, legislative politics is about elections and votes.[72]

When African-American legislators and community activists in Philadelphia and elsewhere announced for school choice it was national news because this could well shift the ground of debate and the balance of power. Reporting on this, *Time* magazine in the fall of 1997 framed the cover story, "What Makes a GOOD School: Special Report," on entirely new grounds, not as a choice story but rather as a question of quality. If a child is attending a public school where violent children attack her, as happened to ten-year-old La-Kia in Philadelphia, something must be done. The story commended Robert Sorrell, of the Urban League, and the Pennsylvania Manufacturers Association for their assistance in providing a $700 private grant to enable La-Kia to attend the St. Thomas Aquinas School. Community cooperation across racial and religious lines solved a simple problem for one child. Noting how small the present public and private voucher efforts were (assisting perhaps 20,000 students nationwide out of 52 million), and how high the survey numbers were for black support of vouchers (86 percent for those aged 26–35 and 57 percent overall), the story was framed as a rescue story. "For the poor, vouchers are a lifeboat."[73]

The politics of it are a different matter as *Time* made very clear. "For the G.O.P., they are a wedge issue." If a number of voters that usually vote Democratic switch because of this issue, close elections lost by Republicans in the past might be won in the future. Politicians are always looking for votes, the article said. *Time* also noted that many suburban Republicans are happy with public schools but it said two groups important in the party were not:

> Vouchers unite two activist segments of the G.O.P. that don't always get along: Christian conservatives who support church-affiliated schools and free-marketers who want to foster competition for the public system as a way to force improvements. What the G.O.P. is also discovering is that vouchers may attract lower-income African Americans, whose votes usually go to Democrats but whose kids often go to the worst public schools.[74]

Essentially the politics of choice leads to new coalitions of groups that only agree on this one thing, yet all of them stand to benefit from collaborating. The article quoted Reverend Floyd Flake of New York in saying, "The N.A.A.C.P. is out of touch. . . . The next wave of the civil rights movement will be demand for choice in schools." Giving idealism its due, yet knowing how difficult it is to get change when the political parties seem interested only in their own success at the polls, the article concluded, as it started, not by discussing choice politics but commenting on the fate of children. La-Kia's grandfather, Jim Lester, said: "I don't care of it's Democrats, Republicans, or chickens—I just want what's best for my grandbaby." This is the kind of reporting Don Eberly of REACH wanted in 1991. It simply was not possible to get it until significant black leaders like State Representative Dwight Evans, of the 203rd Legislative District, who was mentioned in the article, backed school choice.[75]

Mayoral Candidate, State Representative Dwight Evans

Building a mayoral campaign in a major city around school choice is something new. That is precisely what Representative Dwight Evans is doing, setting himself apart as a distinctive candidate, owned not by any special interest or power group, animated by a reform vision, prepared to mobilize public and private resources for parents and children. Selling his plan to city voters before the May 1999 Democratic primary requires more than words, he knows. He must demonstrate to constituents that choice works in real schools. He must out-think his opponents. He must also sell his candidacy to people of power and influence, to campaign contributors, and to the press in establishing his reputation as a reliable leader who will be good for the city.[76]

Evans ran unsuccessfully for lieutenant governor in 1986 and for governor in 1994. An ambitious politician, he was elected to the legislature at age twenty-six in 1980, and is the first African American to be Democratic Chairman of the House Committee on Appropriations, from 1990 to the present. Evans is an issues-driven coalition builder willing to work with Republicans when that suits his purposes. To understand this rising leader and his agenda the *Philadelphia Weekly* published a long and colorful article on his history, present political activities, and leadership style.[77]

Born in 1954 in north Philadelphia, the son of poor parents, "his mother a waitress, his father a laborer," Evans's early memories are of an intact and well-kept neighborhood on 19th Street. The 1960s tore things apart and he points out that nothing remains of his family home except a weed-filled empty lot. Something went wrong for his people and Evans wants to do all that he can do to put it right. For Evans this is his city and his positive early memories reinforce his confidence that the city can be revitalized from within and with outside help. He has not left the inner city, like many of his childhood neighbors, nor has he been content to simply represent his district. Early on in his career, in 1983, Evans formed the Ogontz Avenue Revitalization Corporation (OARC), a non-profit community development company, to help restore an area decimated by urban blight. OARC has helped to put together a fifteen-store strip mall, some apartment buildings, a recreation center, and a local training facility, the Southeastern Pennsylvania Regional Employment and Training Center that teaches technical industrial skills. Helping to improve a neighborhood is a significant start. Schools are the much larger project that Evans now wants to tackle.[78] One reporter commented on his concerns:

> Safety, Evans said, is the most important ingredient in a successful school. The killing of a teacher by a student at a school dance in Edinboro, Erie County, is clear evidence that school violence no longer is a problem reserved for urban districts, he said. Another ingredient is standards, and not just academic standards measured with test results, Evans said, but higher standards across the board.[79]

Evans remembers how his mother obtained school choice for him as a child in Philadelphia. His neighborhood junior high school was overrun by gang violence so she manipulated his address to transfer him out to a mostly white public school. This was far from a perfect solution because he had to confront strangers and race-based prejudice. Yet Evans praises his mother for her initiative and condemns the system for not having the alternative for him of a good black school close to his home. Evans is not against public education, he says, but he does want to change its definition and restore quality. He completed his education at Germantown High School, and, after graduating from LaSalle University in 1975, he taught English for one year in the Philadelphia public schools.[80]

Dwight Evans embraces a comprehensive strategy:

- First, he backed the 1997 state charter school legislation.
- Second, he helped pass legislation providing for the takeover of Philadelphia schools if certain requirements, like balancing the budget, are not met. This controversial act that included the possible use of vouchers placed him in direct conflict with labor unions.
- Third, he supported the formation of a legislative commission on the state's urban schools. The commission spoke favorably on public vouchers.
- Fourth, he worked to establish the largest charter school in Philadelphia.
- Fifth, he led a national tour of Philadelphia civic leaders to cities where they studied choice in education. He also sponsored nationally known education figures to come and make presentations in Philadelphia.

- Sixth, he recommended a change in the law giving the mayor authority and responsibility for the administration of schools.
- Seventh, he advocated school choice on a local option basis.
- Eighth, he involved himself in school choice efforts in the fall of 1998 and subsequently.

The credibility of Evans as a community and state legislative leader is unchallenged. He is banking on this reputation to mount a sustained across-the-board education reform effort to give him the public notoriety, policy credentials, and preparation needed to be mayor of Philadelphia.

First, after years of trying and with Evans's assistance, the legislature in 1997 passed a charter school law with the backing of Governor Ridge and forty-four Democrats. Evans has said that he wished every public school in the city were operated like a charter school. In the fall of 1998, Evans attended a parent's night for two charter schools. Typically parent nights draw about fifty people, he said. On these occasions three hundred and six hundred people showed up, a strong indication of how more parents in charter schools are involved in the life and program of schools. The secret to selling choice to politicians, he said, is to sell it first to the electorate. Once parents find they like choice they will communicate to their elected leaders their wishes.[81]

Second, he helped to craft legislation constraining Philadelphia public schools. Serving in the State Legislature for eighteen years, many of those years as Chairman of the Assembly Appropriations Committee, Evans voted budget increases for the public schools with regularity, giving them what they asked for. There was minimum accountability for how funds were spent. "Never did the legislature investigate the results of increased expenditures. They did not even ask if the system was working." Looking back now Evans is appalled at how irresponsible this was. This is why Evans finally said "no" when Philadelphia School Superintendent David Hornbeck in 1998 asked for $85 million additional dollars from the state to solve his deficit problem. Evans commented that the district already received $848.8 million, which was an increase of $31 million and no more money should be given. He defended his action, arguing that if the school district failed in its most elementary duties, the state Secretary of Education should take it over and be free to innovate and to try new methods, including the use of public vouchers. After Hornbeck threatened to shut the system down, Evans joined with the governor in April to pass the takeover law. This was hardball budgetary politics and unions immediately retaliated against Evans in a way that he sought to turn to his own advantage.[82] He had run unopposed in primaries for years but now he had an opponent, businessman Marvin Smith:

> On primary day next week, teachers, hospital workers and trade unions will be hitting the streets of Evans' 203d District, seeking to convince hundreds of

voters in the mostly black, working-class neighborhood to oust the 18-year Democrat from office. It's the boldest political gamble by organized labor in Philadelphia in years. "This is not about Dwight being a representative—this is about Dwight running for mayor," said Dale Wilcox, a local political consultant. . . . Philadelphia Federation of Teachers (PFT) President Ted Kirsch said of the effort to oust Evans . . . "I believe it can happen." He said the PFT has identified just short of 1000 teachers who live in the 203d, and he's hoping that many will vote for Smith in the low turn out race.[83]

This even made national news in the *Wall Street Journal.* "A mailing from the Philadelphia Federation of Teachers claims that Rep. Evan's legislation 'destroys public education by allowing vouchers, unilateral school closings and privatization by converting public schools to charter schools without approval by teachers and parents.' "[84] The combined forces of PFT, the AFL-CIO, and the hospital workers union ran a radio ad campaign against him, yet Evans saw this as so much free advertising for him, as the *Philadelphia Inquirer* reported:

> For at least the next 10 days, Evans opponents will be, in effect, blaring the message that he is the man to beat next year in the mayoral election. And while the ads will say, "Evans and his Republican pals in Harrisburg are trying to destroy our families and our city," Evans is banking on the possibility that people will hear something else. Something like—"The union bosses don't want you voting for Dwight Evans because Dwight wants to give your kids an even break."[85]

The press noted that Evans's middle-class constituents were leaving the district because of bad schools. Many of them were private-sector union members whose incomes were much lower than the $46,000 paid to the average teacher. Unions divided on school choice. The Teamster union, for example, favors public vouchers. In the end the opposition spent a total of $150,000 to unseat Evans in a district of only 58,000 people, and as it turned out, they failed badly. Undeterred and unruffled, Evans won 75 percent of the vote.[86]

A third initiative by Evans was the bipartisan formation of the Legislative Commission on Restructuring Pennsylvania's Urban Schools that he co-sponsored with Representative John Perzel, House Republican majority leader. This Commission held six public meetings in different cities, two hearings, and a seminar with experts, and reviewed publications on the topic of improving schools in the state's twenty-four urban districts. It made seventeen recommendations. One recommendation was for "opportunity scholarships" for all children who attend a school that failed to meet the performance standards set up by the state. A "failed" school might be closed, put under new management, or a private organization brought in to run it, but all of its students would be provided with the funds to attend any school of their choice. In addition, the Commission called for "opportunity scholarships" for three thousand students from poor families attending low performing schools in cities. The students would be selected randomly or by lottery.[87]

The notion of designating some schools educationally "bankrupt" was a new one in Pennsylvania and it combined the recommendations for standards and accountability with choice. Essentially this plan told specific public schools that if over a several year period they did not produce minimum results the state might abolish them and would give all parents the resources to send their children elsewhere. The idea is that public schools would be at risk, vulnerable to closing if they did not perform and replaced by other schools, including private schools in part funded by vouchers.[88]

Evans's fourth action was to start the West Oak Lane Charter School in his district, opening its doors in August 1998, one of thirteen charter schools in the city. West Oak Lane initially is a grammar school for 600 students K–5. In five years the intent is to expand it through the 12th grade to accommodate 1,300 students. Located in a former grocery supermarket and drug store, Evans arranged for a $2 million refurbishment of the facility with the assistance of his community development corporation, OARC, financing it through a company in Arizona.[89]

> What has emerged are completely refurbished buildings. The smaller of the two, which is in the final stages of completion, will house a library/computer lab with 35 computers. And there will be a multipurpose room, which will double for an exercise and play area during bad weather. The larger building houses 20 classrooms, four special education classrooms, administrative offices, a cafeteria and food preparation room. There are skylights, large windows, new furniture, and wall-to-wall carpeting throughout. For recess, there are fenced-in blacktop and mulch areas. Soon, a fence will also be put around a patch of grass to give the children more room to play.[90]

West Oak Lane Charter School's principal, Dr. Margaret Kenney, is the former principal of the highly praised Dunbar School. Most of the twenty-eight teachers are state certified, the others are in the process of getting certified, and they average eight years of teaching experience. The Drexel University Foundations Technical Assistance Center for Public Charter Schools gives needed advice. Over 90 percent of the parents are African American from the neighborhood. In an August standing-room-only meeting for these parents (there is a waiting list of 200) as the school welcomed them, "There was a modest round of applause for the fact that there will be computers in every classroom, but louder applause for the announcement that security guards will be on hand to greet students."[91]

Commenting on the new school Evans said: "It's one thing to be a legislator and vote on legislation. The question is, "How do you make the connection between voting on something and making it real for the community?" Starting a charter school is Evans' way of winning support for his school choice ideas. Showing his people what school choice is and how it will work is his way of helping to open their eyes to his message. Talk about it, then demonstrate it, and then urge it. People in his constituency test his words by the product, observing the success of their own children. Evans is confident they will agree with him and support his next steps. West Oak Lane Charter School is merely a step in his larger plans for the district, city, and state.[92]

Fifth, throughout the summer of 1998 as the charter school was under construction in preparation for a fall opening, Evans, with John Perzel, put together a multicity tour for a seventeen-member delegation to observe new "best-practices" that might be used in Philadelphia. The Pennsylvania Manufacturers Association, a strong supporter of public vouchers, paid for the trip. Murray Dickman, its President, explained his interest: "We represent a lot of manufacturing companies and there is no question that it is very, very hard getting people trained, people who are educated. We can't run a society where inner-city children are leaving high school without being able to read or write." In cities from Massachusetts to Texas the delegation visited local school experiments and talked with educators and local officials. They were most encouraged by the quality and mix of schools they observed—"public schools operated by private for-profit firms, private schools that operate with public tax dollars in the form of vouchers and even an academy that, under one roof, operates three schools: a charter, public-private partnership, and voucher program." Impressed by the results, including rising test scores and students eagerly learning in orderly classrooms, John Perzel said he wants to experiment in Philadelphia with whatever is working. Disappointed at the two previous defeats of school choice Perzel was hopeful after the trip that the third effort would be successful.[93]

Back in Philadelphia Evans continued to seed his ideas into the public discussion by bringing in speakers to address school reform questions. David Boldt, a commentator for the *Philadelphia Inquirer*, attended a meeting with public school leaders set up by Evans to present Dr. Paul T. Hill, author of *Fixing Urban Schools*. Hill told them not to fear competition but to embrace it. People need to get over their philosophic differences, he said, and new people not polarized by old battles need to seize the initiative and combine strategies. The issue is not public versus private but how to use a host of changes to improve the quality of all schools. Boldt, a long-time supporter of vouchers, came away with a new openness to try reforms in public schools once again.[94]

Sixth, he called for the mayor to be given new authority over education, including the power to appoint school board members and to choose the President and Vice President of the Board. At the heart of his campaign is giving the mayor total responsibility for the running of the schools, as is the case now in Chicago. For decades, Evans relates, mayors did not see an education crisis under their very noses—they saw crime, streets, trash, jobs, and welfare as their responsibility, not children, who were left to the care of professional educators. Yet a successful education system is the biggest issue for the long-term survival of the city, in his opinion.[95]

African Americans can no longer place their confidence in public schools as they once did, Evans asserts. To restore this confidence, he wants his campaign to be a referendum on education reform. "I will be fully responsible for the 217,000 children and 250 buildings." He wants to be like Mayor Giuliani in New York, who promised to clean up the streets and did what he promised. He wants to be like Mayor Daley in Chicago, who is in charge of schools in his city. However, he is committed to no single solution, no silver bullet, and studiously avoids negative attacks on public schools. Essentially he wants support for every kind of school that parents opt to use, from the current public schools to charter schools, parochial schools, and home schools.[96]

Seventh, Evans favors a local district option that would allow each of Pennsylvania's 501 districts to accept or reject public vouchers for their children. School choice then would be largely a local and not a state matter, he says, where it would be up to each jurisdiction to put together a mix of solutions they think will work best for them. The Pennsylvania school code was written in 1949, giving no flexibility to local districts—this must be changed. He also favors accountability standards for every school that accepts a child with public funding.[97]

Today when a young couple have a child that reaches two years old, they flee the city, Evans relates, and the city power brokers are oblivious because their children go to private or suburban schools. "Republicans are not solid for school choice," he says, because their schools are acceptable. Meanwhile the inner city suffers from problems sure to doom the city if they are not solved. Evans says choice is the best way to get at workforce development, giving people the skills they must have to work and providing the knowledge they require to be active intelligent citizens. The local option approach to school choice would allow the inner cities to act swiftly without imposing such changes on districts where parents are presently satisfied.[98]

Eighth and last, Evans joined the former Assemblyman and now state Senator, Anthony Williams, also of Philadelphia, to press for school choice legislation to include vouchers. The two are active members of the larger coalition in the city and state. Their efforts, if choice succeeds in 1999 or 2000, are likely to be crucial.[99]

To conclude, Evans has learned from his experience both in Pennsylvania and travelling outside the state in speaking on behalf of choice—in Indianapolis, Chicago, Cleveland, Milwaukee, Houston, and Dallas—that "people are more ready for school choice than their leaders." He comments, "President Bill Clinton would rather fight Iraq than tackle the school issue in Washington, D.C." To get political and structural change, he says, we need a leader who will seek education responsibility, not shirk it, and a new flexible system to permit local innovation. Simply throwing more money at the issue will not work. Threatening to throw the children on the streets, his characterization of what the Philadelphia leadership did in 1998 (when they ran out of money from the state), will not bring change. Positive solutions are what the times and circumstances demand. Evans says, "Eighty percent of the children in the city are people of color," and he would like to lead them out of the urban desert and into an educational Promised Land.[100]

Winning Additional African-American Support

Most African-American legislators in the twelve districts they represent in Philadelphia oppose school choice. Many of their constituents work in public schools and want to keep their jobs, fear what change might bring, and are loyal to the present system. Evans and Williams are still the exceptions to the rule. Despite the difficulty of doing so, winning over resistant black legislative leaders is the personal vision of long-time community activist Walter Palmer. As quixotic as it seems he wants black legislators to take the lead in asking for a comprehensive voucher program for the whole state.[101]

Palmer, an activist for over forty years, adjunct professor of law, and the head of the Palmer Foundation, once ran an independent private school effort in Philadelphia to prepare children for college. In the last three years he pushed hard for charter school legislation but sees the middle class largely benefiting from charters. His life-long passion, he says, is to help the poor but he does not want to settle for an urban program. Although not Catholic himself, he has close ties to the Catholic Archdiocese and to Cardinal Bevilacqua. The legislation he supports, for example, House Bill no. 2 (1997), called for a statewide phase-in of vouchers, essentially adopting the K.I.D.S. program of Governor Ridge.[102]

In 1995 Palmer formed an African-American organization to support choice in the city. Two years later he broadened it to be racially inclusive in calling it the Philadelphia Coalition for Education Reform and School Choice. How does one persuade legislators to switch sides? Palmer's approach in the fall of 1998 was initially to stir up constituents using a petition drive as his vehicle. He approached CEO America and received some funding for his effort. His goal was to secure over 50,000 signatures in the districts of the twelve black and one Hispanic legislators in Philadelphia. Second, he communicated with legislators using school choice survey information from each district to try to persuade them to be more sympathetic to constituents. In most of the districts this survey showed slightly over 60 percent in favor of choice and 30 percent opposed it; over 75 percent with school age children have them attending public schools; and 75 percent say they would send their children to a private or parochial school if they could afford it. Third, Palmer is sending school choice brochures to households in African-American communities. These are all traditional political tools. As school choice becomes more of an issue in the city, these efforts may even influence legislators, helping to neutralize pressures from the other side. Palmer's realistic goal is to get several legislators to join Evans and Williams in order to increase the chances of winning in Harrisburg.[103]

On another front Palmer is a critic of alternative school choice plans, arguing against them, criticizing what he considers wrong solutions. The Urban Schools Report of the legislative commission, for example, received heavy criticism from him for what it left out. There was no mention of help for children attending Philadelphia Catholic schools, and nothing much said, in his view, about making it easier to start charter schools, two issues he cares about. Palmer functions as a strong advocate for charter schools and vouchers and wants black legislators to take the lead on their behalf. Pilot projects are a sellout from his perspective when the state is so close to getting more.[104]

The Archdiocese of Philadelphia

Anthony Cardinal Bevilacqua is an educator for 111,000 children who attend parochial schools in the archdiocese, more than half the size of the Philadelphia public schools. This huge responsibility, in his view, requires efforts on behalf of choice. Historically there is an ebb and flow to Catholic education policy activity that depends on the priority it is given and the chances of passage in the state legislature. In the past few years, and especially in 1998, that activity increased. The archdiocese is now working hard to educate its parishioners on the value of school choice, mobilizing them in elections. More publicly, Cardinal Bevilacqua offered to take public school students as a way to relieve pressure on the overburdened public schools and to bring relief to taxpayers. He also expresses his views in the newspapers. Lastly, the Office for Public Affairs of the archdiocese is busy pushing its own school choice plan to make sure some alternative plan does not replace it in any legislation put forward.[105]

For the first time in its history the Archdiocese of Philadelphia in 1998 organized a voter registration drive. In its literature for the drive it set the goal of registering 10,000 or more Catholic voters before the fall elections. Archdiocesan voters, it claimed "constitute nearly 30% of Pennsylvanians, elect 64 of 203 State House members, 14 of 50 State Senators, (and) 9 of

Pennsylvania's 21 Representatives in the U.S. Congress." Registration forms were provided and parishioners asked to contact family and friends. "We have a great ability to affect the outcome of elections . . . if we exercise that right." Bumper stickers—"Another Catholic Voter"—were provided, too.[106]

Along with the voter registration campaign, the archdiocese distributed a brochure entitled "The Facts about School Choice," flyers, and videos on school choice to Catholics, calling it a matter of justice. In his personal message "The Voice of the Shepherd" Bevilacqua called his position "Justice in Action" because it was founded, he said, on the parent's right to select the school for their children. Citing recent university studies that confirm improved student performance when students transfer to private schools, he asked Catholics to contact legislators on behalf of school choice bills that he listed.[107]

Starting in 1994 the archdiocese made it a practice to publicly advertise how much parochial schools were saving the taxpayers. Outside of each Catholic school they put a sign listing the name of the school, the sum each student saves taxpayers (e.g. $6,570), and the total dollars saved by that school based on enrollment (e.g. $3,657,600). They updated the signs annually with new figures.[108] In a news release in January 1998, the Archdiocese announced that it was about to put out new taxpayers savings signs at all the schools saying: "Every student in a Catholic school saves the taxpayers Money! This year, Catholic schools in the Archdiocese of Philadelphia will save the taxpayers nearly $1 billion ($949,402,378)."[109]

For decades school choice has suffered from the charge that it is a costly subsidy that increases taxes. The Catholics are now turning this argument on its head saying that public schools need parochial schools because even with vouchers students would be cheaper to educate if more attended private schools. One school board in Pennsylvania faced with rising costs due to expanding enrollments agreed and decided on its own to adopt a voucher program. The South East Delaware County School Board in March 1998 by a vote of 7 to 0 with 2 abstentions set up a voucher plan to allow all students living in the district to have publicly funded scholarships—for kindergarten, $250; grades 1–8, $500; and high school, $1,000. In 1998 over 4,000 S.E. Delco students attended public schools and about 1,900 were in private schools. However, the trend lines for enrollments in local private schools were declining. The plan in the long run would pay for itself, advocates for it argued, because the district would not have to build new facilities.[110]

Cardinal Bevilacqua issued his news release the same day praising the S.E. Delco decision. Then a few weeks later he used it as a precedent. He wrote a letter to the mayor, the School Superintendent of Philadelphia, Edward G. Rendell, and David Hornbeck, offering to take 20,650 students from the city's overcrowded public schools in exchange for a voucher patterned after the S.E. Delco plan. The vacancies in the parochial schools could be filled and the fiscal crisis and classroom shortage in the city eased. Bevilacqua made the same offer to ten suburban districts bringing the total number of students he was prepared to take to 26,000. He said the public schools would save $190 million in one year if they accepted his offer. All refused, some saying they considered this a constitutional church/state issue and others saying they preferred a long-term public school solution. Litigation ensued in S.E. Delco delaying implementation.[111]

In his opinion article in the *Philadelphia Inquirer* explaining his offer, Bevilacqua defended the common sense and constitutionality of his proposal in placing most of his emphasis on savings to taxpayers but also arguing once again for parental choice in education. The tuition costs of parochial schools in Philadelphia range from $800-$2,000 for primary schools and $3,050 for high school. The Cardinal noted this compared to from $7,000 to $13,000 paid for public schools. If one of the districts, the Pottsgrove District in Montgomery County, had accepted his offer they would have saved almost 7 percent of their budget. He concluded:

No one wants larger classes, higher property taxes or overcrowded classrooms. Everyone wants all children to achieve. Vouchers are a viable alternative to ease public school challenges and give parents the choice they deserve.[112]

In the fall of 1998 as school choice once again moved into consideration among its advocates, competing visions vied for preeminence. Cardinal Bevilacqua made it clear that the archdiocese stood behind the plan that had first been proposed in 1995, a phased-in voucher plan that would help both the poor and the middle-class parishioners who had fought so long and hard for it. Other plans may have merit but the Cardinal rejects them. For example, the Commission plan introduced the idea of giving public scholarships to children attending "bankrupt" public schools. John Perzel (R), House Majority Leader, strongly favored targeting the worst urban schools for help but he ran into a stonewall at the archdiocese. Catholics refused any retreat on phased-in statewide vouchers. The friction between the Majority Leader's office and the archdiocese on this issue was fairly intense as parishioners communicated their sentiments to the politician. Clearly any school choice plan put forward in Pennsylvania had to have the backing of the Catholic hierarchy and the politicians. Some accommodation to both sides would be necessary.[113]

In three arenas essential for policy success the Philadelphia Archdiocese showed strong initiatives. First, it took new steps to keep Catholics involved, informing them about choice legislation and presenting reasons for them to get involved. This included encouraging voter registration and old-fashioned direct lobbying by church members. Second, Bevilacqua boldly put forward his offer to help out in the public school crisis of the day, using this as an opportunity to make the case once again for school choice in fiscal terms attractive to most voters, and in his view, in the public interest. Third, the Catholic position on legislation was maintained firmly, forestalling any possible attempt to substitute a different plan for widely available vouchers. Given the political strength of Catholics and their long history in school choice battles in the Commonwealth, this is not surprising. Also, an active Cardinal makes a difference.

Crafting and Passing Pennsylvania School Choice Legislation, 1998–2000

There was no chance that school choice legislation would be put on the table before the 1998 November election. The governor opposed this timing and legislators did not want to stir up union opposition just before the election. The first possible time for it to be passed was in the lame-duck session in November, in a stealthy fashion after the election, or in 1999. Several other factors were also important. Neither the governor nor the legislative leadership was prepared to risk defeat again, the governor because he would like to be a vice-presidential candidate in 2000. John Perzel made it clear that he would have his own vote count, a reference to the narrow defeat in 1995 that he would not repeat. In addition, no final legislative plan would be cast in stone in advance of voting. Cobbling together a bill at the last moment is considered preferable because last minute changes may be necessary to get needed votes.[114]

The present school choice coalition has its strengths and weaknesses. The governor, whose direct intervention is necessary for victory, heads the school choice effort in its push for legislation. Many Republicans who are not supportive will vote for the bill but only if the governor lobbies them personally. Dwight Evans and Anthony Williams provide important Democratic assistance but have not succeeded in winning public endorsement for choice by other black legislators. Catholics and Evangelicals at the Pennsylvania Family Institute are united, although some conservative legislators oppose vouchers as a means of bringing choice because of fears of increased regulation of private schools. The free-market Commonwealth Foundation and the Pennsylvania Manufacturers Association are helpful but the state Chambers of Commerce are neutral at best. With the exception of newcomers Evans and Williams this coalition has worked together for most of the 1990s and all are thoroughly familiar with the political process in the state.

The elements to a bill included the following possibilities in the early fall of 1998:

- K.I.D.S. II, a phased-in voucher backed by the governor and Catholics
- Vouchers for all students in "failed" schools, an Evans/Perzel initiative
- Public school interdistrict transfer, also part of K.I.D.S. II
- Local option choice like that exercised by S.E. Delco
- Full vouchers for the poorest of the poor
- An absolute minimum of additional requirements for private schools

After the election, there were few surprises in the school choice patchwork plan that surfaced. Called the School Choice Pilot Program (terms used previously in 1995) it circulated privately within the coalition and among its legislative supporters. Philadelphia received much and yet predictably it was a broad measure. The program applied to nineteen counties—Philadelphia, Bucks, Chester, Delaware, Montgomery, Allegheny, Butler, Beaver, Westmoreland, Washington, Erie, Dauphin, Lehigh, Northhampton, Berks, Blair, Luzerne, Lackawanna, and Lancaster—covering the suburban and metropolitan areas of the state but not all the rural areas (there are sixty-eight counties in the state).[115]

First, the plan included the phase-in of vouchers starting in the first year with families who earn less than $15,000 income. In five years this income ceiling rose to $75,000. Grants were $350 for kindergarten, $700 for grades 1–8, and $1,000 for high school. For those from the lowest income category the grant was doubled. Second, there were grants equal to the state per pupil expenditure for any students attending an "academically bankrupt" school. This was the commission proposal. Third, provision was made for interdistrict public school transfers as space was available, and by lottery, for those who apply when space was limited. On issues of financial impact and regulations the proposal contained the following: Grants were entirely voluntary so no child had to participate; local districts would suffer no reductions in state funding for four years due to students enrolling in private schools; civil rights laws would apply but no new regulations would be made for private schools; public schools would not be compelled to accept out of district transfers if they lacked room as certified by their superintendent; and after the transition period of four years, money that this program saved the state would be distributed to rural districts and to economically troubled districts.[116]

The only measure not included was a full local option provision that would allow each of the 501 districts to create its own choice program if it wished to do so. Since the S.E. Delco case is still in litigation contesting the issue, this is perhaps why it was omitted.

This proposal was carefully designed to win votes:

- The Catholics and Evangelicals received vouchers and no additional regulations

- The Philadelphia plan for bankrupt schools satisfied the demands of Evans and Perzel
- Suburbs were protected from public school transfers if they had no space
- Rural districts do not have to participate and will eventually benefit financially

Reportedly, Perzel was confident he had the votes in the House and the Senate would go along. Why then did it never see the light of day? There are several explanations that are plausible and sufficient to explain what may only be a delay.[117]

Weeks before the final decision not to put the plan on the floor Perzel was doubtful about the governor's intentions. If Ridge really wanted a bill in 1998 he would push for it in the lame-duck session, making the phone calls that told Republicans they had to line up or else face his displeasure. These calls were never made. The governor went to Florida for the National Governor's Conference in November and chose to be active on another issue, public funding for stadiums, something that he eventually lost. Why did he wait on school choice? Some blame his timid staff, which was unprepared to risk another fight, even one they were guaranteed to win. Perhaps timing was a concern—Ridge wants a big win in the spring for vouchers that will mean a later legal challenge, delaying a final court decision to well after the vice-presidential selection process is completed.

Legislators may share the blame too. Senate Floor Leader, F. Joseph Loeper (R), who carried the legislation in the Senate, is said to have exercised little positive leadership when Senators discussed this. Other issues may also have determined why they waited. Certain legislators want a large increase in their retirement pensions and may be using this delay to put pressure on the governor to be more forthcoming on their behalf. Cloakroom politics prevailed once again in Pennsylvania. Moreover, if it is true that the votes were there this time, which is likely, this is no guarantee that the new legislature will act in 1999. Much will depend on the governor.[118]

Ambition, for the governor to become vice president or the assemblyman to become mayor, propels school choice forward in Pennsylvania. Other factors hold it back, including suburban and rural districts that think school choice primarily benefits the cities. All things being equal, it is reasonable to predict a legislative victory in the period 1999–2000, if Democratic support from black legislators is combined with strong leadership from the governor and the majority leader of the House. Obtaining vouchers for Pennsylvania has been a long and arduous journey.

Conclusion: Building Consensus in Michigan and Pennsylvania

Michigan illustrates the need to come to agreement early on to avoid frustrating the political leadership of the state. Delay can be fatal and internal friction slows everything down. The stronger the interest groups are in their convictions, resources, and leadership, the greater the potential for both success and internal conflict. Civil wars can overshadow the larger purposes of the movement if differences are not respected and accommodated. No group wins if one group loses is a truth coalitions must learn to recognize. Michigan school choice associations are learning how to disagree and still find common ground, with the necessary assistance of strong leaders like Dick DeVos and Governor Engler.

Pennsylvania is, according to some, the perennial bridesmaid of state school choice movements, never the bride. This can change and in the twinkling of an eye if Republicans care enough to get it done with the help of Dwight Evans and presumably when the governor provides necessary leadership.

It would appear from the evidence in Michigan and Pennsylvania that for school choice to succeed, a governor must be ready to do what is necessary, which is to twist arms in the school choice coalitions or in the legislature. Interest groups lobby and legislatures pass laws but governors make it happen. When push comes to shove a governor must expend political capital if school choice is to win. Coalitions form and work hard to insure victory but the grass roots and pressure groups will never be enough to overcome the opposition and inertia that bedevil school choice efforts every step of the way. Legislative leaders also need the extra protection, the political shelter, that strong governors provide.

In the final analysis, winning a big school choice victory is only the beginning of a much longer conflict. Once school choice passes in Michigan and Pennsylvania, it must then be sustained and protected from hostile forces. This is why coalition building is so important. If school choice is to thrive permanent coalitions must be in place to watch over it. When there is a political attack they will be there to respond. Coalitions also can raise money for schools and for lobbying. It takes years for these movements to put in place the school choice programs they desire. It will take many more years to plant them securely. Governors come and go, but strong school choice forces must endure to survive. Pennsylvania points the way for Michigan and other states to follow when it comes to building coalitions.

Notes

1. Paul DeWeese, M.D., interview by Hubert Morken, Lansing, MI, July 23–24, 1998; Joseph P. Overton, Esq., Matt Brouillette, and Dan Cassidy, Mackinac Center, interview by Hubert Morken, Midland, MI, July 24, 1998; Gary Glenn, School Choice Yes, interview by Hubert Morken, Midland, MI, July 24, 1998; "School Choice Programs 1998, Michigan," *Heritage Foundation Online*, November 5 1998.

2. Bruce Fuller, Fordham University, telephone interview by Hubert Morken, October 1998.

3. Constitution of Michigan of 1963, Article VIII, Section 2, p. 36.

4. Paul DeWeese, interview, July 23–24, 1998; Joseph P. Overton, Esq., Matt Brouillette, and Dan Cassidy, interview, July 24, 1998; Gary Glenn, interview, July 24, 1998; Bryan Taylor, TEACH Michigan, telephone interview by Hubert Morken, November 11, 1998; Constitution of Michigan of 1963, Article XII, Section 1.

5. Paul DeWeese, interview, July 23–24, 1998; Joseph P. Overton, Esq., Matt Brouillette, and Dan Cassidy, interview, July 24, 1998; Gary Glenn, interview, July 24, 1998.

6. Bryan Taylor, e-mail message with information on TEACH, sent to Hubert Morken, March 23, 1999.

7. Paul DeWeese, interview, July 23–24, 1998.

8. Bryan Taylor, telephone interview, November 11, 1998; Lansing-based MRG survey of 600 voters, "On Candidates Who Support Vouchers," September 1997.

9. Ibid.; Paul DeWeese, brief professional vita, 1998.

10. Paul DeWeese, interview, July 23–24, 1998.

11. Ibid.

12. Ibid.

13. Ibid.

14. Ibid.; Paul DeWeese, "The Process of Educational Reform in Michigan," March 1995; Paul DeWeese, Remarks for the Jewish Community Council, March 5, 1997.

15. Paul DeWeese, interview, July 23–24, 1998; Joan Richardson, "Paul De-Weese, MD," *Michigan Medicine*, October 1996, 46–47.

16. Paul DeWeese, interview, July 23–24, 1998;

17. Ibid.

18. Ibid.

19. Ibid.; Bill Johnson, "Powerful Baptist Council Leans toward Favoring School Vouchers," *Detroit News and Free Press,* April 20, 1997, 6B–7B.

20. Ibid.; TEACH Michigan, "Empowering Parents to Drive Education Reform," Report of the Council of Baptist Pastors of Detroit and Vicinity, undated.

21. Paul DeWeese, interview, July 23–24, 1998.

22. Ibid.

23. Ibid.

24. Ibid.

25. Mackinac Center for Public Policy, *Publications Catalog,* September 1997. In addition, the following Mackinac Center Reports, La Rae G. Munk, J.D., *Collective Bargaining: Bringing Education to the Table* (August 1998), Patrick L. Anderson, Richard McLellan, J.D., Joseph P. Overton, J.D., and Gary Wolfram, Ph.D., *The Universal Tuition Tax Credit: A Proposal to Advance Parental Choice in Education* (November 1997); Robert P. Hunter J.D., LL. M., *Paycheck Protection in Michigan* (September 1998); National Education Association, *The Real Story Behind 'Paycheck Protection'* (September 1998), 90–91.

26. Ibid.; Joseph P. Overton, Esq., Matt Brouillette, and Dan Cassidy, interview, July 24, 1998; Gary Glenn, interview, July 24, 1998.

27. Joseph P. Overton, interview, July 24, 1998; Gary Glenn, interview, July 24, 1998; Mackinac Center, *Michigan Education Report,* fall 1998.

28. Ibid.; Mackinac Center, *National Summit of Teachers for Education Reform,* Program, List of Participants, and "A Letter to the American People: Our National Crisis in Education," June 12–13, 1998.

29. Mackinac Center, UTTC, 1997.

30. Ibid., 30–32.

31. Ibid.

32. Ibid.

33. Ibid.

34. Ibid., 28–29.

35. Joseph P. Overton, Esq., Matt Brouillette, and Dan Cassidy, interview, July 24, 1998; Gary Glenn, interview, July 24, 1998.

36. Mackinac Center, "Interview by Gary Glenn, President of School Choice YES," *Michigan Education Report,* fall 1998, 11.

37. Ibid.

38. Associated Press, "Black Ministers May Back School Choice," *Battle Creek Enquirer,* personal file, June 8, 1998; Richard Whitmire, "School Choice Moves to Civil Rights Arena," *Detroit News,* clipping in personal file, July 10, 1998; Jodi McFarland, "Group Touts Tax Credits," *Saginaw News,* online clipping in personal file, November 9, 1998.

39. Gary Glenn, e-mail to Hubert Morken, copy of Dr. A. J. Pointer letter sent to pastors on September 23, 1998, November 11, 1998.

40. Gary Glenn, "New Senate Republican Leadership Strong for K–12 Tuition Tax Credit," News Release, November 6, 1998.

41. Tamara Audi and Tracy Van Moorlehem, "Catholic Schools Grow with Enrollment," *Detroit Free Press,* June 25, 1998, 1A, 13A; Mark Mayes, "Week's News Buoys Groups Favoring School Vouchers," *Lansing State Journal,* November 11, 1998; Gary Glenn, "New House, Senate Leadership Strong for K–12 Tuition Tax Credits," News Release, November 12, 1998.

42. Peggy Walsh-Sarnecki, "School Choice Issues Gain Favor," *Detroit Free Press,* online, October 13, 1998.

43. Mackinac Center, "Interview by Gary Glenn," President of School Choice YES, fall 1998, 11; Gary Glenn, "Election Results Boost Drive for K–12 Tuition Tax Credit," News Release, November 4, 1998.

44. Richard Burr, "K–12 Tuition Tax Credit: Choice Plan Takes Surprise Twist," *Detroit News,* detnews.com, March 1, 1998; Chad Swiatecki, "Group Delays Efforts for Tax Credit," *State News,* Michigan State University, April 7, 1998;

45. TEACH Michigan, "Statement Addresses School Choice Collaboration," Fax Alert, June 5, 1998.

46. Michigan Chamber of Commerce, "Official Policy Relating to Parental Choice & Competition in K–12 Education," April 29, 1998; Editorial, "Court Stands Aside," *Detroit News,* November 11, 1998.

47. Richard D. McLellan, Memorandum on school choice negotiations meeting, July 20, 1998.

48. Gary Glenn, e-mail communication on Gallup poll, to Hubert Morken, No-

vember 11, 1998; Teach Michigan, drafts of proposals for a "School Choice Constitutional Amendment" for comparison and consideration, June 22, 1998; TEACH Michigan, notes in preparation for the parental school choice coalition meeting, Lansing, July 15, 1998.

49. Telephone interviews by Hubert Morken, not for attribution, November 1998.

50. George Weeks, "Coalition Plans Drive for Vouchers," *Detroit News*, online edition, April 25, 1999; Patricia Montemurri, "Maida Wants to See Vouchers on Ballot," *Detroit News*, online edition, April 26, 1999; George Weeks, "Time to End Ban on Vouchers for the State's School," *Detroit News*, online edition, April 25, 1999; TEACH Michigan, "Michigan Coalition Announces "Kids First" Voucher Plan," Coalition Fax Alert, April 26, 1999.

51. Ibid.; Bryan Taylor, telephone interview, April 26, 1999.

52. Gary Glenn, telephone interview with Hubert Morken, April 26, 1999.

53. Philip Murren, Esq., interview by Hubert Morken, Harrisburg, PA, November 12, 1997; telephone interview by Hubert Morken, October 19, 1998.

54. Eugene Hickok, Secretary of Education, Commonwealth of Pennsylvania, interview by Hubert Morken, Harrisburg, PA, November 12, 1997; telephone interview by Hubert Morken, October 14, 1998.

55. Thomas Shaheen, telephone interview by Hubert Morken, December 14, 1998; Sean Duffy, telephone interview by Hubert Morken, December 15, 1998.

56. Duffy, telephone interview, September 29, 1998.

57. Shaheen, telephone interview, December 14, 1998.

58. Hubert Morken, "Religious Lobbying at the State Level: Case Studies in a Continuing Role for the New Religious Right," paper presented at the annual meeting of the American Political Science Association, San Francisco, California, 1990.

59. Don E. Eberly, Chairman, REACH Alliance, memorandum, "Pennsylvania's Educational Choice Battle," January 8, 1992.

60. Ibid., 2.

61. Ibid., 3–4.

62. Ibid., 4–6; Michael Geer and Thomas Shaheen, interview by Hubert Morken, Harrisburg, PA, November 13, 1997.

63. Hickok, interview, November 12, 1998; Educational Opportunity Grants: Section-by-Section, May 9, 1995; The K.I.D.S. II Plan Overview, Keystone Initiative for a Difference in Our Schools, November 1995.

64. Ibid.

65. Commonwealth of Pennsylvania, Legislative Journal, Session of 1995, 179th of the General Assembly, No. 53, Friday, June 16, 1995.

66. Hickok, interview, November 12, 1997.

67. Ibid.; telephone interview, October 14, 1998.

68. Mary DeGroot and Gary Huggins, interview by Hubert Morken, Washington, DC, December 12, 1997; Hickok, interviews, November 12, 1997 and October 14, 1998.

69. Hickok, telephone interview, October 14, 1998.

70. Ibid.

71. Sean Duffy, President, The Commonwealth Foundation, "School Choice Is

the Choice of 58 Percent of Pennsylvanians," Memorandum to members of the General Assembly, November 4, 1998.

72. Ibid.

73. Richard Lacayo, "What Makes a GOOD School: Special Report," *Time*, October 27, 1997, 72–74.

74. Ibid., 73.

75. Ibid., 72–74.

76. Representative Dwight Evans, telephone interview by Hubert Morken, September 30, 1998.

77. Eils Lotozo, "The Public Service Candidate," *Philadelphia Weekly*, April 15, 1998, 7 pages; Dwight Evans, professional resume.

78. Ibid.

79. Christopher Keough, "Recipe for Schools: Choice, Standards," *Tribune-Review*, Philadelphia, July 30, 1998 (clipping).

80. Evans, telephone interview, September 30, 1998; professional resume.

81. Ibid.

82. Ibid.; Dwight Evans, Democratic Chair, House Appropriations Committee, "A Message from the Chair," April 22, 1998.

83. William Bunch, "It's Labor vs. Evans—and an Unknown Could Benefit," *Philadelphia Daily News*, May 15, 1998, clipping.

84. Review and Outlook, "Breaking Ranks," *Wall Street Journal*, May 15, 1998, clipping.

85. David Boldt, "Taking Steps to the Mayor's Office, Evans Treads Carefully with Labor," *Philadelphia Inquirer*, May 8, 1998, (clipping).

86. Ibid.; Tom Infield, "Unions Taking on Evans in Radio Ads," *Philadelphia Inquirer*, May 6, 1998, (clipping); Review & Outlook, " Shaking up Schools," *Wall Street Journal*, May 4, 1998, clipping; Report, "Unions Blow $150,000," *Wall Street Journal*, May 21, 1998, clipping.

87. Legislative Commission on Restructuring Pennsylvania's Urban Schools, House of Representatives, Commonwealth of Pennsylvania, Final Report, vol. 1, Findings and Recommendations, December 1997.

88. Ibid.; Representative John Perzel, telephone interview by Hubert Morken, October 20, 1998.

89. Mensah M. Dean, "Teacher: 'Every Child Can Learn' with the Programs," *Philadelphia Inquirer Online*, City and Local, September 21, 1998; Dwight Evans, "Pennsylvania's schools must benefit all students, not just 'shining stars,'" *Tribune Review*, July 25, 1998 (clipping).

90. Ibid.

91. David Boldt, "New School Showcases Commitment by Parents," Commentary, *Philadelphia Inquirer*, August 21, 1998, (clipping); Arlene Edmonds, "Parents Thrilled at Differences in Charter School," *Philadelphia Tribune*, August 21, 1998; Dean, Teacher, September 21, 1998.

92. Dean, Teacher, September 21, 1998; Laura J. Bruch, "At a New Charter School in Philadelphia, the Test Begins," *Philadelphia Inquirer Online*, Front Page, September 18, 1998.

93. Mensah M. Dean, "Voucher Schools Visited," *Philadelphia Daily News*, May

15, 1998, 10; Arlene Edmonds, "Representative's Tour Searches for Solutions to the City's Problems," *Philadelphia Tribune*, August 14, 1998.

94. David Boldt, "To Improve Education, Mix the Fixes," *Philadelphia Inquirer*, September 25, 1998.

95. Dwight Evans, telephone interview, September 30, 1998; Dwight Evans, "First Class Education: A School Reform and Accountability Proposal for the School District of the City of Philadelphia," May 1998, 1–2.

96. Dwight Evans, telephone interview, September 30, 1998.

97. Dwight Evans, panel comments at the annual conference, Association of Educators in Private Practice (AEPP), Northwestern University, Evanston, IL, July 30, 1998, attended by Morken.

98. Dwight Evans, telephone interview, September 30, 1998.

99. Elmer Smith, "Evans and Williams Sounding Alarm," *Philadelphia Daily News*, March 25, 1998, 10.

100. Dwight Evans, telephone interview, September 30, 1998.

101. Walter Palmer, telephone interviews by Hubert Morken, September 28 and October 13, 1998.

102. Walter Palmer, Letter to The Honorable Harold James (copy), September 23, 1998; The General Assembly of Pennsylvania, House Bill No. 2, Session of 1997, Referred to Committee on Education, March 19, 1997.

103. The Philadelphia Coalition for Education Reform and School Choice, "Position Statement on Our Shared Commitment to School Choice," "History of The Philadelphia Coalition for Education Reform and School Choice," undated; The Philadelphia City-Wide African-American Grassroots Coalition, "Petition," on school choice, undated; Walter Palmer, Letter to The Honorable John M. Perzel (copy), October 9, 1998; Precision Marketing, Inc., copies of Commonwealth Foundation School Choice survey by legislative district, undated.

104. The Philadelphia Coalition for Educational Reform and School Choice, Position Statement on the Urban Education Commission Report, undated.

105. Anthony Cardinal Bevilacqua, Letter to Honorable Edward G. Rendell and Honorable David Hornbeck (copy), May 29, 1998.

106. Archdiocese of Philadelphia, Office of Public Affairs, *Voter Registration Drive '98*, pamphlet; voter registration videotape.

107. Anthony Cardinal Bevilacqua, "Justice in Action—Children Succeed with School Choice," *The Voice of Your Shepherd*, vol. 3, issue 11, May 1997; Archdiocese of Philadelphia, Office of Public Affairs, copies of four school choice flyers, undated; school choice videotape; a brochure, *The Facts about School Choice*.

108. Guy Ciarrocchi, "School Choice Information Request," Memorandum to Thomas DeRienzo, February 19, 1997.

109. Archdiocese of Philadelphia, Office for Communications, News Release, "Catholic Education in the Archdiocese of Philadelphia Saves the Taxpayers Nearly $1 Billion," January 23, 1998.

110. S.E. Delco Board of School Directors, "Resolution to Adopt a School Choice Enrollment Stabilization Plan," draft copy, March 1998; Cynthia J. McGroarty and Connie Langland, "Delco Board Approves 1st School-Voucher Plan in Pa.," *Philadelphia Inquirer*, March 19, 1998, A1, 21.

111. Archdiocese of Philadelphia, Office for Communications, News Release, "Cardinal Bevilacqua Applauds School Board Decision to Provide School Vouchers," March 18, 1998; Anthony Cardinal Bevilacqua, Letter to Rendell and Hornbeck (copy), May 29, 1998; Anthony Cardinal Bevilacqua, Letter to Honorable Dr. Charles A. Scott (copy), May 29, 1998.

112. Anthony Cardinal Bevilacqua, "The Voucher Debate," *Philadelphia Inquirer*, September 1998 (clipping).

113. Dennis Giorno, Catholic Conference, telephone interview by Hubert Morken, October 1, 1998; Tom McCormick, staff for Rep. John Perzel, telephone interview by Hubert Morken, October 1, 1998; Perzel, telephone interview, October 20, 1998.

114. Shaheen, telephone interview, December 14, 1998; Sean Duffy, telephone interview, December 15, 1998; Perzel, telephone interview, October 20, 1998.

115. Author not listed, "School Choice Pilot Program," 1998.

116. Ibid.

117. Shaheen, telephone interview, December 14, 1998; Sean Duffy, telephone interview, December 15, 1998.

118. Ibid.

Chapter 4

Entrepreneurial Strategies

Money talks. How can school choice be discussed without mentioning money as a powerful tool to bring about change—in fact, a lot of money and significant change? How can we discuss school choice politics without recognizing the risk takers, that is, the wealthy individuals who want to make it happen? These individuals are essentially policy entrepreneurs: people using money in a variety of ways to leverage school choice for a number of reasons. Their reasons cover the spectrum: some create innovative schools for profit; some found schools or grant private vouchers as a way to make policy changes; and some are philanthropic, empowering parents and helping children with scholarships. Others want to coordinate efforts for change, functioning as quasi-managers of the school choice movement, and some want to influence the political arena, marketing school choice or training activists. Certainly, the purposes and methods of entrepreneurs are varied and complex. In any case, if money talks, so do ideas, and the school choice politics of the 1990's is a powerful fusion of cash, theory, and action. Money follows success; it also precedes it, making it happen. Therefore, this chapter will review some of the most significant entrepreneurial school choice initiatives underway in the United States today.

Creating Innovative Schools for Profit: The Edison Project

One of the most unique organizations involved in the school choice movement is the Edison Project. Located in Manhattan, across the street from the New York Public Library on Fifth Avenue, the office is busy and efficient; and although it is sparse in furnishings, it is filled with innovative ideas. The concept for the Edison Project was conceived and implemented by Chris Whittle, chairman of Whittle Communications, one of America's largest publishers. In 1989 Whittle also founded Channel One, a television news provider for schools, and ultimately sold the company in 1994 for $240 million to K–III Communications Corporation, the owners of the *Weekly Reader*. After the sale, Whittle decided to pursue his dream, and announced publicly that he would reinvent schooling by creating a national network of for-profit schools across the United States.[1]

What makes Whittle different from other "reformers" is that he really is not a "reformer." As founder, president, and CEO of the Edison Project, he is an innovator, a risk-taker, and a venture capitalist all in one; an individual willing to put his reputation and fortune on the line to make meaningful, significant educational change—for *money!*

The kinds of people Whittle has recruited to work with him on his national, for-profit schools reflect his own intensity as well as a variety of other reasons for becoming involved in the company. Among them is Benno Schmidt, Chairman of the Board. Having served as the law clerk to Supreme Court Chief Justice Earl Warren, Dean of the Law School at Columbia University and President of Yale University, Schmidt has extensive legal, academic, administrative, and budgetary experience. Augmenting Whittle's philosophy, Schmidt believes that public education is the "most important enterprise for the future of America," and a "key to justice." These were the notions that led him to believe that he could make an "historic difference," and have a bigger impact on the poorest in society rather than the over privileged."[2] Whittle also brought on John Chubb, a noted Ph.D. in political science, who had taught government and public policy at Stanford University before moving to the Brookings Institution to do research on education. His 1990 work with Terry Moe entitled *Politics, Markets and America's Schools* became one of the most respected, benchmark studies on student achievement. He is committed to change the systems in public schools to provide greater freedom and to demand accountability through competition.[3] Other members of the Edison Project team include Deborah McGriff, former superintendent of the Detroit public schools; Cheryl Wilhoyte, former superintendent of the Madison, Wisconsin schools; Thomas Boudrot, former instructional technology specialist for the state of Texas, Apple Computers, Mindscape and other organizations; Michael Finnerty, former budget director for the state of New York and advisor to former Governor Mario Cuomo; Manuel Rivera, former superintendent of the Rochester, New York, public Schools; James Starr, former senior accountant with Deloitte and Touche; Christopher Cerf, former Associate Counsel to the President of the United States; and Laura Eshbaugh, long-time manager with Whittle Communications.

With his team in place, Whittle proceeded to invest $40 million for research and development before the Edison project began operations. As a result, a comprehensive school design was developed for K–12 education based on the notion that a successful school must be greater than the sum of its parts.[4] Thus, the design team systematically searched out and adopted all

kinds of successful programs that included a wide-ranging curriculum, and
the team supported them by a pervasive use of technology. For students,
Edison stresses basic skill development for those at high risk of academic
failure. It provides each student with a computer in his/her home. It requires
individual accountability while still providing tutors to ensure "success for
all."[5] For teachers, Edison provides laptops and extensive funds for faculty
development while allowing them to work with the same group of students
for a portion, rather than a year, of their education. For administrators, Edison provides a powerful incentive, namely, between $2.5 and $1.5 million
in discretionary funds to control, implement, and tailor the Edison design
for their particular community.[6] Finally, students, teachers, administrators,
and parents are linked together electronically by The Common, a national
on-line service encouraging total participation for the child by those involved
with the Edison project.

The dream of a national network of for-profit schools did, however, have
to be modified as the effort, time, and money involved in creating such an
organization became a reality. In fact, Whittle had originally called for a national system of 200 private or privately managed schools to be in place by
the year 2000, but he had to scale that goal back somewhat in 1994 when
Whittle Communications ran into financial problems. In January 1998, total
investments raised for the Edison Project since 1991 were reported to be
at the level of $161,000,000. Investors included the J. P. Morgan Capital
Corporation ($20,000 000), Investor AB ($20,000 000), Chris Whittle and
Affiliates ($20,000,000), Richmont Leeds ($10,000,000), and other investors ($3,000,000). Although the Edison Project now earns positive operating
margins at the local level, it is not yet defraying the cost of its central expenses. According to Benno Schmidt, the company would be making a
profit within the next year if Edison maintained a steady state of growth, but
instead will produce a profit in two years since it intends to pursue a higher
growth rate. Today, the Edison Project has implemented its school design in
fifty-one public schools, some of which are charter schools. Approximately
24,000 students attend what are now known as Edison "partnership
schools," and the Edison Project calls itself a "comprehensive education
management organization," or a "charter school management organization."

According to Benno Schmidt, the Edison Project is an organization designed to replace the "last of the cottage industries: education." And he emphatically denies that the Edison Project is simply a group of consultants.
Rather, he maintains that the organization works to provide research and
development, to encourage innovations, to integrate systems, and to provide
incentives to teachers and administrators that will, in turn, assure greater
efficiency and higher quality education.

So, how do public schools become part of the Edison Project? They can
apply to the Edison Project for its comprehensive management services and

contract with the Project for the cost of these services or the Edison Project can target a particular area or school in need of its management and attempt to contract with the appropriate authorities for its services. In either case, the scenario remains the same. First, Edison aims to work with schools that are small, focused, professional, collegial, supportive, and individualized. Second, Edison works with multicultural, diverse, and/or special students in schools with a financial need. Third, Edison provides a benefit of $3,000 per pupil, about half of it for technology. Fourth, Edison, outfits each school with free state-of-the-art telecommunications, provides a computer in the home of each student, and supplies a laptop for each teacher.

How are teachers, unions, and administrators being won over to an educational management system that is, in reality, a form of school choice? How are they being won over to what some might even call a system that is an incursion into their business—the business of curriculum design, methodology development, and management? Clearly, it has not been an easy conversion. Schmidt says that "some unions" are opposed to Edison but that most have been supportive and about "one-third have been actively cooperative." Edison thrives on competition and creativity, and sees every challenge as an opportunity. Thus, it has tried to allow union decision making at the local level. First, it assures unions that Edison has no plans to run an entire school system within a particular city. Instead, Edison points out that what it provides is a choice for students and teachers and must, therefore be a fairly modest operation. Second, Edison promises that if it comes to a school district, there will be no job losses. It will hire new teachers or individuals from outside the union only when the old jobs are gone. Third, Edison promises that it will not undercut the teacher's salary structure. In fact, it often asks teachers to work 20 percent more hours, with a 10 percent pay raise because the Edison school year has only a six-week rather than a ten-week summer vacation, and a longer school day. What Edison does offer, however, are incentives as the fourth part of their carrot-and-stick approach to get the teachers, unions, and administrators to buy into their project. They provide significant professional development, including funding for meetings and laptops. They provide contracts that allow teachers to return to their own schools if that is what they want to do. They allow teachers to keep their tenure in the system and so provide them with the same health benefits and state pensions. But, they offer something more—*stock options!*

In October 1998, Benno Schmidt announced that "in order to give teachers a broader sense of ownership in the enterprise, in which they are the key professionals," the Edison Project would make stock options available to its Miami teachers and other school employees at approximately $6.15 per share. The options would be in addition to the teachers' salaries and increases. The idea met with resounding approval from the educational community. Sandra Feldman, President of the American Federation of Teachers, called it "innovative," and praised the fact that it was done in partnership with the union."[7] Pat Turnillo, executive vice president of the United Teachers of Dade County, called it "the first time in the history of American education that teachers have become direct economic stakeholders in the public schools where they work."[8]

Thus, the Edison Project is an innovative attempt to use private investments to re-invent the American educational system. The Project does not see itself in competition with other entrepreneurial attempts to change schooling; in fact, Schmidtt maintains that there is a huge market with plenty of room for a variety of educational options to operate within the schooling market. As a result, the Project does not support vouchers over charter schools, or scholarships over anything else. It is simply a supporter of school choice and the for-profit avenue is the only one that it intends to travel. Edison, therefore, has no political agenda, and the notion that it could form a political action committee, support political candidates who stand for school choice, or in others ways become political to encourage such a movement is not part of its current planning or mission.

While Edison is unique, it should also be noted that there are other for-profit companies also entering the educational "business." The list of organizations proliferates daily, and it includes Advantage Schools, Boston, Mass.; Beacon Educational Management, Westborough, Mass.; Charter Schools USA, Fort Lauderdale, Fla.; National Heritage Academies, Grand Rapids, Mich.; Nobel Learning Communities, Media, Pa.; and Sabis Educational Systems, Eden Prairie, Minn. One of the newer companies, Advantage Schools, is currently creating a stir in for-profit circles by attempting to break into the education market in Massachusetts, New Jersey, Arizona, and North Carolina simultaneously. It has also been hinted that IBM is interested in such a venture.

Creating Schools to Leverage Change: The School Futures Foundation

Non-profit organizations may tend to be more political than profit-oriented companies. Therefore, when Eugene "Gene" Ruffin, president and CEO of the School Futures Research Foundation (SFRF) and retired vice president of Xerox Corporation, faced the huge crowd of 38,000 with trepidation it was another step toward future political involvement on behalf of school choice. He was about to speak to the 1998 Convention of the Church of God in Christ in Memphis, Tennessee. Many in the room were public school teachers. He feared a negative reception from this largely African-American audience. Ruffin is a polished speaker and is black, but he had no experience with church denominational meetings and anticipated a cool reception at best. Then beginning to speak, first of his love for children and his respect for educators, claiming common ground, Ruffin in ten minutes related a vision embracing charter schools and school choice. The response was overwhelming, even electric.[9]

Black denominational leaders are beginning to support choice, and Ruffin notes in particular, C. Edward Jones, of the National Baptist Association, with four million members, and the Church of God in Christ. He thinks that historically this compares to the civil rights movement, which initially had active proponents but was not popular even in churches and was ignored nationally for decades. The school choice issue, too, in his view, has to be taken to the streets. Ruffin expects SFRF to play a supportive role in this process.[10]

SFRF, a California, non-profit, private, (501c-3) corporation, is the brainchild of John T. Walton, businessman and entrepreneur in San Diego, well known for his private voucher program. Shortly after the defeat of voucher initiative Proposition 174 in 1993, Walton created the SFRF. A year later, he approached Ruffin to head up the new organization committed to improve the effective delivery of education to students from preschool through high school, do research and report the results to the public, and develop solutions that could be replicated elsewhere

At first Ruffin resisted joining this effort. He wondered whether Walton could be serious. He made a counter offer suggesting more of a jobs program. Walton refused. The goal that Walton envisioned, a "sustainable free-market solution" to give parents school choice, seemed difficult to achieve, but ultimately Ruffin agreed to join with him. Ruffin is a Democrat, Walton an independent, and they both have a determination to see education reform, starting in California, through to a successful conclusion. This, they believe, is a historic opportunity for entrepreneurs like themselves to serve the public interest.[11]

They affirmed:

Every day more Americans realize that public education is in a state of "Crisis." Over the last 20 plus years, we have seen declining student performance in our urban and rural communities regardless of spending levels and patterns. We have seen heralded "reform strategies and tactics" within the public education system fail miserably and political and union barriers to change escalate.

Although the failure of our public education system is felt in all areas, nowhere is it felt more than in those areas where the education achievement and economic conditions of parents are lowest. Most of these children are trapped in schools with a history of low performance and have little or no hope of receiving the educational foundation they need to function productively in the 21st century. The results of a poor education are manifested in lost generations, a dysfunctional and destructive society and a lost opportunity to maintain leadership in a global economy.[12]

The American Education Reform Foundation (AERF) was then formed by Walton, with Ruffin at the helm, to explore the possibility of a new school choice initiative. In the end they concluded that even if backers spent a large sum buying TV time, matching or exceeding expenditures on the other side, they might not win. This was largely a consequence of the 1992 Proposition 174 campaign, Ruffin reports. "Vouchers at the start of the campaign were perceived as a positive, particularly in the communities that were underserved by the public school system, but by the end of the campaign, they had been demonized. The opposition, led by the California Teachers Association, had outspent supporters 10 to 1." Some in the state school choice coalition wanted to take the risk, to set the agenda for school choice as the civil rights issue of the time. Some opposed the wording of the new initiative. In the end AERF decided an information campaign needed to precede any new initiative and that there was not sufficient time. Ruffin was disappointed with this decision but was reconciled to it, fully expecting another school choice initiative in a few years.[13]

Early on, SFRF worked to try to get at the crux of California's educational malaise. It commissioned research to be done on education costs in order to find out if more money needed to be spent in the state to improve education. One study concluded that money was not the missing ingredient for educational success; systematic reform was what could make the difference. This confirmed for the SFRF the need to provide alternatives at an affordable cost. At the same time, Ruffin also discovered that a healthy, positive coalition for education reform was needed. Instead of pandering to negative politicians and educators, Ruffin insisted that SFRF facilitate reforms that most of the public would welcome.[14]

He also strongly opposes state regulations that politicize education in California and elsewhere. Eight years ago, when the state superintendent of education required that reading be taught using a whole language pedagogy, state reading scores plummeted to the lowest in the nation. As a result, there is now a return to phonics—but the books being used are for the whole language reading system. Setting standards is an acceptable role for state authorities, Ruffin believes, but telling teachers how to teach makes no sense. Ruffin wants to take politics out of the classroom. He says one advantage of charter schools is that pedagogical decisions are left up to the local school.[15]

To summarize, in public policy discussions SFRF supports mandatory state standards that produce accountability, freedom from top-down regulations, and a free market through school choice.

Ruffin critically evaluated different voucher alternatives being considered in the state in 1998. There were divisions in California on vouchers. Milton

Friedman, for example, wanted universal vouchers available to all students, but with the amount of money for each public scholarship low enough so parents must contribute too. John E. Coons and Stephen D. Sugarman thought that the disadvantaged should be given vouchers first because it was politically expedient, and advised a voucher of 80–90 percent of the public school per student daily expenditure, a much larger voucher than Friedman would recommend. Ruffin was not satisfied with either proposal. Instead, he now supports, as a standard, a voucher payment that is equal to the full amount paid per student per day by public schools. Ruffin also advocates full vouchers targeting the poor as a first step followed later by choice for all.[16]

The School Futures strategy entails first to develop, and second to communicate, information supporting legislative and systemic reform initiatives for the year 2000. This includes vouchers, tax credits, and strong charter legislation in California and in the rest of the nation. "Charters and vouchers are not ends in themselves." The goal is justice—a "preferential option for the poor"—in the language of the Catholic bishops meeting at Puebla and reported by Brian Bennett, who works closely with Ruffin at SFRF. Bennett, who calls himself a liberal Democrat, has twenty-six years of experience in California Catholic education as a teacher/administrator. He is SFRF's main public debater for choice and an experienced strategist. He concludes that choice cannot be won without the backing of church leadership, minorities, and the poor, those who are most directly impacted by what he calls "the dismal performance of public education."

Bennett expects substantial assistance in the next effort from black Baptist ministers, AME churches, the Church of God in Christ, Catholic activists, local community organizations, and mayors who have city property and unused buildings ready to be used as schools. He concludes that choice cannot be won without parochial and secular votes, and the backing of nonwhites. Central city support in his judgment is crucial. Bennett would like to win Urban League endorsement and the support of the NAACP. In his assessment of school choice politics in the state, Ruffin comments that old guard black civil rights leaders are less prominent, retiring from the scene. He is hopeful Hispanic legislative leaders might move toward choice. Hispanics traditionally have supported Catholic education and are increasing in numbers and influence.[17]

Speaking realistically, Ruffin expects little help from corporate leaders. He said that in the recent Proposition 226 effort to limit political contributions from labor, the "paycheck protection" initiative, corporations gave little help because they were afraid of unions. In California, Ruffin observed, corporations move with the public mood, doing less to shape it. He thinks that change will come neither from within the education system nor from the top through the corporate or political elites, but from the people and from choice supporters like SFRF who are motivated more by truth and what is needed than by any vested interest.[18]

A school choice initiative, either vouchers or tax credits, is winnable in California according to SFRF. Proposition 174 lost in 1993, according to Bennett, because people feared that cult schools would take advantage of it; that there would be an adverse economic impact on public schools; and that more money was needed to defeat its opponents. Bennett thinks all these objections can be overcome. He is confident that by spending 10 percent more than the opposition a school choice pilot program will win next time.[19]

Charters, Ruffin says, demonstrate that choice works, and they will prepare the way for other free-market solutions. He strongly supported the 1998 AB544 California charter reform law. Private vouchers are good test cases, providing information on how private schools can improve student performance at a fraction of the cost of public schools; and they show how parents with low incomes, when given a choice, make intelligent decisions for their children. Both charters and private vouchers are means to parental empowerment. Looking back on the defeats of public vouchers (1993) and the paycheck protection initiative (1998), Ruffin is convinced that both of these initiatives, which John Walton invested in, helped to open the door to charter schools. He says the threat of vouchers made charter schools a reality in the state of California in 1992. Six years later, the Ab544 charter legislation, with the support of the California Teachers Association, was passed in less than thirty days, partly in his estimation because of initiative pressure. The labor law initiative was the stick that made the new charter school bill look like a carrot.

Charters, however, should not include collective bargaining, according to Bennett, but should have accountability. Charter school control of labor, management, and budget are, in his opinion, necessary for a charter to be different from other public schools. He also strongly favors private accreditation by the Western Association of Schools and Colleges for charter schools.

In the final analysis, Bennett argues, student achievement and cost efficiency are both necessary if charters are to succeed. He is convinced that measurable change in student performance can be demonstrated in one year and for less expenditure than traditional public schools. This will be crucial to building public support. When asked what impact charter schools would have on parochial schools Bennett responded, "Catholic diocesan support for community schools is consistent with the church's position that parents are the primary educators of their children." Furthermore, churches have a large advantage with existing facilities in place, "buildings are expensive," so it is easier to work with churches, plus churches have a ready market of students and teachers. Bennett sees charters as a return to local control of public education, much like the little red schoolhouse of yesteryear, and not destructive to Catholic education. He also wants to see religious communities participate in charter schools. Personally, he says he is committed to good schools of whatever kind.[20]

By the fall of 1998 SFRF had five charter schools in the state and it plans to start four more by January. It intends to have thirty or more schools in three years and to more than double that figure in five years. The SFRF master plan contains a mix of urban and rural schools.

In the first year of operation, 1997–98, SFRF launched three charter schools, in San Diego, Watts, and Palo Alto. Parent satisfaction is generally high and student achievement is encouraging. Some schools have demonstrated dramatic improvement, with two years of measurable progress in reading for first graders accomplished in seven months. SFRF wants to prove that children in poor communities can learn if properly taught.[21]

> SFRF is providing a competitive, performance oriented choice for customers trapped in historically low performing schools by developing and operating charter schools primarily in California. . . . We will develop community schools that are learning centers designed for children and adults in the toughest communities in our country. Within the community we will find visionary leadership and other stakeholders and provide the necessary tools to ensure success. Our facilities will depend on the relationships within the community.[22]

SFRF opened one San Diego charter school in 1997, the Nubia Leadership Academy, and the Chula Visa Learning Community Charter School in 1998. The Sojourner Truth Academy also opened in 1998, replacing Saint Stephens Academy, a church school of 119 students that was about to close for lack of funds. About 150 of the students in the new charter school are Church of God in Christ students, almost half the new student body.

Marvin Threatt, Director of Sojourner Truth, and an administrator for six years in Catholic parochial schools, reports that his Catholic parish is considering supporting a charter school in 1999. This can be done, according to SFRF, by including religion in the core knowledge portion of the curriculum. Under the law, religious schools can also convert to charter schools and this is being done as well.[23]

Dwight Sykes is the principal of the Nubia Leadership Academy. A former math teacher, he was part of the Bay View Baptist Church committee negotiating with School Futures to put a school in the church building in 1997. He was then asked by SFRF to be principal. Sykes is active in youth ministry in the congregation and sees teaching as a good way to get closer to the kids. By working with the church, the school benefits from well-designed, air-conditioned, and carpeted facilities. The church for its part must take down the cross in classrooms and put it back up for church functions. The school operates from 7 a.m. to 7 p.m. and the church takes over from 7 p.m. to 10 p.m. and on weekends.[24]

Nubia Learning Academy is a college preparatory program based on phonics, critical thinking, writing, and reading the classics. It is fully attended, with 300 students and a waiting list of over 125. This partnership, in Sykes view, is beneficial to the school and the church and he would rather have children attend a charter school with influence from church leaders than go to non-charter public schools. A private Christian school seemingly is too costly for his local congregation to build and maintain without external assistance. One advantage of charters over church-based private schools is that teacher salaries in charter schools start at the same level as public schools. In fact, one-third of the teachers at Nubia Academy are teachers from public schools, and only three teachers are from private schools. There are other competitive issues. Starting in 1999 teacher qualifications in charters will be the same as those at public schools. Looking ahead, Sykes said this requirement would make it difficult to keep his teachers because teachers at Nubia work harder and longer hours than do those in public schools. Sykes foresees charter teachers leaving to go to public schools. Early on in the history of charter schools Sykes observed negative impacts on private schools—one nearby closed grades 3–5 as students left to attend charter schools—and he anticipates challenges from public schools. As parents and teachers have more options and exercise them, whichever schools are cheaper to attend or pay higher teacher salaries will have the advantage in market-like competition.[25]

In its third San Diego school, SFRF is partnering with the Chula Vista District, a district led by systemic reform advocate Dr. Libya Gill, who is the superintendent. Working together, they have set up the Chula Vista Learning Academy. The school meets in temporary buildings paid for by the SFRF on land provided by the district. When the Chula Vista Learning Community Charter School soon builds its new $6 million campus these temporary buildings will be turned over to the Rice Elementary School. The Charter Board is made up of five members, including two community leaders, a business leader, an educator, and the CEO of School Futures. The school is largely Hispanic, offers dual language immersion for all students, and has a multicultural curriculum.[26]

Jorge Ramirez, the director of the Chula Vista Learning Academy selected by SFRF, was an elementary public school teacher who helped to create the partnership and the distinctive program of the new school. SFRF strongly prefers starting schools from scratch because existing public schools have teachers used to the old ways. However, this is being done in close collaboration with churches and public schools, with SFRF choosing new staff. To insure academic quality not only will the school conduct pre- and post-testing but it will also keep files with portfolio's and other performance assessments for each child. What sets this school apart is the requirement that all students be able to speak, read, and write in English and Spanish. Other languages will also be taught.[27]

These examples demonstrate that SFRF is flexible in meeting the needs of each local community. Nubia stresses core knowledge in preparation for college; and Chula Vista talks of multicultural competence and sensitivity. Ruffin reports that SFRF's core strategy promotes schools that are distinctive: "The East Palo Alto Charter School led by principal Donald Evans stresses core knowledge and leadership. Dr. Charles Knight, long time advocate for children, helped to envision and to create the east Palo Alto school. On the other hand, Watts stresses early childhood development and multicultural themes." Yet with these differences in school vision and program, all say they work to cultivate morals: "Character and Ethics Standards promote responsibility for one's actions and deeds, self-esteem, sociability, collaboration, integrity and honesty," and each school has as its number one priority the demonstration of superior and distinctive academic results that justify their presence as education alternatives.[28]

SFRF is unique in an entrepreneurial way for two reasons. First, it wants to use charter schools as a laboratory to produce evidence to support more choice and, second, it intends to replicate its school model as widely as possible. Walton, Ruffin, and Bennett are confident that charter schools will work well, helping to justify other alternatives. SFRF plans to move quickly to get vouchers or tax credits by 2000. If this is not done or fails with the electorate, private religious schools will face intense competition from charter schools for students and teachers. However, apparently this is not a major concern to SFRF partly because religious schools have survived thus far without outside help. At the same time, SFRF must decide what it will do if vouchers or tax credits do not become a reality soon. Will it settle for charter schools and build as many as possible? Or might it consider the for-profit option? In the meantime, it will continue to advocate policy change and use its schools to make its point.

Granting Scholarships to Leverage Change: Educational CHOICE

Another entrepreneur working to bring about policy change is J. Patrick "Pat" Rooney, founder and chairman emeritus of the Golden Rule Insurance Company in Indianapolis. He made a singular contribution to school choice in 1991 when he started a pre-college voucher program known as "Educational CHOICE." Rooney was the first businessman to create private tuition vouchers for the poor; a unique way to enable low-income students to attend schools of their choice, including parochial schools. He bankrolled his initial efforts with the slogan—"Let the children go." Soon, major area business leaders and foundations, including Eli Lilly, joined in the project with Rooney pledging money to provide the private voucher grants of up to $800 per student. A devout Catholic, fully and proudly Irish, this Indianap-

olis based entrepreneur attends an all black church. Now 70 years old and
retired from responsibilities at Golden Rule, Rooney continues active in
school choice activities, pioneering in new directions, especially in the African-American and Hispanic communities.[29]

From the start Rooney believed that his efforts represented educational
hope for those in the inner city and that the money from Educational
CHOICE would provide a way for poor families to break their dependence
on the public educational system. Based on the premise that, given a
voucher, many low-income families would choose to send their children to
a private or parochial school, Rooney intended to help poor students receive
a better education than they would receive in a public school. Thus, he created an organization described by his Executive Director, Timothy Ehrgott,
as one "free of government interference, devoid of bureaucracy, and virtually
bereft of rules."[30]

The literature from Educational CHOICE advertises its program as an
"Opportunity to Change Your Child's Future!" Urging parents who qualify
for the reduced-price lunch program to enter the "MILLION DOLLAR
SCHOLARSHIP LOTTERY," it advertises the possibility of winning a
scholarship to the Marion County *church or private school* of your choice!"[31]
Winners are told: "You do *not* have to be present to win." In fact, Ehrgott
proudly claims: "CHOICE makes no judgments on curriculum or academ-
ics. If a child is good enough for the school and the school for the family,
CHOICE cuts a check to the school each month on behalf of the student.
End of our involvement."[32]

By the school year 1998–99, more than 3,800 low-income students "en-
joyed expanded educational opportunities as a result of CHOICE scholarships" with more than 4,200 on its waiting list. And a study performed by
the Hudson Institute found that "students generally achieved better grades
in their new school and recorded higher ISTEP scores in reading, method,
and language." Rooney's ideas have given impetus to an ever-growing number of educational, charitable trusts across the country. By 1998–99, there
were approximately forty other "CHOICE-like programs operating with
more than 13,000 students enrolled and another 40,000 on waiting lists."[33]

Surprised as he is at the recent and rapid expansion of privately funded
education vouchers throughout the nation, Rooney notes there is a limit to
private funds and support. He asks, "What about all those left behind?" He
views private vouchers as a primer for public vouchers. Strategically he thinks
it is important to discern if private funding has peaked or if it will continue
in strength. He hopes private vouchers will grow because they provide the
model for choice where public funds are not yet available—demonstrating
demand for school choice when three or more parents apply for each available scholarship. In his program, in 1998 over 5,500 children applied for
650 positions, nine times the number of grants supplied. Parents living in

poor neighborhoods want choice, he observes. To help to meet this demand Pat Rooney now wants to help create schools.[34]

Rooney expects to receive personal attacks in response to his efforts. There is too much money at stake, he says. When local papers reported that he was involved with Proposition 226, the paycheck protection initiative in California, two big brickbats came through the front window of his home. Rooney hopes future attacks will be verbal only, for by nature he is a peacemaker. When he started private vouchers, he recalls, the Indiana teachers union and the NAACP denounced it. To deflect criticism in Indianapolis, his consistent message is not an anti-public school one, but a positive message that gives people choices—power to the parents to make a decision for the well-being of their children.[35]

Looking back on the last seven years of efforts to provide vouchers (both private and public) Rooney emphatically states that if he could do it all over, in addition, "I would help minority people . . . start and run schools." He laments that generally private vouchers have been fostered by white efforts, with only a few exceptions. Now he understands that programs must start and flourish where African Americans and Latinos have their own movement and have their own schools. Rooney knows that this ownership will create more demand for choice in the community and will change the political situation. If the private school in a poor neighborhood is a success, yet had money problems, the pastor or principal would be inclined to lobby for public vouchers or tax credits.[36]

Rooney agrees with a prominent black leader who told him, "Opposition to choice is all about politics and money, and the elected officials know it." Rooney added, "It's not about children but about money coming from the teachers' union." The number of public and private voucher applications, Rooney believes, proves that parents want choice. Parents who choose vouchers also get a partnership with the school and this is attractive to the parents and beneficial to the children. But, Rooney observed, there are too few private schools owned and operated by blacks and Hispanics. "Black pastors—some are involved but most are scared of the daunting task of running a school." He called this a prodigious undertaking, one to be undertaken with considerable caution, and said he would run from it if he were a pastor.

In 1997 Rooney began to put together a system to encourage and assist black pastors, Methodist, Baptist, and Pentecostal, to start their own schools. Strategically, he felt this would break the school choice issue open—so it would not be a Catholic issue any longer. Yet in spite of this obvious political benefit, he was disappointed to find that affluent whites willing to assist with vouchers or political campaigns are not interested in helping churches start schools. National school choice organizations are also reluctant although he hopes this will change.[37]

Meanwhile, Rooney maintains his commitment to vouchers, the movement he started. Other states, such as Wisconsin and Illinois, also have private voucher programs. The newest development in school choice are national programs that increase funding dramatically and link state programs.

Creating School Choice by Philanthropy: The Children's Scholarship Fund

Another innovative way to leverage school change is to award private scholarships on a national level to a large student population in financial need, rather than simply extending vouchers on a local level. The brainchild of a young, committed, Catholic convert, the Washington Scholarship Fund was started by Douglas Dewey who figuratively "passed around the hat" for its initial funding. Having worked for Secretary of Education Lamar Alexander on a GI Bill of Rights for Parents, Dewey formulated the notion that a private scholarship initiative might be possible if it could bring together a national coalition of business leaders. So in 1993, after leaving the Bush administration, he solicited donations and secured an initial grant of $25,000 from the Bradley Foundation. Soon, he was directing a fledging scholarship organization, and applied to both Ted Forstmann and John Walton for larger grants to bring the program to a higher level. Eventually, when it appeared as though both men were interested, Dewey brought the two mega-entrepreneurs together, forming what is now known as the Children's Scholarship Fund.[38]

Ted Forstmann, the businessman who is co-founder and senior partner of the publishing firm of Forstmann Little, is the chairman and CEO of the Children's Scholarship Fund. In the financial world, he is also chairman of Gulfstream Aerospace, Ziff Davis Publishing, Community Health Systems, Dr. Pepper, and Topps. He serves on the National Commission for Economic Growth and Tax Reform, is a board member of the Cato Institute, and is chairman of Empower America.

Both Forstmann and Walton are interested in, and committed to, helping the poor, with better education for their children. In August 1997, they offered $6 million over three years to Dewey's Washington Scholarship Fund. In October 1997, they sponsored another 1,000 additional scholarships until they finally underwrote a $100 million dollar foundation in June 1998. Renamed the Children's Scholarship Fund (CSF), Dewey's organization now found itself reorganized and financially supported by Forstmann and Walton, both of whom committed themselves to advance school choice through a system of charitable giving.

CSF operates out of New York City in a brownstone at the intersection of 57th Street and 5th Avenue in the heart of midtown Manhattan. In order to project a financial connection instead of a political image, the CSF moved to its prestigious address to be close to Ted Forstmann, who plays an active role in directing the organization's operations and recruiting major financial players. Dewey has become the Executive Vice President. James Courtovich, a leading public relations strategist, is the CSF's president and chief operating officer. Michael Ovitz, the chairman of the world's leading talent agency, Creative Artists Agency, has been named the chairman of the Los Angeles branch of the Children's Scholarship Fund.

Indeed, Forstmann has already begun to bring on other heavy financial hitters to the CSF team. Among them are Bob Mariano of Chicago, owner of Dominick's Fine Food; Steve Barney a top investor; Eli Broad, CEO of Sun America; Joe Robert of Washington, D.C., and Bret Schundler, financier and current mayor of Jersey City. The board of directors includes outstanding individuals from every segment of society: civil rights leaders like Martin Luther King III and the Reverend Floyd Flake; former and current political officials such as Henry Cisneros, Joseph Califano, Sam Nunn, Andrew Young, John Breaux, Trent Lott, Charles Rangel, and Daniel Patrick Moynihan; sports figures such as Pat Riley and Roger Staubach; business leaders such as Dick DeVos, president of Amway; James Kirnsey, founding CEO of America Online; Peter Lynch of Fidelity; entrepreneurs such as Julian Robertson and Stedman Graham; and other well-known individuals, such as Barbara Bush and Colin Powell.

The mission of the Children's Scholarship Fund is to help children by creating a new philanthropic tradition. Based on the notion of providing greater educational opportunities for low-income families, the CSF wants to expand the idea of college giving to the next level of students, those in the K–12 category. Dewey's rationale is that a capable, but needy, student can almost always find some funding to attend college, so why not those in the lower grades as well? In the longer term, the Children's Scholarship Fund seeks to create competition as a natural part of the way people think about education and to stimulate a demand for school choice.

A libertarian, Dewey believes that the movement for school choice is a misdiagnosis of the problem of education in the United States. He believes that the real problem in American education is one of malaise, not a paucity of choices. He believes that parents must become actively involved. He also argues that families must get away from the a priori assumption that education is a government prerogative. He maintains that education is an absolute parental right, one that becomes a derivative right of the state only if parents so choose. Therefore, the Children's Scholarship Fund is based on the philosophy that demands that individual families assert themselves and take responsibility for providing for their children. This keeps the financing of the Children's Scholarship Fund from simply becoming a dole. The organization wants to return primary responsibility to parents and restore their authority for their children's education. Dewey maintains that society has car choice, house choice, and all other kinds of choice. Why not school choice, too?

The Children's Scholarship Fund requires that each family must pay part, usually about half, of the cost of their children's education if it chooses to send its children to a private or parochial school. To be eligible students must be from families whose current yearly income averages $18,000. In case there are more applicants than available scholarships, students are selected by lottery. Students may receive scholarships worth approximately $1,000 for at least four years.

The Children's Scholarship Fund originally offered scholarships to financially eligible students in New York and Washington, but recently expanded its efforts to Chicago, Los Angeles, and other major cities. Letters were also sent to the mayors of hundreds of other cities in the United States introducing the Fund and requesting political support for their scholarship activities. Reaching out to local communities, the CSF seeks to find matching partners and donors from business, industry, and the local sector who will help create local programs across the country.

In stark contrast to its financial matching strategy, however, the CSF works alone; it does not seek to form a financial or political coalition with any other organization. Most important, it does not want to get involved in the political process to advance school choice. CSF does not intend to support legislation or a particular kind of choice. Although it describes itself as non-political and non-profit, the CSF does perceive itself as a "de facto player" in the school choice movement because of it financial clout and its media exposure. Individuals such as Sammy Sosa, Maya Angelou, Oprah Winfrey, Senator Daniel Patrick Moynihan, and General Colin Powell have all helped in Forstmann's efforts to promote the scholarship foundation.

In April 1999, their work was rewarded. The CSF held a simultaneous, computerized lottery in New York and Los Angeles to choose the 40,000 recipients of its scholarships. To the surprise of everyone, including Ted Forstmann, more than one million applications were received! The largest number came from those attending the public schools in New York City, but the largest number of scholarships will go to needy students in Los Angeles. By the final terms of the lottery, each impoverished family must agree to pay $1,000 per year for four years in order for their child to be eligible for a scholarship of between $600 to $1,600 from the CSF for the same period of time.

Forstmann and his supporters have funded a hornet's nest because it has brought both praise and criticism from every segment of society. Some see the numbers of applicants as a reflection of the "deep dissatisfaction among parents with the education their children are getting" while others see it as a "powerful tool"[39] to push state legislatures to fund vouchers for use in private and religious schools. As the *New York Times* noted: "Using an idea that would warm the heart of a free-market economist—leveraging scholarships to help thousands of children seek a better education—Mr. Forstmann has tapped into the deepest fears and hopes of parents about the future of their children."[40]

Coordinating for School Choice: CEO America

Many state private voucher attempts to bring about school choice are tied together through the Children's Educational Opportunity Foundation. An outgrowth of Patrick Rooney's Educational CHOICE Charitable Trust, CEO America evolved from the Texas Public Policy Foundation, an organization founded in 1992 and funded by business leaders and the *San Antonio Express-News*. With the help of a large grant from a Texas businessman, "the groundwork was laid for an organization that would build a network of nonprofit foundations," particularly in Austin, Houston, and Dallas. Two years later, in 1994, the Texas Public Policy Foundation received another major grant. The $2 million award signaled its board that its program could be a vehicle for revolutionary educational change, and that the time was right to create a national entity to lead the private voucher movement.[41]

The umbrella organization was founded as CEO America in 1994, a nonprofit 501 c-3 corporation. The mission of CEO America is to promote parental choice in education through private tuition grants and tax-funded options. With the goal of giving all families the power to choose the K–12 school that will best fulfill the needs of their children, CEO America serves four functions. It provides a national clearinghouse for privately funded voucher program information. It offers and provides support services for each existing program. It provides matching grant monies to help develop theses programs, specifically through the Children's Scholarship Fund. And, it coordinates the development of new programs all across America. In short, it is an umbrella organization that provides support, networking, resources, and training to advance school choice in the United States.

CEO America is managed and directed by Fritz Steiger. Steiger, who was invited by George Bush to work on his presidential campaign in 1979, was also chosen by Sam Walton to head the corporate giving arm of Wal-Mart in 1981, and appointed Executive Director of the Texas Public Policy Foundation in 1992. The chairman of CEO America is James Mansour, a lawyer with a J.D. degree from the Tulane University School of Law, an accountant with a CPA, and the President/CEO of National Telecommunications, a long-distance company.

The current strategy of CEO America is to establish a minimum of ten new affiliates a year and to target the organization's efforts in those states where public policy reform is most likely to occur. These states include but are not limited to: California, Arizona, Texas, Wisconsin, Illinois, Indiana, Ohio, Pennsylvania, New Jersey, and Connecticut. Most recently, the staff of Texas Governor George W. Bush contacted the offices of CEO San Antonio in order for the governor to attend a school choice rally at St. John Berchmans School. Bush spoke to the parents and urged them to continue to fight for school choice even through there are many hardships involved.[42]

The CEO private voucher model basically has eight characteristics. First, it is designed "to provide a model for the legislative/public policy debate." Donors want state legislators, the media, public opinion leaders, and the general public to be able to see how a voucher system works. Second, the program uses the federal government's free or reduced lunch program guidelines. Third, students may use a voucher certificate at any school of their choice. If the student is not accepted at that school, the voucher may be used elsewhere. Fourth, vouchers may be used within city or county limits, although some states allow a regional or statewide choice. Fifth, vouchers are being distributed in a lottery, or random system. Sixth, students in grades 1–8 are the targeted student cohort, although some programs are now including those in junior high and high school. Seventh, the amount of money given in the vouchers varies from 50 percent of the cost of the program with 50 percent paid by the parent, to an 80–20 percent split, with other percentages available as well. Eighth, voucher funds are used mainly in private schools while a few programs allow their use in public schools.[43]

What makes CEO America unique is that it is the only existing private organization whose purpose it is to tie together more than forty affiliate programs across the nation. It does this through challenge grants, training, and networking. Presently, CEO America's policy is to offer matching funds to organizations that want to esablish private voucher programs. These grants include $50,000 for scholarships and $10,000 for administration costs. Using part-time employees to cut operating costs, the organization tries to use 100 percent of the money it raises from the business community for scholarships. Training is also a large part of CEO's agenda. Now conferences are hosted jointly, the most recent held in conjunction with the National Center for Policy Analysis. The purpose of such training meetings is to increase national attention and support for private vouchers, as well as to help raise a broader base of financial support for the *Campaign to Educate America* about school choice. Finally, the networking function enables the affiliates involved to share problems and solutions and to provide support to each organization as needed.[44]

Educating for School School: The Milton and Rose D. Friedman Foundation

The 1998 NEA study, *The Real Story Behind "Paycheck Protection,"* linked the "far right" to school choice but omitted the Milton and Rose D. Friedman Foundation. The Foundation and the Catholic Church were the only two major organizations that escaped identification with political conservatives. The story of the founding of the Foundation corroborates its lack of a political agenda and its unique use of monies to attempt to educate the public and the media about school choice.

Milton Friedman has never liked political labels like "conservative" and sees himself as a defender of basic principles that work in economics and other fields as well. As he puts it, he is "Promoting public understanding of the need for major reform in K–12 education and of the role that competition through educational choice can play in achieving that reform." Gordon St. Angelo, the President and CEO of the Foundation, sees school choice as simply an effort by the Friedman's to carry out a part of their intellectual legacy.

In 1955, the Friedman's were distinct: they advocated market-based school choice and started to help others discover the merits of competition in primary and secondary education. The innovative agenda of the Foundation was, and remains, educational and cooperative.[45]

St. Angelo was chairman of the Democratic Party in Indiana from 1964–74. In 1972 he made up his mind to leave politics, having refused to support George Wallace on the first ballot even though his district supported the Alabaman. Deeply alienated by new egalitarian directions in the Democratic Party, as well as by polarization taking place in the country, St. Angelo went to the Lilly Foundation, where he served as public policy officer for twenty-two years. He found himself to be more conservative than the Republicans on the staff and now considers himself a strict Jeffersonian.[46]

St. Angelo met Milton Friedman early in his career at the Lilly Foundation, and the two developed a lasting relationship, both personal and professional. Showcasing Friedman in the late 1970s, Lilly helped to fund a ten segment TV series titled *Free to Choose,* with one segment on school choice. With these early contacts and a history of professional teamwork, Friedman turned to St. Angelo in 1996 and asked him to head up the Foundation.

In initial discussions about the Foundation, the Friedman's considered a variety of options in defining the purpose of the Foundation. Even famine relief was on its list of potential concerns. St. Angelo was not involved in school choice and had done almost nothing on that issue earlier, but he was looking for a "Friedman type" cause, related to long-term structural change. After thinking over the possibilities, the Friedman's selected school choice as the mission for the Foundation. Since Indianapolis was a hotbed of interest on the subject, St. Angelo, a local, based the foundation there. The Friedman's reside in San Francisco and delegate most of the operational responsibilities to St. Angelo.[47]

St. Angelo considers vouchers to be a tool to bring power to the people, helping the poor first. School choice, he reports, is practiced in Chile, much of Europe, and will soon be in Brazil. He asks, "Why not the United States?"

Milton Friedman gives St. Angelo the responsibility to make grants to other organizations with the basic objective of educating the American public on the value of educational opportunity for all children—this is made possible, he says, only by promoting competition in education. Promoters of school choice receiving grants include the Blum Center, in Milwaukee, which maintains a school choice information base and publishes the *Friedman-Blum Educational Freedom Report,* and the Institute for Justice, in Washington, D.C., which handles most of the school choice court cases.[48]

The Foundation is a strong believer in the Walton/Forstmann scholarship initiatives, but at first St. Angelo was not wholly in favor of private vouchers. Once he saw that they gave the whole choice issue momentum and provided evidence on the impact of choice on parents and kids, he changed his mind. Private vouchers, he thinks, clearly energize the policy issue. St. Angelo also supports the Arizona charter law, the testing of teachers in Massachusetts, and tax credits passed in Minnesota. Friedman is famous for his voucher concept but the Foundation sees the value of all the choice mechanisms being tried in states. Ranking the successes so far, St. Angelo places tax credits in Minnesota put in place by former Governor Arne Carlson at the top of his list. He also praises Mike Joyce of the Bradley Foundation, a fellow Democrat (he has known him for years and he is a classic liberal), as the person most helpful in Milwaukee. Bradley, he says, put necessary financial resources where they were most needed.[49]

Friedman sees the political landscape changing positively on school choice. Some Democrats are breaking ranks, St. Angelo notes that they include Sen. Joseph I. Lieberman (Conn.) and Sen. Robert L. Torricelli (N.J.), who both voted for the Washington, D.C., voucher bill. Sen. Robert Kerry (Mass.) said he would have supported the D.C. bill if it had included an appropriation for physical plant and Sen. Joseph Biden (Del.) promised to look seriously at school choice. St. Angelo also hopes Democrats in the South, particularly in Georgia, Florida, and Texas will also change their minds.[50] His desire, expressed in a speech he gave at Stanford, is to speed up this process. "Simply put, as government-run schools continue to fail and as market-based reform continues to work, our educational Berlin wall inches closer to its inevitable fall." The challenge to the Friedman Foundation, St. Angelo believes, is where does it go from here? "How can the parental choice movement tear this wall down even faster?"[51]

St. Angelo's model for acceleration is fairly simple. First, he believes that it is necessary to lay aside differences and form "broad-based alliances" to include the widest possible variety of groups. Second, he thinks it is important to be respectful of state and regional distinctives, where the pace and direction of change follow no set pattern. Third, he wants to get beyond a public versus private dichotomy and show that parental choice is able to embrace both. "Let the money follow the child" may be the first principle of school choice, as political scientist Quentin Quade urges, but St. Angelo's prescriptions also build on Quade's second maxim, namely, that all steps toward choice are beneficial if they lead in the same direction.[52]

In the fall of 1998 the Friedman Foundation sponsored a major conference in San Francisco on "School Choice and Corporate America" during which the Foundation unveiled its future educational media campaign for choice. This effort bought in such powerful political figures as Governor Pete Wilson (Calif.), Governor Arne Carlson (Mich.), Steve Forbes, Lamar Alexander, George P. Shultz, Mayor Stephen Goldsmith (Indianapolis), Mayor Bret Schundler, Rev. Floyd Flake, and the superintendent of public instruction for Arizona, Lisa Graham Keegan.

The political speaker who brought the most emotional intensity to the conference was former Governor Arne Carlson of Minnesota. As the keynoter for the first evening, the governor urged that it was time for the school choice movement to consolidate: to organize, to put in money, and for those able to do so, to screen candidates and support candidates, because for the first time, according to the Gallup polls, the public "is on our side." He said even vouchers to religious schools are a winning proposition as demonstrated in Wisconsin. We must, Carlson challenged, "bring in choice state by state."[53]

Carlson recounted the Minnesota school choice success story from his perspective as governor. The state had a law forbidding statewide testing. When the education union resisted this reasonable idea, public opinion shifted against the union. The 1997 legislature refused to include the choice tax credits for computers, education summer camp, and tutoring (but not tuition) that he requested. So Carlson pressed the issue, threatening to publish in the papers the picture of those legislators who put their children in private school and opposed the tax credit. "They caved," he said. The majority leader had two children in private schools, Carlson noted, and in the state 20 percent of public school teachers send their kids to private schools. As part of the bargain Carlson also got merit pay, site-based management, and, as a sweetener for the other side, more money for public schools. He asked, "How can educators be so resistant when by his count one-third of the children in the state were deficient in math and reading in the 8th grade?" Carlson ended by thanking the Friedman Foundation for its substantial financial contributions in helping to educate the public in Minnesota.

Lisa Graham Keegan, superintendent of public instruction for Arizona also spoke. Keegan supports all forms of choice—vouchers, tax credits, and charters. Arizona as of 1998 had 300 charter locations and 30,000 students—with full funding, close to $5,000 per student. Some of these schools fail. Arizona grows by 25,000 students per year. Keegan says there is simply too much demand for school alternatives and not enough quality providers. Any more massive choice plan in the state will need support from the financial community. Meanwhile, Keegan lamented, the public needs to be educated on the merits of school choice and the need for quality standards in schools. Her prescription for change as a public servant, she said, is to "annoy someone everyday."[54]

A roster of school choice entrepreneurs also addressed the gathering, including John Walton, Reed Hastings, John Golle, James Mansour, David Brennan, William Hume, and William Oberndorf. Academicians and journalists Thomas Sowell, Paul Peterson, Douglas Carnine, John Fund, and John Marline made presentations. Representatives attended from twelve state governments, including New York, New Mexico, Wisconsin, Ohio, and Minnesota.[55] To say that the Friedman's have clout is an understatement.

Journalists were optimistic as well as realistic. John Fund, a member of the editorial board of the *Wall Street Journal* commented that school choice is "now at a critical juncture about to achieve success." He pointed out that with the Walton/Forstmann national scholarship initiative, the dynamics of the school choice battle had changed—from an intellectual sortie to a political one. He advised building a broad coalition based on principles, and warned school choice advocates to resist compromise, especially at the early stages of negotiations.[56] Fund stressed the importance of studying one's adversaries and of working with Democrats and street smart politicians.[57]

John Merline, member of the editorial board of *USA Today*, noted that opinion among journalists is shifting from skepticism to support for school choice. Younger members especially are more open. Journalists are no longer in lockstep with those who defend the status quo, according to Merline.[58]

The conference leader was Richard B. Wirthlin, President Reagan's pollster and adviser. In terms of long-term influence, it was Wirthlin who was most critical, laying out the basis for educational television and radio advertising. Wirthlin reported on his research and promised a kinder and gentler and more effective image for the movement in the future. As the consultant strategist for Catholic and Protestant efforts to curb abortion, Wirthlin is experienced in packaging controversial messages in non-threatening ways. He is opposed to negative ad campaigns and wants to touch the deep respect the nation has for parents and for the long-term welfare of children.[59]

"Developing Communication Strategies to Promote School Choice" was Wirthlin's message at the San Francisco conference. He called for positive, personal, and relevant terms to get across the message about school choice.[60] "Use stories, anecdotes and real consequences, scenes from class, pictures of satisfied parents, people with less worry," and do it repetitively, he counseled.

The key, said Wirthlin, is to make an emotional presentation backed up by good arguments. They should stress that choice itself is a parental right, tuition costs necessitate public funding, smaller schools with favorable student/teacher ratios work better, and academic performance improves in alternative schools, which test scores prove. Highlight the benefits, he stressed, and *make* public opinion. Wirthlin concluded by reminding his listeners that President Reagan in the air traffic controller strike went up against public opinion, and he won because true leadership works to shape public opinion.[61]

As a result, the Friedman Foundation is producing pro-voucher commercials with positive messages useable anywhere in 1999. These television ads are available for local and state school choice supporters to educate the public about the benefits of school choice. The Foundation also plans to buy media time for its own educational efforts. It is concerned that in the past the movement has suffered grievously from attack ads and wants to seize the media high ground with carefully prepared, credible, accurate, and believable messages. This will be, in this view, an educational effort in every responsible and credible sense yet it will be accessible to the public. Any effort to achieve parental choice, Friedman writes, must not be "episodic," linked to particular elections and ballot initiatives. It must be educational if it is effectively to shape public discourse.[62]

In a vivid contrast if not a rebuke to the Wirthlin positive storyline, on the first evening of the conference, a tall young man in his twenties threw a pie in Milton Friedman's face and was arrested. Over fifty protestors demonstrated across the street from the conference hotel. Yelling and chanting, they accused corporations of taking money away from public schools. Just before the pie incident a conference participant privately warned Friedman that the school choice issue would lead to disruption, even violence—and reportedly, Friedman downplayed the danger.[63]

Supporting Political Activists: The American Education Reform Foundation

Clearly, organizations are finding distinct identities within the school choice movement to avoid unnecessary duplication and even competition. Some build schools (Edison); some build schools and promote choice by every means available (SFRF); some provide vouchers and help others build schools (Rooney); some provide vouchers and promote research (CSF); some provide vouchers, resources, coordination, and consultation (CEO America); some simply educate and propagate (Friedman). But for the movement to be truly effective, one organization and one individual need to care about school choice politics unrestricted by other concerns.

That organization is the American Education Reform Foundation (AERF) and that person is its president, Susan Mitchell. For the past decade, she and her husband, George, have been partners in a public policy consulting firm, the Mitchell Company, located in Milwaukee. Susan Mitchell is a former reporter for the *Wall Street Journal* and the *San Francisco Examiner* and has a history in business as a vice president and president of insurance companies. For the past eight years she has been consumed by school choice politics, and believes that for many children a good education appears to be the luck of the draw. When George and Susan Mitchell adopted two children, one Korean and one Hispanic and African American, Susan saw education through the eyes of her children. Personalizing the issue led to her focusing on it exclusively. She had been active for years in business and in a public policy consulting firm, but nothing has given her the satisfaction she found by working on school choice. This is a long-term commitment for Mitchell; she works on no other issue.[64]

School choice, Mitchell says candidly, is a tough task against long odds. Reflecting on its larger significance, Mitchell sees not only the rescue of individuals but also the future of a democratic republic at stake. In other words, as the schools go, so goes the community and nation. Looking back, she sees her whole personal and professional history preparing her for this battle (Mitchell does read military strategy occasionally). There is no guaranteed success, losses are inevitable, but she likes the risk and she is ready to fail if she must. Mitchell is dedicated to enabling all parents to choose the schools best suited for their children, an opportunity denied in practice particularly to families of limited means. Her commitment to school choice is bound up with her children, her sense of public obligation, and the joys of competing and winning against the odds.[65]

Mitchell sees herself as an air traffic controller for school choice. She much prefers working behind the scenes, eschewing the platform and public eye that she largely avoids for personal and tactical reasons. She likes to help people work together. Excelling in one-on-one negotiations and in small groups within a coalition, Mitchell's management style is result-oriented, organized, realistic, and precise. She is given much credit for expanding and maintaining school choice in Wisconsin.[66]

The AERF Board and its chairman, William E. Oberndorf, hired Mitchell in late 1998. The board includes such school choice notables as Reverend Floyd Flake, Howard Fuller, David Brennan, John Walton, and Arne Carlson. In her new position she is responsible for the AERF, which is a 501c-4 organization, and also the American Education Reform Council (AERC), a 501c-3 involved in education efforts. The purpose of AERF, Mitchell says, is to help in states where local activists welcome assistance and where success or substantial progress is likely. Mitchell, who has worked in Minnesota, Florida, and Texas, is happy to go where her organization "adds value."[67]

What Mitchell brings to AERF is a personal commitment to school choice forged in the heat of local politics. She has intelligence and political savvy, a wisdom gained through experience. The rules she plays by are fully devel-

oped and honed. Her personal perspective on how to win a legislative campaign and how to sustain that victory as the opposition tries to whittle it
away is now being employed strategically. In almost elementary political
terms, Mitchell argues that school choice will live or die not on the basis of
ideas, or advertising, or money alone, but through the long-term commitments of local school choice advocates who are organized and who know
how to work together. The AERF participates in local coalition building by
assessing strengths and weaknesses, providing counsel on how to grow, and
by providing information on how to win campaigns, and invest resources
strategically.[68]

Mitchell cut her school choice teeth in the mid-1980s. At that time, she
began talking seriously with Howard Fuller and her husband about how to
improve education in Milwaukee. Drawing busing maps for a research project, she concluded that the Milwaukee busing program was destructive, unfair, and unworkable. Her experience as a *Wall Street Journal* reporter had
convinced her of the merits of market choices as a stimulus to creativity and
excellence. She is convinced parents need choices. As a consultant, she saw
that so long as the kids and money kept coming, the system wouldn't change
and that "those opposed to choice gave it no hearing because it threatened
their power base." Therefore, she concluded that school monopoly did not
work, that it could be fixed by school choice, and that there was fierce resistance.[69] She liked a fight.

In the early 1990s Mitchell conducted research for the Wisconsin Policy
Research Institute with funding from the Joyce Foundation. She wrote "Educational Choice in Wisconsin: Public Funds for Private Schools Early
Childhood through Post-Secondary," which disclosed that government already funds private pre-school and college education, and "Why MPS
Doesn't Work: Barriers to Reform in Milwaukee Public Schools." Just prior
to Christmas 1993, she presented the latter report to the Metropolitan Milwaukee Association of Commerce (MMAC), using graphic examples to show
how the bureaucracy stifled past reform efforts and recommending school
choice as the solution. Business leaders who had been seeking education reform for some time because of workforce issues greeted her presentation with
silence, she remembers, shocked by the condition of MPS. The Association
then asked her to help in expanding the pilot project enacted four years earlier with the support of state Representative Polly Williams and Governor
Tommy Thompson. Their decision took courage, in Mitchell's view. She
accepted the challenge.[70]

Mitchell was given complete freedom to come up with her plan. Her first
step was to inventory the supporters and potential supporters of school
choice. She assessed their resources and assets to see what each could bring
to the effort. To produce the plan she interviewed all the players seeking a
proposal that met their concerns and objectives. The result was what she

calls "the strange bedfellows coalition," a group of politically, economically, racially, and religiously diverse supporters. Before the effort became public, Mitchell worked for one year behind the scenes. She wanted to ensure that the supporters of choice had a unified plan, defined roles, a budget, and a strategy before they acted. The association approved the plan in June 1994.[71]

Strategically, Mitchell sought to win the support of the governor and then go to the legislature, where school choice is finally won or lost, with a contingent of supporters that would surprise everyone with their good sense, commitment, and diverse community representation. In July 1994, she helped to establish a parents organization called "Parents for School Choice" with the help of Zakiya Courtney, a well-respected former private school administrator active in the African-American community. The first act of the parents group was to sponsor a rally for Governor Tommy Thompson—750 parents attended—and this would demonstrate to him that there was strong grassroots parental support. Two weeks later, a group of Milwaukee business leaders met with the governor to press him to support choice. He was duly impressed. The goal was to win his consent for including school choice in the budget bill. A long-time backer of more choices for parents, he agreed. The team of parents and business leaders proved effective, partly because they represent both the public that votes and established community leadership. In fact she observed that without support of this kind little can be done to persuade politicians to act.[72]

School choice supporters went to work, reinforcing yes votes, persuading the undecided, and neutralizing opponents—a traditional strategy. With volunteers, Mitchell launched a well-organized effort with worksheets, a weekly planning session, and careful targeting of specific legislators for visits from particular people. The team determined who the "best messenger" would be for each legislator. Supporters made from five to ten visits per "yes and maybe" legislator. The legislative leadership received constant attention. Mitchell refused to count a vote as a sure "yes" vote until the legislator promised it positively three times. The lobbying consumed six months of work. Only the inner circle of school choice leaders was informed of the vote count. Outside school choice experts provided some help in lending credibility to the initiative. But during that time, an extended period that lasted for many months, Mitchell never took her eye off the two goals that made it work, support by the governor for school choice in the budget bill and enough votes in the legislature to keep it there.[73]

In 1999 the goal of AERF is to expand the number of successful school choice programs to strengthen the total movement, which is still in its infancy, and to maintain momentum. To do so, AERF probably will search out states where school choice success is most likely to win approval and where there are sufficient leadership and resources. Concentrating AERF efforts in the few states that look most promising would also be a wise use of scarce AERF human and financial resources. It makes most sense to prioritize efforts in any large-scale movement and AERF must target for success if it is to have much impact. As the organization continues to develop its thinking this is a likely strategy.[74]

It does appear that to keep choice alive requires a coalition that is vigilant on its behalf. A variety of people from both political parties, with ideological, racial, social, economic, and religious diversity, must have a vested interest in keeping it alive. Mitchell saw this take place in Milwaukee and wants to see it happen elsewhere. Grassroots coalitions require personal relationships cultivated over time. The care and nurture of a truly indigenous and local choice movement, one that keeps its hands firmly on the levers of political influence, is a Mitchell specialty, and it would be surprising if she did not continue to pursue this strategy with AERF. Mitchell looks for local leaders who are comfortable working with people "ranging from governors to low income parents," and who are able "to draw together people who normally would not work together or agree on most issues and help them see the importance of working together to achieve this goal."[75]

The essence of the AERF contribution, as Mitchell defines it, is to honor the maxim that all politics is local. This is more a bottom-up than a top-down approach, because it assumes the need for an independent support base that works for this one issue. Individual leaders come and go but the base coalition must endure for the long haul or any success one year may easily be washed away the next year.

Mitchell described an anti-school choice event held on December 8 1998 in Milwaukee as an example of the counter-attacks to be expected. After a day of speeches and workshops on what is wrong with school choice, the opposition activities concluded with a dinner and a speech by Congressman Jesse Jackson, Jr. The legislator, who attended St. Albans, the prestigious college preparatory school in Washington, D.C., attacked school choice for low-income families before an audience of public school teachers, many of whom send their own children to private schools. Jackson in his address claimed that school choice roots go back to racist sources in the Deep South. In response, George Mitchell wrote in a local paper, "The idea that giving $4,900 education vouchers to low-income, minority parents is racist was one of many laughable themes that surfaced during the day."

To demonstrate support for school choice, local activists organized a counter-rally of five hundred supporters who gathered to hear Howard Fuller explain the advantages of choice to Milwaukee parents. Fuller was eloquent, Mitchell said, describing to parents how acutely important it is to protect their fledgling program. They foresee many battles to come before school choice is firmly established even in Milwaukee.[76]

Conclusions and an Example of Victory: New York

This chapter points to an ever increasing movement among the corporate, business, and financial leaders of America to provide school choice through a variety of measures—even if it means that these policy entrepreneurs must pay for educational options themselves! The names that are woven throughout the fabric of the school choice endeavor are, indeed, the names of major donors and policy entrepreneurs: Walton, Forstmann, Whittle, Rooney, Freidman, and others, many *wealthy* others who are creating a groundswell for an idea that they believe is part of the capitalistic, democratic way of life. They come out of that mindset, and are used to seeing an opportunity in every challenge.

Creating schools, paying for scholarships, and winning the public and politicians over to school choice are the three main thrusts of the new free-market school choice entrepreneurs. The three goals reinforce and depend on each other. There must be decent alternative schools for choice to work. Entrepreneurs are starting them. The poor especially must be able to afford to go to these schools; entrepreneurs are providing the scholarships for them to attend. The government must help with the funding of educational options if choice is to be universal: entrepreneurs are working to make it happen. These three strategies are all being launched simultaneously. Not every entrepreneur is involved in all three. Some are non-political, scarcely engaged at all in the politics of choice although their efforts at starting schools or helping to pay for scholarships makes favorable legislation more likely. Together entrepreneurs have transformed the school choice movement, using new tools and sending it in new directions.

These are not men to be denied. If they cannot make school choice happen legislatively, they will make it happen financially. The main question is: how long can their money and will endure? Bill Oberndorf, who founded AERF, said that it cost $13 million for a five-year effort in Milwaukee to get a pilot project. Public vouchers in the city for 15,000 children will cost $75 million for just one year. If politics rather than philanthropy is the only solution for a challenge as massive as changing education, when will entrepreneurs put their money and effort into supporting school choice candidates on the local and national level? How long before they will form PACs to lobby Washington and state houses to bring the question of school choice to the fore on state and federal agendas? In New York, some questions have already been answered.[77]

When the New York State Legislature convened on December 21, 1998, in order to get school choice on the agenda of public officials before the government holiday break, it passed both charter school and pay raise legislation. Governor George Pataki had tied the educational reform measure to the politicians' salary increases, vowing to veto the latter if the legislators did not enact the school bill he had supported for so long. What is even more interesting, however, is the fact that the *New York Times* reported a few days later that the governor's pressure was matched by "ardent adherents in the business community [who] made large contributions to lawmakers in the weeks before the charter bill passed."[78]

The newspaper claimed that business leaders associated with the Manhattan Institute, a non-profit policy agency, had been instrumental in getting the legislation passed. The Manhattan Institute, located across the street from Grand Central Station in the Big Apple, is a mainstay of the school choice movement in New York. It had targeted the state legislature, particularly the minority Democratic members of the assembly, early on. Seymour Fleigel, head of the Center for Education Innovation within the Manhattan Institute,[79] was one of the first to realize that the minority legislators would strongly endorse school choice measures, particularly charter schools because their constituents' children were the students losing out the most. He was able to identify a small group of Assembly members who would support charters, such as Roger Green, Laurence Seabrook, Vita Faso, and Carmen Aroyo, a year before the legislation was introduced, and he felt that the movement was beginning to coalesce at that time. The Manhattan Institute, consequently, began to hold conferences in Albany and New York City and at local colleges to discuss and educate community groups and others about school choice.

At the same time, the businessmen who worked with the Institute also believed that things were beginning to happen. Peter Flanigan, a major corporate executive of Warburg, Dillion Read, a Madison Avenue subsidiary of the Swiss Bank Corporation, and a member of the board of trustees of the Manhattan Institute, believed that school choice was in a period of "gestation" in early 1998.[80] He was, obviously, in a position to know. Having founded the Student-Sponsor Scholarship Partnership, he later helped establish the School Choice Scholarship Program in New York State. Working with John Cardinal O'Connor and the Reverend Floyd Flake, Flanigan helped to make scholarships available to financially needy students who wanted to attend religious schools.

He also knew that it was necessary to put a political coalition together, but thought that he could create channels of education and communication while others could carry out the political side of things. But Flanigan is a quick study and he changed his mind. Recognized as a leader of the school choice movement in New York, Flanigan was consulted by Tim Mulhern of United New Yorkers for Choice in Education for advice on how to "shake things up in Albany."[81] By June 1998, six months later, Flanigan knew how, and he put his money where it would do the most good. Along with Roger Hertog, Chairman of the Board of Trustees of the Manhattan Institute and President of Sanford C. Bernstein and Company, and Richard Gilder, an independent entrepreneur, Flanigan founded the School Choice Now Political Action Committee. Hertog, Gilder, and Flanigan each made $25,000 contributions.[82] Reportedly, the committee solicited and contributed more than $100,000 to lawmakers, particularly minority legislators, like Denny Farrell from the Washington Heights section of New York City, and party leaders—both Democrats and Republican—while also lobbying for six months for charter school legislation.[83]

Their efforts paid off. Charter schools are now a reality in New York State. Flanigan believes that this is a step to vouchers, an eventuality that will became a reality for the poor in 2000 or 2001. And, indeed he may be right. Within weeks of the charter victory, Mayor Giuliani began to call for an experimental voucher plan to be implemented in one of New York City's community school districts. He mentioned this first in his "State of the City" address in January 1999. He followed up on it in speeches in Florida and Albany and by March of that year was vigorously lobbying the New York City School Board for support for his voucher plan. The schools' chancellor, Rudy Crew, threatened to resign and for a while it appeared as though the mayor would drop the issue. Then in late April, Giuliani commented that the entire New York City school system was "dysfunctional" and unveiled a new spending plan, one that would include $12 million for a school voucher program. His innovative plan would allow public monies to be used to pay part of the tuition for 3,000 students from low-income families to attend a public or a private school, *but* it would be financed through the mayor's office and simply bypass the funding mechanism of the board of education. Although his critics anticipated immediate legal challenges, the mayor pointed out that "we should not be afraid to basically turn the evaluation of schools over to the consumers, the parents, and the children." Interestingly, he made the remarks after attending a ceremony for the winners of the scholarship program financed by Ted Forstmann and the Children's Scholarship Fund.

Chris Whittle and his for-profit Edison Project are also waiting in the wings. Reportedly, his staff has already begun conversations with people in New York City who want to start charter schools. Others will follow. Ministers are anxious to use their Sunday school classrooms for charter schools. Jewish groups are "studying the possibilities under the law." Even the Catholic archdiocese has "expressed an interest in the potential of the charter law."[84] The moral of the story is simple, and this chapter ends as it began: money talks and it's time for the educational establishment to listen.

Notes

1. For many of his views, see Christoper Whittle, "The Edison Project's Founder's Musings on American Schooling, *The School Administrator,* January 1997, pp. 6–9.

2. Interview of Jo Renee Formicola with Benno Schmidt, December 14, 1998. All reference to him in this chapter come from this interview.

3. For his views, see the interview in "Let There be Light," *Across the Board,* May 1998, pp. 39–44.

4. See information provided on the Edison Project Website (http://www. edisonproject.com).

5. This is a program created by Robert Slavin, a sociologist at Johns Hopkins University. See an account of his work in, Robert Slavin, Nancy Karweit, and Barbara Wasik, *Preventing Early School Failure,* Boston: Allyn and Bacon, 1993.

6. See "Let There be Light," op. cit, p. 41–42. Although this number has been reported here, the May 27, 1998, press release of the Edison Project claims that "typically, Edison invests about $1,500,000 of its own capital to start an Edison school. In many such 'low-spend' districts, philanthropists have concluded that the most effective way to assist a district's school-improvement effort is to fund this start-up capital." See page 2.

7. See the Edison Project Website as cited above.

8. Karen W. Arenson, "Teachers in Miami Are to be Offered Edison Project Stock," *New York Times,* 11 October 1998, p. A6.

9. Eugene S. Ruffin, telephone interview by Hubert Morken, November 12, 1998.

10. Eugene S. Ruffin, interview by Hubert Morken, San Diego, CA, October 6, 1998.

11. School Futures Research Foundation, five-year plan for the School Futures Research Foundation, 1998.

12. Ibid.

13. Ibid.

14. Ruffin, interview, October 6, 1998; SFRF, report, 1998; Brian Bennett, telephone interview, October 14, 1998.

15. Ibid.

16. Ibid.

17. Ibid.

18. Ibid.

19. Ibid.

20. Ibid.

21. SFRF, report, 1998; School Futures Research Foundation, "Charter Schools: Parent Surveys and Achievement Measures, 1997–98.

22. SFRF, report, 1998.

23. Marvin Threatt, Dwight A. Sykes, and Jorge Ramirez, interviews by Hubert Morken, San Diego, October 6, 1998; Ruffin, interview, October 6, 1998.

24. Sykes, interview, October 6, 1998.

25. Ibid.; Rosemarie Vicianti, telephone interview by Hubert Morken, October 13, 1998. Rosemarie Vicianti, is principal of Our Lady of Czestochowa, a parochial grammar school in Jersey City. She has been active for forty-seven years in Catholic education and is a member of the Jersey City Advisory Board on Charter Schools, appointed by Mayor Schundler. There are five charter schools in Jersey City, one run by a for-profit organization and entitled "The Golden Door Charter School."

Vicianti supports charter schools. There are five Catholic grammar schools in the area, with mostly Asian students. Her school in 1997–98 operated two kindergarten classes but this year they only offer one. Vicianti says all five Catholic schools are affected by competition from charter schools. So far they have lost thirty-two students in the five schools, grades 1–5, to the charter schools.

26. Ramirez, interview by Hubert Morken, October 6, 1998; Ruffin, interview, October 6, 1998; School Futures Foundation, The Chula Vista Learning Community Charter School, A Charter School Proposal Presented to the Governing Board of the Chula Vista Unified School District, undated, prior to 1998.

27. Ibid.

28. Ibid.

29. J. Patrick "Pat" Rooney, interview by Hubert Morken, Indianapolis, IN, July 21, 1998.

30. Timothy P. Ehrgott, "School Choice for Inner-City Kids," *The Freeman,* October 1994, p. 553.

31. See the mailings of the Educational CHOICE Trust.

32. Ehrgott, op. cit.

33. Educational CHOICE Update, Winter 1997–98, p. 8; Ehrgott, telephone interview with Hubert Morken, March 16, 1999.

34. Rooney, interview, July 21, 1998.

35. Ibid.

36. Ibid.

37. Ibid.

38. Douglas Dewey, interview by Jo Renee Formicola, New York City, September 16, 1998; interview by Hubert Morken, Washington, DC, November 20, 1997.

39. Anemona Hartocollis, "Private School Choice Plan Draws a Million Aid-Seekers, *New York Times,* April 21, 1999, p. A1.

40. Ibid.

41. See the website of CEO America: www.ceoamerica.org.

42. Ibid., CEO America News, December 8, 1998.

43. Website of CEO America.

44. See the letter of Fritz Steiger to school choice supporters, September 1, 1998.

45. Milton and Rose D. Friedman Foundation, "Educational Choice," a brochure, undated; Gordon St. Angelo, interview by Hubert Morken, Indianapolis, IN, July 27, 1998; Robert Enlow, and Lennore Ealy, interview by Hubert Morken, Indianapolis, IN, July 21, 1998; Robert Enlow, telephone interviews, October 27 and December 17, 1998.

46. St. Angelo, interview, July 27, 1998.

47. Ibid.

48. Ibid.; *Friedman-Blum Educational Freedom Report,* no. 63, September 18, 1998.

49. Ibid.

50. Ibid.

51. Gordon St. Angelo, manuscript of a speech delivered to the Hoover Institution, Palo Alto, CA, August 1998.

52. Ibid.; Quentin Quade, interview by Hubert Morken, Milwaukee, WI, July 29, 1998.

53. Ibid.; Governor Arne Carlson, October 9, 1998.

54. Lisa Graham Keegan, Friedman Foundation Conference, San Francisco, CA, October 9, 1998.

55. Ibid.; Conference Program, San Francisco, CA, October 9–10, 1998.

56. John Fund, Friedman Foundation Conference, San Francisco, CA, October 9, 1998.

57. Ibid.

58. John Merline, Friedman Foundation Conference, San Francisco, CA, October 9, 1998.

59. Richard B. Wirthlin, conversation with the author, San Francisco, October 9, 1998; Friedman Foundation Conference, San Francisco, CA, October 9–10, 1998.

60. Ibid.

61. Ibid.

62. Ibid.; Friedman Foundation, "Educational Choice," a brochure, undated.

63. Eyewitness account and interview with Deborah Devedjian by Hubert Morken, Friedman Foundation Conference, San Francisco, CA, Ocrober 9–10, 1998.

64. Dan McKinley, interview by Hubert Morken, Milwaukee, WI, July 28, 1998; Susan Mitchell, telephone interviews by Hubert Morken, August 24, October 1, and December 23, 1998.

65. Ibid.; Susan Mitchell resume.

66. Ibid.

67. Mitchell, telephone interviews.

68. Ibid.

69. Mitchell, telephone interviews.

70. Ibid.; Wisconsin Policy Institute Report, "Educational Choice in Wisconsin: Public Funds for Private Schools Early Childhood through Post-Secondary," vol. 6, no. 4, May 1993; "Why MPS Doesn't Work: Barriers to Reform in Milwaukee Public Schools," vol. 7 no. 1, January 1994.

71. Ibid.; Susan Mitchell, "MMAC Strategy: Expansion of School Choice," for August to December 1994; Task lists, and other planning documents for 1995.

72. Ibid.

73. Ibid.

74. Mitchell, telephone interviews.

75. Ibid.

76. Ibid.; George Mitchell, "Desperate Measures," *Metro Milwaukee Weekly*, clipping, December 17, 1998.

77. Bill Oberndorf, speaking at the Friedman Foundation Conference, San Francisco, CA, October 9, 1998.

78. Anemona Hartocollis, "Religious Leaders Plan Schools with Public Funds in New York," *New York Times,* 29 December 1998, p. Al.

79. Seymour Fliegel, interview by Jo Renee Formicola, New York, February 12, 1998.

80. Peter Flanigan, interview by Jo Renee Formicola, New York, February 11, 1998.

81. See the letter of Mulhern to Flanigan, February 2, 1998.

82. Hartocollis, op. cit., p. B. 5.

83. Ibid.

84. Ibid.

Chapter 5

Religious Strategies: Catholics and Evangelicals

The two most prominent groups who opposed each other in American politics historically are the Evangelical Protestants, who largely established and dominated the nation from its early settlements to the start of the twentieth century, and the Catholics, who began arriving in great numbers first from Ireland and later from Italy and eastern Europe. Booth Fowler and Allen Hertzke say, "This phenomenon produced the most enduring cultural divide in U.S. history—the Catholic-Protestant split—which shaped partisan political loyalties for over a century and a half." They go on to say that if this history is not appreciated, it is impossible to understand the recent healing of this divide so evident in recent elections, the fruit of "contemporary alliances between Catholics and Evangelicals today." In short, school choice is no longer a Catholic issue, it is now a Catholic-Evangelical concern.[1]

In his book, *Agendas, Alternatives and Public Policies,* John Kingdon talks about seizing the opportunities for political change when they appear, and how to use political connections and negotiating skills to make change happen. Policy advocates, according to him, must work for change as well as broker it; they must be flexible and willing to create partnerships for the sake of policy expediency. This is what religious groups are doing to make school choice a reality—allying with a variety of different groups that will help them to create school choice while using a mix of methods to advance a variety of educational options.[2]

Partnering as a Means to Leverage School Change: Catholics and School Choice

If it is possible to characterize the means being used by Catholics to advance school choice in the United States, it must be described as "partnering." The term as it is used here is meant to describe a political phenomenon that is broader and more practical than coalition building or political alliances for several reasons. First, as it applies specifically to Catholics, it means that the basic thrust of all their efforts to bring about educational options is to support *all* such efforts by *all* groups committed to *all* kinds of school choice. Thus, even if groups are ideologically or economically at odds with one another, it makes no difference to the Catholics. Second, this partnering is usually different from place to place and time to time, depending on the expedient relationship needed in a particular situation to advance school choice. Third, partnering also means that members of the Catholic hierarchy or clergy, who often have the most legitimacy, clout, and resources in relationships, are often in a position to dictate the terms of a school choice coupling with another group or to even veto objectionable alternatives. Fourth, it also means that Catholic attempts to advance school choice will often be difficult to characterize and may often be ad hoc or anecdotal at best.

Catholics, more than any other religious group in the United States, have been traditionally involved in all manner of attempts to leverage change to create freedom of education in America. With more than 8,000 elementary, middle, and secondary schools, enrolling over 2.6 million students in the United States, the Catholics represent a de facto educational force within the United States.[3] Thus, concerns to maintain the church's religious freedom as well as its ideological and educational interests have always motivated Catholic Church-state relations. Since *Pierce v Society of Sisters,* which upheld the right of every parent to choose the education of his/her child, to the most current round of judicial challenges, the church has been heavily involved in the political process. Litigating and lobbying on behalf of particular education benefits at the national and state level to protect its schools and to broaden their financial support in the future, the church has always and still does present a formidable force to challenge the educational establishment.[4]

When speaking of the church, it is necessary to define those organizations, both clerical and lay, whose purpose it is to speak for Catholic educational interests in the United States. Because the church has always been, and remains, a hierarchical institution, its agenda, policies, and methodology are informed by its doctrine and social teachings, and they directed by those most familiar with such teachings—the clergy.

In the United States, the organization that represents the highest Church authority is the National Conference of Catholic Bishops. Made up of the 375 bishops in the country, the general secretary serves the organization at the national headquarters while all the other departments are led by elected bishops who tend to church business from their local diocese.

Located across the street from Catholic University and the National Catholic Cathedral in Washington, D.C., the NCWC building mixes an aura of academe, religion, and politics. It is served by the United States Catholic Conference; a permanent advisory agency meant to assist and represent the church hierarchy in their local dioceses on social concerns. But it does more than that: The USCC carries out the programs and policies set in place by the Bishops at their bi-annual meetings. Its offices are run on a day-to-day basis by religious and lay specialists, who often create a patchwork of policy by their daily decisions.

The chief departments of the United States Catholic Conference deal with communications, domestic matters, world peace, social justice, and *education*. Originally, the latter office was the largest in the USCC, but now Refugee and Immigrant Services have superseded it, reflecting the church's growing commitment to human rights and the poor. Still, the education office commands a budget beyond one million dollars, as it is driven by the bishops' yearly educational agenda. The current bishop in charge of education is Archbishop Francis B. Schulte of New Orleans, and the Secretary of Education for the United States Catholic Conference is Monsignor Thomas Mc-Dade.

Recently, Mc Dade spelled out the purposes, strategies, and methods being used by the NCCB/USCC to advance school choice across the United States.[5] His office is concerned primarily with monitoring legislation for school choice, both in Washington and in the various states. Secondarily the USCC lobbies and gathers information on experimental and demonstration projects. McDade and his staff also work as advocates for school choice and sign off on legal and governmental communications that speak for the Bishops about educational options. He pointed out that his office worked closely with Capitol Hill staffers to help enact the Coverdell-Torricelli Bill to create educational savings accounts in 1998, and that it also interfaced with the White House and Department of Education to enlist their support on the same legislation.

Without a doubt, the bishops are involved at every level of the political process to make school choice happen. The Administrative Board of the United States Catholic Conference justified political activity earlier in this decade.[6] It maintained that the church had the responsibility to educate the faithful on the teachings of the church and to analyze the social and moral dimensions of issues. Further, it held that the church was obligated to measure public policy against gospel values, to participate with other concerned parties in the debate over public policy, and to speak out on issues involving human rights and social justice. Specifically with regard to education, this political involvement was translated into advocacy for:

- Adequate funding for private and public quality education
- Development and implementation of a form of moral education into

public school curriculum that responds to student needs and respects all their beliefs

- Government and voluntary action to reduce inequalities of educational opportunity for the most disadvantaged
- Compliance with legal requirements for racially integrated schools
- Equitable tax support for education of pupils in public, private, and religious schools
- Salaries and benefits for teachers and administrations that reflect the principle of economic justice
- The involvement of private and religious school students and professionals in all government programs to improve education, especially those with educational, economic, and social disadvantages.[7]

These principles have now been supplemented with guidelines for the creation and support of school choice programs. First and foremost, they call for the inclusion and "participation of parents and students who choose private religiously affiliated schools in any federally funded program."[8] They also require a school choice program to give a priority for low- and middle-income families, to respect the policies and practices of existing private schools, and to provide a sufficient level of new federal funds to cover all necessary costs of demonstration programs.

With the bishops' rationale, and the USCC guidelines, McDade was quick to point out that every type of school choice, including charter schools, tuition tax credits, vouchers, magnet schools, and scholarship programs are within the range of options that the bishops will support anywhere within the United States. However, it is also important to point out that the church does have very real reservations about enrollments, religious preferences, funding, and school regulations in any school choice initiatives. And, it cannot be forgotten that individual bishops will require that such questions be answered to their satisfaction, as they are the persons responsible for education in each particular diocese when any experimental or permanent school choice programs come into their jurisdictions for consideration.

Since no definite, hierarchical answers exist yet to cover every potential situation, the concerns of the bishops are varied. Will a particular school choice effort require an open or lottery system of enrollment? Will siblings or parish children be allowed preferences? Will school choice require the inclusion of the educationally or physically handicapped? Will school choice benefits apply only to new students? Will religious education be forbidden? Will some students be allowed to opt out of a religious requirement? Will teacher salaries be paid to teachers of religion? Will vouchers or scholarships be counted as full payment of tuition? What will happen in the case of tuition increases? How will school records be audited? Will civil rights, health, and safety laws be properly assessed? Will programs of health and human sexuality be taught in accord with church teachings? Will school accreditation and teacher certifications overburden the Catholic schools with additional regulations? Recognizing that these issues have many facets to them, the USCC warns those bishops examining various educational choice proposals and school options to review such matters carefully before becoming involved in them.

While all situations are unique and bishops have a certain amount of autonomy, all members of the hierarchy must function within the principles and guidelines of the National Conference of Catholic Bishops and the United States Catholic Conference. The latter operates an Office of Legal Counsel, headed by Mark Chopko. The members of his staff monitor and litigate First Amendment issues from abortion to euthanasia, to religious freedom and speech, to school choice. Most cases are litigated at the merit stage, that is, at the state level. Others are monitored and participation at the constitutional level is usually as *amicus.*

Following in the tradition of the NCWC and its role in landmark cases, such as *Pierce, Everson, Widmar,* and *Zobrest,* the office has moved beyond the days of having to enlist theologians to write *amicus* briefs for the bishops.[9] Currently, it participates in at least six major First Amendment cases as litigant during any given year, participates as *amicus* in as many as possible annually, and works closely with the Office of Education and the Office of Political Affairs within the agency.

On the professional level, the National Catholic Education Association functions separately from the NCCB/USCC and represents the teachers and administrators of Catholic schools. Although it has the potential to be a powerful voice for school choice in the United States, the NCEA's essential responsibility is to carry out the bishops' educational policies and the church's social teachings in the classroom, rather than to formulate its own platforms.

The NCEA is located in Washington, D.C., and is headed by Dr. Leonard DiFiore.[10] Surrounded by his photographs with Presidents Reagan and Bush, as well as souvenirs of the Pope, DiFiore manages a staff of fifty full-time employees and controls an annual operating budget of over six million dollars. Funds come from foundations, private donations, corporations, dues, meetings, and publications. Although he sees school choice as a moral issue, DiFiore also views it as a practical way to remove the financial impediments that have trapped families into having to accept inferior education for their children. He is quite clear in articulating the policy that NCEA supports all types of school choice, just as the bishops do, because it gives parents options and empowers them. Given a choice, however, DiFiore would opt for tuition tax credits and vouchers to leverage school choice because he believes that money is power.

The primary purpose of the NCEA is to serve as an advocate on behalf of Catholic education. At the same time, it is also committed to education about school choice, leadership development, the preparation of teachers, and the advancement of Catholic identity, public relations, and the implementation of the bishops' public policies on education. It has no political role, and, although it monitors legislation for school choice, it does not lobby to influence the issue. In fact the NCEA seeks first to influence teachers and in declining order of importance local, state, and national policy makers, private citizens, and the media. What it does do, however, is to encourage teachers on a local level to create strategies to advance both Catholic education and school choice.

DiFiore, however, is extremely cognizant and respectful of the fact that the involvement of the Christian Right in the school choice debate from 1978–82 raised mutual Catholic and Protestant concerns to a movement, taking it beyond the notion of a "Catholic issue." It is his observation that liberal Catholics in the USCC and members of the conservative Christian Right have formed a "de facto coalition" at all levels in Washington to advance their education agendas. But he believes that school choice must happen at the state level first before their partnership will be able to effect a national piece of legislation to give educational options to all Americans.

Below the National Council of Catholic Bishops (USCC) and the National Catholic Education Association are the fifty state Catholic education agencies who are responsible to their local bishops for education in their particular dioceses. It is at this grassroots level that many of the religious-education battles are fought, where interest groups politics are played out, and where partnerships are often formed or negated. Thus, although the official strategy of the Catholic Church, as an institution, is to support all forms of school choice in all places, that advancement is subject to the interpretation and autonomy of the local bishop who controls the schools in his particular diocese. Thus, in some cases bishops are taking the lead in leverage school choice, while in other cases they will not or cannot accommodate to the kinds of educational options that are being advocated by policy entrepreneurs in their dioceses.

In some states creative initiatives are coming from Catholic Conference staff members who are able to persuade the bishops to go along with their new ideas. This was certainly the case in Chicago with Doug Delaney a recently arrived lobbyist for the Conference. In another state, Wisconsin, creative staff like Daniel M. McKinley could not find sufficient room to operate under the hierarchy and had to move out from under its control to be able to maneuver and build the coalitions and programs necessary to succeed. Massachusetts, in contrast to Wisconsin, preserved an organizational structure that apparently keeps school choice closely tied to the bishops yet is free enough to function with other groups. In Arizona and California the church has to deal with charter schools and deciding to compete with them or to become charter schools is an interesting issue, according to long time Catholic administrator and teacher Bryan Bennett. Pennsylvania is a state where

Catholics have mastered most of the arts of coalition politics yet certain difficulties remain. In all this diversity among approaches there is a consensus among observers that bishops can be active or passive and this makes a difference.

Michael Schwartz, a congressional staffer with decades of experience in Catholic school choice politics, concludes pessimistically that the church is "losing" Catholics on the school choice issue just when other non-Catholics, blacks, and Evangelicals, are waking up to it. He pleads for a revival of school vision and commitment within the Catholic community. Bishops need to lead the effort he suggests, in stating:

> We are losing Catholics on the issue. We need strong bishop-led initiatives on the education budgets, on raising money, on defending the need for choice by arguing for its vital role in Catholic formation and community outreach. We need to articulate the basis for choice more clearly, anchoring it in the authority of parents to educate their children.[11]

Generalizing, however, is difficult when describing an organization as large as the Catholic Church, which functions in such a decentralized environment. Each story has its own dynamics and deserves close study. The stories also vary over time in each state. Leadership changes when new bishops are installed as do the circumstances and opportunities. In most cases, however, commentators in the late 1990s found the interest of bishops in school choice reinvigorated. New York is an example of an archdiocese refusing to give up its parochial schools despite heavy internal pressure to do so from consultants who advised that education was too costly.

New York

In New York, the most powerful bishop of the largest number of Catholics in the United States, John Cardinal O'Connor, has characterized the question of school choice as a "critical subject."[12] Rejecting charter schools because they preclude religious schools and tuition tax credits because they are unfair to the poor, O'Connor supports a voucher/scholarship system as the "cleanest" way to provide school choice to those who need it the most—minorities.

In 1996, watching the New York school system go from bad to worse, even unable to open on time, the archdiocese offered to educate 1,000 of the New York City school system's worst students. It promised to provide both secular and religious instruction and to find private businesses to pay the tuition costs of the students. The archdiocese joined forces with the Student-Sponsor Partnership of Peter Flanigan, the School Choice Scholarship Foundation of Ted Forstmann and the Adopt a School Program of the Reverend Floyd Flake. As a result, it found itself inundated with 17,000 applications during the first year of its operation, and the recognition of New York's school chancellor, Rudy Crew, that the "plan [would] prod the public system."[13] By the second year, the archdiocese provided 1,300 scholarships and had 24,000 applications.[14]

O'Connor believes that scholarships are an idea whose time has come, that the political system cannot resist it, that industry is disaffected with education in New York City, and that parents want it. Therefore, he sees scholarships as an example of pragmatic partnering rather than as an altruistic alliance between business, the media, and governmental leaders, such as New York City's mayor, Rudolph Guiliani and the state's governor, George Pataki. O'Connor sees this partnering as a way to create a stopgap until the public schools can be fixed. He believes that public education will implode, go through a transition phase, and then make a creative breakthrough that will reflect a change in public education as it now exists. Further, he maintains that this will happen if Mayor Guiliani wins a second term, that is, sometime between 2000 and 2004, a prediction that may be correct since charter school legislation has been enacted in New York State with the recent re-election of Governor George Pataki.

Chicago

Over the decades, between 1965 when Chicago had ninety-five Catholic high schools until 1998 when they numbered forty-seven, parochial education in the city has been shrinking. In the last thirty years the archdiocese closed 153 elementary schools, and the elementary parochial school population has shrunk from 289,000 students to 104,000 (there are 27,000 high school students for a total parochial school population of 131,000). In 1998 it closed four schools and more closings are anticipated. For the past thirty years, until 1997, no new schools were built, but this is about to change. Before he died in 1996, Joseph Cardinal Bernardin established an education task force to look into closing an additional thirty to fifty schools in the city and to secure the remaining schools for those children who now attend them.[15] The new archbishop, Francis Cardinal George, presided over the completion of the report of the Special Task Force on Catholic Schools issued in December 1998.[16] George finds the report realistic about funding issues:

> Besides suggestions for continued academic improvement and personnel development, especially in leadership, the report recommends several approaches to financing the schools beyond the present formula of tuition, fundraising, and subsidies from the parishes and the Archdiocese. It recommends some form of

reimbursement or public financial aid to parents who choose to send their children to non-government schools, a major gifts campaign of perhaps one hundred million dollars for all the schools, more aggressive marketing, central purchasing, selective tuition increases and some consolidation of facilities.

My study of the report has engendered two strong reactions. First, the practical impossibility of maintaining the present system with only the present formula for support. The Archdiocese of Chicago kept schools open in poorer neighborhoods as we moved from a system dependent entirely upon volunteers, the teaching Sisters and Brothers, to one dependent on salaried teachers. But we have not kept pace with the salary scale of teachers in public schools, and this continuing inequity of teachers' salaries is for me the single most troubling item in the report. This item alone leads me to the conviction that new forms of funding, even beyond those mentioned in the report itself, must be found.

For over five generations, this city and our state have directly benefited from Catholic schools. They have formed hundreds of thousands of young people to serve society as educated and responsible citizens. This is a public service. But if this service is to continue, citizens should be able to access some of their own tax money to support their choice to educate their children in a non-government school.

In conscience, I cannot indefinitely support a system that pays its teachers, on average, only half of what their peers earn in the government schools. Nor will I watch the system collapse piecemeal until only the wealthy have access to the Catholic schools because of high tuition. Obviously, this conviction will lead others and myself into new conversations in the months to come. The ongoing education of the 131,000 students now in Catholic schools in Cook and Lake Counties, as well as the other students in Catholic schools statewide, is a public concern. Without the richness of educational alternatives for parents and children, Chicago and the two counties would lose a most important civic asset. I hope we can have an informed and civil conversation on this matter.[17]

What is most significant besides the renewed push for school choice calling for "strong lobbying efforts for some form of public reimbursement to parents who choose to send their children to non-government schools," is the equally strong recommendation to build new schools in the suburbs where Catholics now live. More than half of the archdiocesan children live outside the city limits of Chicago. By building new schools for middle-class and affluent Catholics and holding on to old ones heavily attended by poor non-Catholics, despite the financial pressures these decisions entail, the archdiocese insures continued interest in the public funding issue and school choice. With the Hispanic Catholic population approaching one million and growing rapidly in the city this only adds to the funding concerns and sense of mission for Catholic education.[18]

For decades the Illinois bishops held on to their schools as best they could and futilely asked for vouchers. This persistent but fruitless lobbying effort in 1991, 1993, and 1995 ended in 1996 when Doug Delaney became the chief lobbyist for the Catholic Conference. Delaney is an outsider from Colorado with new ideas, and after considerable effort, he was able to persuade the bishops to back tax credits as an interim solution to the funding crisis. The Illinois House subsequently passed a tax credit bill by one vote with the backing, Delaney reports, of four inner-city black Democrats. The bill included refundable tax credits for the poor, and a limit of $500 per family. Delaney was pleased that Evangelical home schoolers who in the past had opposed vouchers stayed neutral on tax credits and Mayor Daley did not oppose it either. Families would have received, Delaney estimates, $70 million a year if the governor had signed the bill. Instead he vetoed it in January 1997. He was from downstate and may have perceived this as a Catholic bill. To soften the blow the governor doubled state aid for parochial school transportation and textbooks to about $13 million.[19]

Delaney was pleased with the progress made in such a short time. The inertia broke. He was delighted at how well Catholics responded; they sent over 20,000 letters to the Senate President in Springfield. The increase in aid also helped and for the first time a school choice bill passed the legislature. The new Republican governor, George H. Ryan, is also supportive of tax credits and Delaney expects to win the next time around. Brother Thomas Hetland, head of the Driscoll School, who worked for years on Catholic school choice lobbying efforts, hopes that eventually a local option voucher law will pass allowing each of the 900 school districts in the state to decide on choice. He thinks, "If the black caucus wanted vouchers we would have them tomorrow." There are two black bishops, Delaney observes, but most African-American voters see school choice benefiting rich, white Catholics.[20]

Politics is all about the "trade-off" and bargaining, Delaney says. The politicians ask, "Do you want money for hospitals, charities, or schools?" Delaney is confident of bipartisan Republican and Democratic support for tax credits but vouchers will have to wait. Free-market Illinois consultant Larry Horist, George Clowes of the Heartland Institute, and Jack Roser, a businessman and school choice activist, agree that the coalition of school choice supporters in Chicago is too weak. "People in Chicago have difficulty working together," they note, and the opposition is too strong to expect more at present.[21]

Looking ahead at the need to pass school choice legislation the archdiocese Task Force management team advised several steps to help build consensus for it in the state. First, "intensify efforts to enact tax credit legislation as well as vouchers."[22] Second, work closely with other Illinois dioceses in lobbying the legislature. Third, study voucher politics closely in other states and monitor court progress on constitutional issues related to vouchers. To execute this strategy the report recommended creating a think tank to provide a mission statement for the future of Catholic education and all education that would be saleable to the general public. This think tank, the report outlined, must include discussion of the value and role of parochial schools:

- To the local community
- To the Catholic Church
- In sustaining a civic dialogue
- To the discourse on public pluralism
- To curriculum and to educational reform
- To preserving Catholic identity and lay leadership
- To the urban minority community
- To public educational policy formation
- In the educational future of the country
- In local financing of parochial schools[23]

The Archdiocese of Chicago has a vision both evangelistic and public and refuses to surrender either. The parochial education mission statements in the report are unapologetically Christian and Evangelical. "To deepen their personal relationship with Jesus as individuals and members of our faith community through prayer, worship, and service, and other activities," and to prepare them to share that faith with "those who do not belong to a faith community."[24] On the surface at least, this is no policy of surrender to secularism. Yet the public benefits of this fully Christian education would be fully explored by this proposed think tank with the intent of securing tax funding for those whose children attend parochial schools.

Milwaukee

Unlike Chicago, people in Milwaukee have learned to lay aside their differences and to forge an effective political coalition. Some of the credit goes to the creativity and restraint of Catholic activist Daniel M. McKinley. In 1987 McKinley came to Milwaukee to set up an independent board interested in Catholic issues. His goal was to keep the parochial schools open and to help in teacher formation. He soon found there was no significant corporate support or interest in K–12 education, public or private. Business, McKinley says, did not want to give to religion and defined civic duties as a secular activity. The Catholic Church, on the other hand, was wrapped up with its own concerns, promoting parochial education. To increase interest both in the church and in the business community and with the encouragement and financial assistance of $1 million from Archbishop Rembert Weakland, Mc-

Kinley helped to found the Milwaukee Archdiocesan Education Foundation.[25]

The Foundation provided assistance to Catholic schools but found it difficult to get more support from the business community and foundations. In 1991 McKinley contacted Tim Ehrgott in Indianapolis to learn about the Indianapolis private voucher choice program, the first in the country. Using the best advise he could get from a variety of organizations, in January 1992 Mckinley and a committed board of businessmen founded PAVE, Partners Advancing Values in Education, a private voucher program that from its inception was designed to be a bridge to an expanding public voucher program. The goal of PAVE was to give poor families access to good schools and to encourage quality schools. Four local corporate leaders—John Stollenwerk, Donald Schuenke, Richard Abdoo, and attorney T. Michael Bolger— all men, all Catholics, and all the products of Catholic schools took the lead. Within three months, three businesses pledged $500,000 each for scholarships K–12. In April 1992 Mike Joyce of the Bradley Foundation met with them and presented a strategy that called for opening up to the whole city and opening up to all schools. He offered $500,000 a year to back the program. This was a critical moment, McKinley recalls, because it helped to tie together all choice efforts in Milwaukee.[26]

PAVE went public on June 10, 1992, in a press conference. In its first year of operation it gave $1.4 million in vouchers, mostly from corporations, targeting the poorest families in the city. By its fourth year PAVE had given half-tuition scholarships to 11,496 students and had raised cumulatively $14.5 million for scholarships. In Milwaukee in 1998 there were 103,000 students in MPS and 23,000 in private schools. Today, McKinley reports, they have over 1,300 donors who have raised over $20 million.[27]

McKinley says the toughest battle in the past eleven years was his effort to win his independence from church control and to restore respect for parents as educators. He was determined to create and preserve the independence of PAVE from the archdiocese and to put the focus on families as partners, with parents as the primary educators, not the parochial schools. It took him six months to create a structure separate from the church; and in the process, he remembers, he was accused of insubordination. His goal, however, was to create a new vehicle for change and the proper theoretical foundation for it, not to destroy a positive relationship with the archdiocese.[28]

> PAVE was conceived as a nonprofit organization, independent of the archdiocesan structure, that could effectively address the educational needs of families in Milwaukee. PAVE could bring together all those with a stake in education reform—corporations, foundations, educators and political leaders—and offer them one of Milwaukee's greatest educational assets: church-sponsored elementary and secondary schools in central city neighborhoods. The indepen-

dent status of PAVE resolved the dilemma that had obstructed the Milwaukee Archdiocesan Education Foundation. At the same time, PAVE could maintain its close ties with the city's large Catholic school system with a permanent seat on PAVE's board for the archbishop of Milwaukee.[29]

Representative Polly Williams's public voucher program for the city had begun in 1991 with 350 students, with none in religious schools. This ceiling was expanded to 1,000, then to 1,500 (including parochial schools), and now to 15,000. PAVE helped to accomplish this expansion. Plans are for 7,500 public vouchers in 1998. As public vouchers increased PAVE planned to downsize the number of private scholarships it gave in 1998–99 from 4,400 to 1,200. With these changes McKinley said it was time to adjust the mission of PAVE. His master plan for the organization includes:

1. Raise $4 million in 1998 for an endowment to provide scholarships for those who have been in private schools too long to qualify for public vouchers
2. Establish an Information Network on the Web to provide parents with information on all schools to help them select the best one for their children
3. Fund research at the University of Wisconsin, Milwaukee, on school choice results
4. Serve as a resource for volunteers and experts to help in schools
5. Be a watchdog to help choice work, facilitating coalition communications[30]

McKinley believes that unity in Milwaukee among school choice supporters has been preserved by a group culture that restrains wild cards. But for this to continue, he says, they need a formal structure. There are ten new choice schools in the city. With such growth in private schools McKinley spends 90 percent of his time building coalitions and raising money. Yet there is no system yet in place to help focus public awareness and keep the resources flowing. He says generally the press gives little coverage; the reporters have no interest. McKinley wishes he could have sports reporters for a time because education reporters in his experience tend to be lazy. Only in recent years, he says, have local reporters caught on to the significance of the issue, and thus have done much better in their reporting. He also wishes the local Catholic hierarchy was more active. He says the passivity of the church on school choice has been a problem for decades.[31]

Quentin L. Quade, the distinguished Catholic scholar and school choice expert who lived for many years in Milwaukee, blamed opposition by the education financial monopoly and social inertia for much of the resistance to school choice. It is always hard, he said, to secure legitimacy for an alternative system based in this case on parental freedom. Over the years Quade found it very difficult to get even devout Catholics who believe in parochial education to push for school choice. This included not only distinguished businessmen and community leaders, many who attended church schools, but the church clergy as well. Even the Catholic bishops, he commented, are victims of this inertia—they give school choice low priority in the list of items on the policy agenda. It gets buried in the middle of the agenda. Bishops, he said, do not see choice as priority, not like abortion, and strive to avoid "single issuism." In response to this problem Quade said he once wrote an open letter to the bishops arguing for the singular importance of choice based on principle. In his experience, he found the Catholic hierarchy to be strategically soft, with no clear solid priority for choice, and tactically rigid, fighting for vouchers when other steps like tax credits or charter schools show more promise of success. The bishops in Wisconsin, he concluded, did little directly to bring choice to the state. Mayor John Norquist, who relied on Quade for counsel and assistance, agreed with his assessment of the weakness of the Catholic role in the Milwaukee school choice effort.[32]

Boston

Politically the biggest obstacle to success for school choice in Massachusetts is the public perception that this is a Catholic issue and public schools will suffer. There is no corporate support for choice in the state. In addition the state constitution has a restriction against using public funds for religious schools.[33]

With such obstacles, Massachusetts, like other states, has a history of failed Catholic efforts to leverage change. Jerry D'Avolio of the Massachusetts Catholic Conference (MCC) reports that in 1982 and 1986 they tried to get the law changed in low budget—$30,000—low profile "let's get out the Catholic vote" initiatives. No coalition building was even attempted, he says, and of course no one else responded. The media and the education unions simply attacked it as parochial aid and it failed miserably with barely 30 percent of the vote in 1986, as he recalls. The Parents Alliance for Catholic Education (PACE) was born out of the ashes of these defeats in the early 1990s. PACE is the only single-issue Catholic organization operating outside the MCC. The Board of Advisors of PACE is made of thirty people appointed by the four bishops in the state. The separation of PACE from the MCC is partly to protect the church from the political and legal fallout so common to education battles.[34]

Steve Perla, a former mayor, member of a school board, teacher, and college administrator, has headed up PACE for five years. He is pushing a four-prong strategy:

- Educate and mobilize Catholic parents on choice—using video, meetings, mailings
- Help to create a broad and diverse coalition
- Promote a court case challenging the Massachusetts constitutional prohibition of a school choice initiative
- Ask for permission of the Court to begin an initiative and gather signatures to start the four-year electoral process to amend the Constitution[35]

Perla sees a rising discontent with public education and he is much encouraged by a shift in public opinion in the state on school choice. He sees this as a window of opportunity. The next step in opening up the state to school choice, in his view, is the private voucher initiative. He noted that Peter Lynch, who headed the Magellan Fund, gives $2 million a year now. Parochial schools are continuing to enroll a large number of students. Bishops, including Bernard Cardinal Law of Boston, are working with renewed interest on choice and Perla is much encouraged.[36]

California and Arizona

An issue of great significance for the future of school choice is the impact of charter schools on private and parochial schools. Bryan Bennett, the Catholic educator now working for School Futures in California where he helps to run charter schools, finds suburban dioceses not cooperative on charter schools as a form of choice. But there are exceptions. Two dioceses, in Los Angeles and Fresno, he reports, have an inner-city constituency and are supportive of charters—they can, he says, teach religion after school hours. Bennett seeks a cooperative relationship between charters and parochial schools. He has no difficulty with religious schools dropping their religious identities and becoming charter schools should they prefer that option or if financial pressures compel them to do so to keep their doors open.[37]

Monsignor Edward Ryle, of the Arizona Catholic Conference, has been active for fifteen years in health, welfare, and education policy in the state. In a state with an aggressive charter program—over 270 charter schools in operation—he says charter schools have had no impact yet on enrollment in Catholic schools. Enrollment in parochial schools is up and they are planning two new primary schools. Earlier efforts in 1993–94 to pass vouchers failed. Currently Governor Jane D. Hull and the education committee chairs of both the state House and Senate support vouchers, Ryle asserts, but there are not enough votes in the Republican-controlled chambers to pass a voucher law. One reason, he thinks, is that last year a tuition tax credit law was passed. Because it does not give a refundable credit to the poor, although he supported the tax credit, Ryle sees value in adding a refundable credit to the law in the future. Most of the poor, he says, pay no state income tax and cannot benefit from the credit.[38]

It is too early to see how the Catholic parochial systems will be affected by charter schools or by tax credits. Tax credits may help and charters may hurt enrollments so that the two may offset each other. Meanwhile the Catholics hope that each step in the direction of more school choice eventually will benefit their schools and all schools.

Conclusion

In Utah, Mormons and other non-Catholics are attending parochial schools because they are preferable to public schools to some parents. Thus, Catholics are in a difficult position. They must organize to win but if the school choice issue is too Catholic in the minds of voters they will lose out in elections and in legislatures.

The preferred solution in the late 1990s is first to form partnerships, then to establish coalitions—inside or outside the church's organizational umbrella—and to settle for half a loaf, tax credits or charters, if necessary. Indeed, the United States Catholic Conference is following this pattern. Moving beyond partnering, it announced the establishment of a diverse coalition to preserve Title One education services for all school children in February 1997, an alliance with other religious and public agencies, including the National Education Association and the American Federation of Teachers. Although the purpose of the coalition is to provide greater support for remediation funds, and *not* school choice, it serves as a learning and networking opportunity to interface with major national, educational organizations on issues involving school funding matters. Such coalition participation, however, does not mean that the church will be diverted from its major school choice goal and give up the voucher issue.

The cost of running parochial schools is so high that in some places parochial high schools cost just about as much to operate as public high schools. It is only the grammar schools that Catholics are able to run cheaply. Cardinal George in his report is clearly warning the leaders of Chicago that the church has limited funds and will not be able to continue paying for the parochial schools in the poorest parts of the city. He makes no bones about his conviction that Catholic schools are private schools rendering a public service and deserve tax support without government controls.[39]

Cardinal O'Connor reports that he thinks and prays for school choice in the middle of the night when he wakes up and cannot sleep. Asked what he prays for, he responded, "For a breakthrough." Asked what a breakthrough might look like, he said something that captures the attention of the press and the city. His concern is that the schools continue to function, that teachers work, and that parents give their support to education. According to O'Connor, inertia prevails and the mentality must be broken before something terrible happens.[40]

In no state do Catholics control the policy process. The church is not strong enough to dominate any legislature. In fact, as Professor Quade points out, the hierarchy has not mounted an effective and winning campaign for school choice anywhere. This is changing as the issue is being given higher priority, as the general climate for school choice improves, and as non-Catholics get involved. In some states, such as Wisconsin and Pennsylvania, where mature coalitions are learning the arts of partnering, archdioceses have surrendered control but not influence in the advocacy process. Catholics typically can veto what they do not like in school choice legislation, but they have to also bend to the wishes of others, accepting tax credits for example, to get along and to win.

The Evangelicals: From the Little Red Schoolhouse to the New Common School

No single group made a larger investment in public schools than Evangelicals, largely Baptist and Methodist, who helped to construct the common school in America. They are now dissatisfied with these schools and some are leaving to attend charter schools, to create private Christian schools, or to home school. In the history of the nation, schools once were created with little help from government. Today, given the high costs of education in teacher salaries and buildings, private schools are hard pressed to make ends meet. Protestants who long opposed state aid to Catholic schools are now considering asking government for tax credits or public scholarships for the parents of children attending their schools. The school choice issue is no longer a Catholic issue and Catholics played a significant role in helping Evangelicals reach this conclusion.[41]

As a group, conservative Protestants bring one concern to the school choice debate that trumps all others, namely, the issue of educational and religious liberty. As school choice is implemented, there is greater political pressure to make requirements of schools that benefit from public funds. Politicians demand accountability and standards as the price of assistance. For Evangelicals, who must deal with this question, the first principle of school choice is treasuring and preserving the independence of private and religious schools. The price of failure would be great: Turning private schools into government controlled schools is the worst possible outcome of school choice reform from an Evangelical perspective. Independence, however is not enough to run a school; there must be sufficient resources too. Securing resources without surrendering education liberty is thus the challenge ahead for Evangelical schools and the organizations and churches that support them.[42]

Entering the political fray for school choice, Evangelicals bring certain strengths and weaknesses to the table. The sheer number of conservative Protestant voters makes them potentially a mighty political force. Internal disagreements on how to approach choice weaken them. There are also organizational deficiencies. Examining how two major Evangelical organizations that favor school choice are working to achieve it begins with the Catholic connection to this Protestant conversion.[43]

The First Principle of Evangelicals

Quietly behind the scenes and also in full view before the Supreme Court of the United States, the distinguished Catholic attorney William Bentley Ball gave aid and counsel to Protestants on education issues. In the case of *Wisconsin v Yoder*[44] (1972), he represented Amish parents who refused to comply with a compulsory school attendance law, preferring that their children learn and work in the home. For almost twenty years Ball served as legal counsel for the Association of Christian Schools International (ACSI), an Evangelical professional organization with a membership of 3,700 schools in America and many overseas. He argued ten Supreme Court religion and education cases. As a senior partner in the firm of Ball, Skelly, Murren, and Connell in Harrisburg, Pennsylvania, Ball served both the Catholic and Protestant leadership for decades. Perhaps no other attorney dealt with school choice policy issues for so long a period of time on both state and federal levels and he understood and shared the concerns of both Protestants and Catholics.[45]

Conservative Christians represented by Ball had lost their customary confidence in public education. Composing about a quarter of the population, these people are torn between loyalty to the public schools they helped to create and still largely attend and other education options, including private and home schools. School choice promises to secure public funds for private education, and young families with limited financial resources need help if they are to pay tuition. However, Evangelicals fear that if they embrace school choice to relieve financial pressure, they will place the independence of private and religious schools in jeopardy. Government will regulate what it pays for.[46]

William Ball agreed that this threat is real, but he was still willing to accept tax support because he thought it is possible to prevent regulations that would compromise the independence and integrity of private schools, especially religious schools. This includes teacher certification (when it comes to credentials, Ball said, who the school hires is up to the school), collective bargaining (Ball referred to *Catholic Bishops of Chicago v NLRB*, and to his quote, "A real liberty position utterly rejects collective bargaining for private schools, especially for religious schools."), opt-out provisions (that allow students attending parochial schools not to participate in religious exercises, something he opposes), and admissions restrictions that the school may wish to impose (and should, he argues, be allowed to impose). Ball thought all these regulatory battles are winnable and that legislative victory can be preserved with vigilance.[47]

Before any voucher or tax credit legislation is passed, Ball strongly advised that statutory protection for private schools be put into state law, as is the case currently in Pennsylvania. The Pennsylvania legislation was passed because some conservative Protestant pastors were concerned that an existing state law placed private schools under the supervision of the State Secretary of Education, who had authority to determine standards for all schools in the state. They objected and came to Ball for help. He advised both Protestant and Catholic authorities that this law was a real threat to the autonomy of all private schools, including the parochial schools. The bishop in Harrisburg agreed and after consultations with his education staff asked them to meet with the Protestants to work out a common set of principles they could all support.[48] A religious education protective amendment to the education law was then passed stating the following:

> It is the policy of the Commonwealth to preserve the primary right and policy of the parent or parents, or person or persons *in loco parentis* to a child, to choose the education or training for such child. Nothing contained in this act shall empower the Commonwealth, any of its officers, agencies or subdivisions to approve the course content, faculty, staff, or disciplinary requirements of any religious school referred to in this section without the consent of said school.[49]

Ball did not object to fire and health code restrictions, to requiring that math and reading be taught, to ensuring that there be minimum academic standards, and to protecting civil rights. But, issues of pedagogy and personnel—how courses are to be taught in parochial schools and how to determine the academic qualifications for the teachers—are not in his view the business of the state.[50]

ACSI and School Choice Politics

Ball started representing ACSI twenty years ago and he continued consulting in this role until he passed away in January 1999. The president of ACSI, Dr. Paul Kienel, for these two decades until he retired as president in the mid-1990s, strongly resisted state regulations and rejected public vouchers, fearing that state regulations would come with financial assistance. Ball disagreed with Kienel on school choice and on vouchers but they concurred on regulations. In fact, Ball thought Catholics could learn a good deal from Protestant resistance to state control. Too often he observed Catholics, "going along to get along," submitting to government direction in exchange for dollars. He also warns that this Catholic "disease" may now be infecting Evangelicals.[51]

In his thinking, Ball connected the independence and autonomy of religious schools to school choice legislation. Each needs the other, he argued, to be fully effective. Having freedom from controls means little if school administrators cannot heat the classroom in the winter or admit a poor student for lack of tuition. On the other hand, if parochial schools were to be no different from public schools, dominated by the state as they are in Holland today, they would hardly be worth attending even if they were tuition free. It is in the public interest, in his view, to use tax revenues or tax credits to assist in the creation of schools over which the government exercises no control and few restraints. Ball was convinced that children well educated in the traditions of their chosen faith by such schools will be civic assets and a credit to their religion as well. ACSI and its new President, Dr. Ken Smitherman, agree, persuaded no doubt partly by the gentle persistence of Ball.[52]

Smitherman was on the Board of ACSI for twelve years before becoming president in 1996. He chaired the Legal/Legislative Committee for most of those years and opposed the position of President Kienel and ACSI on vouchers—he held the minority position. When some claimed that the ACSI member schools took no tax money, Smitherman objected, calling this a misrepresentation because in fact, he said, a substantial number of the schools did get some form of government assistance. Smitherman sees vouchers as a justice issue for the poor and for young and vulnerable families. However, he says, the organization is justifiably concerned about regulation—its members would and should support only vouchers without strings. "This is still a delicate issue." Yet Smitherman's position is that vouchers are worth the risks. Looking out his office window in Colorado Springs at a spectacular view of Pike's Peak, he said, "When you own an old car, when do you decide I am going to take the trip anyway?"[53]

In 1997, the ACSI Board adopted a formal policy on "Tuition Tax Credits and on Vouchers" making clear the boundaries it would seek in any school choice legislation:

> The Association of Christian Schools International recognizes the biblical principle of parental responsibility for the education of their children. The Association therefore supports tuition tax credits and vouchers that further parental involvement and choice in education.

ACSI supports any proposed voucher or tax credit legislation that:

1. Will allow parents to choose an education consistent with their religious beliefs; and that
2. Will not restrict a religious school in:
   - Educational philosophy,
   - Composition of the governing body,
   - Staff selection, or
   - Curriculum content and design.

Such legislation:

1. Should not regulate the school's operational policies and/or student selection or retention policies
2. Should contain language that any such tax credits or vouchers are not direct or indirect aid or assistance to the institution, but rather are a grant-in-aid to the parent(s)
3. Should require participating schools to be nondiscriminatory on the basis of race, sex, national, and ethnic origin[54]

This statement is anchored, philosophically and in the law, in the exclusive authority of parents to determine how and by whom children are to be educated. The intent is to permit aid to parents that does not entangle the government with churches or other religious bodies running schools. Preserving religious liberty, acknowledging parental authority to educate, and calling on civil government to assist in this process is its threefold purpose. Now that they have joined him on choice, Ball hopes Evangelicals will not lose their passion for educational independence or abandon long held principles of educational freedom.

ACSI's Organization and Program

Formed from a merger of several Christian school associations in 1978, ACSI is the largest Protestant school organization. Its rival, the American Association of Christian Schools (AACS), is less than half its size. Housed in a new headquarters building in Colorado Springs, next to Focus on the Family and opposite the Air Force Academy, it offers a full service range of programs to member schools for their selection and participation, including: conventions and conferences (more than 45,000 attend annually); accreditation of schools (approved by the National Council for Private School Accreditation); teacher and administrator certification (for more than 25,000); student assessment in cooperation with Harcourt Brace Educational Measurement (used by more than 200,000 students); student competitions and fairs (300,000 students participate); journals and magazines (*Christian School Education, Legal/Legislative Update, National Notes, Administrator & Teacher,*

National Listing Bulletin, and a website, acsi.org); textbooks in Bible, spelling, and math studies; preschool and kindergarten curriculum; professional consulting and personal counsel; a legal defense fund (spent about $1 million for member schools); a National Preschool Coordinator (full services for Christian preschools); insurance and financial services; and a program for Christian schools in over ninety nations.[55]

There were over 525,000 students in ACSI-USA member schools in 1997–98 (over 200,000 in other nations), which is about 1 percent of the 52.7 million K–12 children in the nation. This is a tiny number, Smitherman says, about 10 percent of the over five million in private schools. Many of these ACSI schools are operating at full capacity with waiting lists. Most if not all are non-profits. Over 1,800 ACSI schools have high schools, but only 300 have more than 100 high school students. More than 2,600 have junior high programs and 3,500 have elementary schools. Smitherman reports that ACSI is growing incrementally every year but not increasing market share, not growing as a percent of the population. He is concerned that they are simply holding their own. Seeing no aggressive entrepreneurial-like initiatives or growth efforts, with regret, he says that ACSI schools currently serve a "remnant" and with their current thinking cannot be considered a launchpad for expansive Christian education.[56]

Most of ACSI's energy goes into helping the schools cope with daily survival—helping them with information and training on how to improve administration and instruction. Too many schools in his estimation have no desire or capacity to grow. They are focused on necessary minimum tasks. Many are content to serve small select student populations. With extremely limited financial resources and facilities, they are often forced to deal only with basic education issues. Frequently, he says, struggling schools are unwilling either to merge or to partner with other nearby schools because of a fear of compromise or loss of denominational or doctrinal distinction. In some areas there has been movement to consolidate, resulting in stronger and more financially viable schools. But an even larger and more serious problem, he relates, are Christian parents who, in placing other priorities above Christian schooling, are often selfish in their thought and behavior, not willing to make the financial commitments to Christian education for their children. Smitherman reports parents who kick and scream when it comes to paying private school tuition.[57]

In 1998 there were seventy million children in the United States—from birth to age eighteen, which is the highest number ever, Smitherman observes. Many are immigrant children. Even with these high numbers, however, children make up just 28 percent of the population; they were 36 percent in 1966. In his view—and with no statistical basis—Smitherman thinks about 25 percent of the children of the nation would attend private schools if they could afford to do so. This is one reason he supports choice. In America education is a public good, like highways and defense, and he commends this, but not the means adopted, the restriction of tax support to secular government schools. Smitherman is confident that his schools do a better job educating children but he wishes more ACSI schools would consider the development of new programs with open admissions policies. By taking any students who apply to such new and innovative programs, and using selective admissions in older established Christian schools, this would, in his view, demonstrate their willingness to serve the general public. He believes that this would overcome much of the resistance to vouchers.[58]

Smitherman is offended when no one points out the enormous savings to taxpayers that private schools bring. This last year, in 1998, they had to beat back a federal effort to tax the teachers who received free tuition for their own children in private schools. He says that "we are a public asset," yet, he notes that politicians were slow to recognize that if the private schools close, the tax burden would have to increase. Smitherman sees his schools constantly on the defensive—protecting their interests and rights in hiring and employment law (hiring Christians only)—where to lose the fight is to lose your identity. ACSI is dealing with the gay issues in hiring. As an example, he noted a state of Washington USDA communication that included a requirement of no discrimination by "sexual orientation" as part of the food/milk program. Subsequently, when ACSI pursued this issue aggressively, he reported that the sexual orientation discrimination policy was rescinded. But some of the biggest issues facing schools dealt with health, safety, and environmental issues such as asbestos and zoning that are not related to First Amendment free exercise of religion concerns. Such regulatory problems are serious and even budget breaking, he says, for schools with limited funds.[59]

ACSI's Lobbying Efforts

For protective and lobbying purposes the ACSI maintains an office run by Burt Carney, Director for Legal/Legislative Issues, in Colorado Springs. In a quarterly journal, *Legal Legislative Update*, a sixteen-page glossy magazine that Carney edits, he keeps member schools up to date on school choice news, on federal and state compliance requirements, Supreme Court cases, and current special issues. He monitors legislation in all fifty states; with 2,200 active legislative bills in his files in the summer of 1998. Following twenty three issues closely, at that moment, he said most were direct threats to the independence and welfare of private Christian schools, including personnel (ACSI favors binding arbitration), honest job reference laws, religious freedom legislation, gay issues, and vans versus buses legislation (schools prefer the vans). Most of Carney's effort addresses adverse state legislation, keeping member schools up-to-date and helping them to strategize on what to do. Carney considers charter schools a real potential competitor to some members.[60]

In the recent Colorado tax credit initiative no one in Colorado contacted ACSI for assistance, Carney reports. He felt ignored. His office is also stretched with its limited resources, and he took no initiatives to contact the tax credit organizers. Carney concludes that most secular supporters of choice do not understand the concerns of religious schools that need vouchers, but will support them only if they come with sufficient protection from unwarranted regulation. Some ACSI schools welcome private vouchers and he hears reports that they are participating in the Walton/Forstmann program.[61]

ACSI is on record in favoring school choice but is sensitive on what kinds of choice to support. It strongly opposes the opt-out provision in the Milwaukee voucher law that allows students not to participate in chapel. Opt-out, Carney remarks, strikes at the heart of the identity of the Christian school. He talked to the attorneys at the Institute for Justice in Washington to see if this was central to the choice argument they were making in the Milwaukee voucher case. When they assured him that this was a marginal question and that opt-out was not likely to be required by the Court's interpretation of the Constitution, he was relieved.[62]

At the federal level ACSI maintains an office in Washington staffed by John Holmes, Director of Government Affairs, who has held this position since 1992. The traditional functions of his office are to keep schools informed of changes in federal law and policy in a newsletter "National Notes"; to lobby; and to network with other groups, including the Family Research Council (FRC), the National Association of Evangelicals (NAE), and other education associations, e.g. Council on American Private Education (CAPE). Much of his time is spent relating to the federal Office of Non-Public Education. He also works with the home-school associations when he is in agreement with them. Holmes observed that home schoolers are the "trip wire/picket fence" early warning system on adverse regulation. He is pleased that ACSI does not cry wolf, issuing false alarms, but is respected as a sober lobby.[63]

ACSI supported the recent 1998 Republican efforts to pass federal school choice legislation, the Washington, D.C. vouchers bill, and the Coverdale A + Education Savings Accounts initiative. Holmes notes it was much easier to lobby against bills in the period before 1995 when Democrats were in control of Congress. Now that the party in power looks favorably on private schools ACSI must help to create a positive agenda, something with which they have little experience. There is no clear school choice leader in Washington, he complains, and school choice groups tend to compete for money from their constituencies by claiming credit for political successes. ACSI as a membership organization does not have to raise money with issue advocacy and this is an advantage and makes for better relations in Washington with other lobbies and with the government. In summary, without legislative experience or leaders to follow, and plagued by fund-raising induced factionalism, there are plenty of reasons for Holmes to anticipate limited legislative success in Washington.[64]

ACSI Contributions to School Choice

During the Proposition 174 voucher battle in California in 1991–92, ACSI in the early going helped to mount the campaign. The organization conducted a survey of all its 732 (800 in 1998) schools in the state—35 percent responded—and 77 percent supported the initiative, most of them "strongly." William Ball worked closely on the wording of the initiative and Burt Carney sat in on planning meetings as an observer/participant to speak on behalf of Christian school interests. But in the weeks before the election ACSI pulled out declaring that it did not support the initiative. In fact, ACSI was divided on the issue and the board opted to remain neutral. Waffling like this was not good for the organization's credibility. This will not likely happen again under the current leadership that cautiously backs vouchers.[65]

How effective is ACSI support for the school choice movement? At the moment ACSI by its own admission is not a full-partner legislative insider when it comes to positive school choice legislation and is not offering answers to general education issues or problems. However, it does have a distinct and positive role in standing up for religious liberty and school autonomy. This contribution will be increasingly important as more school choice laws are passed and governments seize this as an opportunity to increase regulation of private schools in the name of standards and accountability. The lobbying of ACSI at the state level is almost entirely protective in nature. This is its strength and its limitation. But this could change if the organization chose to hire staff to work directly or indirectly on behalf of state school choice measures, something they have not done. This may be a matter of how the leadership chooses to expend scarce resources.

There are two other factors that weaken the organization in this respect. First, member schools are divided on school choice. A number oppose vouchers fearing regulation. Forging unity within ACSI schools on what choice measures to back will be hard to do. Second, and perhaps even more difficult to overcome, is the inertia that Smitherman addressed in his comments. It may well be that ACSI schools lack the strength to mount a major policy reform effort. To change, it must take a different approach not only to public policy but also to how they start and maintain schools.

To move things dramatically, to gain in education market share in the United States, and to lobby state governments effectively, something new is needed from outside of ACSI. Two entrepreneurial possibilities present themselves. First, Christian schools could try a for-profit school model that would encourage the creation of more schools. Second, an Evangelical version of John Walton or a team of entrepreneurs could appear, ready to move aggressively in promoting Christian schools and school choice legislation. Without some breakthrough energy ACSI will benefit or suffer from the school choice successes and failures of others. For the foreseeable future, efforts to leverage school choice will not depend heavily on what ACSI does or does not do. The one exception to this generalization is the guardianship role of ACSI that resists regulation as choice advances.

Focus on the Family and School Choice Politics

Evangelicals and their organizations alarm the National Education Association (NEA) and others who oppose school choice. William Ball for many years worked closely with the Pennsylvania Family Institute (PFI) in Harrisburg, a state-based Family Policy Council with close ties to Focus on the Family (FOTF) and Dr. James Dobson. PFI is headed by Michael Geer and Thomas J. Shaheen, both M.A. graduates of the School of Public Policy, Regent University, Virginia Beach, whose Chancellor is Pat Robertson. In its recent research publication, *The Real Story Behind 'Paycheck Protection,'* the NEA called the conservative Evangelicals the "heart" of the school choice movement, pumping resources and grassroots mobilizing efforts into legislation and elections.[66] Writing about Dobson, this report commented:

> Dr. James Dobson has lobbied Washington more powerfully than any single person of organization on the religious right today and is arguably the most respected man in the social conservative movement. Dobson is president of Focus on the Family, the largest and strongest Religious Right organization both financially and in terms of its grassroots strength and impact. He has the media arm, the grassroots organization, and the lobbying arm to exert his influence.[67]

The list of FOTF organizational assets and activities in 1996 is long, including: annual income well in excess of $100 million, over six million circulation for its print magazines and a similar number listening to its daily radio show, over seventy-eight million items published yearly, multiple conferences, a public policy magazine and research staff, ties to state Family Policy Councils, and a close relationship to the Family Research Council (FRC) in Washington D.C., headed by Gary Bauer until 1999 (he left FRC to run for the Republican presidential nomination). Republican politicians seeking the presidency court Dobson's favor and he is a thorn in the side of legislators who compromise his agenda, not hesitating to attack them behind closed doors and on occasion in public. This mild-mannered psychologist has a significant national political role, and as the NEA points out in its attack on him, they are one of his favorite targets.[68]

Today conservative Protestants with Dobson in a leadership role have begun a search for schools they can once again wholeheartedly support. Critical of public education and its direction, FOTF is in the midst of this search. In principle, Focus supports parental choice in education and is doing much on its behalf, but it has not fully resolved how this is best implemented. Evangelical parents are active in every education reform arena—in public schools, charter schools, private schools, Christian schools, home schools, in efforts to defund public education, and in combinations of all of these. There is no consensus among Evangelicals on how to solve education problems. Even school choice is debated. How will FOTF lead an education reform effort when the constituency it represents is so divided? This is a difficult strategic question that FOTF is attempting to resolve.[69]

First, as a Christian organization, FOTF seeks to base its public policy positions on principles compatible with its theology. The NEA faults Focus for this, arguing that Dobson rejects the separation of church and state and wants a "blending of religion, politics, and government" that is a "Christian Nationalism." No effort is made by the NEA to distinguish between a policy Focus supports and argues for on secular terms and its own theological reasons for doing so. This problem of what kind of public philosophy to adopt on education reform, to help to unify its constituency, is now being addressed.[70]

Second, there is substantial agreement on the problems—declining academic performance, disorder and violence, alienation from religion, lack of morality-based curriculum, centralized control, and high costs. FOTF will continue to bear down on the negative—on what is wrong—with the result that education issues will receive attention. The problems tend to unite any constituency, which helps to strengthen the FOTF base. However, this is more than a top-down process. The author asked Michael Geer and Tom Shaheen at PFI, "What priority are your supporters giving to education issues in their communications to PFI?" Their answer was that 90 percent of the letters and calls they receive from people in Pennsylvania were about education. In response to this overwhelming parental concern PFI started a bimonthly magazine, *Pennsylvania Families & Schools.* Over time FOTF and PFI will likely devote more and more resources to education reform—as a problem to be addressed—because people will demand it.[71]

Third, FOTF as a relatively broad-based organization is slow to side with one reform strategy or another, preferring an open approach that tries most if not all of the available options, including reforming public education, charter schools, public and private vouchers, tax credits, promoting Christian schools, and home schooling. This approach offends the fewest number of supporters. It also has other advantages. For example, it exploits opportunities where and when they arise, but it also weakens the effectiveness of Focus reform efforts. Focus generally follows the initiatives of others who are setting agendas at the state level, an issue not yet addressed.[72]

Fourth, FOTF will over time begin to have a menu of reform preferences, perhaps choosing some and rejecting others, as some options prove their ineffectiveness and others show more promise of success. How long this process will take is questionable and depends on leadership choices and on circumstances related both to schools, the choices of parents, and the politics of education reform. If public schools degenerate more quickly, decisions will have to be made sooner; if Evangelicals opt for private schools, funding questions will accelerate; if legislatures resist choice laws, home schooling will be more attractive; and if charter schools work well, they may be the preferred option. Much has yet to be decided in this highly fluid context by FOTF and by most Evangelical parents.[73]

Fifth, FOTF is working to sort this all out in the wider context of all its other family-related concerns. At issue is the relative importance of school reform. Catholic bishops, for example, have listed school choice as a policy preference for years but because of political defeats and other matters of concern, they have often placed it on the back burner to simmer rather come to a boil. How important is education to FOTF? How much time and money is devoted to it by Focus? It may well be that as education moves up the national agenda, assuming more importance to political parties, it will appear more prominently in FOTF activities as well.[74]

As the solid consensus in support of public education as American's have known it disintegrates, as it will, and before its replacement arrives, Evangelicals have adopted an interim coping strategy that sets the context for an examination of the FOTF role in school choice. This strategy is the following:

- Secure free exercise of religion in public schools
- Exert influence in schools and on school boards
- Protect the autonomy of home schools and private schools
- Provide resources for an alternative to public schools
- Make room for combinations of public, private, and home schools[75]

In broader terms this five-part program, widely accepted among Evangelicals, includes, first, finding a refuge under the Constitution for religious expression in public schools; second, exercising political muscle and powers of persuasion in public debates and elections; and third, crafting new public policies that provide education alternatives for parents. Defending rights came early on, in court cases like *Board of Education v Mergens* (1990) but school board battles and struggles over curriculum in the 1990s, and school choice is looming as a likely Evangelical priority for the first millennial decade.[76]

Education reform activity is necessary for Focus because of its mission. Schooling is so central to family and religion that for it to decline significantly poses immediate and long-term threats. But the critical question remains: "How will FOTF lead a school choice education reform effort when the constituency it represents is so divided?" This requires a five-part answer, which was outlined above.

Constructing a School Choice Public Philosophy

The following is a summarized description of the three-page FOTF philosophy of education policy statement adopted in 1996 by the executive cabinet:

- General Principles—God created children with the rational ability to search for truth and to grow in virtue. Education must help children to do both. Parents are the primary educators.
- Choice in Education—education policy must respect the great variety of parental world-view perspectives, making room for parents to choose how they wish to see their children educated in public, private, or home schools. A Christian ethic requires that a policy that is built on pluralism, choice, and competition will look after the needs of all children, especially the poor and those with special needs.
- Parents and Educators—there is a hierarchy of responsibility for instruction that begins first with parents, then teachers, and ends with local school boards. Teachers, after parents, are to be commended for their role in teaching "principles of decency and truth."
- Public Schools and Charter Schools—public schools will continue to educate most children, but this should be done without help or interference from Washington, therefore, the Department of Education should be discontinued. State controls should be reduced, measurable standards of excellence should be maintained, and unions that are self-serving resisted. Voluntary religious expression by students ought to be allowed and students taught to respect America's religious heritage. Charter schools are a positive development, especially those that allow individuals and groups who are granted a charter to ground a school on a particular educational philosophy.
- Private Schools and Home Schooling—excellent private schools are an invaluable alternative and by their example encourage improvement in all schools. Christian schools made up of committed teachers and like-minded students provide role models and inspiration for each other.

Home schools make possible an education shaped by the needs of the individual child. Evaluation and testing of home schooled children has proven that they can learn as much or more than other children. Non-government schools must be protected from government regulations threatening their well-being.

- The Role of Focus on the Family in Education Policy—the organization must encourage school choice as the best way to help all schools and to minimize conflicts in education that are exacerbated by forcing parents to place their children in educational programs they abhor. Rigorous academics, moral character, and respect for parents and religious liberty are necessary for schools. Charter schools, private schools, and home schools will be promoted against the opposition of those who would argue for a one-size-fits-all-system.[77]

The original FOTF statement as a whole has some inherent tensions because it stresses choice and unity. First, it builds upon a respect for variety calling for a new pluralism in education. This includes giving room for the religious to express themselves within public schools and making it more possible for any and all parents to opt out of public schools. This is choice. Second, it asks for higher academic standards and a consistency of moral purpose to prepare young citizens for their future duties. The latter is the opposite of pluralism and presumes consensus on what is to be taught. This is unity. One way to reconcile this tension is to interpret it as saying, "Give us the quality public school we can embrace or the chance to leave and make our own." This is an improve-it or leave-it strategy. Another view is to see this as a call for a multifront educational war. "We will fight for religious freedom and standards in public schools, to preserve them as best we can for the good of the nation; and at the same time we will seek refuge for a remnant minority in private and home schools."

For the individual parent looking for the best school at a reasonable cost the first interpretation makes sense—"We will start with the public school and move on if necessary." For the public policy maker, which FOTF aspires to be, the second position is a realistic strategy. Realistic because it recognizes the semi-permanence of public schools and wants Christians to be "salt and light" for that context, preserving these schools from destruction. Realistic because it knows that once public schools reach certain levels of decay considered intolerable, Christian parents will be among the first not to send their children to them.

Conspicuously absent from the Focus statement is any mention of school choice preferences, such as tax credits or vouchers. There is explicit support for charter schools. Only indirectly are public vouchers alluded to when providing for the poor and those with special education needs is promised. A simple tax credit system that did not guarantee an education to the disadvantaged or a pure market-based system would appear to be ruled out by this statement, though in general the benefits of competition are extolled. Strategies for adopting school choice are also missing. School choice, it states, will be promoted by FOTH with these ends in mind, but nothing more is said. One clue as to why the nuts and bolts of school choice implementation are neglected, besides the fact that this was meant to be a statement of principles, is the explicit comment at the end. "We recognize the controversial nature of these policies, but we promote them because we believe they serve the best interests of children." Focus backed school choice in Minnesota and Pennsylvania, and it is willing to lose support from constituents who think Focus is too critical of public schools. But vouchers are divisive, so this may partly explain their omission from this statement of principles, though even Focus leadership supports them at least for the poor and defends their use against opponents who fear government regulation. It must be said that Focus supports vouchers as one of several possible school choice options.[78]

Defending What Is Normal, Defining What Is Not

FOTF takes on a breadth of education issues: behavior modification without parental consent, sex education contrary to parental beliefs, reading programs that pretend to use phonics but do not, school boards that fail to hold school administrators accountable, school health clinics that are intrusive, teaching subversive of marriage and family, illegitimate federal controls, school reform fads, NEA politics and influence, lack of measurable standards, and much more. Examples of failing education practices are highlighted constantly and contrasted with what Focus considers normal.[79]

It is normal, FOTF urges, to have discipline and order in the classroom—it is not appropriate for the school to attempt to produce an in-depth adjustment of the thinking and conduct of students using modern psychological techniques. It is proper to teach sexual biology and normative standards of sexual conduct—it is not acceptable to promote adultery or homosexual behavior. Schools must teach reading—but not by methods that can be shown not to work. Elected school boards are necessary—but not if they are simply a rubber stamp for the school administrators. It is good for schools to require immunizations and to test hearing—however, health care is a parental responsibility. Marriage and family are to be promoted—but not redefined, as some would wish to include, for example, friends. Washington may encourage education by, for example, tax credits but, should not be paying for school construction. Changing programs is to be expected—but all changes should be reviewed and discontinued if they do not work. Schools should have ways to measure learning—but setting standards is primarily a local school responsibility.[80]

Defending what is normal and defining what is not is considered by Focus an art or discipline easily and quickly lost if it is not constantly exercised. All its publications ask parents to make judgments on how their children are being or should be educated. There is a constant ferment of debate and controversy stimulated by its publications. Some of this is strongly hostile to the status quo. Much is not. Recommended replacements for current programs and practices keep Focus publications from becoming too bitter or negative. They do this partly by publishing positive materials for use by parents and schools and by looking for good news in public schools or in politics. This balance is designed to encourage hope and activism. FRC publishes *Let Freedom Ring: A Basic Outline of American History* and *Home Remedies: Reading Lists and Curriculum Aids to Promote Your Child's Educational Well-being.* A bimonthly journal of FOTF, *Teachers in Focus,* for example, celebrates good programs in public schools and gives helpful advice on how to protect students on the Internet. But even the positive models are promoted as antidotes or remedies to problem-ridden systems. There is an assumption at Focus that schools must be watched constantly.[81]

At root the strategy of FOTF is to keep parents intelligently and independently active in the education process at home and in the community. They do not want to cede control of education to the experts. By continuing to build up parents as an independent force they hope parents eventually will demand school choice that meets their needs and in the short term will work to improve schools. The opposite of parent-controlled education and local school administration is a centralized system imposed by government. FRC titles its collection of essays responding to the education portion of the 1997 State of the Union address, *Bill Clinton, Superintendent: Micro-Managing Schools From Washington.* Reform of education in the United States will be an arduous process, but James Dobson and his supporters want change, as it comes, to be directed by the families directly involved and by those politicians and educators they trust, not by the current education leadership or by Washington.[82]

Staying Flexible and Experimenting with Change

Focus in 1998 has no preferred plan for school choice, no commitment to one way of doing it, but it does strongly support charter schools, calling them an excellent way to improve public education. In Colorado, for example, Thomas H. McMillan, President of the Rocky Mountain Family Council, related to Focus on the Family, considers charters to be the form of choice most Evangelicals in the state are interested in at the moment, more than tax credits, vouchers, or home schooling. Focus publishes information on how to start charter schools and holds up the liberal Arizona charter school legislation as a model for good charter legislation—one that gives the most room for starting and maintaining charter schools that are unlike other public schools, and one that entails the most autonomy.[83]

Yet each state has its own dynamics, its own preferred school choice solutions, that the local Focus organization tends to reflect, which do not conform to some central directive from Colorado Springs. Michael Geer of the Pennsylvania Family Institute supports vouchers, as do other local reformers, and works closely with Catholic initiatives. Tom Pritchard of the Minnesota Family Council finds most Evangelicals in his state are ignorant of charter schools or vouchers. He strongly supported the tax credit bill put forward by former Governor Arne Carlson, generating calls and letters from Focus people on behalf of the legislation, and he met with individual legislators. But, Pritchard observed it was easier to mobilize the grass roots to fight threats than to back a positive plan. Home school leadership supported the bill too, and, in his opinion, they were the most effective lobbying force for tax credits.[84]

On the other hand, FRC is somewhat divided on solutions, with some staff favoring vouchers at least for the poor and others not liking them at all, preferring tax credits. Bob Morrison is the Senior Director for Domestic Policy, overseeing education. Jennifer Marshall has served as Education Policy Analyst since 1995. In 1996, the FRC agenda concentrated on building connections in Washington and with organizations outside the beltway to have a united front with Congress, but Marshall soon found this left too little time for work on legislation and other pro-family organizations. This included Concerned Women for America (CWA), the Christian Coalition, Eagle Forum, and Traditional Values Coalition groups that at that time lacked staff in Washington for substantial education policy work. FRC shifted tactics in 1997 from coalition building to two policy issues, education savings accounts and testing, favoring the accounts and resisting federal examinations. These two issues, combined with the duty to provide constituent education services, "ran them ragged." Marshall reports that they also resulted in the building of good working relationships and the beginnings of an effective education coalition with a variety of groups.[85]

Marshall gets twenty to thirty phone calls a week on education issues. Her biggest communication tool for FRC education issues is a weekly fax alert that goes out to 5,000 people and includes action items. She also uses press releases and talk radio. Allies in the press include Bob Holland of the *Richmond Times Dispatch*, Matthew Robinson, *Investors Business Daily*, and numerous talk show hosts. Education issues are increasing in importance at FRC and the number of FRC supporters drawn by education is growing.

The education savings account and tax credits are Marshall's preferred way to win new supporters for school choice from among soccer moms.[86]

In 1999 FRC engaged in a coalition effort called EXPECT (Excellence for Parents, Children, and Teachers), involving some thirty reform-minded groups. The coalition also developed a close working relationship with members of the House Education and the Workforce Committee, including Chairman Bill Goodling. The impetus for forming this coalition is the major opportunity afforded by the reauthorization of the Elementary and Secondary Education Act as well as the expiration of Goals 2000. In addition, the EXPECT coalition supports education savings accounts and will likely, Marshall reports, make a statement on parental choice, which she hopes will be useful for state debates. This EXPECT coalition occupied a significant amount of Marshall's time, and, in her view, it constituted a great opportunity to facilitate education reforms and school choice. [87]

On a deeper level FRC is providing its supporters with a critical interpretation of the history of public education together with a new definition of what "public" once meant and, it argues, should once again mean. Public once meant all schools that served the public, most of which were not government operated or even tax supported. Charles Leslie Glenn of Boston University makes this case in the fall 1998 FRC *Family Policy* magazine.[88]

Some efforts are being made to help the Family Policy Councils to coordinate and to share information. FRC had a several day conference on education reform with FOTF and key state councils. There is a desire to concentrate resources in states where school choice initiatives are most promising, but not much progress has been made on this front. Charter schools continue to be viewed as good first steps toward full school choice. Looking ahead, FRC is planning to increase the number of staff dealing with education policy and school choice, hiring at least one additional person in 1999.[89]

Statecraft: Discovering the Right and the Doable

At Focus, Dr. Perry Glanzer, the education and religious liberty analyst for legislative matters, says the number one reason for lack of support for school choice by pastors and parents is a lack of vision for what education can and should be. School prayer (he does not support teacher led prayer in public schools), even when done voluntarily by students, does not come close, he notes, to a mature Christian understanding of education. Evangelicals need a vision for comprehensive Christian curriculums, Glanzer argues, to see the need to fight for choice alternatives free of statist control. Until they do, he thinks most conservative Christians will continue mistakenly to tolerate public schools without considering carefully what needs to be done to supple-

ment what their children receive in public schools, or to reform those
schools, or to go elsewhere.[90]

Glanzer finds coalition building difficult. Free market conservatives and
social conservatives still do not have good working relationships. His phone
calls are not always returned. Philosophically, Glanzer says Focus is committed to parental choice as the cornerstone of education policy and leveraging
choice is the number one priority of the Focus education department. The
three elements of his strategy are (a) to defend and articulate the core principle of choice to help people to understand it (b) to encourage others to create
alternative schools and (c) to reduce barriers to choice by recommending
new laws and policies friendly to choice. Most of his work is pre-political,
laying foundations for a sustained effort to pursue school choice that he believes will come later.[91]

Glanzer is most effective as a theorist who critiques the merits of reforms.
He does engage in some lobbying, for example, in Colorado and Tennessee,
where he testified before legislators on school choice laws. He will also strategize about how best to pass school choice laws using Focus or state affiliate
broadcast and mailing resources. But he is not a policy designer who pushes
specific legislation or forges ground-level state coalitions. In fact, Focus does
not have anyone tasked full-time with helping to get legislation passed. That
role is handled by FRC in Washington or by State Policy Councils, with
some assistance from Focus. On a theoretical level Focus and Glanzer have
been slow to select one reform over another. This strategy has its merits because it leaves them flexible, but it also means that they tend to follow the
lead of others in specific states. However, this will likely change as the merits
and political viability of different reforms become clearer and Focus grows
in its leadership role.[92]

Clearly FOTF wants to give charter schools a chance. They are closest to
reconstituting the public schools of the past where for generations Evangelicals felt at home. They provide full per student tuition, and although full
building and other capital costs are not covered, this is thought to be a small
price to pay for being able to help form a school with an acceptable education program. This option also is more politically viable than alternatives
that risk intense opposition from unions. But Focus is fully aware that many
Evangelical parents, some now and more later, will find charter schools insufficient for their needs, preferring a robust Christian education. For them,
tax credits, vouchers, home schooling, or some combination of the three will
be the answer. Once these programs begin, such as those in Minnesota, Arizona, Wisconsin, and Ohio on a small scale today, there will be pressure to
expand them and to provide more money to cover more children.

It is difficult to imagine pressure for school choice diminishing in the long
run. Actions that reflect evangelical discontent combined with the larger
movement that includes Catholics appear to be gradually building up speed.

Focus has positioned itself to move ahead, but not too far ahead of this un-folding process. This means that FOTF will continue to advocate all options, looking for evidence that one or the other solutions is preferred and work-able. Within the context of school choice this is a pragmatic approach.

Mobilizing Evangelicals: Making Things Happen

Nothing is more frustrating to activists than the slow pace of change. One explanation for the relatively weak school choice lobbying efforts by FOTF, contrasted with its larger school choice education and information efforts through its publications and media and given its tremendous resources and potential, is that it is not a single-issue organization. Evangelicals like Catho-lics have broad social public policy agendas and school choice gets lost in the middle with few resources expended on its behalf. Education is simply not at the top of the list for either group.[93]

Annually James Dobson publishes for his constituents a list of the "sig-nificant family-related developments and events occurring during the previ-ous year." In early 1998 he put the most "encouraging" and "discouraging" in two lists of ten with each story ranked from one to ten with number one being the most important. For 1997, the most welcome event was the Prom-ise Keepers "Stand in the Gap" rally in Washington, which brought, he ob-served, more than one million men to the capital for a non-political moment of spiritual renewal. The most discouraging event was President Clinton's veto of the bill to ban partial birth abortions. Significantly, on both lists, number ten dealt with school choice: the passage of the education tax credits law in Minnesota, which he lauded, and state court decisions adverse to voucher programs in Milwaukee and Cleveland, which he condemned. In 1997, school choice made Dobson's top ten lists for good and bad news. The good news for school choice is that it made the list; the bad news is that it was number ten.[94]

Why is school choice in 1997 less important for Dobson than other issues, including pornography, most favored nation trade status for China, the de-cline of the U.S. military, curbs on religious expression, defense of marriage legislation, gay rights, and tax credits, to name some he listed? He might argue that school choice news was more minor than major, small steps in a long process. However, there is strong evidence that this is where Dobson places school choice on his list of priorities. Focus spends little on education policy per se in its internal system. More money and effort, it would appear, goes to nurture present public school teachers then to change the system.

Focus does not have an education policy journal like the Pennsylvania Family Institute. This could be a matter of tactics—let the states handle the practicalities of education reform because this is a state issue. But there is no obvious reason why Focus could not do both and have an education reform magazine issued from Colorado Springs. There is no full-time education reform person on staff either; education policy is only one of the many hats that Perry Glanzer wears. Until there is more budget for education policy and a more aggressive effort launched, Focus is much more in a "seeding" mode, helping people to get used to the idea of school choice by talking about it, gradually mobilizing people by education efforts. Even FRC was understaffed on this issue up until 1999, with just one person, Jennifer Marshall, dealing full time with education reform.[95]

There are many other reasons why FOTF is not engaged extensively in the political heavy lifting so necessary to bring change:

- The non-profit status of Focus limits direct political efforts. Four percent of its budget goes for public policy-related activities, including research and publications), making them a secondary concern and difficult to pursue.
- Fighting high profile battles that unite conservative Christians is good for an organization—dealing with hotly controversial matters that divide even close families, some opting for home schools and others for the local public school, is problematic and even threatening.
- Choice at Focus advocates every education option, including maintaining quality public schools. This broad perspective may be good and necessary for the long haul but it does not invite swift action by a unified constituency.
- Focus has no clearly worked out strategy to bring choice, no preferred choice option or a plan to get it. Instead it is opportunistic in its approach, helping out where and when there are initiatives made by others.
- Stirring up education unions is a daunting prospect too. However, focus has supported "paycheck protection" in California and written critically of union policies to its constituency, and it has chosen to use some funds for school choice broadcasts and mailings in specific states.
- If getting government money for private education invites regulation, many Focus supporters ask, why do it? This concern to protect the independence of private education adds significant restraint to the Focus approach to choice, a reason for caution widely held by Evangelicals.
- Additionally, FOTF does not have solid ties with free-market /libertarian groups or with the national Catholic hierarchy. It tends to be isolated from the main school choice players, although this may be changing.
- Lastly, there may be a generational issue. Dobson grew up in a period when Evangelicals were comfortable in public schools. His generation

does not grasp in a visceral way the problems faced by young parents today.

In short, Focus now embraces school choice in principle and in its rhetoric, assisting some in campaigns, but it holds back on a full-scale investment to make it happen. The main reason for this is almost certainly the competition with other family concerns. Evangelicals, like Catholics, care about a great many issues. Given this constraint and others (IRS restrictions and budget constraints also play a role), what might occur inside or outside of Focus to speed up more active engagement?

Inside Focus, there could be more aggressive leadership by Dobson; or perhaps Dobson's successor at Focus, when one arrives and if he or she is a younger person with school-aged children will rearrange priorities. Outside Focus, a Republican president with a strong education choice agenda would provide initiatives that FOTF could join, especially if backed by a Republican Congress. Without this political leadership from the top it is hard to see Focus changing fast. Action by governors in Florida, Texas, New Mexico, or Pennsylvania would also help. Another possibility is simply more parental pressure from below, much like what happened in Pennsylvania; this factor, which will vary from state to state, is influenced by the condition, perceived and real, of public education. At some point Focus could decide that public schools are simply not a healthy option for Christian children or any children. Other organizations may also come into play, such as the home schoolers, ACSI, and state and national advocacy groups, encouraging action by Focus.

At present FOTF is not an "800-pound" school choice gorilla that some of its opponents think it is. Its influence on the political process today is helpful in some states, such as Minnesota, Pennsylvania, Indiana, Illinois, and Texas, but it is marginal in most others. Focus does not take the lead on school choice in any state. It plays a supporting role. The future is a different story altogether. Focus is helping to lay a foundation for creative thought and effort by Evangelicals by keeping them from being assimilated into the general culture produced in public schools. By labeling public education such a big problem across a wide range of issues Focus contributes greatly in the long run to school choice. When will Focus's cry of alarm become a call to arms? When that day comes, millions will likely hear it because the issues are so intense and Focus is closely tied to its supporters who are parents with children.[96]

Meanwhile, Focus is working to set the framework for all school reform discussion. School choice—the new pluralism—constitutes its vehicle of choice as an instrument both moderate in methods and yet true to American revolutionary traditions.[97]

Regional and Local Evangelical Responses and Considerations

Why is school choice so weak in southern states where many Evangelicals live? Professor James Carper of the University of South Carolina, a specialist in education history who has written on private Christian schools, responds that "first, there is real concern over regulation, 'the Grove City College mentality'—and for that reason some prefer tax credits." Conservative grass roots Christians in the south are ambivalent on school choice. The pressure for standards and accountability scare southerners hugely, he said, because they could be "the death knell of private schools."[98]

Carper suggested these reasons in addition:

- Public education in the South started fifty to a hundred years behind the North. It is still under construction in much of the South along with the rest of the physical and social infrastructure so necessary to attract business. It is perhaps fifty years too early, he thought, for disappointment with public schools to be substantial and sufficient to turn into a movement for school choice.
- Much of the South is small town or rural where community schools are centers of social activity—Friday night football. In the rural South student numbers and financial resources do not appear to justify having more schools than one per community.
- Private schools are stigmatized as elitist or racist because of the history of desegregation—they are suspect.
- Integrated public schools are "the" victory of the civil rights movement and blacks especially will be slow to abandon them.
- Most of the South does not have the same degree of difficulty with disorder and collapsed standards that schools in large northern cities have.
- There are few Catholic schools in the South—e.g. in Columbia, South Carolina, in a metro area of 450,000, there are only four Catholic grammar schools and one high school. Only Louisiana has substantial numbers of Catholics and some school choice. Florida, where there is considerable school choice activity, is atypical of the South.

There is growing Protestant concern with secularization in the South. This helps to explain, Carper noted, the growing number of home schoolers and private Christian schools in the region. But it will be many years, he thinks, before school choice reaches the southern political agenda.[99]

On the opposite side of the country, in San Diego, pressures for choice are more than offset by difficulties in building private schools. The Foothills Christian Fellowship, a large independent Evangelical church started two schools K–12, bought a building, and plans to start another school K–8.

Reverend Mark Hoffman, senior pastor, reports that the single biggest external obstacle deterring most churches from running schools are problems securing facilities—neighbors complain, there are lawsuits, and zoning board opposition. The cry heard when a church proposes a school is "NIMBY," not in my backyard.[100]

To cope with this pressure Hoffman says churches need to have friends in civic positions just to survive—he strongly encourages his church members to run for local office and some have. His city's general master plan for development omitted any references to churches, and he helped to get this changed so that it was church friendly. Hoffman concludes that Christians who want schools need to be organized and to build majorities. He is convinced, however, that in 1998 the trend in San Diego is for less and not more Christian education. Pastors think schools cost too much money, are damaging to the church's facility if it is used, and simply cause too much trouble—the tail ends up wagging the dog, as the church ends up serving the school.

Hoffman, who has been active in church ministry for over twenty years, disagrees strongly with this pessimistic assessment of Christian education by his peers. He thinks there is no alternative because he sees public schools undermining everything he does with the young. His efforts at mentoring, retreats, classes, conferences, summer programs, and sports, sponsored by the church for the youth in the last decades, were all inadequate, he states, given the destructive power of public schools. "We lose their minds and emotion-based programs are no substitute for learning consistent with Christian teaching." So he supports Christian schools. "Government schools will not teach morals and cannot teach spirituality." Although he will not say this publicly, he considers public education "child abuse."[101]

Hoffman supports school choice. His keenest disappointment is with fellow churchmen and not with politicians. "Pastors have had a hard time going beyond church services measured in numbers to a Kingdom focus. We count people in the pew. Focused on church growth we make no commitment to changing the culture." Hoffman's favorite Biblical passage expressing the scorn he feels for churches without education vision and commitment is Ezekiel 13:4: "Your prophets, Oh Israel, are like jackals among ruins." He considers public schools in a condition of total collapse morally and in bad shape pedagogically, and church leaders are failing to respond.[102]

Many Evangelicals in San Diego agree with Reverend Hoffman, that churches and laity are not mobilized on education issues or on school choice. Most churches do not want the headaches and financial burden. Representative Steve Baldwin (R) California Assemblyman from the 77th District, and past chairman of the Education Committee (1995–96), concurs. He is a young social/economic conservative who attends Hoffman's church. Baldwin reports that Protestants are more active in each election cycle. But for the big picture in California, he sees only small pockets of support for school choice, not a strong coalition—there are few pastors, little business support, no civil rights leaders, no grassroots mobilization, and few Asians or Hispanics ready to work for school choice, which he supports.[103]

The South and the West, to conclude, have a strong Evangelical presence yet each for very different reasons are not ripe targets for choice. In one the need is not evident to most residents and in the other the costs are considered too high. It may well be that the form school choice will take in both regions will be charter schools.

Evangelicals and School Choice Politics Today: Conclusion

School choice is just beginning to show up on the political radar screens but it is not yet, apparently, a hot-button issue for Evangelicals. A good litmus test for just how important conservative Christian advocates consider this issue to be is its prominence in voter mobilization literature put out before elections. In a recent opinion article critical of Republicans and Democrats published in the *New York Times,* Randy Tate, executive director of the Christian Coalition, weighed in on school choice. Tate said, "If President Clinton signs school choice legislation into law in the next two years, it would be a vindication of conservative ideology, as it was when he signed welfare reform, the balanced budget and the $500-a-child tax cut." He faulted Republicans for not making choice a visible part of the 1998 campaign and Democrats for opposing it. Ironically, the Christian Coalition, in its 1998 National Survey of Christian Voters completed just before the election, made education its number two issue just behind number one, key moral issues, yet left out school choice altogether in the list of four education issues. The Coalition asked about condoms, abortions, homosexuality, and prayer in the survey—but said not a word about school choice.[104]

In sheer political terms what is missing from Evangelical social policy circles is an organization that makes school choice its sole reason for being. There is nothing like the Milton and Rose Friedman Foundation, the American Education Reform Foundation, or CEO America, for Evangelicals. ACSI is a broad-based professional organization and has too much on its plate to be effective. FOTF for all of its strengths and visibility has the same problem. FRC is Washington based, has a large agenda, and deals with federal legislation and not state politics where most of the action is. Family Policy Councils can be useful, as Pennsylvania demonstrates, but something more is needed if Evangelicals are to be widely effective in the political process. School choice politics moves very rapidly as the political winds blow in and out of a city and state. What is needed is a national organization that operates in states as flexibly as possible. This may require action by existing structures or some new effort by people of means and vision.

In the meantime, whether or not such an organization springs into existence, Evangelicals appear to be stronger than they are in the policy process. The press gravitates to "Religious Right" leaders and inflates their significance to add conflict and entertainment value to stories. Opponents make them their favorite people to hate and use them to raise money in fund raising letters. Breaking these patterns will not be easy but Evangelicals could learn from the example of people who keep a low profile in politics but carry big sticks. People like John Walton, who is hardly visible, but whose presence is felt through the programs he puts in place and the political battles he fights.

Conclusions

Leadership and structural weaknesses dominate this discussion of religion and school choice politics. Catholic and Evangelical schools exist in large numbers but the churches and organizations that support them have other concerns besides education. As a result, the critical funding questions that underlie the school choice debate tend to be ignored. The Task Force report in Chicago was an effort to address this problem, to give more priority to educating children. Evangelicals are also waking up and giving at least some attention to school choice in their rhetoric, as the example of James Dobson makes clear, and they are beginning to participate in state and local campaigns and in Washington. However, in the future, Evangelicals and Catholics will have to play larger roles in school choice campaigns, if for no other reason than the fact that they operate schools. Their effectiveness will depend on the choices leadership make—assigning higher priority to education; on coalition building, partnering with others for change; on keeping flexible on goals and tactics, willing to take half steps; on achieving common proposals, focusing on what to achieve; on mobilizing the grass roots, seeking the advice and assistance of parents; and lastly, on the strength of the school choice advocacy organizations they help to create.

Notes

1. Robert Booth Fowler and Allen D. Hertzke, *Religion and Politics in America* (Boulder, CO: Westview Press, 1995), 12.

2. John W. Kingdon, *Agendas, Alternatives, and Public Policies* (New York: HarperCollins College Publishers, 1995).

3. Specifically there are 8,223 Catholic schools in the United States. They serve

a population of 2,648,859 students. The elementary distribution is 31.3 percent in urban areas, 13.4 percent in inner cities, 32 percent in the suburbs and 23.3 percent in rural locations. Secondary schools are distributed with 40 percent in urban areas, 9.7 percent in inner cities, 35 percent in the suburbs and 15.3 percent in rural locations. See the statistics of the Department of Education of the National Conference of Catholic Bishops/United States Catholic Conference at their website: www.nccbuscc.org. January 9, 1998.

4. *Pierce v Society of Sisters,* 268 U.S. 510 (1925).

5. Monsignor McDade, interview by Jo Formicola, Washington, DC, March 20, 1998.

6. See "Political Responsibility: Revitalizing American Democracy," and "Political Responsibility: Proclaiming the Gospel of Life, Protecting the Least Among Us, and Pursuing the Common Good," statements issued by the Administrative Board of the USCC in September 1991 and September 1995. Available from the USCC.

7. Taken from the following USCC documents: "To Teach As Jesus Did" (1972), "Sharing the Light of Faith" (1979), "Value and Virtue (1988), "Economic Justice for All" (1986), "In Support of Catholic Elementary and Secondary Schools," (1990), and "Principles for Educational Reform in the United States," (1995). Available from the USCC.

8. "Federal Programs of Parental Choice in Education," Department of Education, USCC. Available from the USCC.

9. This was a common practice prior to the reorganization of the NCWC in 1966. Indeed, John Courtney Murray, S. J., the country's top Catholic moral theologian and specialist on the First Amendment was brought in at the behest of Cardinals Spellman and Stritch of New York and Chicago, respectively. He was charged to protect Catholic educational interests and to assist the legal staff of the NCWC on its preparation of the *amicus* brief in the *Everson* case in 1947. See Jo Renee Formicola, "*Everson* Revisited: This Is Not Just a Little Case over Bus Fares," *Polity,* Vol. XXVIII, No. 1, Fall 1995, pp. 50–51. Murray articulated the argument that still stands in Catholic education circles: that educational choice is an absolute parental right and becomes a derivative right of the state only when granted to another authority by the parents. He also contended that the high wall of separation between church and state was not intended to create a barrier between the church and education. See the *amicus* brief of the National Council of Catholic Men and the National Council of Catholic women as reprinted in Philip B. Kurland and Gerhard Casper, eds., *Landmark Briefs and Arguments of the Supreme Court of the United States; Constitutional Law* (Washington: University Publications of America, 1975), vol. 44, pp. 956 ff.

10. Dr. Leonard DiFiore, interview by Jo Formicola, Washington, DC, March 20, 1998.

11. Michael Schwartz, interview by Hubert Morken, Washington, DC, December 12, 1997.

12. John Cardinal O'Connor, interview by the authors, New York City, October 10, 1998.

13. Jacques Steinberg, "School Choice Program Gets 17,000 Applications, *New York Times,* April 24, 1997, p. B3.

14. O'Connor, interview.

15. Doug Delaney, Catholic Conference, interview by Hubert Morken, Chicago, IL, July 21, 1998; telephone interview, Morken, September 30, 1998; Brother Thomas Hetland, Driscoll School, interview by Hubert Morken, Chicago, August 1, 1998.

16. Archdiocese of Chicago, *Special Task Force on Catholic Schools: Final Report,* summer 1998, p. 7.

17. Cardinal Francis E. George, "Statement on the Report of the Special Task Force on Catholic Schools," Chicago, IL, December 15, 1998, internet, http://www.archdiocese-chgo.org/cardinal/taskforce.html.

18. The Archdiocese of Chicago, news release, "Special Task Force on Catholic Schools Offers Report," Chicago, IL, December 16, 1998; Archdiocese, Report, 1–20.

19. Delaney, interviews.

20. Ibid.

21. Ibid.; Larry Horist, interview by Hubert Morken, Chicago, IL, July 20, 1998; George Clowes, interview by Hubert Morken, Chicago, IL, July 20, 1998; Jack Roser, conversation with Hubert Morken, Chicago, IL, July 31, 1998.

22. Daniel M. McKinley, interview by Hubert Morken, Milwaukee, WI, July 28, 1998; Milwaukee Archdiocesan School Development Consortium, "Goals for 1988–89," unpublished statement; Daniel M. McKinley, "Crisis and Opportunity in Milwaukee," *Momentum,* September 1992, copy in author's possession.

23. Archdiocese, Report, pp. 333–36.

24. Ibid., 3–4, p. 336.

25. McKinley, interview.

26. Ibid.

27. Ibid.; PAVE, *First-Year Report of the PAVE Scholarship Program* (Milwaukee: PAVE, 1993); *Fourth-Year Report of the PAVE Scholarship Program* (Milwaukee: PAVE, 1996); James Traub, "Private Lesson," *The American Benefactor,* spring 1998, reprint.

28. McKinley, interview.

29. McKinley, "Crisis and Opportunity in Milwaukee."

30. Ibid.

31. Ibid.

32. Quentin L. Quade, interview by Hubert Morken, Milwaukee, WI, July 29, 1998; Quentin L. Quade, *A North Star for School Choice,* a pamphlet, The Blum Center for Parental Freedom in Education, Milwaukee, WI, undated; Mayor John Norquist, interview by Hubert Morken, Milwaukee, WI, July 30, 1998.

33. Steve Perla, Parents Alliance for Catholic Education (PACE), telephone interview by Hubert Morken, fall 1998.

34. Jerry D'Avolio, Massachusetts Catholic Conference, interview by Hubert Morken, Boston, MA, September 3, 1998.

35. Perla, telephone interview.

36. Ibid.

37. Bryan Bennett, telephone interview by Hubert Morken, October 14, 1998.

38. Monsignor Edward Ryle, Arizona Catholic Conference, telephone interview by Hubert Morken, September 18, 1998.

39. In Salt Lake City, Utah, for example, some Mormons are attending Catholic parochial schools. Home School Education Supply Store Manager, conversation with the author, Salt Lake City, UT, December 24, 1998.

40. O'Connor, interview.

41. Lawrence A. Cremin, *American Education: The National Experience, 1783– 1876* (New York: Harper and Row, 1980), pp. 50–73.

42. Hubert Morken, "The New Common School: The Evangelical Response to Everson," Jo Renee Formicola and Hubert Morken eds., *Everson Revisited: Religion, Education, and Law at the Crossroads* (Lanham, MD: Rowman and Littlefield, 1997).

43. There are numerous religiously based organizations that support school choice and work for it that are not mentioned in this study, including Ohio Round- table, headed by David Zanotti, the Center for Public Justice, headed by long-time advocate, Dr. James Skillen, and Toward Tradition, a Jewish group headed by Rabbi Daniel Lapin.

44. *Wisconsin v Yoder,* 406 U.S. 205 (1972).

45. William Bentley Ball and Philip Murren, interview by Hubert Morken, Har- risburg, PA, November 12, 1997; Ball, telephone interview by Hubert Morken. Oc- tober 20, 1998; Morken, "The New Common School," pp. 71–72.

46. Robert Woodberry and Christian S. Smith, "Fundamentalism Et Al: Conser- vative Protestants in America," Annual Reviews, Sociology, 1998, 24, pp. 25–56; Hubert Morken, "The New Common School," pp. 59–81.

47. Morken, pp. 71–72; Ball, telephone interview, October 20, 1998.

48. Ibid.

49. Commonwealth of Pennsylvania, Public School Code of 1949, P.S. 13– 1327(b) 75.

50. William Bentley Ball, *Mere Creatures of the State?* (Notre Dame, IN: Crisis Books, 1994): Morken, pp. 71–72.

51. Ball, telephone interview, October 20, 1998.

52. Ibid.; Dr. Ken Smitherman, interview by Hubert Morken, Colorado Springs, CO, October 28, 1998.

53. Smitherman, interview, October 28, 1998.

54. ACSI Position Statement Concerning Tuition Tax Credits/Vouchers, Adopted by the ACSI Executive Board, February 1997.

55. ACSI, . . . *enabling Christian Educators and Schools Worldwide,* two brochures, undated.

56. ACSI Member Statistics, October 23, 1998; ACSI Growth As of December 15, 1997 (1979–97); ACSI Growth-Students 1979–1996; James C. Carper and Jack Layman, "Independent Day Schools Past, Present, and Prognosis," *Journal of Research on Christian Education,* vol. 4, no. 1 (spring 1995): 7–19.

57. Smitherman, interview, October 28, 1998.

58. Ibid.; Smitherman, "The Millennial Generation," research notes with docu- mentation.

59. Smitherman, interview, October 28, 1998; telephone interview, March 3, 1999.

60. Burt Carney, telephone interview by Hubert Morken, September 29, 1998; ACSI, Legal Legislative Update, vol. 8, no. 4 (summer 1998) and vol. 9, no. 1 (fall 1998).

61. Ibid.

62. Ibid.

63. John Holmes, telephone interview by Hubert Morken, August 29, 1998; ACSI, *National Notes,* vol. 1, no. 1–6, 1998.

64. Ibid.

65. Ibid.; ACSI, "Survey Results—CA Voucher Initiative," document, July 7, 1992; ACSI, *Legal Legislative Update,* November 1991; Smitherman, interview, October 28, 1998.

66. Ball, telephone interview, October 20, 1998; Michael Geer and Thomas Shaheen, interview by Hubert Morken, Harrisburg, PA, November 13, 1997; National Education Association. *The Real Story Behind 'Paycheck Protection'* (Washington, DC: NEA, 1998), pp. 13–14, 25–34.

67. NEA, *The Real Story,* p. 25.

68. Ibid., pp. 25–34.

69. Morken, "The New Common School," pp. 66–76.

70. NEA, *The Real Story,* p. 26.

71. Geer and Shaheen, interview, November 13, 1997.

72. Dr. Perry L. Glanzer, *Empowering Parents: Practical Legislative Proposals for Helping Parents Direct Their Children's Education* (Colorado Springs, CO: Public Policy Division, Focus on the Family, 1997); *Better Schools, Better Kids: The Significance of Parental Choice in Education* (Colorado Springs, CO: Public Policy Division, Focus on the Family, 1998).

73. Morken, "The New Common School," pp. 66–76.

74. Dr. Quentin Quade, interview by Hubert Morken, Milwaukee, WI, July 29, 1998.

75. Morken, "The New Common School," p. 65.

76. Ibid., pp. 66–68.

77. Executive Cabinet, Focus on the Family, "What Focus on the Family Believes about Education," adopted, 1996; Bryan D. Ray, *Strengths of their Own: Home Schoolers Across America, Academic Achievement, Family Characteristics, and Longitudinal Traits* (Salem, Oregon: National Home Education Research Publications, 1997).

78. Ibid.

79. Pennsylvania Family Institute, *Pennsylvania Families and Schools,* vol. 1, no. 3, April 1996—vol. 3, no. 4 (September–October 1998); Perry L. Glanzer and Travis Pardo, *Teachers Held Hostage: The Disturbing Agenda of the National Education Association* (Colorado Springs, CO: Focus on the Family, 1997); Perry Glanzer, *Virtue 101: The Strengths and Limitations of Character Education* (Colorado Springs, CO: Focus on the Family, 1997); Family Research Council, "Education Facts," a selection, 1995–1998.

80. Ibid.; Dr. James Dobson, "Family News from Dr. James Dobson," Focus on the Family, April 1998.

81. Family Research Council, *Let Freedom Ring: A Basic Outline of American History,* 2d edition (Washington, DC: FRC, undated); Gina Dalfonza and Jennifer A. Marshall, *Home Remedies: Reading lists and curriculum aids to promote your child's educational well-being* (Washington, DC: Family Research Council, undated); Focus

on the Family, *Teachers in Focus,* vol. 7, no. 4 and 5 (May–June, July–August, 1998).

82. Family Research Council, *Bill Clinton Superintendent, Micro-Managing Local Schools from Washington,* a collection of essays in response to the 1997 State of the Union education program (Washington, DC: FRC, undated).

83. Tom McMillan, telephone interview by Hubert Morken, September 17, 1998; Perry L. Glanzer, *Charting a New Course: A Parent's Guide to the Charter School Movement* (Colorado Springs: Public Policy Division, Focus on the Family, 1997).

84. Geer, interview, November 13, 1997; Tom Pritchard, telephone interview by Hubert Morken, September 29, 1998.

85. Dr. Perry Glanzer, interviews by Hubert Morken, Colorado Springs, July 10, and October 28, 1998; Dr. Mark Hartwig, Editor, *Teachers in Focus* Magazine, interview by Hubert Morken, October 28, 1998; Jennifer Marshall, interview by Hubert Morken, Washington, DC, November 21, 1997.

86. Ibid.

87. Jennifer Marshall, e-mail communication to Hubert Morken, April 7, 1999.

88. Charles Leslie Glenn, Jr., "Where Public Education Went Wrong: Recovering an American Tradition of School Choice," *Family Policy* (Washington, DC: Family Research Council, September–October 1998).

89. Marshall, interview, November 21, 1998.

90. Glanzer, interviews, July 10 and October 28, 1998.

91. Ibid.

92. Ibid.

93. Quade, interview, July 29, 1998.

94. Dr. James Dobson, "Family News from Dr. James Dobson," Focus on the Family, January 1998.

95. Glanzer, interviews, July 10 and October 28, 1998; Marshall, interview, November 21, 1998.

96. National Education Association, *The Real Story,* 1998, p. 26.

97. For another example of this argument see, Robert Booth Fowler, "A Skeptical Postmodern Defense of Multiestablishment: The Case for Government Aid to Religious Schools in a Multicultural Age," *Everson Revisited,* 1997, pp. 167–189.

98. Dr. James Carper, telephone interview by Hubert Morken, Fall 1998.

99. Ibid.

100. Rev. Mark Hoffman, interview by Hubert Morken, San Diego, California, October 6, 1998.

101. Ibid.

102. Ibid.

103. Ibid.; Lynda Hansen, interview by Hubert Morken, San Diego, October 5, 1998; Rep. Steve Baldwin, interview by Hubert Morken, San Diego, October 5, 1998.

104. Randy Tate, "The G.O.P.'s Chance to Reach Out," *New York Times,* Op-Ed on the web, November 12, 1998; Christian Coalition," *1998 National Survey of Christian Voters,* brochure (Chesapeake, Virginia, undated).

Chapter 6

African-American Strategies

Race adds an extra dimension to the imperative for school reform. African Americans are increasingly finding it necessary to deal with the issues of both equality of opportunity *and* quality education in order to revitalize, and in many cases, save their communities. More and more, they are at the forefront of leadership for better, different, and innovative schools to help their children and their neighborhoods.

Being black transcends partisan politics and business as usual. The special nature of the economic, social and, educational needs of minorities challenges all those in public office to think again about what makes a school "public," and what makes an education equal. When schools fail for African Americans, Hispanics, and other ethnic groups in poor neighborhoods that are crumbling and unsafe, at best, minorities demand remedies.

What is to be done to restore education to its community building role? Segregation once excluded all African Americans from good schools; today, poverty in effect does the same for many. When local governments do little to help and instead perpetuate the status quo, refusing to release resources for parents to use for their children to attend other schools, as the affluent can, pressure builds for a solution. In response, black leadership is emerging, anxious to build and operate independent schools and to press for public funding.

School choice movers and shakers, black and white, are determined to bring education change quickly to help minority children in poor neighborhoods. Working for legislation and soliciting funds, they are using public vouchers, private vouchers, and charter schools. These types of school choice can reinforce each other since vouchers, both public and private, can lead to charters and vice versa. A refundable tax credit too, for example, is really a form of public voucher and can be crafted to help the poorest families. These strategies are not mutually exclusive at all. In fact, all can be simultaneously available and functioning within a number of schools. At present, these three methods are used in a variety of venues across the country.

199

This chapter will illustrate the strengths and weaknesses of four African-American programs for school choice and the views of leading individuals who are making it happen: Representative Polly Williams of Milwaukee, Wisconsin; Reverend Floyd Flake of Queens, New York; pastors in Indianapolis, Reverend Steve Gardner, Reverend Marlon Moss, and Reverend Ann Byfield; and educator Dr. Howard Fuller from Milwaukee. Commentary from some community activists is also included.

Williams, Flake, the Indianapolis pastors, and Fuller, as pioneers and innovators, do more than simply adopt an available tool like vouchers or charters and use it. In fact they adapt it, modify it, add to it, and limit it, with their ultimate purposes kept clearly in view. This may cause problems for others. They certainly make school choice politics more interesting. The methods of school choice are less important to them than the outcome, therefore, they are constantly discontented with the status quo, pressing on for better delivery systems when past efforts appear inadequate.

Increasingly African-American politicians, ministers, and citizen activists are exercising school choice leadership roles. They see school choice in different ways and use a variety of means to advance it. Williams, the politician, considers education an equity and justice issue, a matter of community empowerment, and attempts to use the political process to make it a reality. She supports public vouchers for the poor. Ministers like Flake see a better education as a matter of survival for children and the community and as a moral problem—the community must control and fund schools free of bureaucratic controls and they may need outside help to do it. Flake wants vouchers and charter schools. The Indianapolis pastors favor fully religious schools and the freedom to operate them as they see fit for the good of the children. They want vouchers. Citizen activist Fuller and others like him work for school choice because it empowers parents and is the last best hope for education after other reforms have failed. Fuller is infusing new education programs into choice. Judging by the positive responses to these efforts it appears that members of the black community who support choice want it as much as, if not more than, concerned white parents.

Public Vouchers and Equality: The Political Approach of Representative Polly Williams

State Representative Annette "Polly" Williams is a legend in her own backyard of Milwaukee, Wisconsin, and in the school choice movement. Her accomplishment, which includes passing the first public voucher program in the nation (1990), a pilot program for the poor of her city, was upheld by the state Supreme Court in 1998. This program is now expanding under legislation she helped to pass. She stands alone, the true forerunner of a movement. At the moment of triumph, her vindication complete, she is deeply alienated from the leadership of school choice organizations in her city and nation. What happened? Did the school choice movement abandon the poor, leaving out African Americans, as she alleges? Did her own creation, the school choice movement, outgrow the founder, as her former allies claim? A comprehensive and balanced analysis of the Polly Williams role will be written some day. She would like to write her autobiography. What we have at present is a chance to glimpse her thinking, to consider well her positions on parental choice in education, on her terms, and to weigh their implications for the role race and class play in school choice politics.[1]

A number of elected African-American political leaders support school choice, including Representative Dwight Evans (D) and Senator Anthony Williams (D), of Philadelphia, and Ken Blackwell (R), Ohio Secretary of State. Pastors—Reverend Floyd Flake, Reverend Stephen Gardner, Reverend Marlon Moss, Reverend Anne Byfield, et al.—are starting schools and lobbying for choice. There are also black activists and organizers, including Walter Palmer, Gene Ruffin, Dr. Howard Fuller, and Bert Hall. The contributions of these people are great, even indispensable. All are working alongside white supporters of choice. Some strongly disagree with Polly Williams. Williams stirs controversy by boldly raising the issues of class and race with her opponents and allies. She can be a troublemaker in a coalition. By raising difficult questions and being most uncooperative at times, Williams's helps to shed light on important issues easily ignored.[2]

Williams represents the 10th District in Milwaukee, largely poor and African American, one where she has served since 1980. She is sixty-one years old, has four children, six grandchildren, and two great grandchildren. Most people are surprised when they meet her, she says, because this bundle of energy and initiative is "one of those little people" only five feet tall. Her reputation goes before her. Some call her a loose cannon. Williams jokes about what people say of her: "Her driveway does not go all the way to the road; her elevator does not reach the top floor." To this she responds, "Changes made in history are made by people who others considered crazy." When she speaks publicly she never prepares or writes down her comments. Her style is spontaneous and from the heart. Appearances can be deceptive, however, for Polly Williams thinks hard about her community and what actions she must take to benefit them. She denounces unapologetically what she sees as a threat to her community or to her leadership.[3]

"The white people throw their baggage on our train." "Help the needy not the greedy." These two sentences succinctly address race and class, the two issues that so exercise Polly Williams and shape her present positions on school choice. Each is a separate issue. Whites, she thinks, will try to capture the lion's share of public vouchers, and the black poor will not be helped. Both

concerns address the painful facts of inequality in schools and her search for a remedy.[4]

Segregation was terrible, often imposing wretched schools on blacks. Integration of schools, Williams charges, brought with it horrible consequences, too. She opposed forced busing in the 1970s as a remedy for segregation because it exposed black children to racially motivated attacks and abuse and destroyed neighborhood schools. Policies change, she notes, but the white power structures behind them remain the same. In any power battle, Williams comments, she "always looks at who is in charge." Blacks suffered from racism and from its so-called solution, integration, that threatened to steal the community's identity that had long been cultivated in its own schools. "Segregation left blacks with poor facilities and programs—there was no equality—but integration to this day, justified in the name of diversity or multiculturalism, dilutes our strength and weakens our schools." Autonomous community schools not managed or staffed by outsiders, where "We run our own schools," is the Polly Williams' prescription for educational health.[5]

Some call this thinking racism but this is hard for Williams to stomach. Lutherans have schools as do Catholics and small towns and suburbs have schools, all reflecting the local culture. Why then, Williams asks, should blacks have to submit to an education controlled and administered by white outsiders? Her objective is the establishment of "Independent Black Schools," the title of a task force that she heads for the national Conference of Black Legislators, which met in Cleveland in 1998. Cordially inviting the author to attend a panel she will chair on the topic, Williams observed, only blacks would be on the panel. This sensitivity to protecting indigenous leadership and identity at almost all costs shapes everything that Williams thinks and does.[6] She explains:

> The Milwaukee Public Schools (MPS) has 80 percent white teachers and administrators and only 19 percent white kids. No school has more than seven black teachers—with two exceptions, Malcolm X. School and Martin Luther King School, where there are 35 percent black teachers. There ought to be a majority of black teachers in these two schools.[7]

Williams was angry when, to maintain racial balance, MPS transferred two black male teachers from these schools and replaced them with two white female teachers. No, this was not a conspiracy to destroy black manhood by removing positive role models for the youth who need them the most. "Too often government programs are simply jobs programs for the middle-class," says Williams, who sees affirmative action quotas as largely a program for white affluent women. " There is only one black female judge in Wisconsin and only two black male judges," she notes, "and that compares to how many white women?" She wants jobs and parental education choice but she wants them for the poor who need them the most—the blacks in her community. A random survey of blacks in Milwaukee in 1995 revealed that a near majority thought public schools were getting worse in the city and 70 percent said private and parochial schools were superior. Over 70 percent favored school choice for low-income parents. But as school choice expands, Williams declares vouchers must not be allowed to become the "affirmative action" of education reform, benefiting whites largely from the middle class.[8]

Vouchers once had a bad name in the black community of Milwaukee, Williams relates. She once shared the opinion that vouchers were something only Catholics wanted, and these were the very people who fled to the suburbs when African Americans moved into the neighborhood. But then she discovered that "in choice, we could run our own schools just like they do; because blacks lacked resources, they needed voucher help for low-income families." Once she understood this, Polly Williams spearheaded the first successful voucher legislation in the United States—a pilot project for low-income families in Milwaukee that initially excluded religious schools from participating. She explains her success by the fact that she was not afraid, was motivated by her constituency, and stayed close to her people, representing them from the bottom up. To succeed at this, Williams states, you have to have "character" because often people in high places are bought off, selling out their constituency to gain the favor of others. Clearly, Polly Williams is critical of black legislative leadership, which sells out to unions or business or the Catholic Church, all white dominated.[9]

Today, she says, black legislators are killing school choice. To get choice it will take the support of black politicians, yet whites in the school choice movement do not work with the existing black leadership and instead prefer to pick a black they anoint and control. This will not work, Williams warns, because the black community will not respond. But this is not exclusively a white problem. Tragically, in her view, no other African-American legislator will go to the wall to defend school choice in Milwaukee. Her colleagues in the legislature, blacks and Democrats, are afraid or easily co-opted, not sufficiently protective of vouchers for low-income people. Williams now finds herself alone, protected only by her constituency and her sense of mission.[10]

She contrasts her leadership with the Clinton war-room model made famous in the 1992 election where James Carville and George Stephanopoulos sat down, planned strategy, set goals, and worked by any means necessary to get things done. This, Williams says, is done all the time. In her experience, this is how politics usually works. But this form of practical intelligence is built on sand and ultimately fails, she concludes. She wants a different result, one that will last. "If God is in it, it will last forever," she says. In this struggle Williams has no sense that power alone or even coalition building will be sufficient to carry the day. Instead her leadership style is personal and confrontational:

The opposition will fight tooth and nail to hold on to power and money. Those in control of public schools must be forced to make room and change. I have to fight, organize, and intimidate; eye ball 'em and show a big stick, get them to move out of fear. The one who is challenging cannot show fear. My leadership is based on moral authority. Convinced I am right, the opposition people know, "This lady is not going to back down; if you don't move over she is going to move over you." Leadership is based on commitment, once I make up my mind, and I do my own checking first, no one is going to change it, except by facts.[11]

Williams has victories to her credit, but she says that "victory" to her is in the fighting—battles never cease. She is proud of the fact that politicians are afraid of her.

Recently, Mayor John Norquist floated the idea that public school teachers should be allowed to live outside of Milwaukee in exchange for lifting the cap on vouchers. Currently, MPS teachers must live in the city to teach there and vouchers are limited to 15,000 students and by income. Norquist was seeking union support for an expansion of school choice, Williams argues, offering them two plums, the chance to move to the suburbs, if they wished, and, if they preferred to stay in Milwaukee, the opportunity to put their children into private schools. All of this, she says, was designed ultimately to encourage whites to live in the city but not to attend schools with blacks. Immediately she went on talk radio to oppose the mayor's plan as a gift to rich whites, and he backed down. "Vouchers are for the poor," she argues, "and if he wants to help the middle class then pass a tax credit designed for them." Williams said she celebrated the news when Governor Tommy Thompson announced he would not at that time recommend the change.[12]

The whites generally want school choice, Williams maintains, to help their present schools or to create new schools for the white community. The free-market universal voucher supporters are ideologues, she says, with no real concern for her community and no real understanding of the genuine difficulties in bringing change.

> Business wants to take over government schools. Both business and unions are under white control. Even under choice the blacks will lose control if they cannot maintain their independence in the school choice coalition and in their community. Where are the resources for black schools? Charter schools are not the solution because the white controlled unions and government will continue to dominate them. Charters may be a step in the right direction, but will they be under local control?[13]

School choice, Williams asserts, is in danger of becoming just another program for middle-class whites and others who do not need government assistance. In Milwaukee, she observes, private schools still mean Catholic education in practice. So by this logic, school choice is simply helping Catholic schools. When Catholics administrators want the authority to screen voucher applicants for admission, she objects, arguing that "this program is for parent choice not school choice." The parent is to select where their child is to attend from a list of schools willing to participate in the voucher program, and any school that participates must honor the parents' decision. The parochial schools have the right not to participate at all, she says, but if they do, by law they may turn down students only if students have special needs, are severely handicapped beyond the schools capacity to provide services, or if the school has no room. Williams sees Catholic schools outside of Milwaukee as white refuges not open to black students except in small numbers. She does not want to support this system with vouchers because in her opinion they provide little help to her community.[14]

> The whites that promote Reverend Floyd Flake (school choice advocate in Jamaica, Queens, New York) are out to replace public education for their own children, not for blacks. I have a black agenda for black parents. When I attend conferences or have conferences here I want to raise funds for black schools in Milwaukee. Few of the white choice movement are that helpful in my efforts to raise money. They are more concerned to use me to raise funds for their own organizations.[15]

Williams warns that Reverend Flake and others like him are being used to inspire other pastors to start schools, who are told to "follow my example, see what you can do." This is a beguiling message, she says, containing a temptation and a trap. Flake has a large church/school/social services operation with over a $22 million annual budget. Blacks may think, "If I embrace choice I can have a school," giving me jobs and income. These people may not be motivated to help children at all, Williams asserts. They may have no real sense of mission. Furthermore, some pastors may not be capable of building a school even if they are rightly motivated. For them to start a school could be a disaster. So white efforts to inspire others to follow the example of Reverend Flake could backfire, leaving the community no better off.[16]

Black churches have been slow to start schools, Williams observes, for good reasons. Most who are interested are waiting to see if the courts will permit religious schools to participate before they make such a weighty commitment, which entails starting from scratch. Most start-up schools are highly vulnerable, lacking financial backing, and the existing private black schools soak up most of the available community support. Furthermore, she claims, when white outsiders try to help they too often want control. Williams does not know if the latest Walton/Forstmann private voucher initiative would help black schools in Milwaukee. She asks, from her years of seeing promising aid projects fail, "How will it be administered?"[17]

Williams says the vast majority of choice students in Milwaukee in 1998 are white and that before the religious schools were added most were black. "The white people throw their baggage on our train." When the program grew from 1,600 to 6,300 students, the blacks lost out, in her view. Poor black parents she represents face transportation problems if the school is not in their neighborhood. The state will reimburse up to $300 of transportation costs, after the fact, but many cannot afford the up-front costs. She argues that African-American parents are still not well informed about choice programs and others simply do not take the initiative to apply for the voucher. Williams is disappointed with her community's participation rates and wants to remove remaining administrative and financial barriers.[18]

There have been problems with the new check payment procedure for students attending parochial schools. For nine years, Williams relates, the state would cut one check for a school with voucher students. Now Wisconsin cuts a check for each enrolled student, made out to the parent, and eventually sends it to the school. Then the parents have to come to the school to sign it over to the school; all of this red tape is required because the state must not appear to be giving assistance to a church. This is a cumbersome and expensive mess. Rather than go back to the old procedure, Williams wants two payment systems, one for secular private schools and one for the religious. This would clearly work to the disadvantage of the parochial schools.

To a degree Williams is skeptical of all private initiatives, church-based or philanthropic. Speaking as a legislator as well as a community activist she makes it very clear that she supports public education with all of its weaknesses and despite the control of white unions and administrators. She has no desire, she says, to replace public schools with private schools. In fact, Williams will vote to maintain a cap of 25 percent of Milwaukee students in choice schools, up from the present 15 percent. She would expand to this higher cap only after the choice schools are so demonstrably superior that the people in her community demand that the choice program grow. In short, she is saying to private schools, "First prove to us that you are better, then we will gradually phase in more choice." Meanwhile, Williams wants to work to improve public schools.[19]

To help create room for public schools to reform themselves, to be patient with them, Williams rejects a state government takeover of non-performing public schools. However, she sees efforts to reduce class size as just another union ploy to get more jobs. What she does want, and will fight for, are teacher's aids in classrooms, from the same culture as the students, she advises, with the position of teacher's aid considered part of their training to become certified teachers. The aids will help preserve order and give care and concern to students. This proposal, Williams is confident, will motivate people in the community to go into teaching and stabilize and improve public schools.[20]

Limiting school choice to those who need it the most, "Help the needy not the greedy," is the cornerstone of Williams's public policy approach to vouchers. She claims credit for the 1995 expansion of choice for the poor in Milwaukee to include religious schools and to increase the number of vouchers. She backed it against the NAACP and education unions, and she is pleased with the current legislation. It targets low-income families, with an income 75 percent above poverty line or less, about $28,000 for a family of four. She would eventually like to raise the income cap to perhaps $35,000 for a family of four, to bring assistance to young hard-working families, but she rejects efforts to remove the cap altogether. Raising the cap is a way to prevent losing it and it keeps the program for the low-income families. Williams does not want to give the voucher option to low performing schools—many would be white—but rather keep it for poor parents. Once again, she favors parent choice not school choice because she says the latter benefits whites that do not need vouchers if they are not truly poor.[21]

Williams says she is now alienated from the choice coalition of Milwaukee and the nation. She supported expanding the original legislation and initially joined with Catholics, business leaders, foundations, and activists in a coalition. But she was offended when others started an independent organization, Parents for School Choice, with a director and staff dominated by whites (even though she recognizes some of the staff members were black). She felt controlled by the big money funding sources and did not feel herself to be an equal participant. How could she trust their motivation when they have not helped blacks start their own schools? And besides that, she distrusts those with power and money and resists being controlled and the appearance of outside control.[22]

For example, Governor Tommy Thompson and Polly Williams both opposed the appeal of the Milwaukee voucher case to the United States Supreme Court. The Landmark Legal Foundation represented her in the case. She did not want to jeopardize the Milwaukee victory for some larger national purpose. This represented outside control. Rejecting the agenda of attorney Clint Bollick who supported federal review, she claimed that he was too willing to sacrifice Milwaukee cheaply.[23]

The constituency whom Polly Williams feels responsible for representing in the corridors of power is made up primarily of poor African Americans, who, she says, are often left undefended even by their elected leaders. In fact, she is concerned that most middle-class blacks have little concern for low-income blacks. In this context of indifference and betrayal, Williams considers herself a lone voice for targeted vouchers. Let others care about parochial schools or the needs of the middle class, best helped with, for example, tax credits. Vouchers, which she helped design, are for the poor only. Maintaining this standard will help her community the most and eventually other poor people as well.[24]

To sum this up, the Polly Williams's parental choice agenda embraces:

1. Vouchers with an income cap—$35,000 for a family of four
2. Vouchers for no more than 25 percent of the students in Milwaukee
3. Raise the caps on vouchers gradually to preserve the public schools
4. Promote independent black schools, public and private, by all means available
5. Expand the percent of African Americans in public school teaching and administration
6. Bring more order, learning, and respect for ethnic identity to the classrooms
7. Defend the autonomy and distinctive culture of all neighborhood schools, beginning with her own*

Williams is disappointed that her autobiography, in which she expresses her full views, has not yet been written—and she blames white publishers. She would also like to start a school and a foundation to support it, but would need a principal she can trust to submit to her leadership. It is difficult, she says, to find genuine community leaders who combine competence with a clear desire to serve. She wants to secure excellent schools for her community, staffed and attended by African Americans, but she is finding this difficult to do, whether by means of parental choice programs or by public school reforms.[25]

To summarize and review her perspective: Polly Williams maintains that inner-city blacks have left the operation of their schools to whites for too long. She decries the absence in her community of excellent schools staffed by black teachers; she wants them in the public and private schools. Church-run schools, however, are as much a part of the problem to Williams as they are a solution. First, she does not trust the Catholic parochial education system because most of the church members are white and live in the suburbs. Catholic educators want vouchers but they want them for the middle class, she claims, not the deserving poor. Second, she has little confidence in the motivation or abilities of African-American churches and their leaders, who have until recently stood by and done little for education. She also says black pastors have been wise to wait before starting schools, given the legal uncertainties on vouchers. Williams sees greed undermining the motivation of both Protestants and Catholics. In her view churches do not have the answer though they may on occasion be a positive influence.

Note: In addition she acknowledges the place of tax credits for the middle class but does not want this to replace targeted vouchers for the poor.

The business community fares no better in her analysis. Williams sees a huge battle shaping up between for-profit corporations that want to run schools and the education unions fighting to preserve their jobs and exclusive control of public funds. Williams asks why she should trust white free-market conservatives who have done nothing to build black private schools.

Black politicians and the public school establishment get no praise either. Each supports the other to the detriment of children, in her judgment. Power and money tend to rule and the decline of schools is the result.

Even her constituents come in for criticism because they have failed to take advantage of school choice when it is offered to them. Too many parents refuse to act, deterred by simple obstacles like transportation, and many remain ignorant of their options.

The solution Polly Williams proposes is an extended campaign that holds on tenaciously to the gains made thus far. Never surrender vouchers. Never give vouchers to the rich. Never place too much trust in any education provider, public or private. Never lose your separate identity in a coalition. Never surrender the ultimate objective of great independent black schools. Never stop fighting for poor African Americans whose welfare and interests she represents. Never stop believing in your cause.

Williams sharply distinguishes between parent choice and school choice. The former is good. It recognizes the needs of single mothers and others who have few defenders or patrons. The latter is dangerous at best—substituting the interests of schools for those of children—and is fraudulent, pretending to be what it is not, namely, family centered. Nothing in the whole panoply of current school reform efforts fully meets Williams's approval. Perhaps she has not yet discovered a principled solution that she is confident will work in today's world. Ever the political realist and the idealist, with self-deprecating humor, she comments, "My family says I just love to fight."[26]

Private Vouchers Charter Schools, and Morality: The Ministerial Approach of Reverend Floyd Flake

The modern civil rights movement concentrated heavily on obtaining equal rights in public schools. In 1970, 96.4 percent of all African-American students received a public education. In the ensuing decades this figure slowly began to drop, to about 90 percent in 1994. Now there is a growing interest in black private schools estimated to number in the hundreds, many started by local churches. One researcher who studied these "Black-Flight Academies," Professor James Carper of the University of South Carolina, writes that these schools exhibit a remarkable diversity:

Black Christian schools are fascinating in their variety and uniqueness, differing from public schools the way neighborhood stores differ from shopping malls. Schools are located in newly built educational plants; in row houses and frame houses; church basements and large church educational buildings; converted supermarkets, stores, restaurants, and hospitals; and in former public, Roman Catholic, Jewish, and Protestant school buildings. They serve a broad economic and social spectrum of families; they are founded by churches, community committees, and individuals; and they use a variety of academic curricula.[27]

Protestant schools founded in the 1960s and 1970s generally were white. Carper writes that these once exclusively white schools (they are now interracial), are now being followed by black schools founded mostly in the 1990s. This is occurring as part of an almost invisible neighborhood, local church movement, "springing up spontaneously, often unknown to government agencies, public school districts, and secular and religious school associations." Alternative schools like these are of the greatest interest to school choice leaders. With enormous respect for the courage that it takes to start such schools they want to facilitate their growth.[28]

The individuals responsible for these schools are black ministers. Historically, they have been the religious and political leaders of their communities. At times they have been at the forefront in the battles for freedom, equality, and moral righteousness in the United States. Until recently they have been the best-educated and most respected members of their often marginalized societies. They have connections to the white members of their towns and state power structures. They serve as liaisons and buffers between black and white constituencies in local politics.

A prominent African-American minister and former United States Congressman is now a major school choice leader. The Reverend Floyd Flake fits the profile of a traditional black minister. Once in charge of remedial education at Lincoln University in Pennsylvania and Dean of Students at Boston University, Flake has been involved in education for most of his life. He is also a minister and the powerful pastor of the Allen AME Church in Jamaica, Queens, New York. In that capacity, he presides over a twenty-two million dollar annual budget, which funds a church, a nursing/old age home, a housing complex, a series of strip malls and stores, a variety of other real estate holdings, and a parish school. As an educator and the individual in charge of Allen AME's school, he has seen inner-city education with all its strengths and weaknesses. His school is an example of learning and discipline. For $3,400 a year, rather than the $10,000 that is allotted to each child in his district, Reverend Flake's school is immaculate and bustling. Students in uniforms receive basic education skills along with foreign languages enhancement in the early grades, information technology, and quality education in a secure, loving environment.

Flake became involved in politics after he and his parishioners came to believe that he could do more for the poor by promoting their social well-being through the political process rather than by ministering solely to their spiritual needs. Seeking election to the House of Representatives, he was elected and served six terms but came away from the experience disenchanted, returning to Allen AME in 1998. Among his disappointments are the fact that credible black politicians have to compromise with interest group pressures, particularly from teacher's unions, that most politicians only support serious issues for reelection, that politicians feel threatened by ministers, and that they cry "separation of church and state" when ministers challenge them to use their moral persuasion to advance moral issues. And—he sees school choice as a moral issue![29]

While Reverend Flake appears to be a traditional minister his approach to leveraging school choice has been unique. First, he has been using his political expertise gained at the national level, transferring it to the state level in New York, working to support charter schools there. Presently he believes that they are more feasible to enact than vouchers because they are, politically, the more palatable of the two options. But, at the same time, he has been moving in tandem to push both charters and vouchers in order to establish a mechanism for reform in New York State. He understood that it was critical to keep the extreme option i.e., vouchers, on the table for leverage so that, when politicians sought an alternative for major education reform, charters would still be there. Second, Flake has been at the center of a major funding coalition in New York State, and he has joined with many of the entrepreneurs and donors involved in the school choice effort, such as Peter Flanigan and Bruce Kovner of the Student/Sponsor Scholarship Fund, Ted Forstmann and John Walton of the Children's Scholarship Fund, and John Cardinal O'Connor and the Archdiocese of New York's scholarship fund. Flake believes that such interconnections come as a result of funding streams, not political activities. Third, Flake has also developed relationships with minority members of the New York State Legislature and New York's Governor George Pataki. In fact it was Flake who appeared on television with the governor during his re-election bid in 1998 to announce gubernatorial support for charter schools. As a result of Flake's support for charters, his interconnections with the movers and shakers of the New York financial supporters for school choice, and his networking with state politicians, Flake was instrumental in getting charter school legislation passed in New York State in 1998.[30]

It is clear that in his home state, Flake is the straw that stirs the drink. In every interview that the authors conducted in New York, his name emerged as the most influential and high-profile person supporting school choice within the state. Yet, beyond the borders of New York, Floyd Flake, like Polly Williams and Howard Fuller, seems to be fighting an uphill battle by himself. He was disinvited to talk to the black elected officials in Indianapolis in 1998 because he was going to raise the issue of school choice. He was frozen out of the Black Congressional Caucus in 1997 over the same issue.

Although he does not have a national school choice network in place, Flake's chief concern is to help his community reverse itself from within. He is first, last and, always, a minister—but a minister with political savvy and clout. Flake sees economic opportunity and school choice as moral issues. He believes that black ministers must take their moral outrage and, by moral persuasion, do what they are mandated to do by God. Politicians, he believes, do not operate in this environment or hold this mentality. Therefore, he will make his contribution to society, in future, through his ministerial, rather than his political, persona.[31]

Creating Christian Schools in Indianapolis: Steve Gardner, Marlon Moss, and Ann Byfield

Flake is one minister making a difference, but there are many others as well, among them a professor and community activist, Dr. Thomas Brown, of the Institute of Urban Ministries at Martin University in Indianapolis. Brown has a mentoring role with local African-American pastors who are now embracing school choice.

Past racial politics and the fruit of racism, Brown says, none had an impact on the current school choice debate in Indianapolis. In the 1960s, that city went from city-based government to county-based government to dilute the black vote in elections. The county included the white suburban population. However, the old school district boundaries were left intact to preserve de facto segregation—schools outside the city were largely white. To remedy this, in the 1970s, one-way busing was instituted to bring some racial balance. Now this is being phased out, grade by grade, starting with kindergarten. What will replace busing is not yet known. In this time of transition, Brown wants school choice adopted to rejuvenate the schools.[32]

Yet Brown does not see any organization or person that can take the lead to press for school choice in the city. Reports in 1998 on school performance in Indianapolis Public Schools (IPS) were dismal yet the African-American community most affected is not up in arms. When reports are heavily statistical, Brown says they need to be interpreted and communicated to the broader black community in terms they can understand. This has not been done to his satisfaction. Further, positive recommendations are needed to define what are the clear, challenging, and reachable standards for children—otherwise the message is simply condemnatory of schools, parents, and children. Brown blames local reformers for not communicating effectively to the African-American community both the bad news about public school performance and the good news about the opportunities ahead. Reports not properly integrated into a positive school reform effort just add discouragement and condemnation, in his judgment. [33]

Brown also faults the black community for its failure to respond. His explanation is "Generational Entrapment," by which he means the thinking of the civil rights era that still predominates, stressing equal opportunity and equal rights.

> Equality of opportunity has lead to consumerism and consumption but not to creative and productive thinking and deeds. People are living in a comfort zone that makes it difficult to mobilize them for school choice. We need a new generation of leadership concerned about the challenges of the future, not the injustices of the past.[34]

Where will these leaders come from in the black community? From his many years of experience in education and in ministry, Brown observes that pastors are slow to admit that they do not know how to run schools—generally they limit their ministry to preaching and maintaining traditional ministries. Pastors are slow to respond and outside speakers can do only so much. Local leaders are needed and those who are in most need—the young mothers and poorer families—must be mobilized, too. Yet the structure to do this and the public spokesmen to lead the way are not yet visible to him. Meanwhile a quiet grassroots effort to start schools is underway with his encouragement.[35]

Other local pastors, who Brown knows and supports, have a radically Christian school choice vision, related to their commitment to the poor and to the Gospel as they see it. For example, of greatest concern to Reverend Steve Gardner and Reverend Marlon Moss, two Indianapolis pastors of African-American congregations, is what they call middle-class rebellion, an "I have arrived" mentality that looks down on the poor, scorning them. Such people are just getting rich or chasing prosperity, many are not attending church, and as a group they are having few or no children of their own. These successful people have no vision or concern for others less fortunate or for the long-term future of the black community. Churches too are being influenced by this attitude, in their view.[36] Gardner and Moss spoke of several unnamed black churches in the city:

> *Church A*: This church has about 1,500 members, and a weekly income estimated of $7,000. It is traditional. It has no visible support for school choice. Among its members are many IPS teachers. The church runs a large day-care program but nothing K–6.

> *Church B*: With 5,500 members, and an estimated weekly income of $40,000, this church has a weekly local TV show. Members are affluent "boomers" and younger. Some of those members who can afford the expense send their children to private schools. This church is loaded with IPS personnel who live outside of the city, putting their children in suburban or private schools.

Church C: The largest church, with three locations, has an income estimated at $76,000 a week. Members are younger, in their 30's, professionals, middle and upper middle-class, most are living in suburban homes. They are now opening up a school. This is the popular thing to do and they have the resources.[37]

Gardner and Moss say these churches have not yet caught a vision for school choice. The more traditional oppose choice and the more prosperous ignore the plight of the poor left behind even as they start schools for the more well off. What is needed, they say, is a church/school alliance that brings the black community together. They look to Reverend Floyd Flake of New York for help. Gardner and Moss say most pastors are afraid, not knowing how to run schools—dealing with curriculum, costs, and administration—so they avoid the issue of collapsing public schools. Yet, Gardner and Moss are fully confident that smaller classes in smaller schools will produce better performance. Persuaded that they can run such modestly sized schools, they say it will take three to five years to get them fully launched.

Reverend Steve Gardner is an M.A. student of Dr. Brown. He is doing his thesis on the school that his church is starting with the assistance of Pat Rooney and Don Laskowski. Gardner who worked with Reverend Marlon Moss in 1997 to help create one of the first "Safe Haven" schools, Christian Training Academy, is starting a new school in 1998, the Antioch Christian Academy, K–3. Gardner is the pastor of a small church. He has five children, one child in his school, and three in a parochial school. Acting consistent with his opinions, his children have not attended public schools. Moss pastors the Greater Northeast Baptist Church, a small church in the crime zone of the northeast side of the city. Both pastors hold out little hope for children attending public schools in poor black neighborhoods. Their strong desire is to have church-based schools for children K–12, with gospel content, prayer, and quality learning. Private schools that are run in a positive, orderly manner can make the difference, they are convinced, if the students consistently attend them from their earliest school years.[38]

The "Goals" statement of one of these schools reads:

- Creating a safe haven for the children of our community to learn free from drugs, alcohol abuse, and crime
- Create an atmosphere conducive to spiritual and academic growth by incorporating prayer and biblical instruction into daily curriculum
- Provide a quality Christ-centered education through the use of proven high standard curriculum materials that will empower these children for the rest of their lives
- Create a social environment that will foster an appreciation of cultural diversity

- Develop an extended family partnership where school and parents are together working in the child's education
- Provide regular exposure to educational field trips and community leaders, e.g. firemen, policemen, government officials, etc.
- Provide daily hands-on experience with computers for all grade levels, including kindergarten
- Achieve academic excellence and spiritual renewal for our staff by providing retreats, and opportunities for continuing education through university courses, seminars, in-service training, and correspondence courses[39]

The Christian Training Academy has thirty-one students enrolled in 1998, K–1, with two teachers, and a teacher's aid. Each student has a desk and there are fifteen computers in each classroom. Curriculum is a combination of A-BEKA, a traditional Christian program, and RISE, a computer-based teaching system. Teachers use RISE and the computers as a reward for those who have mastered the other materials. Moss is convinced that children need both the personal attentions of teachers—their love and interaction—and the physical contact with paper, blackboard, and books. He does not support a paperless classroom, but rather one that employs a combination of traditional methods where children learn to write by hand and then use the computers. Scholarships—two from Pat Rooney for $800 each and twenty from Laskowski for $1,000 each—pay most of the tuition the school receives. There are six Safe Haven schools in the city similarly supported.

Most of the staff in the Christian Training Academy are church members but many of the students are from outside the church. Gardner and Moss see good schools as a way to interest parents in the gospel—an evangelistic hook, by having parents serve as volunteers in school and then attending church. Yet Moss says it is difficult to get black pastors to support school choice—they are fragmented with no agreed upon leader, "nothing ever gets solved." They hear the teacher union arguments that choice will lead to creaming, are largely ignorant of the contrary arguments, and do not want to be thought radical—"We like to ride the bandwagon but we don't want to drive it or be in front." Pastors do not want to have the responsibility of running a school. Baptists are conservative but if the pastors of the largest churches were to start schools and their pastors were to push for choice, they think others would soon follow.[40]

Gardner and Moss agree that in the larger African-American community you must sell school choice by talking about tuition scholarships for private schools—the word "choice" means nothing now. They say most people are in a rut—they are complacent. People, especially church people, remember the 1960s and do not want turmoil; they fear another civil rights movement. Furthermore, conservative blacks tend to call political activism "not preaching the Gospel," and to wake them up will require, these pastors say, better teaching from pulpits that integrate social concern with spiritual ministry.

Protestant leaders like Gardner and Moss want their own schools. They do not want to send children to Catholic schools and they reject the existing public schools. As a young parent, Gardner was determined to leave his children with a better start in school than he received. He says he wants mature Christian expression in the schools his children attend, the full armor of God, the power of prayer, with all spiritual and educational resources available and mobilized. Quality, he says, not quantity is the issue. As pastors and parents, Gardner and Moss had a vision for quality education long before the school choice issue arrived. Resources, or rather the lack of resources, forced the "choice" issue on to their agenda. They say they always wanted to have their own Christian school but lacked the means to do so.

Black churches need help from corporations and individuals, but such help, pastors argue, must come with no strings attached, no manipulation, nothing that will compel them to compromise their independence. For example, Gardner and Moss do not favor a lottery admissions system for privately- or publicly-funded scholarships. Concerned to preserve order in the classroom and to maintain the integrity of the program, they say, "Let the church select the students to admit." Theirs is a strong concern to associate with those of common vision—quality takes time and agreement to achieve—they maintain, with the goal of forging a bond between schools and the families they serve. They see having teachers who are willing to teach for low pay as a way to preserve the program; teachers must see this as a ministry, not a career, if the school is to succeed in its mission. They are confident that, in the future, fully independent African-American church schools will emerge that will stand even in hard times. Against them, the pastors maintain: "The gates of Hell will not prevail."[41]

In Indianapolis, there are also black middle-class neighborhoods where church members are beginning to start schools because they have already been active in education programs. Starting a school for them seems to be a natural next step in a progression of steps. These churches are neither poor nor rich and have deep traditions. Reverend Ann Byfield, the pastor of the Robinson Community Church (AME) in Indianapolis, with a membership of 400 to 500 people, is well aware of her denominational education heritage.[42]

The African Methodist Episcopal (AME) churches have a long history of interest in schools—Byfield reports they now have sixteen colleges and seminaries. However, as AME members moved north in the 1950s, most went to cities and sent their children to public schools. Today she says they are busy "reclaiming the vision" for church-based schools. Hundreds of AME churches have day-care centers but few have schools. Byfield expects this to change, especially as more private and public funds become available and as the need for alternative schools grows. Some examples of churches with schools are in Baltimore, Los Angeles, and Newark, and she notes Floyd Flake of New York is AME. Some of Byfield's pastor friends and peers are questioning her interest in starting a school—doubting it. She responds that she still supports public education, is not anti-union, and considers choice a "both and" proposition not "either or." Byfield in 1998 was at a crossroads, determined to start a school, confident her past efforts were not in vain.[43]

In 1990 Byfield started Public Education Watch to serve as a watchdog for black parents alarmed at how their children were being treated in public schools. Then she started a back-to-school class to teach children how to get the most out of public school. The public school soon started its own version of a back-to-school program and asked them to stop—they agreed—and then, Byfield reports, the public school version died in two years.

The Robinson Community Church started a seasonal school during vacations; a spring break academic/recreational camp, so popular some had to be turned away; a Christmas break camp with fifty to sixty kids; and a summer camp for forty to fifty children. In 1998 the church received funding from the Lilly Foundation for computers and programs in standard academic courses, including math, reading, and science. Over fifty children five to eleven years old and a few older students enrolled.

In 1993 local businesses sponsored Robinson Community Church students in public schools preparing for college. With this assistance and a generally positive education atmosphere in the church, a high percentage of those in her church who finish high school go to college and graduate. In short, Byfield reports her church has been active in education in almost every way short of having a school. Then in the late 1990s it took some bad experiences with public schools to nudge Byfield toward starting a school and embracing school choice.

Several years ago two children in the church, including her son, got into difficulties in public school and were suspended. Her son, in the 10th grade, had experienced several deaths in the family, and he was in rebellion and angry. He went from school to school, was tested, and labeled a "social deviant." Byfield then took him to a psychologist who tested him and found him bright and bored. The public school he was attending (he is now in college) would not accept the results. His test scores in the IPS testing were borderline, neither disastrous nor good. This unresolved mess led her to rethink her approach to education. Byfield then started travelling and talking to people about private education and school choice. She looked to effective AME schools, like St. James Preparatory, in Newark, New Jersey, for advice and help.[44]

Why should she start a school? There are several reasons that Byfield offers. This had been in the back of her mind; it had always been a vision; and AME churches once ran schools. IPS test results were terrible and most blacks flunked. Black and white children, she said, were fairly close in performance in grammar school and rapidly diverged in higher grades. Something must be going wrong in the classrooms of public schools, she concluded, on the basis of personal experience and by objective measures. The IPS test results were disappointing but then the district also made them public—they posted them on the board for all to see, which added insult and shame to injury and this further stirred Byfield to act.

Byfield asked the Robinson Community Church to start a school by January 1999. Concerned about building code requirements in an old fire station owned by the city that she would like to use, she said she will meet with the mayor to iron out this difficulty if necessary. In a pinch they can use the Robinson church facilities. People in the congregation and community, Byfield comments, are excited about the plans; they will start with pre-kindergarten and kindergarten.[45]

To conclude, ministers who support school choice come to it from a different perspective. Believing that quality education is a matter of survival and a fundamental moral right, they are willing to using moral persuasion as the basis for their mandate to help their communities. They are also coalition builders in their cities. As a result, pastors such as Floyd Flake and the others noted help to bridge the gap between whites and blacks, the haves and have-nots, Democrats and Republicans, to make community and individual success realities.

Some, like the local pastors in Indianapolis—Garland, Moss, and Byfield—are prepared to make this journey with entrepreneurs like Pat Rooney. Their perspective matches his. In May 1997 they together developed the basic idea for "Safe Haven" schools. Funded by Pat Rooney, Don Laskowski, (owner of an international company that makes portable sawmills), and Gordon St. Angelo of the Friedman Foundation, the plan was to help start a new type of private inner-city school. These schools would be open from 6 a.m. to 6 p.m., twelve months a year, with parents who are the recipient of a private scholarship paying $50 a week for tuition and agreeing to volunteer a minimum fifty hours a year of assistance to the school. Their plan is for companies to adopt each school, become a member of the schools' supervising Board, and agree to contribute $1,000 individual scholarships. Laskowski promised to match these scholarships for up to a total of $100,000. By the summer of 1998 one school was completely sponsored and they planned to have nine or more schools opened by the fall in Indianapolis, South Bend, Atlanta, Detroit, and Sacramento. Other cities are also being considered.[46]

The Catholic parochial school model is not what Rooney and his friends are following. Parochial schools require large expenditures on buildings, something Rooney is unwilling to do and, he said, is not needed. There are already facilities readily available in most African-American communities that can and should be used for schools. It is far better, he argues, to use present church facilities, and especially Sunday school rooms. To begin with the minimum of fuss and delay, Rooney recommends a return to the old one-room schoolhouse concept, using only one salaried teacher, and teacher aids (grandmothers), for K–3 with up to four grades in one room if this is necessary. This is his starter model. To begin, all that is required is a sponsoring pastor, a church facility, one teacher, the teacher aids, curriculum, materials, private scholarships, and students.[47]

The intent is to create a school program that can easily be replicated and used elsewhere. The basics are to include: (1) a common curriculum; (2) a life style/character component; (3) an affordable, paperless system using computers (15 per class); and (4) Individualized learning. The schools split the school day into two parts, the first academic, lasting two and one-half to three hours, followed by three hours of instruction in character, lifestyle, and ethics for a six-hour day K–8. Rooney and Laskowski have worked with John Sayre of SayTech Corporation in Indianapolis to develop this program.[48]

Rooney, after his review of curricula in use, concluded that even in Catholic schools there is chaos and confusion on how to teach children in the early grades. He wants to avoid this by looking to home schoolers for suggestions on curricula that work effectively, adapting home schooling material for use in the inner city. Computer-based instruction alone will not do it all, he says. For reading he recommends four different phonics curricula—Open Court; Direct Instruction; Saxon Reading and Math Program; and First Reader, a Phyllis Schlafly program. Rooney says they are all comparable and of good quality. To back up this conclusion he cites an American Federation of Teachers (AFT) report and other authorities. Rooney expects to include additional teacher training in his program but he believes phonics provides the key to reading he believes and computer software to assist in this is not expensive.[49]

To launch the effort, Rooney looked at curriculum, materials, textbooks, and computers ($700 each, using Windows 95). He asked businesses to contribute used computers. It is time, he says, to establish corporate/pastoral connections for a community-based effort. Rooney remembers when most corporations looked askance at his private voucher program and refused to contribute. Now many corporations participate. He hopes the business community will soon learn to work with churches too for the good of the children in the poorest of communities. What is needed is a non-profit foundation that will serve as a funnel for corporate funds to assure donors that the schools are indeed functioning in a responsible way, to assess student progress, and to be a consultant, giving churches information on how to start and run schools. Rooney is confident that substantial sums can be raised from individuals, foundations, and corporations to help churches start schools. He is working to set up this foundation and to partner with other organizations already actively involved in school choice and with pastors and denominational leaders.[50]

To help to stir up interest in school choice opportunities in the African-American and Hispanic community Rooney is teaming up with Ms. Alvita King, niece of Dr. Martin Luther King Jr. to make radio spots aired in Indianapolis and Texas. It is much better, he says, to work with known community leaders to promote school choice. He is also making contacts with local pastors and denominational leaders, including Reverend Raymond Bryant (AME) of Dallas, Texas, and Hispanics in San Antonio. Meanwhile Rooney is working with local pastors in Indianapolis to start schools with the ultimate goal of getting politicians to change, motivated by the need and by pressure from constituents—spiritual conversion he called it.[51]

Thus, while Gardner, Moss, and Byfield have worked with, and accepted funds from, philanthropic businessmen, they have also observed the streets and its temptations, and they are firmly united in a desire to create or to reclaim an education mission for the church. Dr. Thomas Brown nurtures this aspiration for the coming generation in his graduate program. Morals and spiritual realities must be taught, they all believe, in a loving, personal, faith-filled context if children are to resist the temptations on the streets. The severity of education collapse in inner-city public schools made education radicals and innovators of these churchmen.

School Choice and Saving Black Communities: The Activist Approaches of Jackie Cissel and Howard Fuller

Commenting on these developments, Jackie Cissel, Community Relations Coordinator for IPALCO, the local power company, notes that in Indianapolis middle-class blacks are sending their kids to private schools or are moving to the suburbs. African Americans see serious problems in public schools—factories are leaving the city and even the state, immigration is an issue, the schools are dumbing down, and technology demands are increasing. In this fast changing and challenging context, the city is in the process of getting rid of racial busing. Metropolitan leadership is nervous about ending busing because kids will "flow back to the city schools and the inner-city schools are not ready for them." The churches could take up the slack if they would, and some, like Gardner, Moss, and Byfield, are, but black leadership, Cissel says, still sees this as a partisan Republican issue. Her tough and unqualified response is, "If you have a hospital and half the patients come out dead you would close it." The teachers unions and old loyalties persist. Cissel concludes that new efforts by pastors and churches are needed. She is inspired by the example of Reverend Floyd Flake—his 900-student school and 1,500 on the waiting list—but warns that the first commitment must be to the children, not to building lucrative private education empires.[52]

Cissel works with Family Organization for Real Choice in Education

(FORCE), a school choice organization for parents. She set up a meeting with Mayor Goldsmith (R) on education issues but the parents did not show up, perhaps because he is a Republican. This was a big disappointment for her. She supports one-on-one persuasion and radio ads, observing that most poor parents do not know what the phrase "school choice" means and affluent African Americans just pay the money both for taxes and private tuition. Business as a whole, Cissel complains, supports public education; IPALCO, for example, partners with one public middle school. Realistically, she sees the resistance to change by the current corporate authorities as a key reason school choice is so slow in coming to Indiana.

In January 1998, thirty people from different states went to Milwaukee to meet with Dr. Howard Fuller for the purpose of planning a national symposium for African Americans interested in school choice. Cissel attended and reports that he was a big encouragement. Many in the all-black meeting sounded and even looked like 1960s radicals. Black legislators operate in fear of unions, she concludes; mobilizing African Americans to resist white dominated public education institutions will be needed to break this stronghold of opposition. Local politicians disappoint her, as when the Indiana Black Legislative Caucus withdrew an invitation for Reverend Floyd Flake to be a guest speaker in February 1998 because of his outspoken support for choice. There is hope and Cissel observes that legislators like Representative Dwight Evans in Philadelphia, who overcame union opposition in his 1998 election, may lead the way for school choice.[53]

Lennore Ealy, a white professional who until recently worked for a national school choice organization in Indianapolis, offers comments that tend to confirm some of the concerns raised by Polly Williams and others. Wealthy white supporters of choice are entering new and unexplored territory when they try to work in the black community. She is skeptical about the ability of the rich to form effective coalitions with the poor and with black churches to bring school choice. She agrees with the effort to build bridges but does not know if it will succeed. Fundamentally, Ealy sees entrepreneurs having difficulty being partners—they are used to leading—and not functioning as equals. Their goal is for the black community to own its own schools but the means used, assistance with resources, programs, and administrative organization, may undermine the independence of the schools the entrepreneurs help to start. Donors, for example, will demand accountability for funds given, and the churches that start schools may see this as outside interference. Furthermore, outside help can be resented for the inferiority it implies or perpetuates.[54]

Ealy thinks the good intentions and methods of school choice leaders may not be backed up by effective working relationships with those they are trying to help. This is a large issue rooted in history and experience, the painful legacy of racism and poverty. Simply working well with black individuals does not mean an effective bridge reaches to the black community as a whole. Earning the trust of African Americans long disappointed with the solutions offered by liberal and conservative white reformers requires patience, perseverance, extraordinary skills, self-sacrifice, and self-restraint. Ealy thinks school choice reformers underestimate the challenge involved in working with the black community in general and with the poor in particular.[55]

Some activists are pessimistic—they are surprisingly less than sanguine about future prospects for school choice. Jackie Cissel and Lennore Ealy each see grounds for hope but both are disappointed with early efforts and results. Perhaps they are impatient for change. Cissel knows how hard it will be to mobilize black parents and Ealy is sensitive to the historic and cultural barriers that make it hard for the rich to truly partner with the poor. The passive poor and the aggressive entrepreneur cry out for mediators, someone to link them appropriately. Community leaders need to rise up to fulfill this role. Pastors are one answer. Another to be considered are the "rebellious" mentioned by Gardner and Moss. These are the materially successful African Americans who have yet to latch on to a practical vision for the poor they have left behind. Where are the leaders for the next generation, the civil rights movement for education?

Howard Fuller is one such community leader, an accomplished professional focused on getting change by taking full advantage of the present opportunity. His days are half-filled with fundraising and planning for specific programs. The rest of his time he travels and speaks for education reform and school choice. He seeks to inspire others by the example of an education for the poor that works.

Howard Fuller, the distinguished former Superintendent of the Milwaukee Public Schools (MPS), is pioneering new efforts to make school choice more than a dream—a living experiment. He is optimistic. His city, he concludes, is better situated at the moment with more education options for poor people than any other city in America. Vouchers allow parents with incomes below 175 percent of the poverty line to access religious and nonreligious schools. The poor can attend public schools, charter schools, schools with public vouchers, and subsidized private schools. His passion is to make the schools these children attend—whatever the choice they make— the best possible. That for him means getting resources and ideas to the grass roots, and especially to new private community schools, as quickly as possible and exploring programs that already exist, such as Success for All, Chicago Math, or whole school reform efforts, like the New American School Designs, the Edison Project, and the Modern Red School House. It also means promoting the "Milwaukee" example far and wide in speeches and seminars, bringing people to Milwaukee to observe schools and travelling outside the state. Fuller estimates that he gives over fifty speeches and talks each year to a variety of groups, including universities, school boards, pastors, educators, legislators, and conventions of all kinds. He spends about half of his time in local programs sponsored by the "Institute for the Transformation of Learning, Marquette University," and half of it speaking on the road.[56]

The Institute has a practical vision with several elements to it. Fuller spoke first of his new program in seven local churches, the "Neighborhood Technology Learning Centers." Each has a computer learning center set up and staffed by the Institute that provides the necessary equipment and personal instruction for children and adults. "Kids are resilient if you give them a strong adult support structure." Where better to find that structure, Fuller thought, than in churches already connected and committed to people in need. The churches are delighted to participate, and the paid staff put in a twenty-hour week in the learning centers that children attend after school.[57]

The second effort is the Professional Development Center, located at the Institute, accessible to nineteen schools, private choice schools, and partnership schools that contract with the MPS to provide programs for at-risk students. The support is aimed at improving curriculums and teacher practices in the schools. These centers supplement the school programs, providing summer institutes for example, and they are assisting with the regular curriculum. A third program is his Charter School Resource Center designed to help those applying for charters with the application process and with referrals to groups that can assist with curriculum and the running of schools. A fourth program is engaged in advocacy research, studying teacher union contracts for example.

Fuller wants to spend even more of his time in Milwaukee expanding these activities in order to "radically change the one-best system," that he says needs to be replaced. He is getting help to implement this vision. Fuller received grants from the Annie E. Casey Foundation, the Flech Foundation, the Hertzfeld Foundation, the Danforth Foundation, the Bradley Foundation, and others for his Institute programs. Fuller considers outside money necessary as seed money to get things up and running. As of early 1999 some local entrepreneurs have contributed individually and through local foundations.[58]

In the years since he left public education administration in 1992, Fuller says attitudes toward school choice have changed markedly from "universal hostility" to an open interest. The African-American community is especially open, he finds. For over a year Fuller planned a "National Symposium of African Americans" on the subject of school choice. It was held in March 1999, in Milwaukee. He expected over 150 participants to gather to discuss the wide variety of choice options and the best ways to get choice. The purpose of the symposium was to launch a national black school choice network. Fuller notes that most school choice conferences and conventions have few blacks in attendance. He wants to break this de facto color barrier by enabling blacks to organize within the movement.[59]

One issue within school choice reform is the question of how black church-related schools preserve their identity as religious schools if and when they embrace school choice. Fuller reports, for example, that Reverend Floyd Flake will promote the transformation of religious schools to charter schools to gain the benefits of the charter legislation just passed in New York. Fuller is encouraging religion-based schools in his city to accept public vouchers but not to surrender their distinctive nature by becoming charters. African Americans need to discuss this issue among themselves, he says.

Democratic politicians disappoint Fuller by their stubborn refusal to consider the merits of school choice. He has no expectation that this will change in the short term or the long term. Democrats have been on the defensive in the 1990s he says, losing ground nationally and locally to Republicans, and in this period of retrenchment they have grown even more dependent on their base, the education unions. Fuller does not expect this to change and says the exceptions, such as Representative Dwight Evans with whom he is close, only prove the rule that few politicians are genuinely independent of their contributors and financial base. This could, however, precipitate a crisis of conscience in the ranks of African-American public servants if the government-run schools in the inner cities continue to fail and parents and pastors begin to ask for school choice. Meanwhile, Fuller wants to stay close to the neighborhoods that need school choice the most and are willing to work with him and his programs.[60]

Public schools, in Fuller's thinking and experience, have no capacity for real reform unless there is external force that gets their attention. In reality, he says, the education leadership will respond only if they are challenged by loss of control over their budgets. Students who leave, by means of vouchers or charter schools, make a difference because every student lost to the regular public systems means an eventual reduction in revenue. The politics of education reform, he concludes, will follow and respond to the money issues.

School choice in Milwaukee has entered a new phase, according to Fuller. As a movement they used to press for more choice for more students. Now they are concentrating on keeping what they have from being taken away by the regulators. Furthermore, there are not enough private schools operating to provide a quality education to poor students. This must change in his view. He wants more schools so that all 15,000 vouchers authorized will be used instead of the 6,000 currently granted. As many as 70,000 children qualify by income for vouchers, Fuller said, most of them African American.[61]

School Choice and African Americans: Conclusions

The power of Polly Williams's ideas is not so much in her solutions, but in her questions. She wants vouchers for the poor to stay that way but she takes nothing for granted, because she knows that even school choice may fail to produce what it promises. In her ultimate tests for any program she continues to ask: Does it benefit my people? Is the community in control of local schools. Are these schools free of excessive regulation? Are African-American teachers and administrators present? Are they excellent schools in every way, friendly to our culture, preparing our children for every challenge? She presses these questions at every opportunity and scorns false answers. Over the years, Williams has learned to be suspicious of those in power. Of every program, including those she helped to create, she asks, "Where are the results?"

While Polly Williams is a seasoned "pol," black pastors working to build new educational facilities or to turn their Sunday schools into viable full-time private or charter academies are learning the skills and strategies needed to turn their visions into reality. Does this have the potential to become a second civil rights movement, as some urge? It may be more than that if churches succeed at owning and operating schools. For black churches school choice represents tremendous potential for securing greater independence, opportunity, and equality for children. The black religious tradition will also be taking more effective control of its destiny in the next generation, as the reverends Floyd Flake, Steve Gardner, Marlon Moss, Ann Byfield, and others acknowledge.

Reverend Floyd Flake, a forerunner and inspiration to others, sees schools as the means to turn around a child, a neighborhood, and a community. He favors starting charter schools and eventually moving toward a system of vouchers. Working among the poor are other pastors who share an intensity of vision and purpose that cannot be denied. Given even minimal resources, Garland, Moss, and Byfield will manage to start and run schools. Outside help, such as that provided by Pat Rooney and Don Laskowski, may also be indispensable and needs to be given with sensitivity and no strings attached. Keeping those schools truly independent is essential if they are to survive.

Howard Fuller understands that if ideas are to be accepted they must first be demonstrated. "Show me that school choice works," is the challenge he hears and the motivation for his activism. As he sees for himself the good fruit of vouchers and charters and shares this with others he has no doubt that school choice will leap from Milwaukee to other cities. His plan is to spread that good news as it becomes reality and matures in Milwaukee. The next stage, says Fuller, is for African Americans to organize themselves to be an independent force within the school choice movement.

Notes

1. Howard L. Fuller, "School Choice in Milwaukee: 1990–1998," *Current Education Issues: No. 98–1*, Institute of the Transformation of Learning, Marquette

University, June 1998; Rep. Annette "Polly" Williams, telephone interview by Hubert Morken, October 21, 1998; Daniel McKinley, interview by Hubert Morken, Milwaukee, WI, July 28, 1998; Dr. Quentin Quade, Bruce Thompson, and George Mitchell, three separate interviews by Hubert Morken, Milwaukee, WI, July 29, 1998; Mayor John Norquist, interview by Hubert Morken, Milwaukee, WI, July 30, 1998; Susan Mitchell, telephone interview, October 1, 1998.

2. Based on interviews by the authors, specifically documented throughout this monograph.

3. Biography of Representative Annette P. Williams, Wisconsin State Government homepage, December 2, 1998; Williams, telephone interview, October 21, 1998.

4. Williams, telephone interview, October 21, 1998.

5. Ibid.

6. Ibid.

7. Ibid.

8. Ibid.; Parents for School Choice, "The Opinion of Blacks in Milwaukee on Education and School Choice," March 1995.

9. Williams calls Fanny Lewis of Cleveland, another voucher pioneer, a real Christian, a committed innovator, a person of integrity, and he gives high praise to her leadership. Williams, telephone interview, October 21, 1998.

10. Ibid.

11. Ibid.

12. Ibid.

13. Ibid.

14. Ibid.

15. Ibid.

16. Ibid.; Reverend Floyd Flake, interview by Jo Formicola, New York, NY, February 4, 1998.

17. Williams, telephone interview, October 21, 1998.

18. Ibid.

19. Ibid.

20. Ibid.

21. Ibid.

22. Ibid.

23. Ibid.

24. Ibid.

25. Ibid.

26. Williams, telephone interview, October 21, 1998.

27. James C. Carper and Jack Layman, "Black-Flight Academies: The New Christian Day Schools," *The Educational Forum*, vol. 61, (winter 1997): 117.

28. Ibid., p. 116.

29. Flake, interview, February 4, 1998.

30. Ibid.

31. Ibid.

32. Dr. Thomas Brown, interview by Hubert Morken, Indianapolis, IN, July 27, 1998.

33. Ibid.; Community Leaders Allied for Superior Schools (CLASS), A Report on Student Performance: Indianapolis Public Schools, October 20, 1997.

34. Brown, interview, July 27, 1998.

35. Ibid.

36. Reverend Steve Gardner, Reverend Marlon Moss, interview by Hubert Morken, Indianapolis, IN, July 27, 1998.

37. Ibid.

38. Ibid.; Brown, interview, July 27, 1998.

39. Antioch Christian Academy, Handbook, 1998–1999.

40. Gardner and Moss, interview, July 27, 1998.

41. Ibid.

42. Reverend Ann Byfield, interview by Hubert Morken, Indianapolis, IN, July 27, 1998.

43. Ibid.

44. Ibid.

45. Ibid.

46. Rooney, interview, July 21, 1998; Don Laskowski, interview by Hubert Morken, Indianapolis, IN, July 22, 1998; Antioch Christian Academy, Christian School Handbook Kindergarten–3d Grade, 1998–1999; RISE, Script for "adopt a school" marketing video, manuscript, 1998.

47. Rooney, interview, July 21, 1998.

48. Laskowski, interview, July 22, 1998.

49. Rooney, interview, July 21, 1998.

50. Ibid.

51. Ibid.

52. Jackie Cissel, interview by Hubert Morken, Indianapolis, IN, July 27, 1998.

53. Ibid.; Jackie Cissel, "Slap in the Face to the Rev. Flake," clipping, article on opinion page, *Indianapolis News*, February 26, 1998.

54. Lennore Ealy, interview by Hubert Morken, Indianapolis, IN, July 21, 1998.

55. Ibid.

56. Howard Fuller, telephone interview by the author, January 30, 1999.

57. Ibid.; Pastor Robert Harris, "Tabernacle's Computer Connection," *Out of the Box: Explorations in the Transformation of Learning*, newsletter published by Institute for the Transformation of Learning, vol. 3, no. 2, fall 1998.

58. Fuller, telephone interview.

59. Ibid.

60. Ibid.

61. Ibid.

Chapter 7

Scholars, Activists, and Advocacy

Policy wars use the individual contributions of scholars and activists, whose writings or deeds may decide who wins and what prevails, particularly for school choice. Academic disputes over whether or not educational options will work and at what cost influence legislators, judges, and voters. This is the turf of scholars. Citizen involvement, public support, and sentiment for reform, on the other hand, is the territory of the activists. They know how to move people to act. Thus, scholars are committed to study choice in order to inform debate with their findings while activists work for choice by seeking ways to overcome indifference or opposition in people and organizations. Both hope to shape policy by their words and actions.

Change may be justified rationally, but change often occurs in response to political forces. Therefore, scholars do not necessarily decide the outcome but address a host of specific questions. They examine school choice programs and draw conclusions while activists bring motivational and relational skills to bear, working to persuade leaders and followers in communities to believe in school choice and to work for it. School choice has its partisans—professors and others—who make singular contributions to the movement. These people are not simply employees in an organization, hired to do a job. They are better understood as volunteers, though some are paid for their work. Most are not independently wealthy, but instead they contribute words and organizational skills to the cause. Some are professors, some independent scholars, and others do political or administrative work, trying to win and organize support in local communities.

School choice attracts some highly motivated and independent individuals to champion its cause politically. Professors Paul E. Peterson (Harvard), Terry M. Moe (Stanford), and Charles L. Glenn (Boston University) are scholars actively writing on school choice in a way that supports the movement. Independent scholars indirectly affiliated with universities are active, too, including Andrew J. Coulson and Myron Lieberman (Bowling Green State University, Ohio). John E. Coons (emeritus) and Stephen D. Sugarman are law professors at the University of California, Berkeley. They have long been active on behalf of school choice and now have close ties to the Pacific Research Institute, where they continue to be productive. Another group of scholars makes its contribution simply by studying the subject of school choice politics dispassionately, not by conducting any partisan activities. Two scholars at Fordham University, Lance D. Fusarelli and Bruce S. Cooper, are prime examples of professors who strive to give a balanced treatment to divisive controversies.

Activist individuals (and some scholars are activists as well) have a distinct role of pressing for change usually with little more than their wits, energy, and experience to serve them. Their temperaments and abilities vary enormously, as do their tactics and goals. They do make significant contributions and keep the movement from degenerating into the politics of a few well-funded groups. Marshall Fritz and Kevin Teasley, for example, take opposite sides on most school choice issues and have each started their own organization. David Brennan may well be the premier school choice activist in the nation but most of his story cannot be told until he is ready to share it. Bert Hall acts behind the scenes as a school choice administrator, strongly supported by David Brennan and others. Bruce Thompson works from his position as a member of the Milwaukee School Board and James M. Goenner reviews charter school applications in his position at Central Michigan University. Most of these individuals receive occasional press attention. All have a substantial personal stake in school choice, laboring long hours on its behalf.

Both groups, the scholars and the activists, merit attention and deserve to be studied and remembered. Each of the individuals mentioned could be studied at length. Others could have been included. Something distinctive and often of critical value is brought by each to an already diverse movement.

The Scholars: Paul Peterson

Paul Peterson, who is a professor of government at Harvard University and director of the university's Education Policy and Governance Program, thinks school choice is a fifty-year struggle that eventually will be won. He compares it to Jedi fighters against the Death Star in the movie Star Wars "because the activists are so varied and poorly coordinated while the opposition consists of teacher unions, school boards, superintendents, and other well-organized, solidly entrenched interests." This is a battle, he says, between the power of vested interests and new ideas. Peterson is a Democrat. His book on Chicago school reform *School Politics, Chicago Style* (1976) taught him how difficult it was to bring change in a "completely insular" system. He wants to split the close ties between the Democratic Party and teacher organizations by getting support from minority groups and open-minded, thoughtful segments of the Democratic Party. Peterson feels his own personal contribution to this process can best be achieved by conducting compelling research that is authenticated by the best available social science methodology, placing his work beyond reproach. He hopes to demonstrate to impartial observers that school choice works when it is done properly.[1]

Until recently, Peterson was more an observer and sponsor of school choice research than a participant. During the 1960s he became aware of Milton Friedman's ideas on school choice, but he initially saw this as just one of many possible mechanisms for school choice. University of Chicago scholar James Coleman's vilification, after he discovered that students attending Catholic schools outperformed public school students, had a major impact on him. "Coleman, by discovering the positive results of Roman Catholic schools, put the empirical muscle on the theoretical skeleton of Milton Friedman," he says. Jokingly, Peterson refers to Friedman and Coleman and other teachers and students like himself who matriculated there and support choice, "a University of Chicago conspiracy."[2]

Working at the Brookings Institution, a well-known moderately liberal Washington think tank, Peterson sponsored the writing and publication of *Politics, Markets and America's Schools* (1990) by John E. Chubb and Terry M. Moe. He witnessed the violent response of academics as they blacklisted Chubb, in effect cutting him off from academic appointments for which he seemed appropriate. Upset as he was by this apparent discrimination, he was even more impressed with the impact of the Chubb and Moe book.

Peterson wanted to get into school choice research, despite the anticipated persecution—but he had to wait for several years until an opportunity presented itself. He was asked to do a chapter for a book, *Seeds of Crisis: Public Schooling in Milwaukee Since 1920* (1993), with the task of placing the book's discussion of the Milwaukee public schools in national perspective. He remembers thinking, "Urban schools were in trouble, so lets look at voucher alternatives." In the chapter he asked if schools in big cities could be improved sufficiently by incremental and modest reforms or whether the entire structure needed modification at a more fundamental level to shake a debilitating "institutional malaise." He concluded that, although this question could not be definitively answered, "in reality, central city finances are likely to deteriorate, racial segregation can be expected to intensify, school autonomy could well be further eclipsed, and the external pressure on school officials may well become increasingly burdensome." In view of these problems he then asked boldly, "Can choice make a difference?" After critically examining early results of the Milwaukee choice program, which he found were likely to be more positive than others acknowledged, he strongly recommended that school choice experiments be conducted aggressively, unencumbered by restraints designed to make them fail. He wrote, "More and better-established schools need to be given opportunities to participate in choice programs; more funds need to be given students attending choice schools; more students need to be allowed to participate; and crude income limitations on participation should be eliminated."[3]

At the book presentation in Milwaukee where he gave his findings and recommendations, Peterson recalls that he was, to put it mildly, coolly received. However, George Mitchell, the Milwaukee school choice advocate, was in the audience. He subsequently asked Peterson if he would consider writing a full-length paper critiquing the work of Professor John Witte, a strong critic of vouchers. The critique was eventually written, and an ensuing dispute led to the release of data on the Milwaukee choice program, data that Peterson feels justified his original critique. Today, Peterson is grateful to Witte, who unintentionally helped to get him involved in school choice research.[4]

Peterson devoted a summer to preparing his critique of Witte's evaluation. Witte's research, he said, was in need of careful examination because his conclusions were being cited in Washington, D.C., testimony claiming that vouchers did not work. Peterson also asked for the data set used by Witte to evaluate the findings. After some considerable conflict between the two on the issue of access, including exploring possible use of the Freedom of Information Act, Witte agreed to release the information.[5]

When the data were finally released in 1996, Peterson led a team at Harvard, including, as advisory members, Professor Donald Rubin in the statistics department and Northwestern University professor Christopher Jencks, who re-analyzed Witte's data. Peterson and his colleagues maintained that students in private schools were learning more than those remaining in public schools. His findings were based on a comparison of students chosen to participate in the program with those not chosen. Since students were chosen in a lottery, Peterson was confident that this comparison was the most precise available. The findings were reported in the *New York Times* by the end of August 1996, and he presented the results at a meeting of the American Political Science Association in September. He agreed to Witte's participation as a discussant of his paper at the convention. Peterson received an intense negative response from Witte and others; however, he recalls, many others felt his study was of higher quality than Witte's. Overnight Peterson's public profile exploded as a school choice results expert. This in turn gave him credibility with philanthropists Bruce Kovner, Peter Flanigan, and Roger Hertog, who sought his help and counsel in studying the School Choice Scholarship Foundation (SCSF) private voucher program announced in New York City in February 1997.[6]

Peterson had discussed with Terry Moe the possibility of a randomized experiment as the ideal way to estimate precisely the academic value of school choice. Earlier studies by Coleman and others indicated that students who attended parochial schools performed well compared to their peers in public schools from the same neighborhoods and from families of comparable wealth and education. Doubts remained, however, because the excellence of private school results could possibly be explained by differences in the families. Did the families who sent their children to private schools have better educational atmospheres, giving these children superior preparation and more emphasis on learning? The only way to factor out this possibility was to have a large pool of parents who all wanted to send their children to private schools and who shared the same ethnic, income, and social characteristics. This pool needed to be divided randomly into two groups to be able to compare the results of private versus public schools. The SCCF private scholarship initiative provided just this opportunity, and Peterson was quick to seize it.[7]

SCSF in February 1997 offered 1,300 private scholarships worth $1,400 a year for at least three years to low-income families in New York City, selecting the winners from the applicant pool by lottery. The winners who attended private religious and secular schools could then be compared with those who applied, then lost the lottery and remained in public schools. The numbers in the voucher schools and the public school control group must be comparable, the selection must be done randomly, and testing must be done in the same way for both groups. In New York, Peterson reported, 20,000 children applied for these private scholarships. There were easily enough students to be studied using this random selection method. SCSF agreed to support the study, starting the research even before the lottery was conducted. Altogether, Peterson said there would be four locations for this study—New York, Washington, D.C., Dayton, Ohio, and San Antonio, Texas. San Antonio will be somewhat different because 14,000 students from the one district will be eligible for the vouchers (all who meet the income qualification), so no control group will be available.[8]

Peterson reports that initial findings in New York for the first year of the SCSF program are encouraging for academic performance: grades 2–5 demonstrated two percentile points more improvement in math and reading than the control group remaining in public schools, and four points in reading and six points in math for children in fourth and fifth grade. Other measures, including parental satisfaction (higher) and racial isolation (lower), were favorable. Evidence from Dayton, Ohio, and Washington, D.C., data on parents applying for private scholarships shows that they are from lower income and less educated families than those who have attended private schools without such assistance. Peterson is pleased that many of those least able to attend private schools because of cost are now able and willing to apply. They want, his survey's show, a better academic climate. "Applicants with children in public schools said the most important reasons for applying for a private-school scholarship was to find a school with higher academic standards and a better curriculum." Programs built on parental choice must demonstrate that parents, even those with the least education and employment success measured by income, care enough about a quality education for their children to make the necessary sacrifices for them to attend a private school. Peterson argues that even his initial findings support this conclusion.[9]

Peterson, the scholar, has tried to persuade sponsors of privately funded programs to use lotteries in admissions. Activists now understand that if they have a voucher program there are advantages to running it using a lottery instead of on first-come first-serve basis or by a selective admission process. Random selection is better for research purposes and also protects the program from the charge that vouchers deliberately select the best students and leave the problem students for the public schools to educate. Timothy Ehrgott, Executive Director of the Educational Choice Charitable Trust in Indianapolis, reports that for the last two years he has used a lottery for the over 1,000 private scholarships he distributes rather than following the first-come first-serve method of the old system. The advantage of the lottery, he says, lies in the publicity it generates, its fairness, and the popular demand it demonstrates. In the June 1998 Indianapolis lottery, for example, 5,500 children participated in the lottery providing 625 new scholarships to add to the 1,100 already granted. Academic, equity, and political considerations combined to persuade many to favor the lottery approach. Although some private and parochial schools strongly prefer to admit students selectively to preserve standards and school distinctives, this is not compatible with the social science goals Peterson has successfully encouraged the school choice movement to adopt.[10]

Peterson is now active on the school choice speakers' circuit making his case for reform. At a recent conference he reported that in the United States math scores are about as good as most European countries up until the fourth grade. But the longer students are in public schools after fourth grade, the worse they do compared to the children of other nations, as the Third International Mathematics and Science Study (TIMSS) reports. Commenting on this in his essay "School Choice: A Report Card," Peterson suspects the fault lies not with the families and students alone, or with the culture as some charge, but with the schools as well. Is school choice the answer? Peterson intends to find out by compiling and interpreting data from multiple cities where the working poor tend to participate in voucher programs where they are available.[11]

Peterson also reports on recent studies done by his research team as well as by colleagues in different universities, relaying this information to school choice supporters. Why do families apply for vouchers? Peterson reports that from preliminary studies in Cleveland, he knows over 80 percent apply to improve academic quality, over 70 percent are looking for safety, and over

60 percent want a better location. Are families—both parents and students—satisfied with the private schools they select? Much more satisfied, Peterson discovers, in choice schools. Race relations are also better in private schools, he claims, measured in lunch room interaction and by more integrated enrollments—plus there is more fighting between racial groups in public schools and more toleration and community volunteering in private schools. Private schools have less student turn over and less than 1 percent are expelled. Encouraged as he is by these recent research findings, Peterson is confident his new studies just launched will be even more definitive because they use randomized comparisons. He is especially hopeful that his New York study will be accepted as rigorous and objective, and, given New York's location as the media capital, influential for the rest of the nation.[12]

Peterson combines support for school choice with fierce determination to use social science methods honed to a fine edge in its defense. In his estimation, school reform will be a protracted process undertaken over many decades. His scholarly team at Harvard and elsewhere provides the academic muscle to study the results of voucher programs and other differences between private and public schools. This, he says, is in the tradition of James Coleman and the other University of Chicago iconoclasts. The methods he recommends (e.g., the use of the lottery in admissions) become the methods adopted by entrepreneurs pushing school choice. Winning credibility for choice with the press and the public and protecting it from false accusations and adverse attacks are integral to Peterson's work. He hopes politicians eventually will listen, too.

Terry Moe

Terry M. Moe (Stanford), much like Peterson who sponsored him at Brookings in the late 1980s, is an academic willing to speak against the status quo in education and for school choice. But he has no illusions that the policy process is driven by the truth. His experience in the voucher wars in California and elsewhere leaves him with no hope that professional educators in the public school systems will agree with his conclusions and act to break the public school monopoly of tax funds. Education politics, in his view, is interest-group politics in its most elementary form, motivated by money, power, and security.[13]

Moe helped to break new ground in his school choice studies in the 1990s. His book, *Politics, Markets and America's Schools* (1990), written with John E. Chubb, was seven years in preparation. Reflecting on how he came to write the book, Moe says that he was impressed, first, by the merits of *A Nation at Risk: The Imperative for Educational Reform* (1983), a report released by the Reagan administration. Second, he observed that change did not happen subsequently from within the system. As time passed and little improvement occurred during his years of research he concluded that public education, like any monopoly, was intractably resistant to change. As this became more apparent with problems in school mounting, Moe states, by 1990 it was possible to talk about vouchers and be heard.[14]

Chubb and Moe's book hit like a bombshell. The Milwaukee voucher experiment helped to lend credence to his judgments. People were already discussing these ideas, the book came out, and the time was right. Moe then returned to Stanford while Chubb remained in the Washington maelstrom at Brookings and later joined the Edison Company. Moe was called on to lecture and travel. As he looks back Moe relates that he had no intention of becoming an education activist. Yet that is what happened. Soon Moe was active in California in 1993 backing Proposition 174. He edited a book, *Private Vouchers* (1995), and he is working on a book on public opinion vouchers to be published by Brookings (1999).[15]

Moe has a special concern that polls and surveys can be false and manipulated in the policy process often to the detriment of school choice. Good research is needed on school choice and vouchers, he maintains, first and foremost, for the sake of the truth, and second, to protect the policy process from malicious or inadvertent manipulation. No one, Moe claims, has explored in-depth what people really think of this subject. He has recently devised an in-depth survey with many questions that allow him to analyze what people think about vouchers if they consider them more than superficially on a one or two question poll. Moe says he is finding that parents have a personal interest to protect their children, but they also have a social interest in the welfare of the whole community and especially schools.[16]

Speaking at an American Political Science Association (APSA) roundtable on the issue of Politics of Education Reform, Moe gave a starkly negative assessment of school politics as they are presently practiced:

> The new politics of education is poor people and Republicans vs. Democrats. This is a political battle—interest-group politics pure and simple—its all about power and interests—and no truth will make a bit of difference to those opposed to choice. Rhetoric is about how we help kids but the reality is about union power. Institutional interests require unions to oppose vouchers, which are their worst nightmare and a huge threat. This is not a debate but a fight, an incremental fight that will take ten to twenty years. If we could show with 100 percent certainty that vouchers help low-income kids, they would not care because this is the camel's nose and we will go from granting vouchers to poor kids to providing vouchers for all kids.[17]

In Moe's judgment the Milwaukee and Cleveland voucher programs are mutant cases, the exceptions to the rule that unions generally stop vouchers. In the federal separation of powers system there are many points in the policy process where vouchers can be stopped. Even when they are adopted they are vulnerable to assault through regulation. Politicians want reelection and education union money is generally enough to deter really serious choice efforts. Unions, Moe relates, are monolithic and serious about protecting their interests.[18]

Moe is not always happy about the reform efforts of school choice advocates. He is especially critical of those who are too demanding, refusing to be flexible when legislation is being crafted. Also, he finds fault with those too ready to compromise with the opposition. Essentially, he maintains something of a gadfly role within the movement.

After the defeat of Proposition 174, which he considered flawed though he supported it, Moe worked with John Coons and Stephen Sugarman and others, including John Walton, to draft another initiative. This coalition failed to get Milton Friedman's support because he does not favor low-income vouchers. To Moe, school choice is an incremental process and some vouchers are better than no vouchers. Friedman, he observed, was being excessively ideological and rigid. Furthermore, the school choice coalition lost control of the process when the entrepreneurs like Walton got involved. The people with money will make the key decisions in the final analysis, he says. As the coalition split between Walton and Friedman who could not agree, in Moe's view school choice lost out. Disappointed at the temporary stalemate in California, Moe says he fully expects some state to pass a full voucher law.[19]

Moe was encouraged when Silicon Valley entrepreneur Reed Hastings succeeded in liberalizing the state charter school law increasing the number of charters and freeing them from some onerous restraints. He praised Reed's tactics and success but commented that, in his view, Reed gave up too much to win. The phase-in is slow, 100 new charter schools per year after the first year, and Moe believed that in a state the size of California this is insufficient. Charters are just another step along the way to full school choice. However, for some, including Reed, charters may be all they push for. Moe is concerned that half measures may stall further initiatives and so prevent the transformation of schools that he seeks.[20]

Corporate America, Moe relates, generally talks to education experts who see more money for public schools as a cure-all. Meanwhile the religious want religious schools and the intellectual market-oriented leaders of school choice are driven by ideas and not self-interest. The real question, he asks, is: When or how can these diverse groups (with some, like business, not yet on-board for choice) get together to help those who need it the most, the children attending substandard schools?[21]

Charles L. Glenn

Charles L. Glenn (Boston University) is a third scholar who has written extensively on school choice as an advocate. Like Peterson and Moe, he continues to break new ground. Glenn's most recent work deals with the place of religious schools in school choice systems in Europe and the United States.

Glenn worked for the state of Massachusetts beginning in the early 1960s, supervising programs to help achieve racial balance in public schools. In 1974 Massachusetts provided "substantial funding to encourage parent choice that would serve to integrate schools." As a dedicated reformer within the system who was responsible for administering this program, he notes, "Eventually, I came to believe that school choice could not realize its full potential unless the supply of schools among which to choose was opened up with charter schools and even with vouchers." He then wrote *The Myth of the Common School* (1988), a book that dealt primarily with the history of American public education but was designed to lay the foundations for his school choice convictions.[22]

In his graduate seminars at Boston University, Glenn learned that morals are not being taught in public schools. His students, moreover, all agree that public schools have no right to impose morals on students. This is a given, they argued. Yet, in his view, if the schools refuse to teach morals they fail in their most elementary responsibility.[23]

> Two colleagues at Boston University, Kevin Ryan and Edwin Delattre, have helped me to understand how crucial it is that we nourish opportunities for children—and adults as well—to develop the sense of moral obligation and the settled disposition to act virtuously. No social policy question could be more crucial than whether the public assistance, crisis intervention, and criminal justice systems teach those lessons effectively, and no educational policy question could be more crucial than whether schools, early childhood programs, and education of youth and adults based in social agencies does the same.[24]

Glenn concludes from his years of experience in government and study, that government teaches morals badly compared to what he calls the mediating structures of family, church, and private associations. The answer he thinks is for government to rely on private agencies to teach public virtue. Vouchers used by parents to send children to parochial schools, for example, are in this view serving a valuable public role if the students are taught to treat other people respectfully. Europeans have always understood the civilizing influence of religion, he writes, and assist church-related education for this reason. Glenn thinks that even charter schools should be allowed to be religious in their orientation, both accountable for their education results and free from state control in the training and hiring of teachers.[25]

Charter schools are potentially dangerous to parochial schools, competing for students, yet Glenn is on the board of a charter school and thinks the solution is to make religiously distinctive charter schools legal. Constitutional law experts who favor choice, he says, are ready to tackle this issue.[26]

Glenn is known for his excellent studies on school choice in Western Europe and Canada, *Choice of Schools in Six Nations: France, Netherlands, Belgium, Britain, Canada, and West Germany* (1989), and Eastern Europe after its liberation, *Educational Freedom in Eastern Europe* (1995). He has worked with the UN as well as published on language policy. Most recently Glenn has decided to turn to a difficult problem for school choice advocates: How can distinctively private schools, including religious schools, be assisted by vouchers or other public funding mechanisms and preserve their distinctive programs? This issue is crucial for Glenn's whole support of school choice. In short: Why have choice if the "embrace" of government serves to make private schools no different than public schools in what and how they teach?[27]

What gives Glenn the confidence that religious schools can be given public support without losing the capacity to be different? Can they teach morals and the requisite theological and philosophic grounding even as they receive public funding? In his book, *The Ambiguous Embrace* (1999), Glenn tries to be as realistic as possible with his answers, examining the impact of public funding on religious social agencies in the United States and religious schools in Europe. He is cautiously optimistic in his findings. There are many examples of governments giving welfare agencies and private schools room to be different. Schools can operate with some accountability—that racial discrimination not be practiced and academic subjects be taught—with no state control of the curriculum content, religious practices, or personnel. Confident of the feasibility of string-free assistance, Glenn recommends that religious schools be required to have private accreditation to receive public funds, an accreditation that sponsoring religious bodies could provide for themselves. However, he strongly resists state control of teacher preparation or hiring.[28]

What is far more troublesome than government regulation, according to Glenn, are the cultural and spiritual pressures to conform to the standards and assumptions of the dominant public education models and practices. Teachers in Europe who teach in religious schools and even the churches they serve sadly forsake their own traditions and voluntarily secularize programs to fit in or to gain acceptance. The answer to this assimilation into the dominant materialistic culture, writes Glenn, is not to separate from tax-supported funding but to strengthen the authentically religious perspective offered by the schools in all courses and aspects of their programs. The first focus of these schools should be on teacher preparation and nurture, to a sophisticated fusion of theology and pedagogy, not on the tax issues or even regulatory battles that Glenn argues are winnable.[29]

In his recent study of school choice Glenn supports public funding of private religious schools as essential for citizen development. If they are safeguarded from regulatory overreach, thereby preserving their autonomy, this will be positive for religion as well. He does not think government schools can succeed at teaching morals. School choice then for Glenn is the last and best solution for combining skills and academic content with character development.

Looking ahead, Glenn predicts that school choice reform may come fast despite union opposition. He sees two reasons for this. First, he says, the standards issue is exposing how bad the government-operated schools are—public concern and political pressures for change will only increase. Second, teachers over sixty are retiring, and he predicts the quality of learning is sure to drop with younger teachers taking their place who have less ability and no sense of how to teach morals in the classroom. If chaos mounts in the classrooms and student performance declines, reform will accelerate as people look for new answers. A short-term pessimist on the quality of schools, as a scholar Glenn is a long-term optimist. His work is designed to encourage government to find ways to help parochial schools without controlling them and to advise the religious to back school choice and to be different, true to themselves and to their beliefs.[30]

As a scholar/advocate Glenn is now active in promoting his views in publications, conferences, press conferences, and behind-the-scenes consulting with organizations. He brings a multinational perspective to the current discussions heating up in the United States. He also has ties to the Evangelical community. His Calvinist orientation means that he rejects a simple free-market approach to school choice. The market provides some answers but questions of justice, care for the poor, and devising a system that properly nurtures the young in morals are his first concern. Glenn gave half of his professional life to the race question in education. He is committing the remainder to bringing genuine religion back into the education mainstream.[31]

Andrew Coulson

Scholars keep finding particular niches where they make distinctive contributions. Peterson is studying voucher outcomes; Moe is looking at public opinion on vouchers; and Glenn analyzes prospects for preserving the identity of private schools in a mature school choice system. A much different angle, namely, the historic role of the free market in education, is the concern of Andrew J. Coulson, who has written a book entitled *Market Education: The Unknown History* (1999). Coulson is an independent scholar from Canada who recently left his computer work to write on the historic role of the free market in education. At a conference in San Francisco sponsored by The Friedman Foundation he appeared with Milton Friedman on a panel at which his work was showcased. Coulson's book is likely to be influential, certainly in the school choice community.[32]

According to Coulson, school choice is not a new concept, having in fact been tried repeatedly throughout history. In many times and places, parents have sent their children to privately owned, operated, and funded schools, and Coulson argues that these educational markets produced a greater flowering of intellect and creativity than did contemporary state-run school systems. In other words, the historical antecedents of modern public schooling, from the ancient militaristic Greek city-state, Sparta, in the 5th and 4th centuries B.C., to its more benign forms in recent times, did not work well even for elites, and they failed to produce a broadly and liberally educated citizenry. In contrast, free-market education in ancient Athens, in the golden age of Islam, and in eighteenth- and nineteenth-century Great Britain, had all the marks of creativity and greatness.[33]

Based on his analysis of education history Coulson argues for five principles that he says must be present for an education system to succeed. The first is school choice for parents:

> Today, study after study has confirmed that parents who have the opportunity to choose their schools base their decisions on sound academic, discipline-related, and moral grounds. Their ability to choose wisely is demonstrated by the superior academic achievement and stronger community environment they and their children enjoy in independent schools. Parents who take the initiative and opt for independent schooling are more satisfied, on average, with virtually every aspect of their children's education than are parents whose children are assigned to an institution by a public school bureaucracy.[34]

Coulson points out that government run systems tend to reduce the role of parents in education to little more than making sure the child goes to school properly dressed and nourished. "The natural result of the negligible, passive educational role assigned to parents by public schooling is a growing apathy towards that schooling. Parental apathy is the number one reason public school teachers give for leaving the profession, and one of the major complaints of those who stay on." As the needs of the modern world change the parents are most alert to these changes and how they affect children, Coulson suggests, and they will seek adjustments in schooling to meet these new challenges as long as they have not been detached from education.[35]

Coulson's second principle is financial responsibility. By this he means that parents truly control their children's education when they pay for it in whole or in part. Coulson relates that as subsidies increase the scope of parental influence diminishes. In instances of poverty where parents have been unable to cover educational costs, they have historically received an education, private or public, largely designed by others for their children. Coulson wants to find ways of providing financial assistance to low-income families without robbing them of control over their own children's education. One way to achieve that aim, he suggests, is by encouraging the growth of many different scholarship granting organizations, from among which low-income parents could pick and choose. In addition, even the poor, he observes, may be able to volunteer time, learn to participate in the schools, serve as a positive influence, and thereby have some ownership. Coulson does not want schools operated in a way that excludes the active role of parents, who preferably are the ones who select schools, pay for schools, volunteer assistance, and help shape the education their children receive.[36]

The third principle he articulates as necessary for school choice to work is freedom: The freedom for teachers and principals to work where they wish— with a variety of schools from which to choose—and to be responsible for the curriculum and teaching methods. Included is the right to expel students if they refuse to cooperate, a power that improves the conduct and performance of all students when they understand that attendance in that school is a privilege and not a right. Problem students can and should be sent to schools for problem students, Coulson argues, as is the case today in public schools. True freedom in education, he concludes, comes from control by teachers and principals over where they work, how they work, and with whom they work.[37]

Coulson's fourth principle is based on competition between schools. He believes, in other words, that market choices enable parents to gravitate toward good schools and away from poorly performing schools failing to teach. For too long monopoly schools have been dealing with their own failures, Coulson thinks, by labeling children learning disabled (LD) when the school is at fault. Coulson list examples of competitive systems that work in the "supplemental" schools that Japanese use today and in classical Athens. Education, he thinks, would be cheaper and better in such a system.[38]

The fifth principle is the issue of profit making. He thinks profits are necessary for expanding the number of schools offering a quality education. There have been good private schools operating for years, but they have not, in Coulson's view, been as innovative, as efficiently run, or as widely replicated as they could be if they were run for profit. Dynamism is lacking in his view. Good private schools today merely "perpetuate their own existence." Compared to the computer industry, education is moribund, overcome by fads but essentially stagnating as bright people avoid teaching and entrepreneurs ignore the field. Drawing excellence to instruction and to the management of schools and especially expanding the number of them available, in Coulson's opinion, requires reinstituting the profit motive into education.[39]

Coulson not surprisingly, given his strong views, is critical of most current reforms, including publicly funded vouchers, refundable tax credits, and charter schools. All these measures have strengths and weaknesses in his view. Public vouchers, for example, invite fraud as schools could inflate their enrollment figures to receive the government subsidy, and they can be challenged—if not always successfully—on the grounds of church/state entanglement. Refundable tax credits present many of the same problems as do vouchers, and charter schools are too much like public schools to make much of a difference. The alternative he proposes is a greatly expanded private scholarship program, backed up as necessary by means-tested non-refundable tuition tax credits. These credits, as also proposed by the Mackinac Center in Michigan, could be claimed by any taxpayer who pays for any child's tuition at a private school. In other words, middle- and low-income parents could take a credit against their own children's tuition, and taxpayers in general could receive a credit for donating money to a private scholarship program that would use the money to subsidize the tuition of a poor child. He also considers a state education tax a possibility worth considering.[40]

> One approach would be to tax only those citizens who do not already donate to scholarship-granting organizations. For example, consider a couple whose assessed education tax is $500. The couple would have two options: They could either pay the tax *or* donate $500 (or more) to a scholarship-granting charity of their own choosing. In the latter case, they would receive an exemption from the education tax.[41]

These ideas coming from young scholars constitute evidence that school choice possibilities are in the beginning stages of conceptualization. Working out from under a status quo that is hard to change will be difficult. Coulson is good at considering options and assessing their possible consequences. He is a theorist whose historical analysis and proposals will be discussed as the push for school reform intensifies. The entrepreneurial model for education that he espouses looks well beyond the current schools commonly available—public, parochial, and college preparatory—to an outpouring of alternatives generated by for-profit enterprises.

Myron Lieberman

Another independent scholar known for his indefatigable labors on behalf of a competitive education industry is Myron Lieberman. He has concentrated most of his efforts on the education unions and their role in defeating school choice. Lieberman's recent publications include *The Teacher Unions* (1997), and *Teachers Evaluating Teachers: Peer Review and the New Unionism* (1998). What distinguishes these books in the context of school choice politics is that they deal with the structure and nature of teacher union organization and practice. One of Lieberman's criticisms is that too little attention is given to the unions. Few school choice supporters, he says, ever attend an NEA or

AFT national convention or a state affiliate meeting, and most seem ignorant of how they operate. "Know your enemy," could well be the Lieberman credo. He has spent a lifetime, from the mid-1950s, writing about these groups, initially as a strong supporter of collective bargaining in education.[42]

Lieberman performs another role as the activist and advocate Chairman of the Education Policy Institute, which is headed by Charlene K. Haar. In this role Lieberman consults with activists, publicizes his writings, and speaks with legislators. Special interests include promoting pro-school choice teacher association alternatives to the NEA and AFT and getting the school choice message across regularly in major media markets. Lieberman is impressed with how effectively Albert Shanker, President of the AFT from 1974 to 1997 promoted his anti school choice agenda in a weekly column in the *New York Times* entitled "Where We Stand." This column, he says, ran as a paid advertisement, cost the union more that $750,000 per year, and received special treatment by the *Times*. It was the only ad to be included in the *New York Times* index.[43] Impressed with Shanker's chutzpah he writes:

> With unflappable confidence, Shanker used these advertisements to allege that voucher schools would rely on advertising instead of improved educational achievement to sell their services. That is, Shanker alleged that the companies would do what Shanker had been doing for public schools since 1971.[44]

There is no one as effective as Shanker was for his cause, in the school choice movement, according to Lieberman. He wishes someone would take a page from the Shanker playbook and tackle the challenge of writing regularly in the *New York Times*. At an age when most scholars have retired from their research labors, Lieberman remains active, coming up with new and old ideas for better ways to advance school choice. Currently he is working on a new book with Professor John Merrifield (University of Texas at San Antonio) that will deal with the school choice controversy. He is concerned that some programs that are called "school choice" programs will not in fact lead to a competitive education industry. As a scholar who changed his mind about unions in the 1970s he is determined to be an active scholar and player in the present. Lieberman maintains an internet homepage http://www.educationpolicy.org/ that gives the latest union and school choice news along with his analysis.[45]

John Coons and Stephen Sugarman

There are several other scholars whose recent work is useful and merit much more attention than this brief review provides. John E. Coons and Stephen D. Sugarman, legal scholars at the University of California, Berkeley, School of Law, have published extensively on school choice. Their recent work with the Pacific Research Institute for Public Policy in San Francisco, *Making School Choice Work for All Families* (1999), is a detailed proposal for how best to design a school choice public scholarship program. Moving from concept to implementation requires complex planning on the source and size of public scholarships, their method of distribution, the design of schools participating, curriculum, testing, teacher credentials, accountability standards, financial reporting, admissions, and teachers salaries. What is so interesting here is the movement from advocacy to management. Assuming vouchers to be a reality, Coons and Sugarman tackle the subject of how best to implement them.[46]

Coons and Sugarman address the political realities of school choice politics as well. They advise, for example, that home schools, affluent prep schools, and some strict separation church schools have no reason to support school choice but do need protection from government regulation. School choice advocates could at least win favor from these groups by joining in their efforts to secure freedom from regulations. Regulatory battles are common ground, they say, for all non-government education programs. Other "tips" they offer include the need to cultivate ethnic minority and non-conservative leadership for the movement to avoid the middle-class stereotypes and a preference for the term scholarship over voucher. Their primary concern, however, is to see that any school choice program be effective, saleable, and just.[47] Coons and Sugarman recommend the following criteria for any system of scholarships:

- Government schools must be empowered to reconstitute themselves in forms analogous and competitive to private schools.
- Participating private schools must be protected from new regulation affecting curriculum, hiring, discipline, and other elements of "identity."
- Admission and tuition policies must insure all children fair access to participating schools.
- Students in special education must be afforded choice in public and private sectors under admission policies that aim for balance between the family's interest in access and the school's interest in maintaining identity.
- Scholarships must be large enough to stimulate new providers.
- Where transport is necessary to insure access, it should be guaranteed for reasonable distances to families who cannot afford it.
- Adequate information must be assured to less sophisticated parents through private and public agencies.[48]

The Coons and Sugarman administrative and political wisdom gleaned from years in the school choice movement represents their best counsel on how to implement school choice. Activists in the movement and possibly legislators certainly will reference it.

Lance Fusarelli

Another academic work, just completed, is Lance Fusarelli's Ph.D. dissertation on school choice charter school and voucher politics in Texas (1998). Now a professor at Fordham University, Fusarelli explains how and why charter school legislation passed easily in the state and vouchers hit a brick wall. His findings are especially helpful as voucher advocates in Texas continue their efforts in 1999 and beyond.[49]

Debate in Texas on charter schools centered, Fusarelli found, on how many schools to create rather than on whether or not to have them. With bipartisan support for creating charter schools free of "red tape," the legislation passed easily in 1995. Neither extensive research nor study of charter schools elsewhere, preceded the move. A consensus on charter schools emerged in the state by 1994 backed by Governor Ann Richards (D) and candidate George Bush, Jr. (R), and with little formal opposition the bill passed permitting twenty schools as a pilot project. Subsequently, and before the first state charter schools could be studied, in 1997 the legislature pressed ahead to expand the number that could be approved to 100. Fusarelli explains the success of charter legislation as a political compromise, a halfway house designed to preempt vouchers.[50]

Vouchers, proposed by Jimmy Mansour, President of Putting Children First (PFC) and by the Texas Public Policy Foundation, met an entirely different fate prior to 1998. Advocacy groups on both sides mobilized and helped to polarize the political process. Most of the state's newspapers that favored charter schools opposed voucher plans. Minority leadership remained opposed despite some defections like African-American state Representative Ron Wilson (D), and there was some increase in grassroots minority support. Yet voucher supporters were much encouraged. In 1996 for the first time since Reconstruction, Republicans controlled the state Senate and since 1982 nearly doubled their strength in the House to sixty-seven compared to eighty-three Democrats. As electoral tides continued to shift toward Republicans vouchers appeared to be within reach.[51]

What observers familiar with the inner workings of Texas politics know is that the institutional power structures in the legislature make it difficult to get any legislation passed in Texas without a super majority. Democrats control the key legislative positions in the House making it difficult to get a voucher bill but Senate rules are an even higher hurdle despite the Republican majority. Several voucher bills were defeated in the Senate in recent years largely because of the "two-thirds rule." This rule provides in effect that no legislation is put on the floor of the Senate for consideration unless it has two-thirds of the thirty-one Senators voting in its favor at least for consideration. A mere eleven Senators can block new legislation.[52]

In 1997 the Senate Education Committee approved a limited voucher program bill by a 6-4 vote but it died, never reaching the floor. Republicans themselves refused to modify the two-thirds rule because it helps the Senate to control the flow of legislation, limiting attention to bills with strong support. It takes only sixteen Senators to pass a bill but it takes twenty-one to consider it. Since the rules of the Senate favor consensus, charters passed but vouchers did not.[53]

Fusarelli also points out that in Texas the governor has limited legislative influence, the lieutenant governor has even more power over legislation, and there is no provision for an initiative or referendum in the state constitution. He concludes, "The Texas legislature is structured such that policy initiatives which do not have widespread legislative or public support cannot pass through the legislature." Interestingly Fusarelli found that both sides in the voucher debate think vouchers will eventually be adopted in Texas. They expect a limited plan targeting the poor will be most popular and affordable.[54]

Bruce Cooper

Explaining why the movement for vouchers both persists and is thwarted, as in Texas, Professor Bruce S. Cooper (Fordham University) sees the issue much in flux, subject to change. In the long run—fifty years—he is confident that pressure for more choice will prevail in the United States because trends favor market solutions especially where entrepreneurial and religious forces are strong. Cooper studies education union politics in America and Europe and he does not see unions preventing school choice indefinitely. Meanwhile, he explains the failure of vouchers to be adopted widely as a "conspiracy of coincidences."[55]

Cooper finds his explanation not in some master plan orchestrated by unions but in a combination of factors, including: (1) the intense polarization of liberals and conservatives making political consensus impossible to achieve; (2) the divisions between the conservative supporters of school choice, with some opposing vouchers because they fear regulation; (3) the adoption of moderate reforms like charter schools that temporarily preempts further change; (4) the failure to achieve a sufficiently strong and coherent coalition able to work together; and (5) the sustained anti-voucher scholarly research debunking vouchers and their prospects. When he turns to the question of what might happen to change this outcome, Cooper is most sanguine, suggesting: "And surely, the 'conspiracy of coincidences' of political action will break down and changes will occur. The voucher concept is too simple, logical, and real not to take root somewhere."[56]

Looking ahead Cooper speculates on the pressure points likely to end this impasse. He comes up with twice as many possible reasons for a future voucher victory, ten altogether. In Cooper's estimation it will take only some of these to change the outcome politically. The ten reasons why vouchers can win are:

1. The failure of moderate reforms like charter schools to "solve the major problems of the education of the urban poor in the United States."
2. A softening of union opposition and a desire to influence voucher-based programs, much as they have with charter schools.
3. Growing unity among conservatives and acceptance of vouchers properly and carefully crafted to help the poor and to minimize regulatory and other problems.
4. Growing acceptance of privatization as a reasonable way to deliver services including education.
5. The continued failure of public education, jeopardizing the future of cities.
6. Supportive Supreme Court decisions making room for vouchers to be given to parents of children attending parochial schools.
7. The snowball effect with small voucher programs expanding from pilot projects to whole cities and states.
8. Positive research findings with a substantial factual basis indicating that vouchers work well.
9. The redefinition of government's role in education, helping to "break up" monopolies, making room for new experiments in education using the latest on-line technologies that make learning in centralized locations unnecessary.
10. An embrace of vouchers as the moderate solution halfway between total privatization and the current government monopoly.[57]

The strength of this analysis is in its imaginative nature, in its farsighted vision, and in the realism of its plausible scenarios. There is nothing too far-out in each of these ten predictions nor in Cooper's conviction that vouchers have a staying power as an idea that will outlast the opposition. That vouchers will accomplish what supporters envision, the reformation of primary and secondary education, is another matter altogether because vouchers are not sufficient by themselves to guarantee excellence in schools.

Conclusion: The Scholars

Is it ironic that the harder scholars fight for the school choice cause, which is a daunting challenge, the more strict they are with themselves, stressing methodological rigor, and in the case of Paul Peterson and Terry Moe, pressing it to the very limits of their social science discipline?

There is an insightful and necessarily defensive discussion by Myron Lieberman on the issue of partisanship and its relationship to scholarship and to the canons of academic integrity. He and most of the scholars just discussed are proponents of school choice and are willing to speak, write, and lobby for its adoption. In his book, *The Teacher Unions*, Lieberman argues that this is natural for anyone who makes judgments or recommendations concerning what they know so much about. Having strong feelings about what is right does not mean a scholar can no longer think clearly and write honestly.

Lieberman distinguishes between being "partisan," something he freely admits to, and being "biased," a fault he wishes to avoid if it is defined as avoiding "significant evidence, or weighs it on a double standard, or ignores arguments that belong in the discussion." Lieberman considers it not only possible but also admirable to be both objective and partisan:

> I regard "bias' as a pejorative term, which I hope is not applicable to this book. My goal has been to provide an objective analysis of the teacher unions, but "objective" is not synonymous with "nonpartisan." On the contrary, objective analysis of an issue often results in a partisan position with respect to it. . . . Furthermore, objectivity is not to be confused with a subjective state of mind. In countless situations, analysts reflect bias even if they are not aware of it. My plea is that the analysis not be dismissed as "biased" simply because it is partisan.[58]

Lieberman knows that his positions on education issues are unpopular among most scholars writing on his subject. This is a most intense partisan struggle. He, however, wants a wider audience and defends the academic canons that in his view not only protect his reputation as a scholar but also gain credibility for his argument. If he does shoddy work why should anyone pay attention to him at all? If he is dishonest, ignoring facts and good reasons to change his views, he should be rebuked and ignored. But if he plays fair with the evidence and interprets it responsibly, he says, those with open minds should at least consider what he has to say.

The Activists

Scholar and activist Professor Quentin L. Quade of Marquette University, past Director of the Blum Center for Parental Freedom in Education, founded in 1992, studied school choice activists and was a recorder and reporter of their activities. Quade passed away in January 1999. He named the Center in honor of Virgil C. Blum, S.J., who was Professor of Political Science at Marquette, a scholar-activist who created Citizens for Education

Freedom (1956), with headquarters in Saint Louis, and also wrote *Freedom of Choice in Education*. The Center maintains a depository of information and a data base on school choice efforts organized by states. It also publishes the *Educational Freedom Report*, a monthly publication.[59]

For Quade the "North Star" of school choice is the principle that the same amount of public money spent per pupil should follow the child no matter where her/she attends school. As a matter of practical politics he favored a two-step process for legislative initiatives. First, give the legislature the authority to act, however they see fit, on choice. Keep the unity initially, he argued, and do not get caught up in the minutiae of different school choice plans that tend to divide people. Second, work on legislation (which always tends to be divisive) to implement choice—by stages if necessary. Quade was confident that any step toward choice was preferable to inertia. He found it easy to support a school choice plan as long as it could be adopted and its proponents were dissatisfied with anything less than full school choice—his "North Star." The Center that Quade created and that the Friedman Foundation helped to fund, starting in 1998, is designed to give aid and comfort to all school choice activists and to be of assistance to the scholars who study them.[60]

Another person who surveys the work of activists in the school choice movement is Dr. George Clowes, Managing Editor of *School Reform News* (SRN), published by Joseph L. Bast, President, of the Heartland Institute. The Institute is a fifteen-year-old, free-market, libertarian think tank focused on study of state and local issues. SRN is a national monthly designed to collect and disseminate school choice news that is sent to over 10,000 people, including all state and federal legislators. Clowes is convinced that ignorance of what school choice is and what it can do to improve education is widespread and deep. Few know much about it at all. Obtaining support for school choice, in his view, depends on getting the school choice message and news out to opinion makers who in turn can educate the public. Clowes considers grassroots support stirred up by activists to be crucial for the future. His role is to report on the work of these activists to stimulate interest and encourage further efforts. [61]

Marshall Fritz

Marshall Fritz, the founder and Director of The Separation of School and State Alliance, and publisher of *The Education Liberator* (honoring William Lloyd Garrison the abolitionist and his newsletter, *The Liberator*), is dedicated to what he considers to be real school choice, i.e., to non-statist education, and not false school choice like vouchers or charter schools. Education that he loves—the word love is not too strong in this instance—must have no taint of government and its coercive power to be truly free. The very basis for a true and acceptable education policy, Fritz believes, is love, the sacrifice of parents and not the coercion of the state via taxes.[62]

Government schools, Fritz argues, are paid for by compulsory taxes, and they clearly engage in indoctrination that constitutes, in essence, propaganda and manipulation. To be consistent, Fritz also opposes charter schools and vouchers as government-controlled solutions that will not work. In fact, even tax credits that are popular because they may involve less regulation, in his judgment, generally compromise the school funding issue. He favors private funding only and rejects compulsory school attendance laws, resisting almost all current school choice proposals and programs. In his staunch opposition to statism, Fritz functions as a critical gadfly in the school choice movement, challenging common assumptions and warning of potentially disastrous consequences from reforms. He asserts a threefold definition of the mission and nature of the Alliance.[63]

- The "Separation Alliance" is a grass-roots non-profit organization.
- Our mission is to inform Americans how education can be improved—especially for the poor—by the full separation of school and state.
- As an organization, we have no political or religious affiliations. We are strictly educational and leave to others any ballot initiatives, lobbying, litigation or electioneering needed to accomplish Separation.[64]

Most of the Alliance efforts—95 percent of them, he says—go into encouraging parents to send their children to private schools or to home school them. The remaining 5 percent, he dedicates to opposing school choice efforts like tax credits or vouchers: Fritz calls them bribes. Fritz is a Roman Catholic and a long-time libertarian. He formed the Alliance in January 1994, convinced that no tax money should be used for education. He opposes vouchers for four basic reasons. One, they use taxes, which are obtained by coercion and not by charity; two, they create dependency and are an entitlement very like welfare programs already proven to be so destructive; three, they will bring regulation by the state for schools that use them, not true independence; and four, legislation establishing vouchers will be a compromise—"your enemies will write the law," so it will be corrupted from the start.[65]

The Alliance has drafted a Proclamation that spells out the principle of privately operated and funded education. As of March 1999, 6,500 individuals have signed it, including a cross section of people the Alliance categorizes as religious leaders (Protestant, Catholic, Jewish, and Muslim), "public" and private school educators, policy leaders (conservative and libertarian), business leaders, and home school leaders. The list of proclamation signatories includes, to name a few, Dr. D. James Kennedy, Coral Ridge Ministries; Fr.

John A. Hardon, S.J., author of *The Catholic Catechism;* Rabbi Daniel Lapin, President of Toward Tradition; Douglas Dewey, who is active in the private voucher movement; Marvin Olasky, author of *The Tragedy of American Compassion;* Joel Belz, publisher of *World* magazine; Charles Rice, Professor of Law at the Notre Dame University School of Law; John Taylor Gatto, 1991 New York State Teacher of the Year; D. Bruce Lockerbie of A Passion for Learning (educator and author for many years at the Stony Brook School); Ron Trowbridge, Vice President, Hillsdale College; Edward Crane, President, Cato Institute; John Fund, columnist, *Wall Street Journal;* and author and home school advocate Samuel Blumenfeld.[66] The Proclamation, which is the cornerstone of Alliance school choice efforts, states:[67]

> **Whereas** parents have both the responsibility and the right to provide for education for their children, and
>
> **Whereas** a state-financed school system—even one that is well funded and staffed with talented, caring teachers—cannot address the differing expectations that parents hold for their children, and
>
> **Whereas** assumption by government of parents' financial responsibility and consequent undermining of their authority leads to weaker families and social decline, and
>
> **Whereas** the politically strongest factions inevitably use schools to shape attitudes and control the content of children's minds,
>
> **Thus**, it is clear that **mere** reform of state schooling will not solve the education crisis.
>
> **Therefore**, we must end government **involvement** in education funding, attendance, and content. Separation of school and state is essential to restore parental responsibility and create an environment of educational freedom in which both students and teachers can flourish.
>
> **By my signature below, I proclaim publicly that**
> **I favor the Separation of School and State**

X_____

The primary purpose of the Alliance is to promote understanding and adoption of this principle that government should neither fund nor control schools. Just as home schooling is now accepted whereas once it was considered foolish and outside the pale of civilized discourse, Fritz wants, first, to establish basic respect for his position and organization. So far he indicates that three publications have endorsed his principles—*World Magazine*, the *Orange County Register*, and the *Molokai News*. Second, the Alliance wants to encourage other organizations to sign the Proclamation. As a first step, the Alliance is co-sponsoring conferences with other groups, e.g., for its 1998 Colorado Springs Annual Conference: American Family Policy Institute Exodus Project, Colorado for Family Values, Concerned Women for America of Colorado, Exodus 2000, Landmark Books, the Plymouth Rock Foundation, and seven other groups. Fritz uses the conferences to reach out to people who share at least some of his views, and he attempts to persuade them to adopt a full *Separationist* position. He finds Evangelicals, Catholics, and libertarians particularly congenial to his views but he excludes no one. He tends, by his own admission, not to respect politicians but he would very much like to influence opinion makers and theorists like Congressman J.C. Watts (R–Okla.) and Dr. Alan Keyes.[68]

Fritz sees a huge shift toward private education options as the current system implodes. It does not work, in his view, and efforts to reform it will fail. Radical movements like his own, he comments (citing the views of Arthur Schopenhauer), first seem absurd and are ridiculed; then they are a threat and are attacked; lastly they are adopted and accepted. Fritz says this movement, which is five years old, is still ridiculed but soon it will be attacked as more parents move their children out of public schools. He is not comfortable on the margins, outside the general discussion of school choice, its principles and purposes. To be attacked is progress and is much better than being ignored or ridiculed. Lastly, he says the Alliance and the Separationist positions will be respected and then accepted.[69]

Fritz reports that in his estimation about 6.5 million children are in private schools and home schooling out of fifty-two million children K–12 in 1998. Many more are considering private education. He says the goal of the Alliance is to help the marginal to switch by telling them the truth about how bad public schools are—he intends to influence by every means at his command some fifteen million children toward private schools. As the better parents and their children leave, the tax-supported schools will decline faster. At some point Fritz believes the current public education system finally will be undermined, discredited, and there will be a rush to private schools. This will occur in stages. First, innovators precede early adopters, who are followed by an early majority, a late majority, and finally the laggards. The truth and a proper understanding of principle motivate innovators. Early adopters, the next group to act, are motivated by a desire to protect their own children; they make great sacrifices and are six million strong now. These two groups—the truth seekers and the children protectors—are the groups Fritz targets. Once the current system falls apart, the majority will reluctantly follow, their indifference shattered by public school disasters.[70] Fritz contends:

> At some moment we'll reach that "Whoosh Point" when a society quickly sweeps into the new paradigm. Victor Hugo called it "an idea whose time has come." We saw the Whoosh in East Germany and the Berlin Wall fell. We saw it in Russia and the Soviet Union is no more. We saw it in the Philippines and Marcos left. When we reach the Whoosh Point, "public school" educators

and major religious leaders will stand and announce that the time has come for the separation of school and state. The transition will be easier than you think, because by the time the Whoosh begins, we will already have a third of the children in home and campus schools that are built on the true premise of parental responsibility. We will have created 100,000 new schools, so the process of converting the remainder will not seem as daunting as it seems today.[71]

Fritz sees the need to start and run more Christian schools and private schools generally—he wants to encourage school entrepreneurs. He predicts that schools will be much smaller, perhaps one-fifth the average size of the present government schools. His expectation initially is for "5,000 charitable scholarship foundations providing a billion dollars a year to one million children," followed by a massive $300 billion tax cut that will allow the private scholarships to be expanded to fifteen million children. In short, this plan is for the partial and then full privatization of education.[72]

In his advocacy tactics Fritz tends to be rhetorically tough, especially with private school leaders or school choice advocates with whom he disagrees. He may, according to some, make more enemies then he needs to. He wants to avoid ad hominem attacks on public schools at all costs because he believes this will impede later conversions and he is working to be conciliatory where possible, giving special recognition, for example, to the school choice efforts of William Bentley Ball, the school choice attorney who was also a fervent supporter of vouchers.[73]

As public education problems increase and as change comes incrementally with too few children helped, the plausibility of Fritz and his views increases. He has little or no incentive to compromise his position for principled or practical reasons; the worse things are the less he has grounds for trusting halfway solutions. As time passes, however, and should inertia seem to rule, as it likely will in many communities, his principles and sense of history will be tested. Fritz considers all the other tax-funded school choice answers, including vouchers, tax credits, and charter schools, to be subversive of his goal—ways to delay the deluge and not the true lifeboat of a private education exclusively funded by parents and charitable giving.

Kevin Teasley

Things have come full circle for Kevin Teasley, an Indiana University journalism and political science graduate, who is one of the most active school choice proponents of the 1990s. First, Teasley has returned to Indiana after working in Washington for three years at the Heritage Foundation, then moving to California to the Reason Foundation for four years, and subsequently heading up the Proposition 174 campaign in 1993. In January 1992,

Joe Alibrandi, Chairman and CEO of the Whitaker Corporation, asked him to help run the initiative campaign. Teasley learned much from this experience and the eventual California defeat. He went on to participate in the establishment of a private voucher program in southern California (CEO), was a co-founder of the American Education Reform Foundation (AERF), and currently he is President of Greater Education Opportunity Foundation (G.E.O.) in Indianapolis. In this whirlwind of activity some things have not changed for him. When he started to work for school choice in California Teasley put on forums to educate people on school choice. He is doing the same thing today in his old backyard of Indiana but with a new sense of purpose and strategic vision born of years of experience. He hopes to export elsewhere what works in Indianapolis.[74]

Teasley says that he does not lobby. He wants to specialize in grassroots mobilization and in elections, including helping with candidate selection. Politically he likes to think systematically and sequentially—"Failing to prepare is preparing to fail." He advises, "You have to help to make this issue a priority—you are competing with fifty other issues." Churches and family groups each have fifty issues. Not one of them, Teasley observes, makes school choice its top priority. "We make school choice our only priority. We ask daily who has or has not been impacted by this issue or touched by our message."[75]

Teasley does not spend time thinking about the opposition. "The only thing I think about them is that they do a good job. I ask how do they do a good job? They are worth studying to see how they do policy making—they stay focused and they have a financial collection system, an information distribution system, and relationships." He wants to do the same, except that, unlike them, he does not wish to become bureaucratically driven but rather action and mission driven.[76]

Staying focused for Teasley means not losing sight of his objective—greater education opportunities for children. No means or method should be allowed to take precedence over this goal. Vouchers and tax credits are means only and, in any case, most people, he says, do not understand them. The school choice movement puts the cart before the horse in his view when it takes to the air in an ad campaign talking abstractions. Teasley argues that choice needs to be brought down to the level where most people think.

To accomplish this, Teasley proposes a good product that he can sell, namely, an *assignable, refundable tax credit*, modeled on the Minnesota law and 1998 Colorado initiative. Tax credits unite more than they divide, he argues, unlike vouchers, and they can be given to all families with children, including those who attend public schools. Teasley supports tax credits for most school-related expenses, including books, tutors, computers, education summer camps, and tuition. By assignable he means a guarantee can be given to a private school—he assigns the money to the school in advance, so the school can go to the bank with this as collateral and borrow money on it to operate. By refundable he means simply that the poor who pay no taxes still receive the full tax credit. This is a program that Teasley says he can sell to voters and politicians. In the fall of 1998 he sent out a 100,000-piece mailing to families in Indianapolis. "Free books, free computers, free tutors, free schools," read the headline. "Parents in Wisconsin, Ohio, Minnesota got these things for their children. Don't your children deserve these things too?"[77]

Collecting money sufficient for grassroots organizing and political activity is essential. Teasley shoulders this responsibility for his own organization. He does not want to rely on one or two donors. In any sustained effort there needs to be, he asserts, a strong financial base to begin with, so that activists do not worry about paying the bills tomorrow. Major donors are now aware that this is true. However, he points out that "most of the state organizations are one and two persons shows." They are undermanned, compared to private voucher organizations that employ, he says, as many as twenty people. Public policy campaigns, Teasley reflects, are very labor intensive, requiring that you build corporate, minority, political, grass roots, and funding support. He explains:

> These are the things you need to be successful, and you are trying to do all that with one or two people? Sound a little disheartened? You better believe I am! No one has focused on the political/policy making side of things. They think it is just going to happen through osmosis. It is not going to happen through osmosis.[78]

As important as finances are Teasley is convinced that the greatest lack in school choice mobilization efforts is the absence of an internal information distribution system and the personal community relationships that sustain it. More top-down leadership in this view will not do the job. Not until school choice breaks out of its own self-imposed box (relating to those who already agree on choice) does Teasley think it will succeed. His strategy is local, personal, and communitywide with a stress on reaching those people whose children attend the worst schools and the leaders who represent them. This will take time, he knows, but it also offers the greatest chance for building the base needed to sustain school choice over the long haul.[79]

Coalition building is an obvious part of this process. In his state, Teasley formed the Greater Education Opportunities Alliance of Indiana. This coalition includes the Indiana Chamber of Commerce, the Indianapolis Chamber of Commerce, the Indiana Non-Public Education Association, Indiana Family Institute, the Hudson Institute, the Milton and Rose Friedman Foundation, Families Organized for Real Choice in Education, and his own organization, GEO. Teasley wants to organize. He is writing articles for these

member organizations and their magazines. For example, he is convinced
Indiana home educators can be won over to support tax credits if they are
approached properly. Teasley is trying to get home schoolers at least to consider that they should benefit from all the money they have spent on education taxes.[80]

Teasley suggests that the Washington-based think tanks begin a grassroots
educational campaign in their own backyard. They need, he thinks, to organize local support and to network with other community organizations. This
will increase credibility for the programs they advocate. They have abundant
resources—ideas, money, and staff—so think tanks, he concludes, should
put these resources into action at the grass roots.[81]

What can corporate Indiana do? In Teasley's opinion it lacks boldness. He
says, "They will help to expose the problems with the system," and the
Chamber of Commerce is part of the alliance. "But we do not want them
leading the battle. They have been leading the battle for education reform
for a long time and we have not seen much result." Teasley affirms that he
wants people who are in the schools to support choice. "In last year's legislation discussion the people leading the debate had their children in private
schools. They have already saved their kids." This cannot, he argues, be a
private school subsidy; it has to be a solution that those kids in public schools
and their parents want. "That's what we and the legislators want to hear."
Indianapolis has a history of little grassroots effort for education reform;
Teasley is trying to rectify that dismal record.[82]

In the Teasley approach, talk should be directed toward the goal of forming listeners and former opponents into a cadre of activists and their friends.
His favorite term is "drumbeat," with all of its martial connotations. The
call is for the school choice vision to be recreated in public at least once a
month, he says, in an open forum that encourages questions and debate. He
prefers a debate format that makes it easy for those who oppose school choice
to attend. His goal is political conversion. Teasley has little interest in big
conferences with multiple speakers that tend to bore people because they are
repetitive, give too little time to each speaker, and fail to attract minority
Democrats. He advises showcasing different speakers and is regularly bringing the best to Indianapolis. "You put on a good show, get an expanding
audience, and concentrate on inviting the public, neighborhood associations,
pastors, and community groups."[83]

> Then you develop relationships with those who attend. Find out their needs.
> Go on fact finding trips. Take these people to Milwaukee and Cleveland—see
> the schools attended by choice students to dispel the myths that school choice
> is sponsored by the KKK or is racist. They are working. Let them make up
> their own minds. I say go and see for yourself and you make up your own
> mind. We should not be in the business of pitting public schools performance
> against private schools performance, rather we should be selling choice itself.[84]

Teasley is showcasing black Democrats when he can. Representative Dwight Evans from Philadelphia was his first speaker. Mrs. Bert Holt, an African-American school choice administrator from Cleveland and a political independent, was the second. John E. Brandl, Dean of the Hubert H. Humphrey Institute of Public Affairs, University of Minnesota, a former state Senator and a white liberal Democrat was the third. Brandl recently wrote a book, *Money and Good Intentions Are Not Enough: Or, Why a Liberal Democrat Thinks States Need Both Competition and Community* (1998) on why he supported school choice. Teasley also planned to have Howard Fuller, a black Democrat from Milwaukee, speak.

When Bert Holt spoke, Teasley relates, he invited a group, Families Organized for Real Choice in Education (FORCE), a group of parents, to have dinner with her at his expense. FORCE is an all-volunteer organization with no paid staff and little time to get things done. A group of fifty to sixty parents attended. "We have become facilitators," Teasley said. Several of the pastors who also attended Holt's public presentation were hearing the pro-school choice side for the first time. He blames lack of communication for their ignorance—no one had made the effort to reach them before.

"To many times this discussion, this debate over school choice has been done over the air waves, or in newspapers, over the air, or in the op-ed pages." People are not getting out there and meeting each other and embracing one another and saying we have a common goal here, which is children getting a good education.[85]

Shortly after hearing Holt these pastors changed their minds on school choice. Teasley offered to help them to start schools of their own, Safe Haven Schools, backed by grants from local philanthropist Don Laskowski (five such schools were in operation in the city in the fall of 1998). Then Teasley held a meeting with these pastors and told them that Indianapolis schools get $9,500 per student. In his own effort to help them to start a privately run church school all he could offer in assistance was $1,000 per student. He told them about the state budget surplus of $2 billion. They quickly made the connection and formed a pastor's council. They then planned a trip to Milwaukee where Teasley said they would find out about how Milwaukee church schools can get a $4,500 voucher. These pastors soon held a press conference pressing for vouchers and got significant TV coverage. When pastors have schools and know how public resources can be obtained they will be active for choice. He comments:

Republicans in Indiana are talking about a tax credit of $1,000 per child. We are not. We are talking about real school choice, i.e., real opportunities for children. But it is too early to push for legislation. I want to get behind grass-roots people who are pushing and an aggressive program. I would rather start from a $9,500 voucher and work down from there then to work up from the lower figure—would rather end up with $4,500 then $1,000.[86]

Reverend Ann Byfield (AME) called him up to go to have lunch together. She said, "Kevin, I want to know why you feel the way you do about this issue? Your answers will decide whether I want to work with you." She liked his answers, both regarding private assistance and public policy. Teasley comments, younger blacks especially, are breaking the mold. Some pastors who are pro-school choice have members who are public school employees. "We have to prepare the pastors," he says. Pastors start schools—they can promise parishioners that "we will get you jobs." The secret to success, Teasley relates, is to help them to understand that choice is something they can own—not an abstraction that benefits already existing private schools. "Sell them on the benefits for the children, and the members of the church." In public schools—people unknown to the church, often from outside the community, serve as teachers. In a church school the church can screen its own teachers. Start with the need for private schools. Help the pastors to understand that need and to articulate it for the community. Start those schools. Then get to the solution of school choice.[87]

Teasley is also reaching out to black Democratic legislators, journalists, and community leaders. He is inviting them to his forums and to go on fact-finding trips. Recently he got on the phone with a black reporter for the *Indianapolis Star*, who was quite hostile to school choice. He said to the reporter, "I am not for tax credits or vouchers—but for greater education opportunities for children. Let's talk." The reporter warmed to the whole subject after this conversation. The person who had disinvited Reverend Floyd Flake from attending a function for black legislators in the city accepted Teasley's invitation to go to Milwaukee. Things are moving, the climate for school reform is warming. A lot of things are changing peoples' minds besides his efforts, says Teasley; public schools are continuing to fail and choice schools are working. His plan is to help influential community leaders see this for themselves and then to make their own judgments.

Teasley is convinced this will work. He affirms that with personal relationships throughout the community and a measure of trust, you can then develop your own internal information distribution system. "Then when they see your fax now they will read it. When there is a story to be written in a paper the reporter and those they interview can vouch for you as a good man." This is a form of friendship politics: Win friends and impact reporters. As the existing network of blacks give choice a chance the movement will snowball in Indianapolis as friends communicate. "Hopefully we can broaden the debate."

"Educationally you can do a lot politically or politically you can do a lot educationally," he notes. Because G.E.O. is a 501c-3 non-profit, it is careful to avoid direct political involvement. Direct mail is a Teasley forte. He sent out the 100,000 pieces of mail to families in Indianapolis and concluded his pitch with, "call now to help your child's future," giving the phone number to the G.E.O. Foundation. He included in the package coupons for pizza and chicken. "Parents are looking for deals." They will call, Teasley expected, and he will secure their name, address, and phone number. G.E.O. sends parents who respond information on what is happening in other states on school choice, telling them the position their legislator or candidates are taking on this issue. This is all educational Teasley relates, "and by the way November 3 is election day." He does not ask those who write or call to vote or tell them how to vote.

Building an information distribution system means cultivating and identifying supporters. His goal is to broaden the base and to cultivate community leadership for school choice. Teasley comments, "I am free to do what I want to do now, right here. If I can't get it done here why do I think I can get it done anywhere else?" His primary job is to get the funding and to make sure it all happens. So far in his own estimation he has enough success with black Democrats to be encouraged that his methods have merit and can be exported and be used in any ethnic context.

Teasley continues to function as a consultant outside the state, most recently in Colorado but also in Minnesota and Washington, D.C. Replicating what he is doing in Indiana in other states, building grassroots leadership and support, is his primary objective. He is convinced that the way to win is not to wage a negative campaign, attacking education unions—he says that only stirs up the opposition, including their whole informal network of family and friends—but rather to stress the positive benefits of school choice for everyone, including the public schools. This is one reason his tax credit proposal has benefits for public school parents too. He is also convinced that national resources need to be invested in state campaigns and is concerned that the string of losses in state initiatives will discourage donors. Out-of-state donors need to be brought in early in the process, in his view, to give them some ownership:

> I don't know Colorado but I know the issue. Probably the biggest role I am playing is getting them the financial support. Helping them put everything in place so that when they go asking for that support they have a better chance of getting it.[88]

If New York school choice leaders, he says, have a multiyear plan to bring in tax credits to their state, they must ask how a big loss for tax credits in another state like Colorado or Michigan will delay progress or speed it up in New York. One big win, Teasley argues to potential big donors, like Peter

Flanigan and Bruce Kovner, could sweep the country quickly, including New York, and save years of effort in other states.[89]

Teasley says that to win an initiative a triangle of support is needed:

- Politicians need to be supported. They need to know there is financial support available for political campaigns and the necessary votes to keep them in office.
- Donors need to see politicians out front on the issue, ready to fight for it.
- Grassroots participants need financial and organization support provided by full-time activists to stay involved.
- All three need support and coordination. Initiatives are not primarily a media campaign in his view—not an air war; but a ground war using mail and phone banks.[90]

In his view, politics in the United States works on the basis of momentum. Schools still have not improved despite five to ten years of effort. People know that change is needed and more money is not the silver bullet. In the nation there is a momentum—in Milwaukee (verified by Harvard analyzed test scores), Cleveland, and Minnesota. Public vouchers in these two cities and tax credits in one state demonstrate that choice works—and the accusations of the opposition are a smoke screen. You have to educate everybody, he says, on these positive results.

Looking ahead, Teasley hopes for successful results in Florida, Texas, Pennsylvania, and Indiana, where he anticipated legislative battles in 1999. Another effort will be waged in California after that, he surmises. Even when every defeat, as in Colorado, tends to delay change elsewhere, leadership by governors, he observes, is critical in most cases and can overcome obstacles and defeats elsewhere.

This is a long battle and it is wise, according to Teasley, to push for incremental change. Charter school legislation allows you to develop relationships. It requires you to get your fingers dirty by starting and running schools, helping those who need it the most. Teasley supports charters because he thinks they are good for the movement and for students, but he says charters are often a delaying tactic, more a wall than a bridge, to more school choice. "The verdict on whether charters are a bridge or a wall is still out."[91]

Teasley is not sure private vouchers will lead to public policy changes. He observes that PAVE, the private voucher effort in Milwaukee, came after the 1989 public voucher legislation. However, PAVE was committed to expanding the public vouchers from day one of its existence, and it saw private vouchers as a way to prove that vouchers work. "It is unfortunate that the PAVE model is not being followed across the country because most of the private voucher programs are not getting anywhere close to public policy."

Teasley strongly disagrees that philanthropy by itself is the way to go. He even questions the motives of those who oppose public vouchers. "Some people want a perpetual job. I want to be put out of business." Teasley remains a hardcore supporter of school choice, first for the poor and then for everyone—and he wants public means used to accomplish it.[92]

David Brennan

All students of school choice in Ohio agree that it would never have happened without the efforts of David Brennan. One day the full story of how he accomplished that feat will be told. Brennan, who donates heavily to Republican Party and conservative causes and who is the mover and shaker for school choice in the state, became involved in school choice when he found that many of his employees were illiterate and innumerate—he said they could not count, add, subtract, multiply, do simple arithmetic. Having started training programs for his employees, Brennan was subsequently exposed to the notion of school choice in 1988 by the Heritage Foundation. In 1990 he raised over $500,000 for the gubernatorial campaign of then Governor George Voinovich, and he was later appointed to head up a school reform commission for the state. Brennan concluded, among other things, that students were not learning disabled but that teachers were teaching disabled![93]

Brennan then became active in the 1994 state elections and succeeded in helping ten school choice candidates to get elected. He was instrumental in securing subsequent reforms. On June 30, 1995, Governor Voinovich (R) signed a two-year budget package that created a $5 million pilot voucher program in Cleveland, a program championed by Councilwoman Fannie Lewis (D). With his signature, the governor made Ohio the first state in the country to enact a school choice program that included religious schools. The program, which began in September 1996, allowed parents of 2,000 Cleveland elementary students to use vouchers for tuition at a private, public, or religious school of their choice.

David Zanotti, chair of the Ohio roundtable, reports that in 1997–98, there were 4,000 students in fifty-seven schools who received up to $2,250 in vouchers. The voucher program in Ohio is limited to schools of twenty-five students or more, thus excluding home schoolers. Teachers must be certified with a college degree and have an annual criminal background check, but they do not need educational degree certification as in public schools. This program was immediately contested in state courts but is awaiting a decision and allowed to continue.[94]

In 1997, community or charter school legislation became a reality in Ohio, but Brennan views these charter schools as a positive development but flawed because they exclude parochial schools from public funding. He supports voucher schools because they cannot be co-opted as easily as charter schools by the education establishment, and because they will have to make room for parochial schools.[95]

Brennan may well be the premier state-based activist in the nation. In addition to his legislative and electoral victories, he started two voucher schools, the Hope Academies, and five charter schools. When Brennan spoke of lessons learned in Ohio that are useful elsewhere he said that, to win, one must support legislators who back choice with long-term political commitments. "Get them elected and help keep them elected." He noted the size of the oppositions' political contributions and complained that the public in America is largely indifferent.[96]

Brennan says that if the U.S. Supreme Court passes vouchers he will strongly favor them (Charter schools, in his view are only a halfway house toward full school choice). This will take new aggressive legislation in Ohio. The biggest reason for opposition to choice, in his opinion, is the NLRB decision that religious schools do not have to engage in collective bargaining with a union. Unions know they cannot organize religious schools. People for the American Way, Brennan alleges, is now helping to pay for black ministers to travel and speak out against choice. He wants private religious schools included in choice. However, despite Brennan's dedication, school choice in Ohio was delayed by an adverse state Supreme Court decision on vouchers.[97]

Bert Holt

Bert L. Holt, once a leader in the desegregation of Cleveland schools, was placed in charge of administering the Cleveland voucher program. When first asked to head this office under the Ohio Department of Education, she was about to retire. A person of independent means, great savvy, and political connections, Holt had no personal need to take this position with all of the headaches that went with launching school choice in the city. Without her expert assistance school choice may well have failed in Cleveland. Her example demonstrates the importance of good administration for future voucher programs.[98]

The law itself eased the transition for Holt. Governor Voinovich, with ties to Cleveland, made sure vouchers did not cut into the public school district education budgets. All funds for this pilot project came from the state, and none would be lost to the public schools for students who transferred with vouchers to choice schools like the Hope Academies. This certainly made things easier, Holt says, with all of her local contacts in the education community. She could reassure people that school choice was not a direct and immediate budget threat to existing programs.

Early on Holt engaged in behind-the-scenes politicking. She went to the NAACP leadership and secured their agreement not to wage a mud-slinging fight against vouchers or to vilify her; they agreed to disagree with her civilly, based on her old personal ties. She also went to corporate leaders for advice and some support—selling choice to them as an agent of change and not as a betrayal of public schools. She spoke to leaders of the University School, a nationally recognized local preparatory school, to get some understanding; and different pastors groups, asking them to give her a chance for the sake of the children. No base went uncovered; she even contacted corporate, university, and college presidents.[99]

The biggest obstacle Holt initially ran into was the belief that poor people could not fill out applications or verify their eligibility. Her first task was to get applications into the hands of the poor—she distributed 30,000 at public housing centers, headstart programs, preschools, libraries, all K–2 parents in Cleveland public schools, medical facilities, girl scouts, YMCA, groceries, and church groups. To give information and to build ties she went into public housing projects at night, driving in a luxury car, dressed as a professional, with never a problem. They collected 6,000 applications for 1,500 openings to be selected by lottery.

The next tough job was documentary verification of income, rent, and ownership, which must be redone every year. Her office of three full-time staff was responsible for this. In hindsight Holt wishes the private schools had this task. However, to sell the schools to participate she assured them that her office would carry the logistical and paperwork load. Fifty-seven schools joined in, most of them in the Catholic parochial system. Throughout this whole process Holt had to answer many questions, and if she hoped to succeed, she had to do so quickly to the satisfaction of the questioner. Delay could be fatal, she thought, to any part of the effort.[100]

The next step was to rent the Convocation Center to hold a school choice "fair" for prospective parents and qualified schools. Holt organized the fair so as to have all the schools present themselves to the lottery winning parents, who would select the school for their child or children to attend. She used sign-up tables and let the parents circulate. This fair, which was her idea, was a smashing success for the parents and a media bonanza, but, to pull it off, she had to arrange for transportation and parking.

Throughout the whole launch phase of the program Holt said that she worked closely with the Hope Academy leadership and was not helped at all by the Department of Education. To this day, she reported, the Department ignores her and has put up many difficult and undermining barriers. When she had her first emergency, she clearly remembers, on September 26th, 1996, the date of the first voucher payment, the office computer crashed.

Hackers had done it (she reports this was confirmed by computer contractors who maintain the systems), yet she completed it and schools were paid. Holt has learned to document everything and to fear no accountability check; always be honest, she says, welcome scrutiny, and solve every problem instantly.[101]

The biggest problem in implementing school vouchers in Cleveland, Holt reports, was transportation. The Cleveland Public School District in Ohio is responsible for providing transportation to all private schools if the school is more than one mile from the residence of the child. The Cleveland District balked at providing transportation. The program then used a combination of buses and taxis. Since the school district was under the jurisdiction of the Ohio Department of Education, the State Superintendent could have ordered the Cleveland schools to provide buses. But since this was not done, Holt soon found it necessary to set up a logistical trouble-shooting position in her office, which tracked each child. A Navy veteran with aircraft-carrier experience ran this job superbly, in her view. Subsequently, and long overdue in her estimation, on January 20, 1998, the governor's office issued the order for over 1,000 of these students to be taken out of taxis and put on school buses. Transportation, however, continues to be a political football, she says, that is used by those who oppose choice. A Hope Academy principal confirmed that two years into the voucher program transportation was their biggest problem.[102]

Cleveland's pastors, Holt reports, were quietly supportive. Most have public school teachers and staff as members who fear for their jobs, and church facilities often are not capable of handling a school. Holt sees the black middle class, who are newly out of poverty, as not supportive of school choice. The black upper middle class or rich, together with the poor, were each more likely, in her view, to support choice.

Although Holt has traveled out of state to speak for choice, only a few state governments contacted her to ask about the feasibility of administering a school choice program. She thinks the Ohio Department of Education may block invitations. Facing such sustained indifference or hostility to her program by the state civil service, Holt has not crumbled for many reasons she says, including, her seniority—she will retire in a year or so—her financial independence, age, experience, maturity, contacts, the support from school choice entrepreneur David Brennan, a strong family heritage, and frequent prayer. In Holt's estimation a younger person without these protections might have resigned.

Looking ahead five years Holt predicts a multiplicity of community choices among independent schools. There will be, she expects, more activity by corporate sponsors and more specialization in public education. Vouchers will no longer be an issue; they will be accepted. Privatizing of other government services, including education, will be common. Teachers in all schools will be empowered to take responsibility. Unions are afraid. She says they will resist and it will take a strong governor and legislature to push the state Board of Education and Department of Education to embrace change. The opposition has used all the old tactics employed in the desegregation battle— isolation and attacks—but these will fail, Holt is convinced, just as they did when the schools embraced integration.[103]

Speaking before a large group of pastors in Cleveland, Holt charged that public education today preserves racial and class divisions. She said 3,000 parents involved in the voucher schools are convinced that they are safer, teach morals, and promote good behavior. She warned, "Woe to those who take legal action against parents who want choice for their children." Holt is not prepared in any fashion to accept or expect defeat for school choice despite bureaucratic opposition.[104]

Bruce Thompson

Some school choice activists are school board members who work on its behalf from inside the system. Bruce Thompson, Professor at the Milwaukee School of Engineering and former owner of a Montessori school, is a member of the Milwaukee Public Schools (MPS) School Board, who fell into the school choice movement quite by accident. His three-year-old daughter attended a Montessori school that the IRS took over for failure to pay back taxes. Thompson bought the school and after investing in it looked for ways to increase enrollment. When he saw that kindergarten students qualified for public vouchers, he recruited voucher students. Soon he got to know other inner-city schools besides his own and found them to be inspiring in their distinctive approaches varying from counterculture to conservative. Meanwhile liberals he knew moved to the suburbs and opposed choice. Eventually Thompson met David Reimer, a staff member in Mayor John Norquist's office and an articulate liberal who supported choice. Thompson was drawn gradually toward school choice. He recalls writing letters for the *Wall Street Journal* in 1993 and wrote a letter to the local paper.[105]

To help lobby for an expansion of the voucher program Thompson, along with John Gardner, started a parents' organization, Milwaukee Parents for Schools and Choice, with 200 parents from three downtown schools. Then Susan Mitchell, supported by the local Association of Commerce, started a parents' group with funding and paid staff, which succeeded so well that he saw no purpose in continuing the volunteer effort. Meanwhile Thompson looked for his niche. The Milwaukee School Board has eight district seats and one at-large seat. In late 1994 he assisted in a campaign, electing a pro school choice candidate, John Gardner. In 1996 he ran for a district seat and won on an aggressive reform platform:

- To allow high schools to select their students to create quality schools (this measure thought by some to be elitist was implemented in the fall of 1998)
- To have more specialty schools (there are not sufficient schools doing this)
- To promote vocational education[106]

An underlying theme for his whole campaign was support for all means available to reverse the flow of middle-class children leaving the MPS and the city. Confronting this problem and looking for solutions, Thompson found that in the past the school board ethos was passive—they delegated to superintendents and took little initiative. This has changed. In principle, he favors public money following the student to the school of their choice, a universal voucher program that includes MPS. But at present there are 100,000 students in the system with vouchers authorized for 15,000, and he says even if vouchers were made available to everyone, there are not enough private schools available to take all potential voucher students. Elementary students in the city are short on classroom space (although he says this is changing with choice and charters); even bad schools are full. High schools on the other hand have space. He says high schools can put in place admissions standards, and they can be shut down if no one wants to attend them.

There are four "choice" programs in place in the state of Wisconsin: (1) Interdistrict public school transfer; (2) Vouchers for private schools; (3) charter schools; and (4) an integration program for large cities and suburbs. The politics of school choice remain somewhat unstable with continued resistance from the State Department of Public Instruction. At issue now are regulatory problems. However, there is progress in his judgment. A statewide public choice program went into effect in the fall of 1998 allowing interdistrict transfers. This means all inner-city residents may attend suburban schools and not have to move. Charter schools, on the other hand, he considers a real threat to private schools like the Montessori school that he owned. There are four charter schools downtown in Milwaukee and all were formerly choice schools. Four more charters are slated for 1999. The advantage of charters, Thompson notes, is that there is no income restriction, permitting a more diverse student body, but there is also more regulation.[107]

Thompson sees a three-legged stool arrangement for education in Milwaukee—regular public schools, charters, and voucher schools. He favors allowing regular schools to convert to charter schools to give them more freedom. To summarize, he says MPS is moving toward more autonomy for good schools, more supervision of bad schools, and multiple solutions. Milwaukee prefers varied choices and loose coalitions, with lots of cooperation across ethnic, confessional, and ideological lines. Even single-sex schools are now possible, he says. The key to school reform success in Milwaukee, according to Thompson, is that most people supporting school choice succeded in submerging their differences to work for the common program. Despite disagreements on policy that he observed, people as different as Polly Williams and Susan Mitchell combined to bring progress. Thompson is optimistic about reform in Milwaukee. Once parents have choice, Mayor Norquist comments, they will not give it up; this is a one-way street, therefore, this will not always be a political football.[108]

James N. Goenner

Behind the scenes in a position critical for the success of charter school program in Michigan sits James N. Goenner, Director, Charter Schools Office, Central Michigan University (CMU), and President of the Michigan Association of Public School Academies (MAPSA). Like Bert Holt and Bruce Thompson, Goenner seeks to create educational opportunities, in his case, by working within the public school system.

There are two chartering methods in Michigan: state universities may charter anywhere in the state, and community colleges, county school districts, and local school districts may charter within their school boundaries. The state cap on charter schools was 150 in 1998 when there were already 138 charters, 110 granted by state universities, one by a community college, fourteen by county districts, and thirteen by local districts. Central Michigan University, the first university to issue a charter in Michigan in 1994, by the fall of 1998 chartered forty-six schools. Detroit Public Schools allowed ten to be licensed, seven in 1997–98 after there was so much interest.[109]

Michigan's chartered schools do not have to engage in collective bargaining. Goenner reports that all charters are granted to non-profits, but these bodies may hire staff and teachers or contract out to either for-profit or non-profit providers to assist with these administrative services. For-profit school management companies are rapidly growing. They can replicate themselves. Others, he comments, have a hard time because there are no start-up costs provided by the state. In fact the first state funding check does not arrive until October each year. The per pupil charter payment in 1998 was capped at $5,962.

Chartered schools cannot levy millages or issue bonds like other public schools, which makes careful fiscal management and cost effectiveness an imperative for them to survive, Goenner commented. Not surprisingly, schools turn to service providers who can offer a proven system at an affordable price because of economies of scale. In effect, this encourages those with capital to get into the business of running schools. Such organizations are operating in Michigan and nationally, and they include National Heritage Academies, JCR and Associates, the Edison Project, and more. As this for-profit movement grows, Goenner predicts, there will be strong efforts made to control and limit them—like HMO's.[110]

There are 1.7 million school age children in Michigan—more than 35,000 in charters, and 14,000 in schools chartered by CMU. However, there are five charter schools with 2,000 students in Lansing out of 20,000 in the district. Goenner reports there is a real impact on the community when 10 percent of the students attend chartered schools. In response to the charter movement, the mayor brought together a blue-ribbon panel designed and empowered to improve the public schools. There is substantial pressure now to raise the cap on charters. Few Democratic legislators publicly support charters, according to Goenner, but more are visiting charter schools and warming to the idea—sometimes even putting their own children in charter schools.[111]

The role of CMU beyond granting charters is to provide ongoing oversight to ensure the fiscal and academic integrity of these schools. CMU also provides ongoing education and training for school boards, administration, teaching, staffing, and curriculum, through its development and performance institute. In a brochure, the university describes its role and vision for charter schools using strongly positive terms appropriate for a promotional campaign:

> CMU intends to be the pre-eminent charter school authorizer—a lofty goal, for certain. Being an authorizer doesn't mean operating schools each day. Rather, we provide broad oversight and assistance. We make sure the school boards uphold their charter contracts, and we monitor their compliance with laws and regulations. We strive to ensure schools have the necessary resources and are positioned for success . . . before they open. We visit the schools regularly. We work on their behalf with governmental entities and policymakers, and we help administrators navigate state and federal educational regulatory systems. We pursue our oversight responsibilities with diligence. In doing so, we believe CMU-licensed schools will make tremendous progress and pioneer educational breakthroughs that benefit all. These schools must make the grade under intense public scrutiny, proving their value to families and taxpayers alike.[112]

Goenner says the Michigan Education Association (MEA) and its supporters have made attempts to intimidate Central Michigan into dropping the program. In a well-publicized incident in 1995–96, the superintendent of the Lake Orion Community Schools, Robert W. Bass, on his own authority, instituted a boycott of CMU student teachers and asked the guidance counselors in the high school not to recommend CMU to prospective students.

Bass then sent a letter to CMU President Leonard Plachta informing him of this action. Plachta objected strongly. Eventually Bass backed down and the Michigan legislature in 1995 responded by passing a law making this kind of action punishable by a loss of state funds. To this day, Goenner says, CMU feels legislative pressure over its role in promoting charter schools. The University budget can be reduced if the legislature chose to do so.[113]

Democratic gubernatorial candidate, Geoffrey Fieger, received the endorsement of the MEA in 1998, Goenner says, partly because he advocated shutting down charter schools. Goenner predicts with confidence that there will be increased conflict over education choice. A monopoly is being threatened, and, in his opinion, the monopoly will fight back. He is concerned the social fabric will tear, leading even to destructive acts, as the pace of change accelerates. As the number of students in choice schools goes from 1 percent to 20 percent, opposition will heat up. Others in the choice movement do not see the risks of disorder like Goenner does, but his perspective is that of a front-line administrator dealing daily with the supporters of school choice and charter school applicants.[114]

Goenner helps to implement charter schools confident of their present and future success, but he is pessimistic about the conflicts and assaults he expects will continue and even accelerate in the near future. Positive testing results by Michigan charter schools in 1997–98 is welcome news and will certainly help to solidify public and legislative support for charters, but they will also be another source of angst, according to Goenner, for opponents who desire to prevent charter school success.[115]

Conclusion: The Activists

The most interesting thing about these individuals is how they stand out, somewhat alienated from the groups with which they are associated. Quentin Quade as a loyal supporter of parochial education, for example, was clearly and forthrightly critical of Catholic efforts on behalf of school choice. Marshall Fritz might be called the apostle of "individuation"; he is both libertarian and Catholic, which make him predictably unpredictable, a friend to Evangelicals, but above all one who abhors statist imposed conformity. Kevin Teasley, who appears secular because of his long association with free-market organizations, now works closely with pastors. Bert Hall, the civil rights revolutionary, is allied with David Brennan, the entrepreneur capitalist, an odd couple arrangement that works extremely well. Bruce Thompson, a liberal democrat, is now the consummate coalition-building school board member who works closely with conservative Catholics. James Goenner, who is employed by a state university, objects when public schools resist charter schools. All are critical of their home constituencies for having done too little for children, or for hurting them, and they reach out to find like-minded people to leverage school choice. They are both individuals and coalition builders, people with a mission who are not fully at home in any political or social group.

Conclusion: Scholars and Activists for School Choice

Individuals make a difference in school choice politics. Milton Friedman, a scholar we have not discussed here but whose work for school choice is well known, helped to change the whole framework for debate when he wrote about vouchers. Today scholars and activists are examining and assisting in the implementation of Friedman's ideas. How the movement develops may depend as much on a Paul Peterson, a Marshall Fritz, or a Kevin Teasley than on the efforts and investments of large organizations. Measuring the impact of scholars and activists may be difficult, but it is impossible to imagine school choice succeeding without them. As long as this issue captures the imaginations of inspired and creative people they will be scarce resources for this movement.

Politicians cite scholars as experts. Mayors like John Norquist seek their advice and counsel, and they testify at congressional hearings. Activists, on the other hand, exert the influence behind the scenes and in public that get the hearings scheduled in the first place. With out the political pressure that activists help to unleash school choice might not even be on the policy agenda.

Above all, individuals provide a critical function. These people often are out of step or one step ahead of others more conventional in their thinking. They also pay a price for this independence—they no longer fit in—they are the *odd balls* who make the impossible eventually seem possible. Each is not exclusively right, they have their differences, but they each bring vitality to the mix.

Notes

1. Paul E. Peterson, interview by Hubert Morken, Boston, September 4, 1998.

2. Ibid.; Paul E. Peterson, presentation at the Rose & Milton Friedman Foundation Conference, San Francisco, October 9, 1998.

3. Ibid.; Paul E. Peterson, "Are Big City Schools Holding Their Own?," in *Seeds of Crisis: Public Schooling in Milwaukee since 1920*, Eds. John L. Rury and Frank A. Cassell (Madison: University of Wisconsin Press, 1993), pp. 269–301.

4. Peterson, interview, September 4, 1998.

5. Ibid.; written comments sent to Hubert Morken, March 1999.

6. Ibid.; Paul E. Peterson and Chad Noyes, "School Choice in Milwaukee," in *New Schools of a New Century*, Eds. Diane Ravitch and Joseph P. Viteritti (New Haven: Yale University Press, 1997), pp. 123–146; Jay P. Greene and Paul E. Pe-

terson, "Effectiveness of School Choice: The Milwaukee Experiment," Occasional Paper, Program in Education Policy and Governance, March 1997; Jay P. Greene, William G. Howell, and Paul E. Peterson, "An Evaluation of the Cleveland Scholarship Program," in Education Policy and Governance, September 1997; Jay P. Greene, William G. Howell, and Paul E. Peterson, "Lessons from the Cleveland Scholarship Program," Program in Education Policy and Governance, December 10, 1997.

7. Ibid.; Paul Peterson, panel, American Political Science Association Annual Meeting, Boston, September 4, 1998.

8. Ibid.

9. Paul E. Peterson, David Myers, and William G. Howell, "An Evaluation of the New York City School Choice Scholarships Program: The First Year," October 1998; Paul E. Peterson, Jay P. Greene, William G. Howell, and William McCready, "Initial Findings from an Evaluation of School Choice Programs in Washington, DC and Dayton, OH," October 24, 1998, p. 4.

10. Timothy Ehrgott, interview by Hubert Morken, Indianapolis, IN, July 22, 1998.

11. Peterson, presentation, San Francisco, October 9, 1998; Paul E. Peterson, "School Choice: A Report Card," in *Learning from School Choice*, eds. Paul E. Peterson and Bryan C. Hassel (Washington, D. C.: Brookings Institution Press, 1998), p. 3.

12. Ibid.; Paul E. Peterson, "A Report Card on School Choice," *Commentary*, October 1997, pp. 29–33.

13. Terry Moe, interview by Hubert Morken, Boston, September 5, 1998.

14. Ibid.

15. Ibid.

16. Ibid.

17. Terry Moe, roundtable, American Political Science Association Annual Meeting, Boston, September 4, 1998.

18. Ibid.

19. Moe, interview.

20. Ibid.

21. Ibid.

22. Charles L. Glenn, a manuscript provided by Hubert Morken, *The Ambiguous Embrace: Government and Faith-Based Schools and Social Agencies*, to be published by the Princeton University Press in 1999, p. 3.

23. Glenn, *The Ambiguous Embrace*, p. 5.

24. Ibid.

25. Ibid.; Glenn, manuscript, 1999.

26. Ibid.

27. Charles L. Glenn, interview by Hubert Morken, Boston, MA, September 3, 1998.

28. Ibid.

29. Ibid.

30. Ibid.

31. Ibid.

32. Andrew J. Coulson, roundtable at the Rose and Milton Friedman Foundation Conference, San Francisco, October 10, 1998.

33. Andrew J. Coulson, *Market Education: The Unknown History* manuscript provided by its author to be published by Transaction Publishers, 1999.

34. Ibid., 178.

35. Ibid., 179.

36. Ibid., 179–81.

37. Ibid., 181–82.

38. Ibid., 182–83.

39. Ibid., 183–85.

40. Ibid., 194–219.

41. Ibid., 227.

42. Myron Lieberman, interview by Hubert Morken, Virginia Beach, VA, March 9, 1998; Myron Lieberman, *The Teacher Unions* (New York: The Free Press, 1997); *Teachers Evaluating Teachers* (New Brunswick, NJ: Transaction Publishers, 1998).

43. Lieberman, *The Teachers Unions*, pp. 191–206.

44. Ibid., 202.

45. Lieberman, interview, March 9, 1998.

46. John E. Coons and Stephen D. Sugarman, *Making School Choice Work for All Families*, manuscript provided by the Pacific Research Institute, fall 1998.

47. Ibid., 141–45.

48. Ibid., 146.

49. Lance Darin Fusarelli, *The Interplay of Advocacy Coalitions and Institutions on School Choice in Texas: A Case Study of Charter Schools and Vouchers*, Ph.D. Dissertation, University of Texas at Austin, 1998.

50. Ibid., 57–67.

51. Ibid., 82–129.

52. Ibid., 121–26.

53. Ibid.

54. Ibid., 141, 145.

55. Bruce S. Cooper, telephone interview by Hubert Morken, October 1, 1998.

56. Bruce S. Cooper and E. Vance Randall, "Critics Stop Vouchers in Their Tracks: A Conspiracy of Coincidence?" a paper presented at the Education Between State and Civil Society Conference, Boston, November 13–16, 1997, pp. 3–31.

57. Ibid., 42–51.

58. Lieberman, *The Teacher Unions*, x-xi.

59. Quentin L. Quade, interview by Hubert Morken, Milwaukee, July 29, 1998.

60. Quentin L. Quade, "A North Star for School Choice," a pamphlet, The Blum Center for Parental Freedom in Education, Milwaukee, WI, undated; "All Roads Lead to Educational Choice without Financial Penalty," a pamphlet, The Blum Center for Parental Freedom in Education, Milwaukee, WI, undated.

61. George A. Clowes, interview by Hubert Morken, Chicago, July 20, 1998.

62. Marshall Fritz, telephone interview by Hubert Morken, September 28, 1998; and interview by Hubert Morken, Fresno, California, October 8, 1998; The Separation of School and State Alliance, *The Education Liberator*, vol. 1, no. 1, (September 1995), vol. 3, no. 2 (February/March 1997); vol. 4, no. 1 (September 1998).

63. Ibid.

64. The Separation of School and State Alliance, organization stationary, undated.

65. Fritz, interviews by Hubert Morken, 1998.

66. Ibid.; Douglas Dewey, "How to Separate School and State: A Primer," *The Freeman*, vol. 46, no. 7, (July 1996): pp. 480–85.

67. The Separation of School and State Alliance, "Proclamation for the Separation of School and State," in a pamphlet, *Who Should Control a Child's Education? Parents or Government?* undated.

68. Fritz, interviews by Hubert Morken, 1998; The Separation of School and State Alliance, "Readings of Interest to Protestants and Catholics Considering Separation of School and State," October 16, 1996; "Separation Solution Resource Binder, The Compendium," articles collected by staff and volunteers, November 8, 1997.

69. Ibid.; Marshall Fritz, "Director's Letter," *The Education Liberator*, February/March, 1997, p. 2.

70. Ibid., interviews; Marshall Fritz, "Director's Letter," *The Education Liberator*, September 1998, p. 2.

71. Fritz, "Victory," *The Education Liberator*, September 1998, p. 3.

72. Ibid.; Fritz, interviews.

73. Fritz, "The Cement Canoe," *The Education Liberator*, September 1995, 6.

74. Kevin Teasley, interview by Hubert Morken, Indianapolis, IN, July 22, 1998; telephone interview by Hubert Morken, September 14, 1998.

75. Ibid.

76. Ibid.

77. Kevin Teasley and Danielle Underwood, "Home Educators Speak out on Tax Credits," *The IAHE Informer*, September/October, 1998, p. 6.

78. Teasley, telephone interview, September 14, 1998.

79. Ibid.

80. Ibid.; Teasley and Underwood, "Home Educators," September/October, 1998, 6; Kevin Teasley and Danielle Underwood, "Education Tax Credits," *Indiana Family Institute Citizen*, vol. 9 no. 8 (August 1998): pp. 1–2.

81. Ibid.

82. Ibid.

83. Ibid.

84. Ibid.

85. Ibid.

86. Ibid.

87. Ibid.

88. Ibid.

89. Ibid.

90. Ibid.

91. Ibid.

92. Ibid.

93. David Brennan, interview by Hubert Morken, Cleveland, OH, June 2, 1998.

94. David Zanotti, interview by Hubert Morken, June 2, 1998.

95. Brennan, interview, June 2, 1998.

96. Ibid.; David Brennan, panel comments, Milton and Rose Friedman Conference, San Francisco, October 10, 1998.

97. Ibid.; Linas Vysnionis, Managing Director, Hope Central Academy, interview by Hubert Morken, Cleveland, OH, June 2, 1998.

98. Bert Holt, interview by Hubert Morken, Cleveland, OH, June 3, 1998.

99. Ibid.

100. Ibid.

101. Ibid.

102. Ibid.; Linas Vysnionis, Managing Director, Hope Central Academy, interview by Hubert Morken, Cleveland, OH, June 2, 1998; Holt, interview.

103. Ibid.

104. Bert Holt, speaking at a meeting for pastors, co-sponsored by the Ohio Roundtable and David Brennan, chaired by David Zanotti, Cleveland, OH, June 2, 1998.

105. Bruce Thompson, interview by Hubert Morken, Milwaukee, WI, July 29, 1998; Bruce R. Thompson, "Ideologies Spoil School Choice Debate," and " Vouchers Offer a Choice of Problems," Letters to the Editor, *Wall Street Journal*, January 7 and May 17, 1993.

106. Ibid.

107. Ibid.; Public Policy Forum Debate, John Gardner and Leon Todd, Italian Community Center, Milwaukee, WI, July 29, 1998.

108. Ibid.; Mayor John Norquist, interview by Hubert Morken, July 30, 1998.

109. James N. Goenner, telephone interview by Hubert Morken, fall 1998; *Central Michigan Charter Public Schools, 1998–1999*, a pamphlet; Michigan Association of Public School Academies, *Joining a Union*, a pamphlet, undated; conversation by Hubert Morken at the Milton and Rose Friedman Conference, San Francisco, October 1998; Central Michigan University, *CMU & Charter Schools*, a pamphlet, undated.

110. Goenner, telephone interview.

111. Ibid.; Roland Wilkerson, "Charter Schools See Large Jump in Enrollment," *Grand Rapids Press*, Grand Rapids, MI, September 67, 1998.

112. Central Michigan University, *CMU & Charter Schools*.

113. Scott Anderson, "CMU Boycott Threatened over Charter Schools—University Promises 'Assertive' Response," *Central Michigan LIFE*, Mount Pleasant, MI, May 31, 1995; Margaret Trimer-Hartley, "Charter Schools Spark NEw Battle," *Detroit News and Free Press*, Detroit, MI, May 27, 1995; Avi Stern, "SVSU Students in Crosshairs of MEA Threat," *Saginaw News*, Saginaw, MI, June 2, 1994.

114. Goenner, telephone interview; Julius A. Maddox, Michigan Education Association, letter to members, August 25, 1998; MAPSA, *Charter School MEAP Scores Uphold Promise of Improvement*, pamphlet, June 12, 1998.

115. Ibid.

Chapter 8

Trends and Analyses

Throughout this book, a variety of methods were used to articulate and analyze information for its central research question, namely, what are the strategies being used to leverage school choice in the United States today? The techniques employed to try to find this out included an extensive literature study, an overview of federal and state judicial decisions and legislation, interviews; primary source documents, newspaper accounts, and a survey. The questionnaire, developed in 1998, collected data from organizations working to advance school choice. It included a sampling of not-for-profit foundations, think tanks, interest groups, and religious, racial, and ideological organizations as well as state departments of education that had offices of charter or alternative educational affairs. The sample was put together from lists that the authors had gathered from directories, the school choice literature, and bibliographies, as well as from recommendations from individuals working in the field or others being interviewed for specific informational purposes.

Two hundred and forty organizations were identified and contacted by first class mail to participate in this survey. Three mailings were conducted: one on May 12, a second on June 2, and a third on August 18, 1998. In each of the three mailings, the same forty letters were returned. Thus, about one-sixth of the original sample were either out of business, had moved, or had been subsumed into another organization. This seemed significant, of itself, since no forwarding addresses were given, and follow-up phone calls yielded no responses or other information. Questions remain. Was the issue of school choice no longer relevant to these organizations? Did they run out of money to fund its purposes? Were workers lacking? The answers are unknown.

Of the 200 organizations left in the sample, 105 sent back responses,[1] giving the survey a credible response rate of 52.5 percent. It is important to point out, however, that not every respondent answered every single question on the questionnaire. In fact, some organizations, viewing themselves strictly as non-profits with 501c-3 tax status, and some state Departments of

Education charged with charter schools or alternative educational programs felt that it was inappropriate for them to answer the survey. Some claimed that even though their agencies were involved politically for purposes of budgeting, negotiating contracts, and other matters, their peculiar status precluded them from giving any information on the survey. Thus, the number of organizations answering every question dropped to eighty-seven, and the percentages of all cross tabulations and t-tests represent an adjusted response rate.

At the outset, it is important to realize that this survey, like every other, is merely a snapshot in time. It is not meant to be definitive, and, indeed, the landscape is changing so quickly that it is incumbent to say the data here only evidence *trends* for, and *directions* within, the school choice movement. Its value comes from the fact that the data covers a wide range of school choice organizations, among them foundations, think tanks, state agencies, and entrepreneurial companies; and that the cohort is a national one, which includes organizations from Alaska to Florida and Maine to California.

The survey was designed to uncover two types of information. First, demographic facts that would identify and characterize the size, resources, and purposes of school choice organizations. Second, data about the impressions, accomplishments, and perceptions of the respondents about the movement for school choice in the United States.

The demographic information revealed some of the basics about school choice organizations. Regarding size, the survey showed that most school choice organizations are relatively small, with about 77.1 percent reporting that they had between one and nine full-time employees. Agencies of this size also stated overwhelmingly—95.2 percent—that they had part-time employees, as well as volunteers—81.7 percent—to help them in their efforts. Only three of the largest organizations, with budgets of over one million dollars, reported a paid and volunteer staff of over 500 persons. Therefore, the numbers tell us that most of the school choice organizations in the United States are relatively small operations, with only about a third reporting staffs of more than ten employees.

The budgetary data of the organizations was also interesting. The survey showed that most of the respondents received funding from more than one source. More than half—57.3 percent—received some funds from private sources; 46.3 percent reported getting some monies from foundations; 41.5 percent indicated some corporate donations, and another 41.5 percent of school choice organizations listed "other" sources of funding as well. However, when viewing the funding sources of smaller versus larger organizations, the larger ones, i.e, with budgets over one million dollars, reported that they were receiving almost two-thirds of their funding from corporations and "others," such as state, federal, and church dollars. On the other hand, smaller organizations, i.e., those with budgets of $500,000 and under were receiving their funding mainly from private sources and foundations. This information suggests two important things: first, that major corporations in America are interested in school choice, and second, that they are willing to fund the larger school choice organizations that they believe will have the clout to make a difference on the issue.

The largest organizations, in terms of budget, fall into three categories. The first group of organizations included foundations, institutes, and research centers such as the Tesseract Group, the Leona Group, the Cato Institute, and the Heartland Institute. The second category included state agencies, such as California's Department of Education Office of Policy and Education, the Wisconsin Department of Public Instruction, and the Department of Charter Schools of the North Carolina Department of Education. The third category was comprised of religious agencies, such as Parents Advancing Values in Education (PAVE), the Catholic League for Religious and Civil Rights, the Catholic Education Association, the United States Catholic Conference, the Family Research Council, and the National Association of Evangelicals. With regard to the last category, this study garnered information from the major religious agencies by either survey or interview.

The survey questionnaire presented the respondents with questions about seven possible functions and asked whether or not they participated in them. Some of the functions were political, and some were non-political, i.e, to raise awareness about school choice. The organizations were asked whether or not they carried out education, monitoring, research, advocacy, lobbying, litigation, or "other" activities. The overwhelming response to the two most significant political functions, lobbying and litigation, was that most respondents did not participate in these two activities at a rate of 75.9 percent and 77.1 percent, respectively. Only about 25 percent of the groups indicated that they were involved with lobbying or litigation, but this number rose to 33 percent or greater among groups with budgets of over one million dollars. As expected, then, three things are clear. *Most school choice organizations do not participate overtly in political activities per se. That among those that do, larger rather than smaller groups are more involved politically to advance school choice, and that lobbying and litigation require more funds and larger organizational bases.* Concomitantly, then, respondents reported greater participation in "awareness" activities as follows: education (50.6%), monitoring (43.4%), research (42.2%), advocacy (41%), and other (43.4%).

One caveat needs to be mentioned here, however, with regard to these statistics about political activities. Field research has shown that many organizations do not like to report political undertakings for strategic, as well as for legal, reasons. Some organizations simply do not want the opposition to know what they are doing! In other cases, there is close collaboration between groups that are working to engineer legislation or to win initiatives and elections. This is true in Wisconsin, Ohio, Michigan, and Pennsylvania, to name only four states. Often, there are off-the-record meetings and communications between state-based and other groups. Sometimes there is a division of labor. One organization might lobby in the traditional sense while another will "educate" legislators. At what point, though, does education become political, particularly in the eyes of the IRS? Differences in understanding are potentially a legal problem for school choice organizations due to the 501c-3 tax exempt status that most enjoy. Thus, it is possible that for tax reasons, some groups simply reported that "we do education work," on the survey, especially if the organization is only marginally political.

The survey also showed that, to a varied degree, organizations wanted to influence a diverse audience—from government officials to students, from religious groups to the media. One would have expected that all of the organizations would have wanted to advance the school choice agenda politically. But surprisingly, when viewing the group as a whole, only about one-third of the responding organizations indicated that they wanted to influence federal, or local, lawmakers, and only a slightly larger number (42.2%) wished to influence state officials. However, the larger organizations, i.e., those with budgets over $500,000, indicated that they were pursuing activities to influence all levels of government. Sixty percent of those organizations reported that they wished to influence state officials and at least 50 percent of the groups indicated interest in influencing national and local lawmakers. A similar trend could be seen with regard to the respondent's desire to influence the media. Fifty per cent of the larger organizations wished to influence the media, whereas only 35 percent of the smaller groups wanted to do so. In general, about one-quarter of the respondents indicated an interest in influencing students (24.1%), minorities (28.9%), and religious groups (27.7%). Almost a third or more of the organizations aim to influence teachers (30%) and parents (41%). What do all these numbers mean? It is hard to say. It can be argued that there is a patchwork of organizations looking to influence school choice among a variety of different constituencies, and that, in so doing, influence may be uneven, scattered, and fragmented across the economic, ideological, social, racial, and political spectrum. The information also reveals what might be expected, namely, that the larger groups are the ones mainly concerned with influencing government, particularly state governments, where they believe their actions might have the most impact.

One of the goals of the survey was to try to find out if there was unified support for a particular type of school choice. The respondent's answers clearly showed that no type of school choice received either overwhelming support or even a meaningful consensus. More important, the lack of support for many types of school choice could also be interpreted as a reason for a serious fragmentation of efforts and resources, necessary components of a potential educational and political movement. Thus, while the survey found that school choice organizations supported charter schools (43.4%), tuition tax credits (34.9%), vouchers (37.3%), magnet schools (22.9%), scholarships (39.8%), and other kinds of school choice (26.5%) the numbers, when turned around, also reveal that significant numbers of organizations do not support charter schools (56.3%), tuition tax credits (65.1%), vouchers (62.7%), magnet schools (77.1%), scholarships (61.2%), and other kinds of school choice (74.5%). This internal lack of cohesion indicates a fledging movement, one not yet totally developed at the policy level. Of the reporting organizations with budgets of over one million dollars, it is interesting to note that 42.9 percent supported "other" or their own particular type of school choice. These included their own versions of public and private scholarship and voucher programs, such as those of Children's Scholarship Fund. In comparison to the general cohort, these organizations with more than million dollar budgets supported charter schools at 31.4 percent, scholarships at 33.3 percent, tuition tax credits at 34.5 percent, vouchers at 35.5 percent, and magnet schools at 36.8 percent. The point is quite clear: school choice organization with larger financial backing support a different kind of school choice—*their own kind* of school choice. Whether or not they will support other groups and other types of school choice in the future, other than their own and particularly at a political level, in order to advance the movement is unknown at this time.

Part Two of the survey consisted of seven questions designed to identify trends and perceptions about school choice. Again, not every respondent answered every question in this section of the survey. However, since these questions were totally subjective, the fact that some were not answered led to broad speculation as to why they were left blank. In some cases it can be conjectured that the respondents did not think the questions were appropriate to their organization, or they simply did not understand them. In other cases, it can be speculated that respondents simply did not have an answer. In attempting to quantify the results of this section of the survey, the percentages regarding each question were calculated according to the number of answers received to each particular question. Thus, if 100 out of 108 respondents answered a particular question, the percentage was calculated on those replies. If fifty out of 108 answered a particular question, the percentage was figured based on those numbers.

Grounded on the realization that power, particularly national dominance, is a key to advancing the school choice agenda in the United States, this survey attempted to find out what national organization was perceived as the most influential in the country and why. Fully 47 percent of the respondents could not or would not identify any organization, or any reason for their answers. One simply replied "none," and left the "why" part of the question unanswered as well. The lack of responses raised more questions than answers. Why did almost half of the respondents, the most knowledgeable and committed of the school choice advocates in the country, leave this part of the survey blank? Were they unconnected or unfamiliar with organizations outside their own sphere of interest and concern? Did they lack information about other school choice organizations? Did they simply see themselves as equals among the groups? Does this reflect a need for greater networking among school choice organizations so that there is a perceived or visible movement able to give support and credence to smaller state and regional organizations? Or is it simply possible to conclude that school choice groups do not think that there is a national organization that is the most influential for school choice in the United States? Absent any other compelling information, the latter seems to be the answer.

Of those organizations that did answer the question about national school choice leadership, 22 percent identified scattered names of diverse organizations, none of which were mentioned more than once by any of these respondents. They also had a variety of reasons for naming the various organizations, which included vague notions such as they "know what they are doing" to the fact that they were perceived as "hav[ing] influence."

The Center for Education Reform, however, was identified by a number of respondents as the most influential national school choice organization—but only with a 14 percent response rate. Survey participants agreed that CER had clout because of its resources, newsletters, website, accurate, topical information, publications, and in one case, "aggressiveness." Yet on the whole, the school choice organization, located in Washington, D.C., is only recognized as the chief leadership organization by a very small minority of the school choice community across the United States. Headed by Jeanne Allen, CER describes itself as a "national, non-profit education advocacy group and an active broker in providing resources, support and guidance for school reform to communities across the United States."[2] Although it provides publications, an educational forum, education news analysis, and an annual ranking and analysis of charter laws and legislation, CER is yet to have the name recognition within its intended constituency to be considered a dominant force to advance school choice.

Another 12 percent of the respondents listed the Children's Educational Opportunity Foundation (CEO America) as the most influential national school choice organization in the country. They perceived the Arkansas-based foundation as an organization that could actually implement school choice, as one that helped children and provided school choice information. Some respondents indicated that CEO America was experienced, had resources, and had a grassroots organization. Headed by Fritz Steiger, CEO America has a twofold mission: the promotion of parental choice in education through private tuition grants and tax-funded options, and the empowering of all parents to have the right to choose the elementary schools that best suit their children's needs. It serves as a clearinghouse for school choice news and facts and provides support services ranging from administrative training to programmatic consulting and to technical support. It creates a forum for networking, provides specialists in certain fields to organizations that need them, and produces resources, such as videotapes, manuals, software, brochures, and other materials.[3] Again, however, CEO America is not perceived by a significant number of its peers as being the most influential national organization advancing school choice.

Finally, with regard to the question of national influence, respondents named the Institute for Justice (2%) in Washington, D.C., the Heritage Foundation (2%) also in Washington, D.C., and the Blum Center (1%) in Wisconsin, as distant runner ups. They were identified generally as having national influence due to their media clout, persistence, resources, and publications. In short, however, *no organization was identified or perceived as 'influential' nationally, by a majority of the school choice organizations in this survey.*

This questionnaire also attempted to find out if there was any recognizable national school choice leader in the United States working among the organizations pursuing that agenda and why. It was assumed that if someone could be identified, organizations could rally around the individual either professionally or politically and support that person to move the school choice agenda along on a national level. Again, 45 percent of the respondents simply left this question blank, and one answered "none." All these respondents left the reason "why" unanswered as well. In short, many respondents overwhelmingly would not or could not identify an influential national spokesperson for choice in the United States.

Of those who did list individuals, the most influential person emerged as the Reverend Floyd Flake, former Congressman and pastor of the Allen AME Church in New York—but with only 8 percent supporting him on this question within the school choice community. He was perceived as an influential national leader because of his understanding of the need for school choice, his high profile in the media, and his respect and credibility among his peers. Jeanne Allen of the Center for Education Reform came in second (6%). Described by respondents as personable and well informed with a solid philosophy, they believed that her "non-commercial" position at a well-funded organization gave her influence in the national school choice movement. Howard Fuller of the Institute for the Transformation of Learning in Milwaukee received 3 percent for being articulate and experienced. William Bennett of Empower America, Clint Bolick of the Institute for Justice, Mayor Bret Schundler of Jersey City, and former Governor Arne Carlson of Minnesota each received 2 percent for their media exposure and commitment to school choice. Finally, Fritz Steiger, President of CEO America, Chester Finn of the Fordham Foundation, and David Kirkpatrick of the Pennsylvania REACH Alliance each received 1 percent of the vote for their experience, with Finn being singled out for his "sense of humor!" Others mentioned, who composed 18 percent of the responses included Representative Dick Armey (R-Tex.); Pat Rooney, President of the Indianapolis-based Choice Charitable Trust; Richard Reily, Secretary of the Department of Education; Eric Premack, head of the Institute for Education Reform at the California State University; Joe Nathan, Director of the Center for School Change at the Hubert Humphrey Institute of Public Affairs; Rush Limbaugh of talk show fame; Lamar Alexander, former Secretary of Education; Milton Freidman, President of the Freidman Foundation; Ted Kolderie, of the Center for Policy Studies; President Bill Clinton; Lisa Graham Keegan, Secretary of State for the state of Arizona; John Taylor Gatto, a New Jersey lobbyist; Peter Du Pont, Policy Chairman of the National Center for Policy Analysis; Bill Andrews, a Republican state legislator from Florida; and a few other unidentifiable individuals. Again, *no single person was identified or perceived as being 'influential' nationally by a majority of the school choice advocates in this survey.*

It was also important to find out if there were any influential school choice organizations within the states since many in the school choice movement perceive educational options and experiments as a state, rather than a federal, issue. On this question, 52 percent of respondents left the question blank, and three answered "none." All respondents left the question "why" blank as well. In short, respondents, once again, could not or would not identify an influential organization within their own state working to advance school choice. Perhaps, again, some of the respondents considered themselves equals at the state level. However, of those who did respond, most listed *themselves* as the most influential and no organization received more than one vote except for Minnesotans for School Choice.

The results of this question were particularly perplexing, given the field research of the authors on specific state organization and activities. Their inquiries showed that grassroots efforts are growing, some coalitions are developing, and there is both knowledge and communication among school choice groups about what it going on in some states. How do the authors reconcile the statistics with their field research? It is possible to explain this discrepancy by the fact that, since the authors pursued their investigations in those states where school choice was both viable and volatile, the information that they uncovered was state specific and does not necessarily apply to the whole United States. Keeping that in mind, then, it is possible to conclude from this survey *that there currently appears to be no school choice group in a large number of states that can identify itself or any other group as the most dominant or influential on the issue.*

Two questions were also designed to find out if school choice organizations were interfacing with their peer groups, and if such involvement was leading to some sort of developing political movement for the issue. The survey asked: "With which national, state, and/or local political organizations does your organization interact? And how?" While 44 percent left this question blank and 10 percent responded "none," it is important to realize, again, that many of the organizations in the sample were non-profits with 501c-3 tax-status, and were thus limited as to the kinds of activities they could pursue. Virtually all the state offices of education responded that they could not participate in the political process and found this question to be inappropriate for them. Of those who answered this question, 16 percent responded by naming a number of groups that they interacted with, such as "other religious groups," their "national chapters," the U.S. Department of Education, "numerous" and "many" organizations. The type of involvement school choice organizations cited as "interaction" with other, similar organizations included efforts to pursue grants and information sharing. Another 11 percent named specific organizations with which they interacted, but none appeared with any regularity. Their answers as to "how" they interacted were described as telephone and conference calls, e-mail contact, attending meetings, sharing newsletters and mailings, networking, promoting discussions and endorsements, co-signing letters, providing speakers exchanges, seeking organization and legal advice, discussions, and personal communications. *Political* interaction, which would normally consist of strategizing, lobbying, and attending policy briefings, was reported only three times within this cohort of respondents. A few, 5 percent, reported that they interacted with the political parties in their state legislatures and 4 percent answered that they interacted with "everyone" or "all" political groups. But again it is clear that *most school choice groups are not pursuing political strategies.*

What does this say then, about the potential of school choice organizations to advance school choice in the political arena at the state level? It seems clear. If school choice groups continue to function as they are now, with little direct political involvement, the chances of school choice becoming a priority on the policy agendas of most states are slim to none. School choice organizations cannot compete with the money, resources, or clout of unions, who are organized politically and who have a vested interest to maintain the educational status quo, or of the politicians, who are beholden to the unions for campaign funds. School choice cannot happen by simply raising awareness, believing in principles, or desiring change.

Another question on the survey was designed to find out if the respondents were part of, or perceived themselves to be part of, some burgeoning political movement toward school choice in their state or across the nation. They were asked if school choice was coalescing politically in the respondent's state and why; or if school choice was coalescing politically at the federal level and why. Fully 52 percent of the respondents simply did not answer this question with regard to their particular state. Of those who did, however, 26 percent did see some movement at the state level, 12 percent saw no movement, 8 percent saw "some," "a little," or a "growing" movement, and 2 percent saw the situation as not applicable to them. With regard to school choice coalescing on a national level, 65 percent opted not to answer the question and left it blank. Of those responding, 15 percent felt that it was becoming a national issue while 9 percent did not and 9 percent did not know or thought it might be gaining ground as an issue "moderately" or "somewhat." Of all, 2 percent did not feel it was applicable to their situation. Thus, it can be reported that, of the organizations that answered the question, most believed that the beginnings of a political movement for school choice was starting to occur at the state level, but that clearly nothing was really happening on the national level. Again, this answer is revealing, especially in light of the fact that, for the first time, school choice legislation in the form of the Coverdell-Torricelli Bill for Educational Savings Accounts (ESA's) passed both the House and the Senate during the 105th Congress. School choice organizations obviously did not see this as a sign of crystallizing national legislative concern for the issue.

Another question was designed to find out if the school choice organizations felt that they were making a difference or having some impact on the movement for educational reform in the United States. They were asked: "What is your organization's major school choice accomplishment?" Of the respondents, 32 percent left the question blank, 2 percent saw the question as not applicable to them, and one simply answered "none." This question had the highest response rate on the survey, most likely because those surveyed felt that they had indeed accomplished something in the area of school choice.

Of the respondents, most were quite informative, and most were quite clear in explaining their achievements. Twenty-one percent of the respondents felt that their major accomplishments had been in the areas of educating and communicating with the public. They had created newsletters, videos, websites, and publications, and they had sponsored rallies and gave tours of alternative educational facilities. They had put together school choice conferences, written and received grants, and some even felt that they had created a presence, one to whom the media could turn for information on school choice. Another 17 percent saw their major accomplishment as playing a role in advancing charter schools. They reported doing this through education and awareness raising within the public and legislatures about the issue, assisting in charter school development by writing charter school legislation in various states, or actually establishing charter schools themselves. Six percent reported that they had established scholarship programs, and one organization alone could point to 6,000 recipients of such financial assistance. Five percent felt that their support of tuition tax credits and vouchers was their major accomplishment. A variety of "other" accomplishments also surfaced, representing 16 percent of the total. They included combating anti-Catholicism, challenging the public school monopoly, advocating, monitoring, collecting information, helping children and families, representing parents, raising school choice awareness among black parents, recruiting minorities for education reform initiatives, and securing bus transportation, remedial assistance, loan forgiveness, and teacher scholarships. With regard to *political* accomplishments, only 8 percent reported such activities or interpreted them as a kind of achievement. Two respondents recounted that they had lobbied for the Coverdell-Torricelli Educational Savings Accounts Bill, two reported getting school choice issues on state ballots, two discussed their success in developing relationships with state legislators and building grassroots organizations, one talked about creating coalitions for school choice, and one could point to efforts at litigating school choice matters.

Finally, the survey concluded with an open-ended question to elicit additional comments about any aspect of the school choice organizations' work or the educational reform movement. Although 74 percent had nothing more to report, many appended literature, videos, phone numbers, websites, and other contacts for this study. Some pointed out that school choice was only one part of their reform agenda, or issues list. One interesting point that did emerge, however, was the notion of one respondent: that there was a disconnect between black families and black leadership, a separation that could be overcome with a voucher vehicle designed to put an end to the de facto public system of educational inequality. Several organizations also blamed the lack of school choice success on teachers' unions. One claimed that the government intrudes on parochial schools, one maintained that few understand the principles of the school choice movement, and one very proudly ended with the fact that although their particular organization did not have money, it had respect.

What then is the significance of this survey? Put into perspective, it shows some startling information. *First, the school choice issue, at this time, is a developing special interest rather than a powerful and dominant movement.* The reasons for this are varied, and, although this book has showed some successes in advancing educational options, it is important to realize that in the grand scheme of things school choice is progressing, but it is proceeding relatively slowly and in an uneven and sporadic way.

The reasons for this kind of movement are varied. As this survey has showed, most school choice organizations are small, with budgets that are dwarfed by those of their opponents. They cannot compete in terms of personnel or finances with, for example, the National Education Association or the American Federation of Teachers. They cannot and do not support political candidates publicly or formally, as most school choice organizations have 501c-3 tax-exempt status. Overwhelmingly, then, the statistics show that school choice organizations are *not* pursuing overt political activities or agendas. Although a very small percentage are carrying out litigation and lobbying tactics, the major organizations are counting on acknowledged, non-political means to advance school choice: education, monitoring, and advocacy. These activities do have the potential to move education reform and funding to a variety of state and even federal policy agendas, but they will remain a relatively long time in coming.

Thus, these numbers bear out what our other research has shown, namely, that the smart money is now looking to bypass the political process and to finance and support education reform in its own way. Larger school choice organizations are attracting corporate support, and smaller ones are attracting private funding. And, surprisingly, this survey has shown that private funding is being used increasingly to support a variety of school choice programs, particularly scholarships and other options that are different depending on whom the private sponsor happens to be. Indeed, scholarship programs private vouchers, and for-profit schools may be the wave of the future to leverage school choice until a political solution can be developed to move educational reform forward.

Second, this survey has also showed that there is currently *no preferred type of school choice* that has emerged as "the one" that can engender or ignite the movement. There is no rallying point among school choice advocates for a particular type of program. Indeed, there are those who would argue that the very smorgasbord of options is good, that a one-size-fits-all mentality is not what school choice is about. Yet, without some unity or standard of school choice, there is the possibility of always having to reinvent the wheel within the movement. Perhaps, if charter schools were the starting point, steps to public and private vouchers, tuition tax credits, and total choice in education could be leveraged. However, there is no unity among the existing educational reform groups as to what the best kind of school choice is. The result is that there is a fragmentation among the organizations as to what is the most practical type of school choice to support financially or politically.

Third, this survey has showed that there is *no identifiable school choice leader* on the federal or state level. Thus includes both professionals in the field and politicians in the public arena. Thus far, none of the front runners for national political office has placed this issue on the top of his or her agenda. It is anticipated that the school choice movement could get support if either George Bush Jr. or Elizabeth Dole were the Republican candidate for the presidency in 2000, since they have both sent signals that they will support vouchers in the future. Currently, there is no national Democratic candidate who might put school choice on his agenda, as Al Gore, the heir apparent, is on record supporting President Clinton's reform measures for public schools. It is also important to remember that both Clinton and Gore won the overwhelming support of the teachers' unions in both the 1992 and 1996 campaigns.

At the state level, there are some Republican governors who are working to advance school choice. Most notably these include, Tommy Thompson (WI), John Engler (MI), Tom Ridge (PA), Garry Johnson (NM), George W.

Bush (TX), and Jeb Bush (FL). In general, though, most gubernatorial efforts have supported a variety of experimental school choice programs and have advocated compromise proposals between public and private calls for educational change. Others have been implemented simply as a valve to let off some of the pressure for school choice within states. Thus, the lack of national and state leadership leaves school choice an orphan in most political campaigns.

Fourth, the school choice movement also *reflects an immature understanding of its power position.* In general, participants in this survey do not see themselves as being dominant on either the national or state level. Although most can point to small accomplishments, only a very few can point to significant victories. More important, the majority of organizations do not see themselves as part of a larger movement able to advance a unified goal. Instead, this survey reveals that most of the smaller organizations see themselves functioning alone within a small parameter, and even the largest organizations appear to be "going it alone" and pushing their own particular brand of school choice program. They are unaware of the potential strength of the movement and of the steps needed to bring it to a position of political viability.

Nevertheless, this survey should not leave the impression that school choice is either a weak or a dying issue in the United States. Rather, it is growing and vital, albeit slowly and deliberately, much like a child trying to find its way. But just as an adolescent often does not understand his strength or how to use it, school choice will eventually, if not inevitably, come into its adulthood, connecting its vision to its growing political experience to create a new generation of educational options.

Notes

1. The list of respondents and all charts are located in the appendices at the end of the book.

2. Self-description of the Center for Education Reform. See its website: http://edreform.com/political.htm up-dated July 1998.

3. Self-description of CEO America. See its website: http://www.ceoamerica.org/about.html received December 28, 1998.

Conclusion

After more than two years of extensive study of the variety of strategies used to implement school choice, it is now possible for us to synthesize and articulate our research findings. First, it is clear that school choice is an idea whose time is coming. It is very different from an El Niño, whose powerful moving current of warm water can change whole weather patterns. We found, instead, that in the case of school choice, there are currents of discontent and waves of reform but not an aroused school choice public. All our research confirms that there is growing parental and public frustration with America's schools and that this dissatisfaction is beginning to achieve critical mass, but only in certain areas of the country. This is particularly true in the inner cities and among blacks and Hispanics, but it is not limited only to urban areas and minorities. Across the nation, we studied white, suburban parents and politicians, activists and scholars, religious leaders and businessmen, who are promoting school choice. They are bringing the problems of American education to the public consciousness and conscience. We were amazed at the breadth of the school choice debate and the diversity of those who participate in it. These people are putting alternative schools and ways to fund them on state and federal policy agendas.

We interviewed and surveyed so many committed and interested people. We listened to and noted their frustrations, their visions, and their solutions to what they perceived as America's underlying educational problem. And although they see different aspects of that problem, those participating in this movement all see the need to provide greater school choice as the solution, to meet the individual educational needs of each child. We found this nationwide, and we are confident of the staying power of these advocates, who, despite the difficulty of bringing change, remain so optimistic about the future education of America's young.

The public, however, including the voters and most politicians, consider education reform reluctantly. One explanation for this is that this generation contains a majority of people who have positive memories of neighborhood schools: They do not yet want school choice to be adopted wholesale. Incremental experiments can be considered, but they do not want a complete overhaul of the system. Circumstances, too, like a strong economy, are not conducive to a dramatic shift in public thinking on education or on a host of other issues from social security to taxation.

There are exceptions—local storms, where schools are so bad that no reform, even school choice, seems radical enough to solve the problems. The inner city schools face a potential breakdown—when on any given day one-fourth of the students are not in school and one-seventh of the teachers fail to show up. This is reportedly a typical school day in Philadelphia, but it is indicative of many other urban schools as well. As school choice is tried in areas of greatest need, and it works with the least educable, it will be tried elsewhere. As more parents opt for private education or charter schools it is clear that a rethinking process will begin. Behind the school choice effort lies a growing number of people who see it as the only education reform that will succeed in the long run. This effort is young, only ten years old in its latest phase, but old enough to have encouraging victories, disappointing defeats, and new reinforcements.

Second, our research confirmed the fact that school choice is beginning to coalesce as a topic of public debate, but not as a full-fledged political movement—yet. This is due in part to the philosophical and political fragmentation that challenges the development and maturation of any public policy, and school choice in particular. A clear consensus has yet to emerge among the diverse interested parties as to what kind of school choice they should advance. Many different proposals are made. So in a troubled sea, where the public is concerned about education but not alarmed, there are waves of change that keep pushing up on the beach. Absent a storm, and there is no sign of one on the horizon, change comes on the margins, incrementally, on the beaches.

In 1997 and 1998, education reform pioneers who are school choice advocates cajoled and persuaded politicians and voters to act, people who would otherwise do little or nothing. Sometimes they succeeded and sometimes not. These leaders brought the subject of school choice to the attention of the public despite indifference and opposition, and this resulted in a variety of approaches to advance school choice. Pragmatic politicians and activists want to settle for a functioning "half a loaf:" experimental, magnet, or charter schools operating and funded within the public educational system. Visionaries want to insist on holding out for total educational autonomy and the right to send their children to any school at public expense through the implementation of vouchers. Purists wish to privatize education altogether, with no public funding or accountability to civil government. Parents and community leaders are in the middle, many of whom are willing to accept the difficult personal responsibility of paying part of the cost of parochial or private education while gratefully accepting scholarships provided by the wealthiest in society. They do not want to lose their current financial help. Herein lies the paradox: While there is a *political* need to reconcile these views for the simplicity of legislation and programming there is a *philosophi-*

cal need to create a system that can virtually accommodate all sides for school choice. For school choice as a movement, *in and of itself,* must necessarily include and support differences. Thus, we believe that school choice still has to play out, both philosophically and politically, in order for it to emerge as a natural consequence of heterogeneous educational needs in a variety of places with distinct programs for the future.

Decisions have to be made about the forms, sequences, and kinds of school choice to pursue. Should the movement push first for charter schools, then tax credits, and lastly for vouchers? Or are each of these so distinctly different that they are really competing plans? Political costs also have to be weighed against the benefits and likely outcomes. Answers to three questions are necessary: (1) what school choice reform is best? (2) what public or private mechanisms should be used to implement it? and (3) what tactics will be most effective to achieve it?

Third, we also conclude that in order for school choice to become established policy it will be necessary for a national leader to emerge who will champion the cause for choice and give it the impetus it needs to get on the national agenda. Without political support from the White House down, school choice may well linger as a second-rate domestic priority. We note, without judgment, that this will be extremely difficult to achieve because there are many powerful groups, particularly the teacher's unions, that have a vested interest to maintain the status quo. Predictably they will act to protect their profession and their jobs, and they can do it with huge infusions of union money and political activity to support those local, state, and national candidates who reflect their view on public education. Reports indicate that the NEA and the AFT each have political action committees and that they ranked sixth and sixteenth, respectively, among the top contributors to political campaigns in 1996.[1] Further, one of every eight delegates to the Democratic National Convention was a member of a teachers union.[2] This kind of political clout makes it extremely difficult for any fledging, fragmented organization or group of organizations trying to advance school choice to match or surpass the public education lobby in terms of resources and influence. It also forces school choice groups to have to work within the Republican infrastructure, on both a federal and state level, in order to find supporters for its issue, since teachers' unions are so closely allied with the Democrats. Advocates of school choice are in a difficult political place at this time because Republicans give half-hearted support and Democrats oppose them.

Fourth, our research deals with recent events that lead us to also conclude that advances are occurring in almost every kind of school choice. Vouchers for failing schools passed in Florida. Statewide public vouchers are being considered in Pennsylvania. Varieties of tax credits have passed in Minnesota and Arizona. There is an expansion of charter schools in California. Ted Forstmann and John Walton have promoted private vouchers in the form of scholarships nationwide. Public vouchers have been approved for the poor in Milwaukee to attend parochial schools. African-American ministers have established numerous new schools. The Congress for the first time passed public voucher and educational savings account legislation and will try again despite a promised White House veto.

Fifth, the scope of our research makes it possible for us to see that school choice is being advanced by a wide variety of public and private mechanisms. In Pennsylvania, for example, partisan legislation is evolving, but there is now some Democratic support. A constitutional amendment using the initiative process has been attempted in Colorado. Bipartisan legislative action has made possible an expanded charter law in California. Private philanthropy is making school choice a reality in a number of states. Grassroots efforts are gaining momentum, especially efforts being made by pastors. Coalition building and political support for candidates is starting, particularly in New York. A positive state Supreme Court decision has been handed down in Wisconsin assuring the continuance of a scholarship system in Milwaukee. Federal laws are being enacted by the Congress that portend that certain aspects of school choice will continue to get attention and possible passage.

Sixth, our travels and interviews confirmed part of our hypothesis, namely, is that the use of varied tactics for the advancement of school choice could be seen as a sign that there is potential for it to develop into a political movement. Old-fashioned coalition politics are alive and well in Pennsylvania. Grassroots politics have a new face in Colorado. Entrepreneurial politics have been infused with Silicon Valley software money and have created political leverage in California while investment bankers, mega-retailers, and stockbrokers have pumped money into New York politics to get charters enacted in that state. There is unprecedented funding and organizational support for private vouchers. Appeals from lower state courts to federal courts and even a writ of certiorari to the Supreme Court attest to the pressures being put on the judiciary to establish legal guidelines for school choice. Partnerships among business leaders, foundations, and local churches are beginning to proliferate. The Republicans are attempting to define a distinctive federal education agenda, and they have the potential to do so with possible presidential candidates such as George Bush Jr. and Elizabeth Dole.

Seventh, we have found that the different strategies to advance school choice have resulted in mixed success. Legislation in Pennsylvania looked as though it would pass, but was then delayed until 1999. The school choice initiative in Colorado lost for a second time, but with an increased number of votes. Charters were victorious in California with concessions, but school choice advocates believe that there is more to be done. Vouchers have been launched in thirty-five cities, demonstration projects are being studied, and in some places are being replicated. The United States Supreme Court has allowed the Wisconsin pro-voucher decision to stand, prompting other suits for a variety of school choice actions to go forward. Many new charter, experimental, and magnet schools are up and running.

What do we see, then, as the implications of our study for the immediate future? From a practical standpoint, we believe that it is highly unlikely that the American private educational system could survive the onslaught of demand that would follow if total school choice were to occur all at once in the United States. Cardinal O'Connor assured us that, if New York suddenly adopted vouchers, the Catholic school system would be overwhelmed and that it could not handle all the children who would choose to leave public schools. Thus, it appears to us that a political movement for school choice must be one that supports change in stages. Public education, for all practical reasons, cannot be abandoned overnight because there is nothing with which to replace it. Programs, either federal, state, or local, that would provide individual educational choices will have to be phased in; and the educational "business" that might develop in the future will have to grow incrementally as well as experimentally. At the same time, whether this is desirable or not, any type of school choice public funding will also be subject to some kind of state accountability and regulation in order to assure educational competency and credibility. Therefore, we conclude that state-by-state and step-by-step changes for school choice are the only possible ways for the U.S. educational system to transition to something different.

We also believe that there will be more and different school choice plans put forward, permutations, experiments, and combinations of what has been tried with what might work better in the future. And we believe that all the mechanisms that now exist for school choice will be used to try new and different methods of school choice.

Like successive waves on a beach, each school choice campaign leads to others. This is partly because people are studying them like battles, trying to learn from past successes and failures to identify what works best. But there are reasons for the interest in school choice besides the size, cost, and market domination of government-run schools that some object to. If parents conclude that one size does not fit all, there is ever more pressure for school choice, either to escape public education altogether because they don't like it or simply to find a better school. Poor academic quality, disorder in classrooms, and controversial curriculums are all matters of dispute disturbing the waters. When latent discontent, running largely beneath the surface more like an ocean current than a wave, finally connects with school choice visions for a better way to teach the young, and this then attaches itself to leaders, there will be a school choice movement with a momentum capable of overturning the status quo. An El Niño could then develop and that expectation is certainly the hope of those pressing for school choice, which also helps to explain their persistence.

This is not a unified movement. Reforms conflict. No organization or combination of groups controls or dominates as state efforts proliferate backed by local funding. We have discussed:

- The Federal government, the courts, and the contest for school choice politics
- The latest efforts to implement school choice in the United States in its varied forms, including, tax credits, charter schools, public vouchers, private scholarships, and starting new schools
- The influence of entrepreneurs and the organizations they have founded on the school choice movement
- Political, judicial, entrepreneurial, corporate, religious, scholarly, activist, ethnic, and grassroots efforts to leverage policy change, their relative merits, their success and failure
- The chosen mechanisms and tactics of the movement, public and private, initiatives and legislation, partisan and bipartisan, local and statewide, covert and controversial, and their effectiveness given the different goals of activists
- A survey of school choice organizations and activists

As authors we do not argue the merits of school choice. Other writers do that from all points of view. What we study are the politics of this diverse movement and its search for ways to leverage change. This is a relatively young movement in our opinion. The next ten years will see it expand with more resources to expend at its command. With new leaders it will defend previous victories from efforts to roll them back or regulate them. It will seek to establish school choice as a reality in more states.

The federal government has begun to move in this direction, particularly the Congress. Educational Savings Accounts, or something like them, are the wave of the future. As far as the judiciary is concerned, it is simply a matter of time before the Supreme Court deals with the significant number of school choice cases wending their way through the appellate process. Attorneys general in the various states and public-interest law firms are straining the system, bringing increasing numbers of claims and demanding the establishment of federal guidelines for a variety of school choice questions, particularly the state funding of religious schools.

No matter how much protection the Constitution gives to school choice or how much national support comes from Washington, it will be difficult to establish, as each of the state stories (Colorado, California, Michigan, and Pennsylvania) covered in detail indicate. Colorado proves once again that initiatives are hard to pass. California shows that legislation to create charter schools is passable when enough political muscle is exerted and when vouchers force accommodation. Michigan demonstrates the internal stresses that must be overcome within the school choice movement before progress can be made. Pennsylvania is a prototype of an ambitious coalition politics that presses for vouchers but has yet to win. Each state, including some mentioned in less detail, i.e., Wisconsin, Ohio, Indiana, Illinois, Minnesota, Arizona, New Jersey, and New York, have stories to tell because all politics is indeed local.

Entrepreneurs changed school choice politics most dramatically in the past ten years, starting with Pat Rooney in Indiana. John Walton and Ted Forstmann have since expanded private vouchers to a national program. They have been followed by private and charter schools, for-profit ventures like that of the Edison Company and non-profit schools like that of School Futures, then expanding with public vouchers in Milwaukee and Cleveland, with promoting and coordinating choice efforts in many states by CEO America, and lastly with efforts to promote school choice in using public information strategies by Friedman Foundation, and with direct political consulting and training by AERF.

The motives of entrepreneurs defy simple description, ranging from simple altruism, "give a scholarship to a child," to seeing every gift as a step toward leveraging a change in the education policy of the nation, and to profit making in the huge untapped education markets. Intentions vary with the person, and they change over time. Even those who have no personal financial ambitions whatever, like Milton Friedman, see the free market solution as the best way to provide quality schools to children.

Catholics and Evangelicals have great potential to help leverage change if they were ever fully to embrace school choice and organize for its passage. Each are weighed down by limitations. Catholics have such large policy agendas that it is hard for the bishops to give it priority. Evangelicals at ACSI and Focus on the Family have the same problem. Besides, the Catholic and Evangelical parents are now in the suburbs where public schools remain acceptable to many of them, where there are magnet and charter school options, and where the deeply disenchanted have home schooling available. At times Catholics have been too rigid, demanding vouchers only, but this obstacle is much reduced today, for example, in Illinois with the bishops recent adoption of tax credits. Evangelicals remain ambivalent because of regulatory issues—demanding that educational and religious liberty be preserved—and are underorganized. There is no Evangelical organization devoted to the promotion of school choice as its sole agenda. However, Catholics and Evangelicals remain critical of public education and these groups are a latent pool of potential support for school choice. They are likely to be mobilized for school choice in the future.

African Americans are the prime candidates to serve as the fulcrum of school choice; the point where the lever of change will rest as the opposition is moved. Black children in poor neighborhoods were the first to benefit from choice in Milwaukee, Indianapolis, and Cleveland. African-American leaders such as Polly Williams, Dwight Evans, Fannie Lewis, Floyd Flake, and Howard Fuller, are point people who have led the way locally and nationally. They are each contributing pressure and momentum, breaking the white, Catholic, and Republican stereotypical image of the school choice movement. As black pastors join in and create schools, the benefits of school choice become tangible to people—they want some form of assistance to attend a local nonpublic school they see and like. Opposition to school choice from within the black community comes directly from those who work in public schools and from loyalty to the memory of a civil rights movement that fought so hard to get equal access.

Scholars, like Paul Peterson, Terry Moe, and Charles Glenn to name only three of those we examined, are fighting a battle to establish the credibility of school choice for policy makers. If school choice results are bad in existing voucher programs school choice can hardly advance. But if they are good—and preserve the distinctives of private schools intact—this silences some arguments and accusations and opens the door for potentially friendly legislators to come on board. Scholars and research projects are in place to examine in minute detail the fruits of public and private voucher programs and charter schools. These scholars are not neutral observers of the policy process but active participants. They even shape the programs they study, as is the case with admissions lottery systems now used to facilitate research.

Individual activists make contributions over and above their affiliations and organizations. These people stand out because they keep their independence and use their activism to leverage change. Some like Marshall Fritz are well know for their views. Others like Kevin Teasley are masters at getting people active in the grass roots, winning conversions to school choice and preparing for campaigns. The activists keep the movement alert to new possibilities and warn of paths that might prove to be wrongly taken.

Our survey confirms that most school choice organizations do not engage directly in politics by lobbying for school choice. Many are occupied in grassroots educational efforts and are limited by IRS restrictions from doing so. Some we know are more active in politics then they are prepared to discuss, not wanting to disclose information to the opposition. But even if they were all political, and most are not, they do not agree on what form of school choice to adopt—charters, tax credits, public vouchers, or private vouchers. The movement divides on this issue as much perhaps as it is willing to unite behind a specific measure at any place and time. Furthermore, no single school choice organization or individual nationally or at the state level is clearly dominant, holding the position of greatest influence. It might be argued that this is a strength in a coalition but it also leaves it open to fragmentation. In its assessment of school choice movement influence the survey found some confidence of growing influence on the state level and some pride in the accomplishments of individual organizations.

We concluded from the survey that the school choice movement as a whole is not yet an effective political movement. Much of it is engaged in what might be called pre-political activity. The leadership is widely held by a variety of people. There are strong internal disagreements and a lack of legislative lobbying experience. We concluded that the survey reveals, with all of the limitations of this kind of statistical research, a developing special interest that is not yet a "powerful and dominant movement."

What is truly amazing is how much is getting done in such a short time. In less than ten years public vouchers and private vouchers have been launched. For-profit schools have secured a foothold and are expanding. Charters schools, the lesser form of school choice, are taking hold widely. Tax credits too have begun. Florida, under the leadership of Governor Jeb Bush (R), in a few short weeks in the spring of 1999 passed $4,000 individual "opportunity scholarship" legislation for students attending failing public schools. Many more children are being educated in home schools and in newly started church schools. Assigning credit for this progress is impossible. So many different people are now involved. A few stand out, such as Polly Williams, William Bentley Ball, David Brennan, Pat Rooney, Milton Friedman, Cardinal O'Connor, John Walton, Floyd Flake, Susan Mitchell, Kevin Teasley, Marshall Fritz, Clint Bollick, and Jeanne Allen, to risk offending those we fail to mention here, but many more, including newly elected Governor Bush, deserve recognition and close study.

The next ten years will contain even more surprises. Impacts of existing programs will be studied. Adjustments will be made. Pressures are sure to build for more choice. Resistance will increase, too, as more choice leads to more political conflict. Court battles are not over. Public vouchers for parochial schools have yet to be adjudicated by the Supreme Court. There is no evidence, however, of any slackening of effort for choice—only new energy and opportunity for its use. How this will all play out is by no means clear. That there will be a school choice movement seems inevitable because the tension between the current system and its monopoly of public resources and the needs and desires of parents who want to have education alternatives for their children is increasing. Funding school choice, protecting the autonomy of private school options, and providing quality education for all children are the primary goals of the movement. The waves of school choice reform may yet turn into a powerful current, an El Niño of staggering potential. But at the moment school choice must settle for incremental change.

Notes

1. See "Top 50 PAC's—Contributions to Candidates Jan. 1, 1995–Dec. 31, 1996," http://www.fec.gov/finance/paccnye.htm

2. "Clinton Chooses Union Cash over Our Children's Future," press release of Bob Dole, 27 August 1996, p. 1. Available from http://web.Lexis-nexis.com/unwerie/doc

Appendix A

Survey Questions and List of Respondents

Survey Questions

I. ORGANIZATION INFORMATION:

Name of Organization _____

Name and Title of Person Completing Survey _____

No. of full-time employees __ No. of part-time employees __ No. of Volunteers __

Date organization founded _____ Founder(s) _____

II. WHAT ARE THE PURPOSES OF YOUR ORGANIZATION? (Rank order 1–7 with one the highest)

(a) advocacy for school choice _____
(b) monitoring legislation for school choice _
(c) lobbying for school choice _____
(d) education about school choice _____
(e) research about school choice _____
(f) litigating about school choice _____
(g) other _____ What? _____

III. WHO DOES YOUR ORGANIZATION WANT TO INFLUENCE? (Rank order 1–10, with one the highest)

(a) local policy makers _____
(b) state policy makers _____
(c) national policy makers _____
(d) teachers _____
(e) parents _____
(f) students _____
(g) media _____
(h) minorities _____
(i) religious groups _____
(j) others _____ who? _____

IV. WHAT TYPE OF SCHOOL CHOICE DOES YOUR ORGANIZATION SUPPORT? (Rank order 1–6, with one the highest)

(a) charter schools _____
(b) tuition tax credits _____
(c) vouchers _____
(d) magnet schools _____
(e) scholarship programs _____
(f) other _____

If "other," please explain or attach copy of plan to survey _____

297

V. ORGANIZATIONAL FUNDING:

Budget Sources: (Rank order 1–4 with one the highest)

(a) foundation(s) _____ (c) corporation(s) _____
(b) private donation(s) _____ (d) other(s) _____

Budget Size: (Please check one)

(a) between $1–100,000 _____ (c) between $500,001–1,000,000 _____
(b) between $100,001–500,000 _____ (d) beyond $1,000,000 _____

VI. ORGANIZATIONAL INFLUENCE:

The most influential *national* school choice organization is _____

Because _____

The most influential *national* spokesperson for school choice is _____

Because _____

In your *state,* the most influential school choice organization is _____

Because _____

With which national, state, and/or local *political* organization does your organization

interact? _____

_____

How? _____

Is school choice coalescing politically now in your state? and/or on the federal level?

_____

Why? _____

VII. THE MAJOR SCHOOL CHOICE ACCOMPLISHMENTS OF YOUR ORGANIZATION ARE:

_____

_____

VIII. ADDITIONAL COMMENTS: _____

_____

List of Respondents to Survey

Three mailings were sent out in order to solicit responses from school choice organizations that were identified for the survey. Originally 240 organizations were contacted. Forty surveys were returned for being "undeliverable," for a change of address, or for having no forwarding address. Ninety-five organizations did not respond at all. One hundred and eight organizations* responded totally, in part, or where they felt it was "appropriate." The first mailing was sent out on May 12, 1998; the second on June 2, 1998, and the third on August 18, 1998.

1. Achelis and Bodman Foundations
2. Alaska Department of Education
3. Aesthetic Realism Association
4. American Family Association of New York
5. Americans for Tax Reform
6. Arizona School Choice Trust
7. Arizona State Board for Charter Schools
8. Austin CEO Foundation
9. Baptist Joint Committee
10. Becket Fund
11. Blum Center for Parental Freedom in Education
12. Bison Scholarship Fund
13. California Department of Education, Office of Policy and Evaluation
14. CATO Institute
15. Center for School Change, Hubert Humphrey Institute
16. Children's Education Opportunity Foundation, Inc.
17. Catholic League for Religious and Civil Rights
18. Christian Coalition of Monmouth County
19. Center for Education Change
20. Center for Education Reform
21. Center for Governmental Research
22. Center for Market-Based Education, Goldwater Institute
23. CEO Foundation of Connecticut
24. CEO Foundation, Main Office
25. Choice in Education Foundation
26. Change, New York
*27. Children's Scholarship Fund
28. Heartland Institute
29. Coloradans for School Choice . . . for All Kids, Inc.
30. Colorado League of Charter Schools
31. Colorado Department of Education
32. Committee for Oklahoma Educational Reform
33. Commonwealth Foundation
34. Competitive Enterprise Institute
35. Connecticut Department of Education
36. Conservative Caucus
37. Delaware Department of Education
38. Education Commission of the States
39. Education Policy Institute
40. Empower America
41. Ethan Allen Institute
42. Family Research Council
43. Florida Department of Education
44. Floridians for School Choice
45. Fordham Foundation
46. Free Congress Foundation
47. Friends of Choice in Urban Schools
48. Georgia Department of Education
49. Georgia Public Policy Federation
50. Harmony School Center
51. Home Education Resource Center
52. Hope for Cleveland Children, Inc.
53. Independent Institute
54. Indiana Non-Public Education Association
55. Institute for Education Reform
56. Houston CEO Foundation
57. Illinois State Board of Education
58. Institute for Justice
59. James Madison Institute
60. Kentucky Board of Education
61. Kentucky League for Educational Alternatives
62. Kids First Scholarship Fund of Minnesota
63. Kolderie, Ted
64. Leona Group
65. Louisiana Board of Education
66. Maine School Choice Coalition
67. Massachusetts Charter School Resource Center
68. Memphis Opportunity Scholarship Trust
69. Minnesota Department of Children, Families and Learning
70. Minnesota Governor's Office
71. Morriston Institute
*72. National Catholic Education Association
73. National Center for Policy Analysis
74. National Parents Alliance
75. New Citizenship Project
76. New Hampshire Department of Education
77. New Jersey Catholic Conference and N.J. Alliance of Catholic School Families and Supporters
78. New Mexico State Department of Education
79. North Carolina Department of Public Education
80. Odysseus Group Inc.
81. Parents alliance to Protect our Children
82. Partners Advancing Values in Education
83. Pennsylvania Federation—Citizens for Education Freedom
84. Parents Rights Organization
85. Parents Alliance for Catholic Education

86. Parents and Taxpayers for School Choice
87. Philanthropy Roundtable
88. Pioneer Institute
89. Progressive Policy Institute
90. Public Interest Institute
91. Public Service Research Foundation
92. Reach Alliance
93. Resources for Vermont Education
94. Rhode Island Department of Education
95. Scholarship Fund for Inner City Children
96. Star Partnership
97. Taubman Center, Program on Education Policy, JFK School of Government
98. Teach Me, Inc.
99. Tesserat Groups, Inc.
100. Texas Education Agency
101. Texas Justice Foundation
102. United in Spirit Coalition
*103. United States Catholic Conference
104. United Taxpayers of New Jersey
105. Urban Family Council (formerly Philadelphia Family Policy Council)
106. Washington Institute
107. WKBJ Foundation
108. Wyoming Board of Education

*The responses from three organizations were gained from personal interviews in which the respondents answered the questions verbally rather than in writing.

Appendix B

Survey Tables

Table 1 Functions By Funding

Function	ALL† Yes	ALL† No	Yes/Yes Cross Tabulation N=20 1–100,000	N=16 100–500,000	N=10 500,000–1.0m	N=21 >1.0 mil
Advocacy	41.0%	59.0%	50.0%	50.0%	40.0%	52.4%
Monitoring	43.4%	56.6%	35.0%	50.0%	60.0%	61.9%
Lobbying	24.1%	75.9%	25.0%	25.0%	20.0%	38.1%
Education	50.6%	49.4%	50.0%	30.0%	50.0%	72.6%*
Research	42.2%	57.8%	30.0%	43.8%	60.0%	71.4%*
Litigation	22.9%	77.1%	25.0%	18.8%	20.0%	42.9%*
Other	43.4%	56.6%	45.0%	31.3%	50.0%	71.4%
Missing			3.0	3.0	3.0	3.0

†All = 83
*Statistically significant

Table 2 Number of Employees in School Choice Organizations

Employees	ALL Percentage	(N)	Mean
0–9 Full Time	77.1%	64	*
0–9 Part Time	95.2%	79	2.8
0–9 Volunteers	81.7%	67	7.4

*Too great for meaningful mean

Table 3　School Choice Preference By Funding

	ALL		N= 20	N= 16	N= 10	N= 21
Type of School Choice	*Yes*	*No*	*1–100,000*	*100–500,000*	*500,000–1.0m*	*>1.0 mil*
Charters	43.4%	56.6%	40.0%	43.8%	70.0%	52.4%
Tuition tax credit	34.9%	65.1%	50.0%	43.8%	20.0%	47.6%
Vouchers	37.3%	62.7%	45.0%	43.8%	30.0%	52.4%
Magnet schools	22.9%	77.1%	25.0%	31.3%	30.0%	33.3%
Scholarships	39.8%	61.2%	45.0%	50.0%	40.0%	52.4%
Other	26.5%	73.5%	45.0%	31.3%	50.0%	71.4%*
Missing			3.0	3.0	3.0	3.0

*Statistically significant

Table 4　Influence By School Choice Organizations

	ALL		N= 20	N= 16	N= 10	N= 21
Seek to Influence	*Yes*	*No*	*1–100,000*	*100–500,000*	*500,000–1.0m*	*>1.0 mil*
State officials	42.2%	58.8%	40.0%	37.5%	60.0%	61.9%*
National officials	31.3%	68.7%	20.0%	37.5%	50.0%	52.4%*
Local officials	34.9%	65.1%	30.0%	31.3%	60.0%	52.4%
Teachers	30.1%	69.9%	25.0%	31.3%	50.0%	47.6%
Parents	41.0%	59.0%	45.0%	37.5%	60.0%	52.4%
Students	24.1%	75.9%	20.0%	25.0%	40.0%	38.1%
Media	35.0%	62.7%	35.0%	37.5%	50.0%	57.1%*
Minorities	28.9%	71.1%	40.0%	25.0%	30.0%	38.1%
Religious groups	27.7%	72.3%	35.0%	37.5%	30.0%	33.3%
Others	25.3%	74.7%	30.0%	18.8%	40.0%	38.1%
Missing			3.0	3.0	3.0	3.0

*Statistically significant

Table 5　Source of Support

		N= 20	N= 16	N= 10	N= 21
Source	*ALL*	*1–100,000*	*100–500,000*	*500,000–1.0m*	*>1.0 mil*
Foundations	46.3%	45.0%	81.3%*	70.0%	52.4%
Private	57.3%	90.0%*	81.3%*	50.0%	57.1%
Corporations	41.5%	50.0%	50.0%	40.0%	61.9%*
Others	41.5%	45.0%	43.8%	40.0%	66.7%*

*Statistically significant

Appendix C

Internet Homepages with Information on School Choice Issues

American Federation of Teachers
A teacher's union resource site.
http://www.aft.org//index.htm

Anti-Defamation League
A social and civil rights organization.
http://www.adl.org

Arizona Charter Schools Association
An information web site for charter schools in Arizona.
http://www.azcharters.org

Arizona Charter Schools Organization
An information web site for charter schools in Arizona.
http://www.azcharterschools.org

Brookings Institution
A policy organization that focuses on various political issues.
http://www.brookings.org

California Education Reform Alliance
An organization that seeks to end the governmental monopoly in public education.
http://www.getrealed.org

Baptist Joint Committee on Public Affairs
A Baptist organization focused on different political issues.
http://www.bjcpa.org

Blum Center for Parental Freedom in Education
An organization focused on studying school choice.
http://www.marquette.edu/blum/

California's Local Choice2000.Com
A grassroots organization for educational change in California.
http://www.localchoice2000.com

California Network of Educational Charters
An information web site for charter schools in California.
http://www.canec.org

Capital Partners in Education
An organization that promotes educational vouchers for at risk children.
http://www.cpfe.org

Cato Institute
A policy organization dedicated to free-markets and limited government.

A wealth of information with scholarly research on school choice.
http://www.cato.org

Center for Education Reform
An advocacy group for reform in education providing many resources for the school choice movement and charter schools.
http://edreform.com

Center for New Black Leadership
An organization focused on developing the inner city through faith and skills.
http://www.cnbl.org

Center on Reinventing Public Education
A research and development organization that concentrates on school choice and charter schools.
http://www.crpe.org

Charter Friends National Network
Founded by Hamline University to help communication between state to state charter school initiatives.
http://www.charterfriends.org

Charter School Developers, USA
An information site on charter schools throughout the United States.
http://www.topschools.com

Charter School Project
A Colorado based organization that seeks to expand school choice throughout the state.
http://www.charterproject.org

Charter School Research
A research tool for charter schools throughout the United States.
http://csr.syr.edu/index.html

Charter School Resource Center of Texas
A resource tool for charter school information in Texas.

http://www.charterstexas.org

Children's Educational Opportunity Foundation
An organization that seeks to foster vouchers for parents to choose the best school for their children's needs. This site provides a tremendous amount of resources on the subject.
http://ceoamerica.org

Children's Scholarship Fund
An organization that promotes scholarships to low income families.
www.scholarshipfund.org

Colorado Alliance for Educational Excellence
An organization that seeks to promote tax credits or scholarships for those outside of the public school system.
http://www.cafee.org

Colorado Free Market Schools
An organization that believes that the free market system should run schools.
http://www.coloradoschools.com

Education Week
An education magazine on the web with a large section on school choice and vouchers.
http://www.edweek.org/context/topics/choice.htm

Education Policy Institute
An organization that seeks greater choice in education—chaired by Dr. Myron Lieberman.
http://www.educationpolicy.org

Effective Education
An alphabetized collection of essays on choice in education.
http://www.interlog.com/~klima/ed/charters.html

Family Research Council

A private organization that seeks to foster Judeo-Christian values and school choice nationally.
http://www.frc.org

Floridians for School Choice

A Florida organization with the goal to create public scholarships to follow each child into the school of the parents' choice.
http://www.floridians.org

Thomas B. Fordham Foundation

An organization that seeks to change the current educational system.
http://edexcellence.net

Milton and Rose D. Friedman Foundation

Milton Friedman's foundation for educational choice.
http://www.friedmanfoundation.org

Freedom Works

Home page for Majority Leader Dick Armey.
http://freedom.house.gov

Greater Educational Opportunities Foundation

An organization that promotes educational opportunity for all children.
www.geofoundation.org

Harvard University

A major source of school choice research.
http://data.fas.harvard.edu.PEPG

Heartland Institute

A nonprofit public interest group.
http://www.heartland.org

Heritage Foundation

A policy research organization committed to conservative issues, it has a large resource of information on school choice issues throughout the United States.
http://heritage.org

Institute for Justice

A legal group seeking limited government political solutions.
http://www.ij.org/index.shtml

Works of David W. Kirkpatrick

An informational website with links to articles and information on school choice.
http://schoolreport.com

Landmark Legal Foundation

A national public interest law firm that seeks conservative objectives.
http://landmarklegal.org

Little Hoover Commission

A private foundation in California that seeks to promote efficiency in California's government.
http://www.lhc.ca.gov/lhcdir/138rp.html

John Locke Foundation

An organization that seeks to foster free-market ideals for North Carolinians.
http://www.johnlocke.org

Mackinac Center

A policy research group that educates Michigan's citizens on a variety of policy issues.
http://www.mackinac.org

Manhattan Institute

An organization focused on various social reforms.
http://www.manhattan-institute.org

Michigan Association of Public School Academics

A grassroots coalition for the support of charter schools in Michigan.

http://www.charterschools.org

Michigan Resource Center for Charter Schools

A resource tool for charter school information in Michigan.

http://charter.ehhs.cmich.edu/html/us.html

National Alliance of Business

A business organization focusing on improving education in America's workforce.

http://www.nab.com

National Center for Policy Analysis

A policy research institute.

http://www.ncpa.org

National Education Association

A nationwide association of teachers that represents their rights and objectives.

http://www.nea.org

North Carolina Charter School Resource Center

An information web site for charter schools in North Carolina.

http://www.nccsrc.org

New York Charter School Resource

An information web site for charter schools in New York.

http://www.nycharterschools.org

Pacific Research Organization

A research organization focused on education with emphasis on charter schools.

http://www.pacificresearch.org

Paradigm Alternative Centers Inc.

A political information site with many resources on charter schools and vouchers.

http://pacsystems-curriculum.com

Parents Coalition of Texas

A political action parents organization in Texas focused on excellence in education.

http://www.parentscoalition.org

Partners Advancing Values in Education

A private organization that offers scholarships to low income children in Milwaukee.

http://www.pave.org

People for the American Way

A civil and social rights organization.

http://www.pfaw.org

Reach Alliance

A grassroots organization for school choice in Pennsylvania.

http://www.paschoolchoice.org

Rethinking Schools Online

A nonprofit publisher of materials on education.

http://www.rethinkingschools.org

School Choices

A research site for school choice. Andrew J. Coulson leads this organization.

www.schoolchoices.org

School Choice Yes

A Michigan based school choice organization.

http://www.schoolchoiceyes.org

Brett Schundler Mayor of Jersey City

An extensive resource of Mayor Schundler's involvement in school choice.

http://www.schundler.org

Separation of School and State Alliance

An organization that wants education to be in the hands of the parents.
http://www.sepschool.org

Teach Michigan Education Fund

An organization that seeks to educate the public on school choice issues.
http://teach-mi.org

Texas Charter Schools

An information web site for charter schools in Texas.
http://www.texascharterschools.net

Alexis de Tocqueville Institution

An organization focused on research that promotes democracy throughout the world.
http://www.adti.net

Toward Tradition

An educational foundation created by Rabbi Daniel Lapin promoting conservative ideals.
http://www.towardtradion.org

Town Hall

Conservative news and information web-site.
http://www.townhall.com

U.S. Charter Schools

A research tool for the study of charter schools nationwide.
http://www.uscharterschools.org

Vermonters for Educational Choice

A school choice organization focused on Vermont schools
http://www.act60.org

Washington Scholarship Fund

An organization that provides scholarships to low income families.
http://www.wfs=dc.org

Appendix D

Federal and State Education Agencies

U.S. Department of Education
400 Maryland Avenue, SW
Washington, DC 20202-0498
(800) USA-LEARN
E-Mail: CustomerService@inet.ed.gov
URL: http://oeri.ed.gov

Alabama
Alabama Department of Education
Gordon Persons Office Building
50 North Ripley Street
P.O. Box 302102
Montgomery, AL 36130-2101
(334) 242-9700
FAX: (334) 242-9708
E-Mail: erich@sdenet.alsde.ed
URL: http://www.alsde.edu

Alaska
Alaska Department of Education
Suite 200
801 West 10th Street
Juneau, AK 99801-1894
(907) 465-2800
FAX: (907) 465-4156
URL: http://www.educ.state.ak.us

Arizona
Arizona Department of Education
1535 West Jefferson
Phoenix, AZ 85007
(602) 542-5460
FAX: (602) 542-5440
URL: http://www.ade.state.az.us

Arkansas
Arkansas Department of Education
General Education Division
Room 304 A
Four State Capitol Mall
Little Rock, AR 72201-1071
(501) 682-4204
FAX: (501) 682-1079
URL: http://arkedu.state.ar.us

California
California Department of Education
Second Floor
721 Capitol Mall
Sacramento, CA 94244-2720
(916) 657-2577
FAX: (916) 657-2682
E-Mail: dholt@cde.ca.gov
URL: http://www.cde.ca.gov/iasa/

Colorado
Colorado Department of Education
201 East Colfax Avenue
Denver, CO 80203
(303) 866-6600
FAX: (303) 830-0793
URL: http://www.cde.state.co.us

Connecticut
Connecticut Department of Education
Room 305
State Office Building
165 Capitol Avenue
Hartford, CT 06106-1080

(860) 566-5061
FAX: (860) 566-8964
E-Mail: ctsde@aol.com
URL: http://www.state.ct.us/sde

Delaware
Delaware Department of Education
John G. Townsend Building
P.O. Box 1402
Federal and Loockerman Streets
Dover, DE 19903-1402
(302) 739-4601
FAX: (302) 739-4654
URL: http://www.doe.state.de.us

District of Columbia
District of Columbia Public Schools
The Presidential Building
415 12th Street, NW
Washington, DC 20004
(202) 724-4222
FAX: (202) 724-8855
URL: http://www.k12.dc.us

Florida
Florida Department of Education
Room PL 08
Capitol Building
Tallahassee, FL 32399-0400
(850) 487-1785
FAX: (850) 413-0378
URL: http://www.firn.edu/doe/
    index.html

Georgia
Georgia Department of Education
2054 Twin Towers East
205 Butler Street
Atlanta, GA 30334-5001
(404) 656-2800
(800) 311-3627
Toll Free Restrictions: GA residents only
FAX: (404) 651-6867
E-Mail: help.desk@doe.k12.ga.us
URL: http://www.doe.k12.ga.us

Hawaii
Hawaii Department of Education
#309
1390 Miller Street
Honolulu, HI 96813
(808) 586-3310
FAX: (808) 586-3234
URL: http://www.k12.hi.us

Idaho
Idaho Department of Education
Len B. Jordan Office Building
650 West State Street
P. O. Box 83720
Boise, ID 83720-0027
(208) 332-6800
(800) 432-4601
TTY: (800) 377-3529
FAX: (208) 334-2228
URL: http://www.sde.state.id.us/Dept/

Illinois
Illinois State Board of Education
100 North First Street
Springfield, IL 62777
(217) 782-4321
TTY: (217) 782-1900
FAX: (217) 524-4928
URL: http://www.isbe.state.il.us

Indiana
Indiana Department of Education
State House, Room 229
Indianapolis, IN 46204-2798
(317) 232-6665
FAX: (317) 232-8004
URL: http://www.doe.state.in.us

Iowa
Iowa Department of Education
Grimes State Office Building
East 14th and Grand Streets
Des Moines, IA 50319-0146
(515) 281-3436
FAX: (515) 281-4122
URL: http://www.state.ia.us/educate

Kansas
Kansas Department of Education
120 South East 10th Avenue
Topeka, KS 66612-1182
(785) 296-3202
TTY: (785) 296-6338
FAX: (785) 296-7933
E-Mail: atompkins@ksbe.state.ks.us or
lasnider@ksbe.state.ks.us
URL: http://www.ksbe.state.ks.us

Kentucky
Kentucky Department of Education
1930 Capital Plaza Tower
500 Mero Street
Frankfort, KY 40601
(502)564-3421
(800)533-5372
Toll Free Restrictions: KY residents only
FAX: (502)564-6470
E-Mail: kwilborn@kde.state.ky.us
URL: http://www.kde.state.ky.us

Louisiana
Louisiana Department of Education
626 North Fourth Street
P. O. Box 94064
Baton Rouge, LA 70704-9064
(504) 342-4411
FAX: (504) 342-7316
E-Mail: webmaster@mail.doe.state.la.us
URL: http://www.doe.state.la.us

Maine
Maine Department of Education
23 State House Station
Augusta, ME 04333-0023
(207) 287-5800
TTY: (207) 287-2550
FAX: (207) 287-5900
URL: http://www.state.me.us/
education/homepage.htm

Maryland
Maryland Department of Education
200 West Baltimore Street
Baltimore, MD 21201

(410) 767-0462
FAX: (410) 333-6033
URL: http://www.msde.state.md.us

Massachusetts
Massachusetts Department of
Education
350 Main Street
Malden, MA 02148
(781) 388-3300
FAX: (781) 388-3396
E-Mail: www@doe.mass.edu
URL: http://www.doe.mass.edu

Michigan
Michigan Department of Education
Hannah Building
Fourth Floor
608 West Allegan Street
Lansing, MI 48933
(517) 373-3324
FAX: (517) 335-4565
URL: http://www.mde.state.mi.us

Minnesota
Minnesota Department of Children,
Families, and Learning
1500 Highway 36 West
Roseville, MN 55113-4266
(651) 582-8200
E-Mail: Cfl.Library@state.mn.us
URL: http://cfl.state.mn.us

Mississippi
Mississippi State Department of
Education
Suite 365
359 North West Street
Jackson, MS 39201
(601) 359-3513
FAX: (601) 359-3242
URL: http://mdek12.state.ms.us

Missouri
Missouri Department of Elementary
and Secondary Education
P.O. Box 480

Jefferson City, MO 65102-0480
(573) 751-4212
TTY: (800) 735-2966
FAX: (573) 751-8613
E-Mail: pubinfo@mail.dese.state.mo.us
URL: http://www.dese.state.mo.us

Montana
Montana Office of Public Instruction
P.O. Box 202501
Helena, MT 59620-2501
(406) 444-2082
FAX: (406) 444-3924
E-Mail: cbergeron@opi.mt.gov
URL: http://www.metnet.state.mt.us/
MAIN.html

Nebraska
Nebraska Department of Education
301 Centennial Mall South
P. O. Box 94987
Lincoln, NE 68509-4987
(402) 471-7295
TTY: (402) 471-7295
FAX: (402) 471-0017
E-Mail:
Eduneb@NDE4.NDE.State.NE.US
URL: http://WWW.NDE.State.NE.US

Nevada
Nevada State Department of Education
700 East Fifth Street
Carson City, NV 89710
(702) 687-9141
FAX: (702) 687-9101
E-Mail: fsouth@nsn.K12.unr.edu
URL: http://www.nsn.k12.nv.us/nvdoe/

New Hampshire
New Hampshire Department of
Education
101 Pleasant Street
State Office Park South
Concord, NH 03301
(603) 271-3144
(800) 339-9900
TTY: (800) 735-2964

FAX: (603) 271-1953
E-Mail: ksanborn@ed.state.nh.us
URL: http://www.state.nh.us/doe/
education.html

New Jersey
New Jersey Department of Education
P.O. Box 500
100 Riverview
Trenton, NJ 08625-0500
(609) 292-4469
FAX: (609) 777-4099
URL: http://www.state.nj.us/education

New Mexico
New Mexico State Department of
Education
Education Building
300 Don Gaspar
Santa Fe, NM 87501-2786
(505) 827-6516
TTY: (505) 827-6541
FAX: (505) 827-6696
URL: http://sde.state.nm.us

New York
New York Education Department
111 Education Building
Washington Avenue
Albany, NY 12234
(518) 474-5844
FAX: (518) 473-4909
URL: http://www.nysed.gov

North Carolina
North Carolina Department of Public
Instruction
Education Building
301 North Wilmington Street
Raleigh, NC 27601-2825
(919) 715-1299
FAX: (919) 715-1278
URL: http://www.dpi.state.nc.us

North Dakota
North Dakota Department of Public
Instruction

11th Floor
Department 201
600 East Boulevard Avenue
Bismarck, ND 58504-0440
(701) 328-2260
FAX: (701) 328-2461
E-Mail: wsanstea@mail.dpi.state.nd.us
or tlalonde@mail.dpi.state.nd.us
URL: http://www.dpi.state.nd.us/

Ohio
Ohio Department of Education
Room 810
65 South Front Street
Columbus, OH 43215-4183
(614) 466-3304
FAX: (614) 644-5960
URL: http://www.ode.ohio.gov

Oklahoma
Oklahoma State Department of
Education
2500 North Lincoln Boulevard
Oklahoma City, OK 73105-4599
(405) 521-3301
FAX: (405) 521-6205
E-Mail: sgarrett@phoenix.osrhe.edu
URL: http://sde.state.ok.us

Oregon
Oregon Department of Education
255 Capitol Street, NE
Salem, OR 97310-0203
(503) 378-3573
TTY: (503) 378-2892
FAX: (503) 378-4772
URL: http://www.ode.state.or.us

Pennsylvania
Pennsylvania Department of Education
10th Floor
333 Market Street
Harrisburg, PA 17126-0333
(717) 787-5820
FAX: (717) 787-7222
URL: http://www.pde.psu.edu/

Rhode Island
Rhode Island Department of
Elementary and Secondary Education
255 Westminster Street
Providence, RI 02903-3400
(401) 222-4600, Ext.
FAX: (401) 222-6033
E-Mail: ride0015@ride.ri.net
URL: http://instruct.ride.ri.net

South Carolina
South Carolina Department of
Education
1006 Rutledge Building
1429 Senate Street
Columbia, SC 29201
(803) 734-8492
FAX: (803) 734-3389
URL: http://www.state.sc.us/sde

South Dakota
South Dakota Department of Education
and Cultural Affairs
700 Governors Drive
Pierre, SD 57501-2291
(605) 773-3134
TTY: (605) 773-6302
FAX: (605) 773-6139
E-Mail: janelle.toman@state.sd.us or
jolene.brakke@state.sd.us
URL: http://www.state.sd.us/deca/

Tennessee
Tennessee State Department of
Education
Andrew Johnson Tower, Sixth Floor
710 James Robertson Parkway
Nashville, TN 37243-0375
(615) 741-2731
FAX: (615) 741-6236
URL: http://www.state.tn.us/education/

Texas
Texas Education Agency
William B. Travis Building
1701 North Congress Avenue
Austin, TX 78701-1494
(512) 463-8985

FAX: (512) 463-9008 ·
URL: http://www.tea.state.tx.us

Utah
Utah State Office of Education
250 East 500 South
Salt Lake City, UT 84111
(801) 538-7500
FAX: (801) 538-7521
URL: http://www.usoe.k12.ut.us

Vermont
Vermont Department of Education
120 State Street
Montpelier, VT 05620-2501
(802) 828-3135
FAX: (802) 828-3140
URL: http://www.state.vt.us/educ

Virginia
Virginia Department of Education
P. O. Box 2120
101 North 14th Street
Richmond, VA 23218-2120
(804) 225-2020
(800) 292-3820
Toll Free Restrictions: VA residents only
FAX: (804) 371-2455
E-Mail: cmakela@pen.k12.va.us
URL: http://www.pen.k12.va.us/go/
   VDOE

Washington
Office of Superintendent of Public
   Instruction (Washington)
Old Capitol Building
600 South Washington
P. O. Box 47200

Olympia, WA 98504-7200
(360) 586-6904
TTY: (360) 664-3631
FAX: (360) 753-6712
URL: http://www.ospi.wednet.edu

West Virginia
West Virginia K-12 Schools
Building 6
1900 Kanawha Boulevard East
Charleston, WV 25305-0330
(304) 558-0304
FAX: (304) 558-2584
E-Mail: wvde@access.k12.wv.us
URL: http://wvde.state.wv.us

Wisconsin
Wisconsin Department of Public
   Instruction
125 South Webster Street
P.O. Box 7841
Madison, WI 53707-7841
(608)267-9153
(800) 441-4563
TTY: (608) 267-2427
FAX: (608) 267-1052
URL: http://www.dpi.state.wi.us

Wyoming
Wyoming Department of Education
Second Floor
2300 Capitol Avenue
Cheyenne, WY 82002
(307) 777-7675
FAX: (307) 777-6234
E-Mail: jcatch@educ.state.wy.us
URL: http://www.k12.wy.us/
   wdehome.html

Territories

American Samoa
American Samoa Department of
   Education
Pago Pago, AS 96799
(684) 633-5237
FAX: (684) 633-4240

**Commonwealth of the Northern
   Mariana Islands**
No Entry

Federated States of Micronesia
No Entry

Guam
Guam Department of Education
P.O. Box DE
Agana, GM 96932
(671) 475-0460
URL: http://www.doe.edu.gu/

Puerto Rico
Puerto Rico Department of Education
P. O. Box 190759
San Juan, PR 00919-0759
(787) 753-2062
FAX: (787) 250-0275

Republic of Palau
No Entry

Republic of the Marshall Islands
No Entry

Virgin Islands
Virgin Islands Department of Education
44-46 Kongens Gade
St Thomas, VI 00802
(340) 774-2810
FAX: (340) 774-4679
E-Mail: ldavis@sttj.k12.vi.us

Bibliography

Adler, Michael, Alison Petch, and Jack Tweedie. *Parental Choice and Educational Policy.* Edinburgh, UK: Edinburgh University Press, 1989.

Aguirre, Robert B. *Educational Choice: A Privately Funded Model: School Choice with a Bite.* San Antonio, TX: The Foundation, 1992.

Allen, Jeanne, and Angela Dale. *The School Reform Handbook.* Washington, DC: Center for Education Reform, 1995.

American Federation of Teachers. *Charter School Laws: Do They Measure Up?* Washington, DC: The Federation, 1996.

Anderson, Patrick L. *The Universal Tuition Tax Credit: A Proposal to Advance Parental Choice in Education: How Educational Freedom Will Help Michigan Students, Schools, and Taxpayers.* Midland, MI: Mackinac Center for Public Policy, 1997.

Armor, David J., and Brett M. Peiser. *Competition in Education: A Case Study of Interdistrict Choice.* Boston: Pioneer Institute for Public Policy Research, 1997.

Arons, Stephen. *Short Route to Chaos: Conscience, Community, and the Re-constitution of American Schooling.* Amherst, MA: University of Massachusetts Press, 1997.

Ascher, Carol, Norm Fruchter, and Robert Berne. *Hard Lessons: Public Schools and Privatization.* New York: Twentieth Century Fund Press, 1996.

————. *Free to Choose: The False Promise of School Privatization.* New York: Twentieth Century Fund Press, 1996.

Barr, Robert D., and William H. Parrett. *How to Create Alternative, Magnet, and Charter Schools That Work.* Bloomington, IN: National Educational Service, 1997.

Bastian, Ann. *Choosing Equality: The Case for Democratic Schooling.* Philadelphia: Temple University Press, 1986.

Bates, Stephen. *Battleground: One Mother's Crusade, the Religious Right, and the Struggle for Control of Our Classrooms.* New York: Poseidon Press, 1993.

Beales, Janet R. *Given a Choice: A Study of the PAVE Program and School Choice in Milwaukee.* Los Angeles, CA: Reason Foundation, 1995.

Berliner, David C., and Bruce J. Biddle. *The Manufactured Crisis: Myths, Fraud, and the Attack on America's Public Schools.* Reading, MA: Addison Wesley, 1995.

Billingsley, K. L., ed. *Voices on Choice: The Education Reform Debate.* San Francisco, CA: Pacific Research Institute, 1994.

315

Blackman, Julie. *Voucher Schools, Who Participates?* New York: ERIC Clearinghouse on Urban Education and Institute for Urban and Minority Education, 1975.

Blumenfield, Samuel. *Is Public Education Necessary?* 2d ed. Boise, ID: Paradigm, 1985.

Boaz, David, ed. *Liberating Schools: Education in the Inner City.* Washington, DC: Cato Institute, 1991.

Bonsteel, Alan, and Carlos A. Bonilla. *A Choice for Our Children: Curing the Crisis in America's Schools.* San Francisco, CA: ICS Press, 1997.

Bracey, Gerald W. *Transforming America's Schools: An Rx for Getting Past Blame.* Arlington, VA: American Association of School Administrators, 1994.

Breger, Marshall J., and David M. Gordis. *Vouchers for School Choice: Challenge or Opportunity? An American Jewish Reappraisal.* Washington, DC: Susan and David Wilstein Institute of Jewish Policy Studies, 1998.

Budde, Ray. *Education by Charter: Restructuring School Districts: Key to Long-Term Continuing Improvement in American Education.* Andover, MA: Regional Laboratory For Educational Improvement of the Northeast and Islands, 1998.

———. *Strengthen School-Based Management By Chartering All Schools.* Andover, MA: Regional Laboratory For Educational Improvement of the Northeast and Islands, 1996.

Carnegie Foundation for the Advancement of Teaching. *School Choice: A Special Report.* Princeton, NJ: Carnegie Foundation, 1992.

Center for Public Policy Research. *School Choice in North Carolina? A Pro/Con Discussion.* Raleigh, NC: Center for Public Policy Research, 1995.

Center for the Study of Public Policy. *Education Vouchers; A Report on Financing Elementary Education by Grants to Parents.* Cambridge, MA.: Center for the Study of Public Policy, 1970.

Chubb, John E. *Choice Is a Panacea.* Reno, NV: Nevada Policy Research Institute, 1993.

———. *Designing a Public School Choice Program That Can Pay for Itself.* Reno, NV: Nevada Policy Research Institute, 1992.

———, and Terry M. Moe. *Politics, Markets and America's Schools.* Washington, DC: Brookings Institution, 1990.

Clinchy, Evans. *Planning for Schools of Choice: Achieving Equity and Excellence.* Andover, MA: New England Center for Equity Assistance, 1992.

Clune, William H., and John F. Witte, eds. *Choice and Control in American Education, Volume 1: The Theory of Choice and Control in Education.* London: Falmer, 1990.

———. *Choice and Control in American Education, Volume 2: The Practice of Choice, Decentralization and School Restructuring.* London: Falmer, 1990.

Cobb, Clifford W. *Responsive Schools, Renewed Communities.* San Francisco, CA: ICS Press, 1992.

Cohn, Elchanan. *Market Approaches to Education: Vouchers and Schools Choice.* Tarrytown, NY: Pergamon, 1997.

Colopy, Kelly W. *Minnesota's Public School Choice Options.* Washington, DC: Policy Studies Associates, 1994.

Colorado Department of Education. *The Colorado Charter Schools Evaluation Study.* Denver, CO: Colorado Department of Education, 1999.

Commission on California State Government Organization and Economy. *The Charter Movement: Education Reform School by School.* Sacramento, CA: Little Hoover Commission, 1996.

Cookson, Peter W., Jr. *School Choice and Urban School Reform.* New York: ERIC Clearinghouse on Urban Education, 1997.

————. *Recent Experience with Urban School Choice Plans.* New York: ERIC Clearinghouse on Urban Education, 1997.

————. *School Choice: The Struggle for the Soul of American Education.* New Haven, CT: Yale University Press, 1994.

————. *The Choice Controversy.* Newbury Park, CA: Corwin Press, 1992.

Cookson, Peter W., Jr, and Barbara Schneider. *Transforming Schools.* New York: Garland Publishing, 1995.

Coons, John E., and Steven D. Sugarman. *Scholarships for Children.* Berkeley, CA: Institute of Governmental Studies, 1992.

————. *Education by Choice: The Case for Family Control.* Troy, NY: Educator's International Press, 1978.

————. *Family Choice in Education: A Model State System for Vouchers.* Berkeley, CA: Institute of Governmental Studies, 1971.

Corwin, Ronald G. *Private Schools and Parental Choice: Dubious Assumptions, Frail Claims, and Excessive Hyperbole.* Los Alamitos, CA: Southwest Regional Laboratory, 1993.

Corwin, Ronald G., and John F. Flaherty. *Freedom and Innovation in California's Charter Schools.* Los Alamitos, CA: Southwest Regional Laboratory, 1995.

Coulson, Andrew J. *Market Education: The Unknown History.* New Brunswick, NJ: Transaction Publishers, 1999.

————. *Forgotten Wisdom: The Historical Case for a Free Market Educational Market.* Cambridge, MA: Education Policy and Governance, Harvard University, 1997.

Dale, Angela, and David DeSchryver. *The Charter School Workbook: Your Roadmap to the Charter School Movement.* Washington, DC: Center for Education Reform, 1997.

Darby, Jaye T., and Amy S. Wells, eds. *The Choice on School Choice: California Confronts Its Educational Future.* Los Angelos, CA: UCLA, GSE&IS, 1996.

Darling-Hammond, Linda, Sheila N. Kirby, and Priscilla M. Schlegel. *Tax Tuition Deductions and Parent School Choice.* Santa Monica, CA: Rand, 1985.

DeVore, Adam. *Michigan's Experiment with Public School Choice: A First Year Assessment.* Midland, MI: Mackinac Center for Public Policy, 1993.

Doerr, Edd, Albert J. Menendez, and John M. Swomley. *The Case against School Vouchers.* Amherst, NY: Prometheus Books, 1996.

Domanico, Raymond J. *Bringing School Choice to the Nations's Largest School System.* Washington, DC: The Heritage Foundation, 1993.

Dudley-Marling, Curt, and Dennis Searle, eds. *Who Owns Learning? Questions of Autonomy, Choice and Control.* Portsmouth, NH: Heinemann, 1994.

Dunne, Danielle. *School Choice Pros, Cons, and Concerns.* Washington, DC: ASPIRA Association, Inc., 1991.

Education Commission of the States. *State Policy Makers Guide to Public School Choice.* Denver, CO: Education Commission of the States, 1989.

Everhart, Robert B., ed. *The Public School Monopoly: A Critical Analysis of Education and the State in American Society.* San Francisco, CA: Pacific Institute for Public Policy Research, 1982.

Feintuck, Mike. *Accountability and Choice in Schooling.* Philadelphia, PA: Open University Press, 1994.

Figlio, David N. *School Choice and Student Performance: Are Private Schools Really Better.* Madison, WI: Institute for Research on Poverty, 1997.

Finn, Chester E., Jr. *Charter School Accountability: Findings and Prospects.* Bloomington, IN: Phi Delta Kappa Educational Foundation, 1997.

————. *We Must Take Charge: Our Schools and Our Future.* New York: Free Press, 1991.

Finn, Chester E., Jr., and Herbert J. Walberg, eds. *Radical Education Reforms. The Series on Contemporary Educational Issues.* Berkeley, CA: McCutchan Publishing, 1994.

Finn, Chester E., Jr., and Theodore Rebarber, eds. *Education Reforms in the '90s.* New York: Macmillan, 1992.

Finn, Chester, E., Jr., and Marci Kanstoroom. *New Directions: Federal Education Policy in the Twenty-First Century.* Washington, DC: Thomas B. Fordham Foundation, 1999.

Finn, Chester E., Jr., Louann A. Bierlein, and Bruno V. Manno. *Charter School Accountability: Findings and Prospects.* Bloomington, IN: Phi Delta Kappa Educational Foundation, 1997.

————. *Charter Schools in Action: What Have We Learned?* Indianapolis, IN: Hudson Institute, 1996.

Flam, Samuel, and William G. Keane. *Public Schools, Private Enterprise: What You Should Know and Do about Privatization.* Lancaster, PA: Technomic Publishing, 1997.

Fliegel, Seymour, and James MacGuire. *Miracle in Harlem: The Fight for Choice in Public Education.* New York: Times Books, 1994.

Formicola, Jo Renee, and Hubert Morken. *Everson Revisited: Religion, Education, and Law at the Crossroads.* Lanham, MD: Rowman and Littlefield, 1997.

Friedman, Milton. *Capitalism and Freedom.* Chicago, IL: University of Chicago Press, 1962.

Fuller, Bruce F., Richard Elmore, and Gary Orfield, eds. *Who Chooses? Who Loses? Culture, Institutions and the Unequal Effects of School Choice.* New York: Teachers College Press, 1996.

Gaffney, Edward. *Private Schools and the Public Good: Policy Alternatives for the Eighties.* Notre Dame, IN: University of Notre Dame Press, 1981.

Gallagher, Richard. *The Status of School Choice in Arizona, 1991–1992.* Phoenix, AZ: Arizona Department of Education, 1992.

Gatto, John Taylor. *The Exhausted School: The First National Grassroots Speakout on the Right to School Choice.* New York: Oxford Village Press, 1993.

————. *Dumbing Us Down: The Hidden Curriculum of Compulsory Schooling.* Philadelphia, PA: New Society Publishers, 1992.

Gewirtz, Sharon. *Markets, Choice, and Equity in Education.* Philadelphia, PA: Open University Press, 1995.

Glanzer, Perry L. *Better Schools, Better Kids: The Case for Parental Choice in Education.* Colorado Springs, CO: Focus on the Family Public Policy Division, 1998.

Glatter, Ron, Philip Woods, and Carl Bagley. *Choice and Diversity in Schooling.* New York: Routledge, 1997.

Glenn, Charles. *The Myth of the Common School.* Amherst, MA: University of Massachusetts Press, 1988.

Godwin, Kenneth, Frank R. Kemerer, and Valerie Martinez. *Educational Outcomes and Educational Equity: Lessons from San Antonio's Choice Programs.* Cambridge, MA: Program on Educational Policy and Governance, Harvard University, 1997.

Goldberg, Bruce. *Why Schools Fail.* Washington, DC: Cato Institute, 1996.

Goldring, Ellen B. *Parental Involvement and Public Choice in Education.* New York: Pergamon, 1991.

Gorard, Stephen. *School Choice in an Established Market.* Brookfield, VT: Ashgate, 1997.

Guthrie, James W., Walter I. Garms, and Lawrence C. Pierce. *School Finance and Education Policy: Enhancing Educational Efficiency, Equality, and Choice.* 2d ed. Boston, MA: Allyn and Bacon, 1988.

Hakim, Simon, Paul Seidenstat, and Gary W. Bowman, eds. *Privatizing Education and Educational Choice: Concepts, Plans, and Experiences.* Westport, CT: Praeger, 1994.

Halstead, Mark J., ed. *Parental Choice and Education: Principles, Policy and Practice.* Philadelphia, PA: Kogan Page, 1994.

Hanus, Jerome J., and Peter W. Cookson, Jr. *Choosing Schools: Vouchers and American Education.* Lanham, MD: American University Press, 1996.

Harmer, David J. *School Choice: Why You Need It—How You Get It.* Washington, DC: Cato Institute, 1994.

Hassel, Bryan C. *The Charter School Challenge: Avoiding the Pitfalls, Fulfilling the Promise.* Washington, DC: Brookings Institute, 1999.

Henderson, David R. *The Case for School Choice.* Stanford, CA: Hoover Institution, 1993.

Henig, Jeffrey R. *Rethinking School Choice: Limits of the Market Metaphor.* Princeton, NJ: Princeton University Press, 1994.

Hill, Paul T., Lawrence C. Pierce, and James W. Guthrie. *Reinventing Public Education: How Contracting Can Transform America's Schools.* Chicago, IL: University of Chicago Press, 1997.

Hirsch, Donald. *School: A Matter of Choice.* Washington, DC: OECD Publications and Information Center, 1994.

Holland, Peter F. *Education Vouchers: The Radical Approach to Education Reform?* Sheffield, UK: PAVIC Publications, 1985.

House, Ernest R. *Schools for Sale: Why Free Market Policies Won't Improve America's Schools, and What Will.* New York: Teachers College Press, 1998.

House, H. Wayne, David W. Smith, Kenneth O. Gangel, and Gregg Harris. *Schooling Choices.* Portland, OR: Multnomah Press, 1988.

Hughes, David. *Trading in Futures: Why Markets in Education Don't Work.* Philadelphia, PA: Open University Press, 1999.

Hulsey, Angela. *School Choice Programs: What's Happening in the States.* Washington, DC: Heritage Foundation, 1993.

Johnson, Daphne. *Parental Choice in Education.* Boston, MA: Unwin Hyman, 1990.

Kelly, Elizabeth A. *Education, Democracy, and Public Knowledge. Interventions: Theory and Contemporary Politics.* Boulder, CO: Westview Press, 1995.

Kirkpatrick, David, W. *School Choice: The Idea That Will Not Die.* Millersburg, OH: Bluebird Publisher, 1997.

————. *Choice in Schooling: A Case for Tuition Vouchers.* Chicago, IL: Loyola University Press, 1990.

Kober, Nancy. *Private School Vouchers: What Are the Real Choices?* Arlington, VA: American Association of School Administrators, 1996.

Koprowicz, Constance L. *School Choice and Charter Schools.* Denver, CO: National Conference of State Legislatures, 1995.

Ladd, Helen F., ed. *Holding Schools Accountable: Performance-Based Reform in Education.* Washington, DC: Brookings Institution, 1996.

LaNoue, George R., ed. *Educational Vouchers: Concepts and Controversies.* New York: Teachers College Press, 1972.

Larson, Colleen. *Educational Choice.* Bloomington, IN: Indiana Education Policy Center, Indiana University, 1990.

Levine, David P. *Rethinking Schools: An Agenda for Change.* New York: New Press, 1995.

Lieberman, Myron. *Public Education: An Autopsy.* Cambridge, MA: Harvard University Press, 1993.

————. *Public School Choice: Current Issues/Future Prospects.* Lancaster, PA: Technomic, 1990.

————. *Privatization and Educational Choice.* New York: St. Martin's Press, 1989.

Lindelow, John. *Educational Vouchers.* Reston, VA: National Association of Secondary School Principals, 1980.

Lines, Patricia M. *Compulsory Education Laws and Their Impact on Public and Private Education.* Denver, CO: Education Commission of the States, 1985.

Lowe, Robert, and Barbara Miner. *Selling Out Our Schools. Vouchers, Markets, and the Future of Public Education.* Milwaukee, WI: Rethinking Schools, 1996.

————. *False Choices: Why School Vouchers Threaten Our Children's Future.* 2d ed. Milwaukee, WI: Rethinking Schools, 1993.

————. *Selling Out Our Schools: Vouchers, Markets, and the Future of Public Education.* Milwaukee, WI: Rethinking Schools, 1996.

Lowell, Stephen S. *Parent and Student Choice of Schools: Strengths and Weaknesses.* Portland, ME: J. Weston Walch, 1991.

Lytle, R. J. *Property Tax Cut and School Vouchers.* Farmington, MI: Structures, 1978.

Madsen, Jean. *Private and Public School Partnerships: Sharing Lessons about Decentralization.* Washington, DC: Falmer Press, 1996.

Malone, Mike. *Facts, Figures and Faces: A Look at Minnesota's School Choice Programs.* Minneapolis: Center for School Change, Hubert H. Humphrey Institute of Public Affairs, University of Minnesota, 1993.

Maranto, Robert, Scott Milliman, Frederick Hess, and April Gresham. *Frontiers of Public Education: Lessons from Arizona Charter Schools.* Boulder, CO: Westview Press, 1999.

Marshall, James S. *School Choice: A Time and Place to Begin.* Tallahassee, FL: Floridians for Educational Choice, 1995.

Marshner, Connaught, ed. *A Blueprint for Education Reform.* Chicago, IL: Regnery/Gateway, 1984.

Mateer, Dirk G. and Robert N. Mateer. *Education and Freedom: Restoring Judeo-Christian Values through Parental Choice.* Lynchburg, VA: CEBA, 1993.

McChesney, Fred S., and William F. Shughart II, eds. *The Causes and Consequences of Antitrust: The Public-Choice Perspective.* Chicago, IL: University of Chicago Press, 1995.

McGroaty, Daniel, and William J. Bennet. *Break These Chains: The Battle For School Choice.* Rocklin, CA: Forum, 1996.

Miller, Ron, ed. *Educational Freedom for a Democratic Society: A Critique of National Goals, Standards, and Curriculum.* Brandon, VT: Resource Center for Redesigning Education, 1995.

Millot, Marc D. *Autonomy, Accountability, and the Values of Public Education: A Comparative Assessment of Charter School Statutes Leading to Model Legislation.* Santa Monica, CA: Rand, 1994.

Moe, Terry M. *Private Vouchers.* Stanford, CA: Hoover Institution Press, 1995.

Molnar, Alex. *Giving Kids the Business: The Commercialization of America's Schools.* Dunmore, PA: Westview Press, 1996.

Morgan, Kerry L. *Real Choice, Real Freedom in American Education: The Legal and Constitutional Case for Parental Rights and against Governmental Control of American Education.* Lanham, MD: University Press of America, 1997.

Murphy, Dan, F. Howard Nelson, and Bella Rosenberg. *The Cleveland Voucher Program: Who Chooses? Who Gets Chosen? Who Pays?* Washington, DC: American Federation of Teachers, 1997.

Murphy, Joseph. *Pathways to Privatization in Education.* Greenwich, CT: Ablex Pub. 1998.

———. *The Privatization of Schooling: Problems and Possibilities.* Thousand Oaks, CA: Corwin Press, 1996.

Nash, Ronald H., and Ron Taber. *The Case for School Choice: How to Improve Our Schools.* Olympia, WA: Triune Press, 1995.

Nathan, Joe. *Charter Schools: Creating Hope and Opportunity for American Education.* San Francisco, CA: Jossey-Bass, 1997.

Noll, James W. *Taking Sides. Clashing Views on Controversial Educational Issues.* 9th ed. Guilford, CT: Dushkin Publishing Group, 1997.

O'Neill, Dave M., and Sue G. Ross. *Voucher Funding of Training: A Study of the G.I. Bill.* Arlington, VA: Public Research Institute, 1976.

Ott, Attiat F. *Education through Choice: Elementary and Secondary Education.* Worcester, MA: Institute for Economic Studies, Clark University, 1981.

Palmatier, Larry L. *Crisis Counseling for a Quality School Community: Applying Wm. Glasser's Choice Theory.* Washington, DC: Accelerated Development, 1998.

Patrinos, Harry A., and David L. Ariasingam. *Decentralization of Education: Demand-Side Financing.* Washington, DC: World Bank, 1997.

Pearson, Judith. *Myths of Educational Choice.* Westport, CT: Praeger, 1993.

Peterson, Paul E., William G. Howell, and David E. Myers. *An Evaluation of the*

New York City School Choice Scholarships Program. Cambridge, MA: Program on Educational Policy and Governance, Harvard University, 1998.

Peterson, Paul E., and Bryan C. Hassel, eds. *Learning from School Choice.* Washington, DC: Brookings Institution Press, 1998.

————. *Why Not School Choice?* Washington, DC: Brookings Institution Press, 1998.

Pierce, Ronald K. *What Are We Trying to Teach Them Anyway? A Father's Focus on School Reform.* San Francisco, CA: ICS Press, 1993.

Policy Analysis for California Education. *Description and Analysis of Proposition 174: The Private School Voucher Initiative.* Berkeley, CA: Policy Analysis for California Education, 1993.

Quade, Quinton L. *Financing Education: The Struggle between Government Monopoly and Parental Control.* New Brunswick, NJ: The State University of New Jersey, 1998.

————. *Paths to Parental Freedom and School Choice.* Milwaukee, WI: Blum Center, 1995.

————. *School Choice and Parental Freedom: A Challenge to All Catholics.* Milwaukee, WI: Blum Center, 1994.

Randall, Ruth E., and Keith Geiger. *School Choice: Issues and Answers.* Bloomington, IN: National Educational Service, 1991.

Randall, Vance E. *Private Schools and Public Power: A Case for Pluralism.* New York: Teachers College Press, 1994.

Rasell, Edith, and Richard Rothstein, eds. *School Choice: Examining the Evidence.* Arlington, VA: Public Interest Publications, 1993.

Ravitch, Diane, and Maris A. Vinovskis, eds. *Learning from the Past. What History Teaches Us about School Reform.* Baltimore, MD: Johns Hopkins University Press, 1995.

Ravitch, Diane, and Joseph P. Viteritti, eds. *New Schools for A New Century. The Redesign of Urban Education.* New Haven, CT: Yale University Press, 1997.

Rehfuss, John. *Privatization in Education.* Alexandria, VA: National Association of Elementary School Principals, 1995.

Reimer, Everett. *School Is Dead: Alternatives in Education.* Garden City, NY: Anchor, 1972.

Rich, John Martin, and Joseph L. DeVitis. *Competition in Education.* Springfield, IL: Charles C. Thomas, 1992.

Richman, Sheldon. *Separating School & State: How to Liberate America's Families.* Fairfax, VA: Future of Freedom Foundation, 1994.

Riddle, Wayne C., and James Stedman. *Public School Choice Recent Developments and Analysis of Issues.* Washington, DC: Congressional Research Service, Library of Congress, 1989.

Rinehart, James R., and Jackson F. Lee, Jr. *American Education and the Dynamics of Choice.* New York: Praeger, 1991.

Robinson, Peter. *School Days: An Essay on the Hoover Institution Conference 'Choice and Vouchers: The Future of American Education?'* Stanford, CA: Hoover Institution, 1993.

Rogers, Martin. *Opting Out: Choice and the Future of Schools.* London: Lawrence and Wishart, 1992.

Rouse, Cecilia E. *Private School Vouchers and Student Achievement: An Evaluation of the Milwaukee Parental Choice Program.* Princeton, NJ: Industrial Relations Section, Princeton University, 1998.

Saks, Judith B. *The Basics of Charter Schools: A School Board Primer.* Alexandria, VA: National School Boards Association, 1997.

Sarason, Seymour B. *Charter Schools: Another Flawed Educational Reform?* New York: Teachers College Press, 1998.

Schwartz, Wendy. *How Well Are Charter Schools Serving Urban and Minority Students?* New York: ERIC Clearinghouse on Urban Education, 1996.

Shanker, Albert. *Politics, Markets and America's Schools: The Fallacies of Private School Choice.* Washington, DC: American Federation of Teachers, 1991.

Shapira, Rina, and Peter W. Cookson. *Parental Choice and School Ethos, from Theory to Practice.* New York: Elsevier Science, 1997.

Shires, Michael A., Cathy S. Krop, C. Peter Rydell, and Stephen J. Carroll. *The Effects of the California Voucher Initiative on Public Expenditures for Education.* Santa Monica, CA: Rand, 1994.

Shokraii, Nina H., and Sarah E. Yousseff. *School Choice 1999: What's Happening in the States.* Washington, DC: Heritage Foundation, 1999.

———. *School Choice Programs: What's Happening in the States,* Edition 1998. Washington, DC: Heritage Foundation, 1998.

Skillen, James W. *The School Choice Controversy: What Is Constitutional?* Grand Rapids, MI: Baker Books, 1993.

Smith, Kevin B., and Kenneth J. Meier. *The Case against School Choice: Politics, Markets, and Fools.* Portland, OR: Book News, 1995.

Smrekar, Claire. *The Impact of School Choice and Community: In the Interest of Family and Schools.* Albany, NY: State University of New York Press, 1996.

———. *The Impact of School Choice and Community: In the Interest of Families and Schools.* New York: State University of New York Press, 1995.

Smrekar, Claire, and Ellen B. Goldring. *School Choice in Urban America: Magnet Schools and the Pursuit of Equity.* New York: Teachers College Press, 1999.

Solo, R. A. *Economics and the Public Interest.* New Brunswick, NJ: Rutgers University Press, 1955.

Stedman, James B. *School Choice Status and Issues.* Washington, DC: Congressional Research Service, 1992.

Steinberg, Laurence. *Beyond the Classroom: Why School Reform Has Failed and What Parents Need to Do.* New York: Simon and Schuster, 1996.

Steuerle, Eugene C., Van D. Ooms, George Peterson, and Robert D. Reischauer. *Vouchers and the Provision of Public Services.* Washington, DC: Brookings Institution, 1999.

Sweeney, Mary E. *Planning a Charter School: One Colorado Group's Experience.* Denver, CO: Angel Press, 1994.

Tannenbaum, Margaret D., ed. *Concepts and Issues in School Choice.* Lewiston, NY: E. Mellen Press, 1995.

Thernstrom, Abigail M. *School Choice in Massachusetts.* Boston, MA: Pioneer Institute for Public Policy Research, 1990.

Thies, Clifford F. *Parental Choice in Education: Forecasting the Impact.* Washington, DC: Heritage Foundation, 1993.

Tucker, Allyson M. *School Choice Programs, What's Happening In the States, 1994.* Washington, DC: Heritage Foundation, 1994.

United States Department of Education. *The Charter School Roadmap.* Washington, DC: United States Department of Education, 1998.

University of New York. *Charter Schools: A Comprehensive Overview.* Albany, NY: University of New York, 1994.

Van Treese, James B., ed. *School Choice: Why We Need It, How We Get It.* Kent, WA: Northwest Publishing, 1993.

Vergari, Sandra, and Michael Mintrom. *Charter Schools Laws Across the United States.* East Lansing, MI: Michigan State University, 1996.

Walford, Geoffrey. *School Choice and the Quasi-Market.* Oxford, UK: Triangle, 1996.

Wells, Amy Stuart. *Time to Choose: America at the Crossroads of School Choice Policy. New Frontiers in Education.* East Rutherford, NJ: Putnam Publishing Group, 1993.

West, E. G. *Education and the State: A Study in Political Economy,* 3d ed. Indianapolis, IN: Liberty Fund, 1994.

Whitty, Geoff, Sally Power, and David Halpin. *Devolution and Choice in Education: The School, the State, and the Right to School Choice.* Bristol, PA: Open University Press, 1998.

Williams, Scott, ed. *The Alternative School Choice.* Bloomington, IN: Phi Delta Kappa Educational Foundation, 1991.

Witte, John F. *The Market Approach to Education: An Analysis of America's First Voucher Program.* Princeton, NJ: Princeton University Press, 2000.

Witte, John F., and William Clune, eds. *Choice and Control in American Education.* Vol. 1. New York: Falmer, 1990.

Wohlstetter, Priscilla. *First Lessons Charter Schools as Learning Communities.* Philadelphia, PA: University of Pennsylvania, 1997.

———. *Creating and Sustaining Learning Communities Early Lessons from Charter Schools.* Washington, DC: U.S. Department of Education, 1997.

Woods, Philip A., Ron Glatter, and Carl Bagley. *School Choice and Competition: Markets in the Public Interest?* New York: Routledge, 1998.

Young, Timothy W., and Evans Clinchy. *Choice in Public Education.* New York: Teachers College Press, 1992.

Index

About the Authors

Jo Renée Formicola, Ph.D. is an associate professor of political science at Seton Hall University in New Jersey. She teaches American parties and politics as well as church and state and combines both interests in her research and writing on the Catholic Church in the political process. She is the author of *The Catholic Church and Human Rights* (1988) and numerous articles on religion and politics and is also the co-author of *Everson Revisited: Religion, Education, and Law at the Crossroads* (Rowman & Littlefield 1997).

Hubert Morken, Ph.D. is professor of government at Regent University where he teaches in the public policy graduate program. The focus of his recent work is on education reform efforts in the United States. He is the founder of the Religion and Politics section of the American Political Science Association and has written extensively on grassroots political activism and religion. He is the author of *Pat Robertson* (1988) and co-author of *Everson Revisited: Religion, Education, and Law at the Crossroads* (Rowman & Littlefield 1997).